ROBERT C. CROKEN is the assistant director of the Lonergan Research Institute in Toronto.

ROBERT M. DORAN is the director of the Lonergan Research Institute and a professor at Regis College, University of Toronto.

COLLECTED WORKS OF

BERNARD LONERGAN

VOLUME 17

PHILOSOPHICAL AND

THEOLOGICAL PAPERS

1965–1980

COLLECTED WORKS
OF BERNARD
LONERGAN

PHILOSOPHICAL AND
THEOLOGICAL PAPERS
1965–1980

edited by
Robert C. Croken and
Robert M. Doran

Published for Lonergan Research Institute
of Regis College, Toronto
by University of Toronto Press Incorporated
Toronto Buffalo London

© Bernard Lonergan Estate 2004
Printed in Canada

ISBN 0-8020-8963-1 (cloth)
ISBN 0-8020-8638-1 (paper)

Printed on acid-free paper

Requests for permission to quote from the Collected Works of Bernard
Lonergan should be addressed to University of Toronto Press.

Canadian Cataloguing in Publication Data

Lonergan, Bernard J.F. (Bernard Joseph Francis), 1904–1984.
  Collected Works of Bernard Lonergan.

  Contents: v. 17. Philosophical and theological papers, 1965–1980 /
  edited by Robert C. Croken and Robert M. Doran.
  Includes bibliographical references and index.
  ISBN 0-8020-8963-1 (v. 17 : bound). – ISBN 0-8020-8638-1 (v. 17 : pbk.)

  1. Theology – 20th century.   2. Catholic Church.   I. Crowe, Frederick E., 1915–

  II. Doran, Robert M., 1939–   III. Lonergan Research Institute.   IV. Title.
  BX891.L595 1988   230   C88-093328-3 rev

The Lonergan Research Institute gratefully acknowledges the generous
contribution of THE MALLINER CHARITABLE FOUNDATION, which has made
possible the production of this entire series.

The Lonergan Research Institute gratefully acknowledges the financial
assistance of JAMES AND ANNA MEYER toward the publication of this volume of
the Collected Works of Bernard Lonergan.

University of Toronto Press acknowledges the financial assistance to its
publishing program of the Canada Council for the Arts and the Ontario
Arts Council.

University of Toronto Press acknowledges the financial support for its
publishing activities of the Government of Canada through the Book
Publishing Industry Development Program (BPIDP).

Contents

LECTURES AT MASSACHUSETTS INSTITUTE OF
TECHNOLOGY

THE LARKIN-STUART LECTURES AT TRINITY COLLEGE, UNIVERSITY OF TORONTO

Editors' Preface

Like volume 6 in the Collected Works series, *Philosophical and Theological Papers 1958–1964*, this volume parallels the better known 'Collections' of Lonergan papers that have enriched students for many years. In this particular anthology, we gather a number of papers that reveal the 'later' Lonergan. These papers document his development in philosophy and theology during the years leading up to the publication of *Method in Theology*, and beyond to 1980, when he was more engaged in his writings and seminars on macroeconomics.

Some of the papers in this volume have been published elsewhere but are included here, with editorial notes, because of the exigencies of Collected Works. Again, some of these papers were published only posthumously, and indeed one very important piece ('Philosophy and the Religious Phenomenon') was discovered by the General Editors only after Lonergan's death.

The book is divided into five sections. The first and last of these form units only on the basis of dates, while the three central sections are each a set of lectures, the first at the Massachusetts Institute of Technology, the second at Gonzaga University in Spokane, and the third at Trinity College in the University of Toronto. Readers will find some repetition both internally to the volume itself and in relation to other more familiar works, particularly *Method in Theology*. Yet even in this repetition there are occasional new turns of phrase that the careful reader will note, and in at least one instance (chapter 7, with its distinctions of formal system, referential system, and empirical system) familiar material suddenly opens out onto expressions not to be found anywhere else in Lonergan's work. Other very interesting developments regard the movement from speaking of the immutability of dogmas to their permanence of meaning (chapter 5) and the permutations among 'real self-transcendence' (chapter 2), 'performative self-transcendence' (chapter 3), and 'moral self-transcendence' (chapter 17).

Like its companion volume 6, this volume should also serve as a useful tool in the classroom. In some cases a single chapter (for example, 'Self-transcendence: Intellectual, Moral, Religious,' which is also available in audio form on compact disc) may provide a good introduction to Lonergan's thought. For students more familiar with his thought, a lecture or a series of lectures from the volume might elaborate more fully a subject or theme dealt with in other volumes of the Collected Works.

No doubt the relative importance of the items collected here varies from one instance to another. The importance of the lectures on 'Philosophy of God and Theology' has long been acknowledged. There is a great deal of still untapped material in the Larkin-Stuart Lectures. And in the view of the editors, chapters 19 ('Questionnaire on Philosophy: Response') and 21 ('Philosophy and the Religious Phenomenon') are among the most important pieces Lonergan ever wrote. Every reader will have her or his favorites, no doubt, and that is one of the values of an anthology such as this.

As is our policy we have used the *Oxford American Dictionary* and the *Chicago Manual of Style* as basic (but not rigid) guides to editorial minutiae. We have added a lexicon of Latin and Greek words and phrases.

We wish to single out for special thanks Richard Liddy, William F.J. Ryan, s.j., and Heather Stephens, for bibliographic information; Walter Conn for the tape of 'Faith and Beliefs' and responses, and William A. Shea and Sister Rose Tadsen for a transcript of the same material; Mary Gerhart for the tape of 'Self-transcendence: Intellectual, Moral, Religious'; Frederick E. Crowe, s.j., for consultation, advice, and the previous editing and publication of some of the papers; Daniel Monsour and Michael G. Shields, s.j., for consultation and advice; Nicholas Graham, for transcribing lectures from tapes; Marcela Dayao, for the laborious work of transferring the transcriptions to computer; and Greg Lauzon, for the audio restoration onto compact disc of 'Self-transcendence,' 'Horizons and Transpositions,' and an edited version of 'The Human Good.'

This is the first volume in the series to be published with the help of a very generous donation from Mr Robert Mollot and the Malliner Charitable Foundation. We wish to express our deep gratitude.

THE EDITORS

1967–1971

1

The General Character of the Natural Theology of *Insight*[1]

Professor Gilkey was kind enough to suggest the topic for this talk, 'The General Character of the Natural Theology Contained in My Book, *Insight*.'[2] The natural theology in that book is found in chapter 19, and it consists in an argument for the existence of God.

1 Presuppositions

Before attempting to outline that argument, I had best say something about the general character of its presuppositions, worked out in the previous eighteen chapters.

1 Based on notes on a lecture given at the Divinity School, University of Chicago, towards the end of March, most likely 30 March 1967. What are available are 'reportationes' of uncertain origin that were in circulation soon after the lecture. Two copies are in the Lonergan Research Institute Library (LB 195.1), one dated November 1973, the other February 1974. Lonergan himself refers to a 'reportatio' on the lecture in a letter dated 25 November 1972, to Bernard Tyrrell and William Ryan, who were then engaged in editing *A Second Collection*: 'The talk at the Divinity School in Chicago is contained only in a Reportatio. I never wrote it out; I never corrected the Reportatio; I do not think it should be included [in *A Second Collection*]' (Archives, Correspondence, Lonergan Research Institute). The present version is based on the two 'reportationes' available at the Institute, but where these transcriptions are sketchy and in outline form, complete sentences have been composed by the editors. Divisions and section headings are editorial, and are not the same as those found in the two reports (which themselves vary somewhat). Footnotes are, of course, also editorial.

2 Bernard Lonergan, *Insight: A Study of Human Understanding* (London:

In the main, they are concerned with three rather basic and closely connected questions: (1) what am I doing when I am knowing? – cognitional theory; (2) why is doing that knowing? – epistemology; and (3) what do I know when I do it? – metaphysics.

The use of the first-person pronoun is deliberate: the book invites the reader to a self-appropriation, to come to know and take possession of himself; at the same time it is an invitation to authenticity, to take possession of his true self, to an intellectual conversion. The basic task is to acquire familiarity with one's own cognitional operations, to find out from performing the operations what the operations are and how they are related to one another.

The reader is presumed to be sufficiently familiar with seeing, hearing, touching, smelling, tasting. The act of understanding, however, is set up for scrutiny throughout the whole first part of the book. Chapter 1 investigates mathematical understanding, where the act of understanding is clearest, most sharp; chapters 2–5 study scientific understanding and its development; chapters 6 and 7 scrutinize commonsense understanding, its development and aberration; chapter 8 asks about the notion of the thing; and chapters 9–11 focus on reflective understanding and judgment, including the judgment, 'I am a knower,' in the sense that I perform such and such operations related in such and such a manner.

Whence it follows (a) that human knowing is not some one type of operation but a compound of different types: roughly, experience, understanding, judging; (b) that the objectivity of human knowing is not some single property but a compound of different properties proper to different types of operations: experiential, normative, absolute; and (c) that the proportionate object of human knowing is not some simple object but a compound of different partial objects assembled in the compound of different operations.

Hence, there is the possibility of open system. In the domain of basic terms and relations, mutually determined basic terms refer to my operations, and basic relations are the dynamic relations between my operations. Isomorphic to these are terms and relations in the proportionate object.

2   *Insight*'s Argument and Traditional Formulations

In chapter 19 of my book, *Insight*, I worked out an argument for the existence

---

Longmans, Green & Co., 1957); 2nd, revised ed., 1958; 5th ed., vol. 3 in Collected Works of Bernard Lonergan, ed. Frederick E. Crowe and Robert M. Doran (Toronto: University of Toronto Press, 1992, 1997, 2002) 366–71.

of God. It is presumably this argument that constitutes any 'natural theology' I happen to have. And so an account of this argument follows.

Briefly the argument reads as follows. If the real is completely intelligible, God exists. But the real is completely intelligible. Therefore, God exists.

Substantially this argument is quite traditional, but it differs from the old proofs of the existence of God in two manners, and in each case it does so to meet later developments.

First, the hypothetical premise 'If the real is completely intelligible, God exists' is a variant on the appeal to causality. In the medieval period, theology, philosophy, and science were distinguished but they were not separated. The distinction of theology and philosophy became a separation with Descartes; he wanted his philosophy based on certitudes quite distinct from his religious faith. However, in Descartes philosophy and science were not yet separated; he proved the conservation of momentum by appealing to the immutability of God. That separation, however, was effected virtually by Newton's *Philosophiae naturalis principia mathematica*,[3] and formally by Laplace's proof of the periodicity of planetary motion and his famous remark about the First Mover, 'Nous n'avons plus besoin de cette hypothèse.'[4] With the separation of philosophy and science, there was developed a scientific notion of causality, a notion that relates effects only to causes within the observable, created universe. Accordingly, if God's existence is to be proved, there has to be formulated a complementary, philosophic notion of causality. Within the Scholastic tradition this commonly is done by a metaphysical formulation. My

3 Sir Isaac Newton, *Philosophiae naturalis principia mathematica*; trans. Andrew Motte, *Sir Isaac Newton's Mathematical Principles of Natural Philosophy and His System of the World*, 1729; revised, Florian Cajori, vol. 1: *The Motion of Bodies*, vol. 2: *The System of the World* (Berkeley: University of California Press, 1934, reprinted 1962).

4 The major scientific work of Pierre-Simon Laplace is *Traité de mécanique céleste*, 5 vols., 1799–1825; trans. Nathaniel Bowditch, *Celestial Mechanics*, 4 vols. (Boston: Isaac R. Butts Press, 1829–39), reprinted Bronx, NY: Chelsea Publishing Co., 1966.
    The occasion of the quotation was an interesting exchange with Napoleon, recounted by Eric T. Bell, *Men of Mathematics* (New York: Dover Publications, 1937, reprinted 1961) 181: 'The story of Laplace's encounter with Napoleon over the *Mécanique céleste* shows the mathematician as he really was. Laplace had presented Napoleon with a copy of the book. Thinking to get a rise out of Laplace, Napoleon took him to task for an apparent oversight. "You have written this huge book on the system of the world without once mentioning the author of the universe." "Sire," Laplace retorted, "I had no need of that hypothesis."'

own formulation is, however, gnoseological: it speaks of the complete intelligibility of the real. It does so because, for me, a metaphysics is not first but derived from cognitional theory and epistemology.

In other words, my position is transcendental, in the sense that I would say that our knowledge of objects is constructed by the subject's activities.

I said that the argument departed from the traditional proofs in two manners. The first was a variant on the principle of causality. The second is a matter of taking a precise philosophic position.

It is not from the world as interpreted in any philosophy that the existence of God can be proved. One cannot prove the existence of God to a Kantian without first breaking his allegiance to Kant. One cannot prove the existence of God to a positivist without first converting him from positivism. A valid proof has philosophic presuppositions, and the presuppositions of the argument set forth in *Insight* are indicated in the antecedent, 'The real is completely intelligible.'

So much for my first remark on the general character of my position. Substantially, it is the traditional manner of proof. But it departs from older formulations, first, inasmuch as it assumes a precise philosophic stance or horizon by stating that the real is completely intelligible, and secondly, by departing from the medieval view of causality (which did not differentiate philosophy and science) and from the subsequent Scholastic formulations in terms of metaphysics, to a transcendental formulation in terms of the manner in which our apprehension of the universe is to be constructed, namely, with an exigence for complete intelligibility.

3   'The Real Is Completely Intelligible'

Let us now devote a little more attention to the categorical premise, 'The real is completely intelligible.' Its meaning may be clarified by introducing a middle term and arguing as follows. Being is completely intelligible. But the real is being. Therefore, the real is completely intelligible.

3.1   'Being Is Completely Intelligible'

3.1.1   Being and Questioning

Basically, being is what is intended in questioning. Such intending is not knowing. When a question is genuine, the answer is not yet known. When one questions, then, one intends what as yet one does not know.

On the other hand, such intending is not complete ignorance. At least one knows enough to know that one does not know and to ask the questions that would bring the remedy.

Such intending, then, is somewhere between knowing and total ignorance. It is the conscious dynamic element in the process of man's coming to know. Moreover, such intending presupposes something previously given, presented, somehow known. But it goes beyond that to an unknown. Such going beyond is a priori; it is just the opposite of the a posteriori that is given, perceived, known, for its concern is going beyond to the as yet unknown.

3.1.2 Further Properties of the Notion of Being

Some further properties of the notion of being had best be noted.

First, the use of the a priori intention has to be intelligently controlled. There is a strategy in our choice of questions, a tactic in the order in which they are to be raised, limits to the questions that can usefully be investigated now, and so on.

Second, the necessity of such control arises from the fact that the a priori intention of itself is unrestricted. It is not limited to some genus as sight is limited to color or hearing to sound. We inquire about any genus or species whatever. It is not limited to what we can know. Man's knowing is limited. Just where the limits lie is a matter of dispute, but no matter where the limits are placed, there can and does arise the question whether there is beyond the limits anything to be known.

Third, the a priori intention is not abstract. People think of metaphysics as abstract. Scotus and Hegel agreed that the notion of being coincides with the minimal concept 'not nothing.' But just as our questions, of themselves, are unrestricted in extent, so too they are unrestricted in intent. As we may ask about everything, so too we may ask everything about anything. What is the concrete? One knows a thing concretely when one knows it completely. One intends the concrete by the intention of being.

Fourth, the a priori intention is not optional. It is the nerve of all questioning, of all learning, of all correcting mistakes, of all inquiry and insight, of all reflection and judgment, of all deliberation and reasonable choice. Human living is solving problems and living out the solutions.

3.1.3 Intelligent Grasp and Reasonable Affirmation

As being is intended by asking questions, so it is to be known by answering them correctly. Asking and answering suggest a dialogue, a catechism, at least a flow of words. But the verbal aspect is posterior. Prior to the formulated question there is the surprise, the wonder that Aristotle described as the beginning of all science and philosophy. Prior to the answers there are the insights formulated in hypotheses or hunches, and the reflection that weighs the evidence and comes to affirm or deny with probability or at times with certainty. So being may be redefined as what is to be known by intelligent grasp and reasonable affirmation.

3.1.4 The Complete Intelligibility of Being

So being is completely intelligible. It is by the exercise of our intelligence that we come to know. Mere gaping (unintelligent looking) is not human knowing. We have to look, but we also have to inquire, investigate, come to understand. Merely understanding is not human knowing; insights are a dime a dozen; they have to be developed, corrected, complemented, rounded out. To get beyond myth to science, astrology to astronomy, alchemy to chemistry, legend to history, it is not enough to understand. One has to reflect, critically weigh the evidence, judge reasonably.

What is known by the exercise of intelligence is the intelligible. The sensible is potentially intelligible, what can be understood. Ideas are formally intelligible, the content of insight. The affirmed is actually intelligible, the intelligibility that is so.

What is known by the exercise of intelligence is completely intelligible, for every obscurantism is reprobated. While there are illegitimate, mistaken, inopportune questions, still no question can be brushed aside without some reason being assigned; and questions do not stop: they keep coming, and libraries continue to fill up.

3.2 'The Real Is Being'

Next, the real is being. I remember being surprised as a boy by a companion who assured me that air was real. Astounded, I said, 'No, it's just nothing.' He said, 'There's something there all right. Shake your hand and you will feel it.' So I shook my hand, felt something, and concluded to my amazement that air was real.

Whether my conclusion was correct, we need not consider. The point is that all of us in childhood have to solve implicitly and pragmatically a whole series of questions in cognitional theory, epistemology, and metaphysics. We have to distinguish dreaming and waking, imagining and seeing, stories and what really happened. We have to discover the possibility, and learn to suspect the occurrence, of a sibling's joke, trick, fib.

So it is, perhaps, that we arrive at the manifest, unquestionable, self-evident certitudes that later make the problems of philosophers seem so absurd to us. But the fact is, it seems to me, that besides retaining not a little of the mythical world of childhood, we also move into the universe of being. We know by experiencing and inquiring, by understanding and reflecting, by weighing the evidence and judging. The world mediated by language also is a real world. When, then, I say that the real is being, I am saying that we have to recapitulate in ourselves the old Greek breakthrough from mythos to logos; that we have to do so consistently, completely, rigorously; that unless we do so, we shall be forever caught in the coils of a Kantianism, an idealism, an existentialism, or a positivism; that if we are so caught, then we cannot find any valid proof for the existence of God.

4   The Existence of God

The realities of this world are of themselves not completely intelligible. That is, questions arise that are not to be answered in terms of the nature of causality of minerals, plants, animals, men; again, questions arise that are not to be answered by the use of scientific method, or by the use of empirical science. From that use, one event or existence can be accounted for by appealing to other events or existences, but no attempt is made or can be made to meet the questions, Why does anything exist? Why does anything occur? Existence and occurrence are known in judgment; judgment rests on a virtually unconditioned; a virtually unconditioned is a conditioned whose conditions *happen* to be fulfilled.

If the real is to be completely intelligible, we have to go beyond this world to a completely intelligible being that accounts for the existences and occurrences of this world. That completely intelligible being would be an unrestricted act of understanding. And such an act has the properties traditionally associated with God.

Moreover, this apprehension or notion of God is open; it admits of further determinations from revelation. And so from it we can go on to the theological treatise 'De Deo trino.'

2

Horizons[1]

My topic is horizons. Literally, the horizon is the line where apparently earth and sky meet. It is the boundary of one's field of vision. And, as one moves about, this boundary recedes in front and closes in behind so that, for different standpoints, there are different horizons. Moreover, for each different standpoint and horizon, there are different divisions of the totality of visible objects. Beyond the horizon lie the objects that, at least for the moment, cannot be seen. Within the horizon lie the objects that can now be seen.

1 A lecture given at the Thomas More Institute, Montreal, 21 March 1968. It was the first in a spring lecture series under the general title 'The Drama of the Sensible and the Drama of the Real: Consciousness in Tension.' The title of Lonergan's lecture as reported in the flyer for the series was 'Horizons of Fact,' but the lecture has long been listed in primary-source bibliographies with the more accurate title that is given it here. We are grateful to Dr Heather Stephens of the Thomas More Institute for unearthing the background information on the lecture. The experienced reader of Lonergan's works will recognize that parts of the lecture eventually found their way into *Method in Theology* with little or no alteration.

A transcription of the tape recording of the lecture and the question period (File 473, Lonergan Research Institute Library, Toronto) was made by Nicholas Graham. The present edition relies on both the tape recording and the transcription. Divisions and section titles are editorial, as are all footnotes, though reference was made to parallel works of Lonergan's for the information in the footnotes.

Fr Eric O'Connor, then president of the Thomas More Institute, introduced the series and the speaker for the opening lecture. Lonergan began the lecture by acknowledging the introduction and expressing his pleasure at having been invited to speak in the series.

As our field of vision, so too the range of our interests and the scope of our knowledge are bounded. As fields of vision vary with one's standpoint, so too the range of one's interests and the scope of one's knowledge vary with the period in which one lives, with one's social background and milieu, with one's education and personal development. In this fashion, there has arisen a metaphorical or analogous meaning of the word 'horizon.' In this sense, what lies beyond one's horizon is simply outside the range of one's interests and knowledge: one knows nothing about it and one cares less. And what lies within one's horizon is in some measure, great or small, an object of interest and of knowledge.

Such, in very general terms, is what I mean by horizon. And I propose to treat the topic very incompletely, but in some way comprehensively, under four headings: first of all, self-transcendence as the possibility of horizon; secondly, intentional response as revealing values and carrying us to self-transcendence; thirdly, judgments of value, for it is our values that largely settle our horizons; and fourthly, faith, for religious values are the supreme values.

1   Self-transcendence as the Possibility of Horizon

First, then, self-transcendence. One can live in a world, have a horizon, just in the measure that one is not locked up totally within oneself. The first step in this liberation is the sensitivity we share with the higher animals. But while they are confined to a habitat, we live within a universe, because beyond sensitivity we question, and our questioning is unrestricted.

First, there are questions for intelligence. We ask what and why and how and how often. And our answers unify and relate, classify and construct, serialize and generalize. From the narrow strip of space-time open to immediate experience, we move towards the construction of a worldview and towards the exploration of what we ourselves could be and could do.

On questions for intelligence follow questions for reflection. We move beyond imagination and guesswork, idea and hypothesis, theory and system, to ask whether or not this really is so or that really could be. Now self-transcendence takes on a new meaning; it not merely goes beyond the subject but also seeks what is independent of the subject. For a judgment that this or that really is so reports, not what appears to me, not what I imagine, not what I think, not what I would be inclined to say, not what seems to be so, but what is so.

Still, such self-transcendence is only intentional, only cognitional; it is in the order not of doing but only of knowing. On the final level of questions, questions for deliberation, self-transcendence ceases to be intentional and becomes real.[2] For when we ask whether this or that is worth while, whether it is not just apparently but truly good, then we are inquiring, not about feelings of pleasure or pain, not about comfort or ill ease, not about sensitive spontaneity, but about objective value. Because we can ask such questions and answer them and live by the answers, we can effect in our living a real self-transcendence. That real self-transcendence is the possibility of benevolence and beneficence, of willing what is truly good and doing it, of collaboration and true love, of swinging completely out of the habitat of an animal and of becoming a genuine person in a human society.

I have spoken of value and, indeed, of objective value. I have distinguished between what truly is good and, on the other hand, what only apparently is good. But the basic fact is the subjective fact of self-transcendence, and the basic distinction is between achieving self-transcendence and failing to do so. The true good, the objective value, is what is judged to be good by a person achieving self-transcendence, being authentic; and the merely apparent good is what is judged to be good by a person failing to transcend himself.

2 There are data here for an interesting bit of history. This paragraph is echoed (with a few changes) in *Method in Theology* 104, but by the time of *Method in Theology*, these sentences came to read, 'Still such self-transcendence is only cognitive. It is in the order not of doing but only of knowing. But on the final level of questions for deliberation, self-transcendence becomes moral.' Bernard Lonergan, *Method in Theology* (London: Darton, Longman & Todd, 1972; latest printing, Toronto: University of Toronto Press, 2003) 104. Later in the paragraph, too, *Method in Theology* has 'moral self-transcendence' where the current text reads 'real self-transcendence.' We will see other evidence in this volume of Lonergan's attempt to find the appropriate term (eventually, 'moral') to describe activity and self-transcendence at the fourth level. See below, p. 35 and note 9. Similar evidence can be found in the earlier typescripts of the text of *Method in Theology* (from which some of the paragraphs and sections in this chapter and in other selections in this volume may have been taken). For some time, he referred to fourth-level self-transcendence as 'real.' Below, p. 35, we will see him using the term 'performative.' And see *Method in Theology* 241 for at least one instance in which the expression 'real self-transcendence' is retained.

The exclusive identification here of 'intentional' with 'cognitional' is also a problem that, for the most part (but not completely), his later language transcends. Fourth-level activity is also the achievement of intentional consciousness, as is clear even in the next section of this lecture ('Intentional Response and Values'). But see below, p. 23, in Lonergan's response to the first question raised after this lecture.

This may be thought to be a subjective rather than an objective view of value; but subjectivity and objectivity are themselves quite ambiguous terms, and the solution of the ambiguity once more is to be found by reverting to the basic fact and the basic distinction. There is a subjectivity to be blamed because it fails to transcend itself, and there is a subjectivity to be praised because it does transcend itself. There is an objectivity to be repudiated because it is the objectivity of those that fail in self-transcendence, and there is an objectivity to be accepted and respected, and it is that achieved by the self-transcending subject.

Our position, then, parallels that of the existentialists, inasmuch as it can conceive man's mere existing as his capacity for existing authentically or unauthentically; but it differs inasmuch as it discerns in self-transcendence both genuine subjectivity and the principle of genuine objectivity. However, the objectivity it affirms is not the objectivity of positivists and pragmatists, which existentialists deplore, but the objectivity of intentional self-transcendence, to which existentialists have failed to advert.

Again, the subjectivity it affirms, so far from being opposed to genuine objectivity, is its prolongation, for it consists in moving on from intentional, cognitional, to real self-transcendence. Finally, the continuity of the intentional and real is in principle the reconciliation of truth and value, and so of science as concerned for truth with religion as concerned for value.

In brief, we have the capacity both to judge things as they are and to respond to them for what they are. This brings us to our second topic, intentional response.

2   Intentional Response and Values

Here, with Dietrich von Hildebrand, there is a distinction to be drawn between different types of feelings.[3] Some are nonintentional states and trends, while others are intentional responses. The former may be illustrated by such states as fatigue, irritability, bad humor, anxiety, and by such trends or urges as hunger, thirst, sexual discomfort.[4] The states have causes, and the trends or urges have goals. But the relation to the cause or the goal is merely causal or

3 Dietrich von Hildebrand, *Christian Ethics* (New York: David McKay, 1953).
4 Lonergan's expression here avoids an ambiguity that appears on p. 30 of *Method in Theology*, where parallel material is found: '... and distinguish nonintentional states and trends from intentional responses. The former may be illustrated by such states as fatigue, irritability, bad humor, anxiety, and the latter by such trends or urges as hunger, thirst, sexual discomfort.'

teleological; it does not presuppose and arise out of perceiving, imagining, representing the cause or the goal. First one feels tired, and then, perhaps belatedly, one discovers that what one needs is a rest. First one feels hungry, and then one diagnoses the trouble as a lack of food.

Intentional responses, on the other hand, respond to what is intended, apprehended, represented. The feeling relates us, not to a cause or an end but to an object. Such feeling gives our intentional consciousness its mass, momentum, drive, power. Without our feelings, our knowing and deciding would be paper thin. Because of our feelings, our desires and fears, our hope or despair, our joys and sorrows, our enthusiasms and indignation, our esteem and contempt, our trust and distrust, our love and hatred, our tenderness and wrath, our admiration, veneration, reverence, our dread, horror, terror, we are orientated massively and dynamically in a world mediated by meaning. We have feelings about other persons, we feel with them, we feel for them. We have feelings about our respective situations, about the past, about the future, about evils to be lamented or remedied, about the good that can, might, must be accomplished.

Feelings, not as mere states but as intentional response to objects, respond to two main classes of objects: on the one hand, the agreeable or disagreeable, the satisfying or dissatisfying; on the other hand, to values: to the ontic value of persons and to the qualitative value of beauty, of understanding, of truth, of noble deeds, of virtuous acts. In general, response to value both carries us towards self-transcendence and selects an object for the sake of whom or of which we transcend ourselves. In contrast, response to the agreeable or disagreeable is ambiguous. What is agreeable may very well be what also is a true good. But it also is true that the true good may be disagreeable. Unpleasant work, privations, pains have to be accepted gladly by most good men.

Not only do our feelings respond to values, but also they do so in accord with some scale of preference. So we may distinguish vital, social, cultural, personal, and religious values, in an ascending order. Vital values, such as health and strength, grace and vigor, normally are preferred to avoiding the work, the privations, the pains involved in acquiring, maintaining, restoring them. And that preference is spontaneous. We feel contempt for a person who destroys his own health. Social values, the good of order that conditions the vital values of the whole community, are preferred by the community to the vital values of single individuals: not, indeed, in the sense that the community will sacrifice individuals but that the community will expect and demand them to be willing to sacrifice themselves. Cultural values do not exist without the underpinning of social and vital values, but nonetheless they rank higher. Not on bread alone doth man live. Men live and operate, but they also have to find a meaning and a value in their living and operating, and it is the function of culture to discover, express, validate, criticize, correct, develop, improve such meaning and value. Personal value is the person in his self-transcendence, as loving and being loved, as originator of values in himself and his milieu, as an inspiration and invitation to others to do likewise. Religious values, finally, are at the heart of the meaning and value of man's living and man's world, but to them we shall return presently.

Besides the development of skills, studied so painstakingly by Piaget,[5] there is also the development of feelings. It is true, of course, that fundamentally feelings are spontaneous. They do not lie under the command of our will[6] as do the motions of our hands. But, once they have arisen, by advertence and approval, or by disapproval and distraction, they may be reinforced or curtailed. Such reinforcement and curtailment not only will encourage some feelings and discourage others but also will modify one's spontaneous scale of preferences. Again, feelings are enriched and refined by attentive study of the wealth and variety of objects that arouse them, and so no small part of education lies in fostering and developing a climate of discernment and taste, of discriminating praise and carefully worded disapproval, that will conspire with the pupil's or student's own capacities and tendencies, enlarge and deepen his apprehension of values, and help him towards self-transcendence.

I have been conceiving feelings as intentional responses but I must add that they are not merely transient, limited to the time that we are apprehending a value or its opposite, and vanishing the moment our attention shifts. There are, of course, feelings that easily are aroused and easily pass away. But there also are feelings so deep and so strong, especially when deliberately reinforced, that they channel attention, shape one's horizon, direct one's life. Here the supreme illustration is loving. A man or woman that falls in love is engaged in loving not only when attending to the beloved but at all times. Besides particular acts of loving, there is a prior state of being in love, and that prior state is, as it were, the fount of all one's actions. Mutual love is the intertwining of two lives. It transforms an 'I' and a 'thou' into a 'we' so intimate, so secure, so permanent, that each attends, imagines, thinks, plans, feels, speaks, acts in concern for both.

So our feelings, whether momentary or deep and lasting, both reveal to us

---

5 For Lonergan on Piaget, see *Topics in Education*, vol. 10 in Collected Works of Bernard Lonergan, ed. Robert M. Doran and Frederick E. Crowe (Toronto: University of Toronto Press, 1993) 193–207.

6 *Method in Theology* (32) replaces 'our will' with 'decision.'

where values lie and give us the power and momentum to rise above ourselves and accomplish what objectively is good.

We have come, then, to our third topic, the judgment of value.

3   Judgments of Value

Judgments of value are simple or comparative. They affirm or deny that some *x* is truly good or only apparently good. Or they compare distinct instances of the truly good to affirm or deny that one is better, or more important, or more urgent, than the other.

Such judgments are objective or merely subjective inasmuch as they proceed or do not proceed from a self-transcending subject. Their truth or falsity, accordingly, has its criterion in the authenticity or the lack of authenticity of the subject's being. But the criterion is one thing and the meaning of the judgment is another. To say that an affirmative judgment of value is true is to say what objectively is or would be good or better. To say that an affirmative judgment of value is false is to say what objectively is not or would not be good or better.

Judgments of value differ in content but not in structure from judgments of fact. They differ in content, for one can approve of what does not exist, and one can disapprove of what does. They do not differ in structure, inasmuch as in both there is the distinction between criterion and meaning. In both, the criterion is the self-transcendence of the subject, which, however, is only intentional in judgments of fact but is heading towards real self-transcendence in judgments of value. In both, the meaning is or claims to be independent of the subject: judgments of fact state or purport to state what is or is not so; judgments of value state or purport to state what is or is not truly good or truly better.

True judgments of value go beyond merely intentional self-transcendence without reaching the fullness of real self-transcendence. That fullness is not merely knowing but also doing, and man can know what is right without doing it. Still, if he knows and does not perform, either he must be humble enough to acknowledge himself a sinner, or else he will start destroying his moral being by rationalizing, by making out that what truly is good really is not good at all. The judgment of value, then, is itself a reality in the moral order. By it the subject moves beyond the purely intentional order of knowing.[7] By it the

---

7 At the parallel place in *Method in Theology* (37), the text reads, 'By it the subject moves beyond pure and simple knowing.'

subject is constituting himself as proximately capable of real self-transcendence, of benevolence and beneficence, of true loving.

Intermediate between judgments of fact and judgments of value lie apprehensions of value. Such apprehensions are given in feelings. The feelings in question are not the already described nonintentional states, trends, urges that are related to efficient and final causes but not to objects. Again, they are not intentional responses to such objects as the agreeable or disagreeable, the pleasant or painful, the satisfying or dissatisfying. For, while these are objects, still they are ambiguous objects that may prove to be truly good or bad, or only apparently good or bad. Apprehensions of value occur in a further category of intentional response, which greets either the ontic value of the person or the qualitative value of beauty, of understanding, of truth, of noble deeds, of virtuous acts, of great achievements. For we are so endowed that we not only ask questions leading to self-transcendence, not only can recognize correct answers constitutive of intentional self-transcendence, but also can respond with the stirring of our very being when we glimpse the possibility or the actuality of real self-transcendence.

In the judgment of value, then, three components unite. First, there is knowledge of reality, and especially of human reality. Secondly, there are intentional responses to values, feelings that reveal values. Thirdly, there is the initial thrust towards real self-transcendence constituted by the judgment of value itself. The judgment of value presupposes knowledge of human life, of human possibilities proximate and remote, of the probable consequences of projected courses of action. When knowledge is deficient, then fine feelings are apt to be expressed in what is called moral idealism, that is, lovely proposals that don't work out and often do more harm than good. But knowledge alone is not enough, and, while everyone has some measure of moral feeling (for, as the saying is, there is honor among thieves), still moral feelings have to be cultivated, enlightened, strengthened, refined, criticized, and pruned of oddities. Finally, the development of knowledge and the development of moral feeling head to the existential discovery, the discovery of oneself as a moral being, the realization that one not only chooses between courses of action but also thereby makes oneself an authentic human being or an unauthentic one. With that discovery, there emerges in consciousness the significance of personal value and the meaning of personal responsibility. One's judgments of value are revealed as the door to one's fulfilment or to one's loss. Experience, especially repeated experience, of one's frailty or wickedness, raises the question of one's salvation, and, on a more fundamental level, there arises the question of God.

The fact of development and the possibility of failure imply that judgments of value occur in different contexts. There is the context of growth, in which one's knowledge of human living and operating is increasing in extent, precision, refinement, and in which one's responses are advancing from the agreeable to vital values, from vital to social, from social to cultural, from cultural to personal, from personal to religious. Then there prevails an openness to ever further achievement. Past gains are organized and consolidated but they are not rounded off into a closed system but remain incomplete and so open to still further discoveries and developments. The free thrust of the subject into new areas is recurrent, and as yet there is no supreme value that entails all others. But at the summit of the ascent from the initial infantile bundle of needs and clamors and gratifications, there are to be found the deep-set joy and solid peace, the power and the vigor, of being in love with God. In the measure that that summit is reached, then the supreme value is God, and other values are God's expression of his love in this world, in its aspirations, and in its goal. In the measure that one's love of God is complete, then values are whatever one loves and evils are whatever one hates, so that, in Augustine's phrase, if one loves God, one may do as one pleases, *Ama Deum et fac quod vis.* Then affectivity is of a single piece. Further developments only fill out previous achievement. Lapses from grace are rarer and more quickly amended.

But continuous growth seems to be rare. There are the deviations occasioned by neurotic need. There are the refusals to keep on taking the plunge from settled routines to an as yet unexperienced but richer mode of living. There are the mistaken endeavors to quieten an uneasy conscience by ignoring, belittling, denying, rejecting higher values. Preference scales become distorted. Feelings sour. Bias creeps into one's outlook, rationalization into one's morals, ideology into one's thought. So one may come to hate the truly good, and love the really evil. Nor is that calamity limited to individuals. It can happen to groups, to nations, to blocks of nations, to mankind. It can take different, opposed, belligerent forms, to divide mankind and to menace civilization with destruction.

In his thorough and penetrating study of human action, Joseph de Finance distinguished between horizontal and vertical liberty.[8] Horizontal liberty is the exercise of liberty within a determinate horizon and from the basis of a corresponding existential stance. Vertical liberty is the exercise of liberty that

---

8 Joseph de Finance, *Essai sur l'agir humain* (Rome: Presses de l'Université Grégorienne, 1962) 287–304.

selects that stance and the corresponding horizon. Such vertical liberty may be implicit: it occurs in responding to the motives that lead one to ever fuller authenticity, or in ignoring such motives and drifting into an ever less authentic selfhood. But it also can be explicit. Then one is responding to the transcendental notion of value, to the question, Is it worth while? by determining what it would be worth while for one to make of oneself, and what it would be worth while for one to do for one's fellow men. One works out an ideal of human reality and achievement, and to that ideal one dedicates oneself. As one's knowledge increases, as one's experience is enriched, as one's reach is strengthened or weakened, one's ideal may be revised, and the revision may recur many times.

In such vertical liberty, whether implicit or explicit, are to be found the foundations of the judgments of value that occur. Such judgments are felt to be true or false insofar as they generate a peaceful or an uneasy conscience. But they attain their proper context, their clarity and refinement, only through man's historical development and the individual's personal appropriation of his social, cultural, and religious heritage. It is by the transcendental notion of value and its expression in a good and an uneasy conscience that man can develop morally. But a rounded moral judgment is ever the work of a fully developed self-transcending subject or, as Aristotle put it, of the virtuous man.

4   Faith

There remains the fourth topic, faith. I would describe faith as the knowledge born of religious love.

First, then, there is a knowledge born of love. Of it Pascal spoke when he remarked that the heart has reasons which reason does not know, *le coeur a ses raisons que la raison ne connaît pas.*[9] Here by reason I would understand the compound of the activities of the first three levels of intentional consciousness, namely, of experiencing, of understanding, and of factual judging. By the heart's reasons I would understand feelings that are intentional responses to values; and I would recall the two aspects of such responses, the absolute aspect, inasmuch as the feeling is a recognition of value, and the relative aspect, inasmuch as feelings express preference of some values over

---

9 Blaise Pascal, *Pensées, d'après l'édition de L. Brunschvicg* (Londres: M. Dent & Sons, n.d.; Paris: Georges Crès et Cie, n.d.) no. 277, p. 120: 'Le coeur a ses raisons, que la raison ne connaît point; on le sait en milles choses.'

others. Finally, by the heart I understand the subject on the fourth, existential level of intentional consciousness and in the dynamic state of being in love.

Now such being in love may be total. Then it is without conditions, reserves, qualifications; it is otherworldly, for only idolatry would bestow it on anyone or anything of this world; it is a state reached through the exercise of vertical liberty, the liberty that chooses, not among objects within a horizon but between different horizons, different mentalities, different outlooks. It is a state that, once reached, is distinct from, prior to, and principle of subsequent judgments of value and acts of loving. It is the fulfilment of man's capacity for self-transcendence, and as fulfilment it brings a deep-set joy and a profound peace. It radiates through the whole of one's living and acting, opening one's horizon to the full, purifying one's intentional responses to values, rectifying one's scale of preference, underpinning one's judgments of value, simplifying issues by moving them to a deeper level, and strengthening one to achieve the good in the face of evil.

Such being-in-love is religious. Of it St Paul spoke when he exclaimed that the love of God is poured forth in our hearts by the Holy Spirit that has been given us. Of it Paul Tillich spoke when he conceived the religious man as one grasped by ultimate concern.[10] But it is experienced in many ways. It can be the quiet undertow of one's living that reveals itself only in a deep but obscure conviction that one cannot get out of trying to be holy; it can be nurtured by a life devoted to prayer and can transitorily redirect consciousness away from the world mediated by meaning. But however personal and intimate, it is not solitary. It can be given to many, and the many can recognize in one another a common orientation in their living and feeling, in their criteria and their goals. From a common communion with God, there springs the religious community.

Community invites expression, and the expression may vary. It may be imperative, commanding love of God above all and love of one's neighbor as oneself. It may be narrative, the story of the community's origins and development. It may be ascetic and mystical, teaching the way towards total otherworldly love and warning against the pitfalls on the journey. It may be theoretical, teaching the wisdom, the goodness, the power of God, and manifesting his intentions and his purposes. It may be a compound of two or three or all four of these. The compound may fuse the components into a single balanced synthesis, or it may take some one as basic and use it to interpret and manifest

10 Lonergan refers in several places to D.M. Brown, *Ultimate Concern: Tillich in Dialogue* (New York: Harper & Row, 1965). See, for example, *Method in Theology* 106, note 3, and below, p. 40, note 21.

the others. It may remain unchanged for ages, and it may periodically develop and adapt to different social and cultural situations.

Communities endure. As new members replace old, expression becomes traditional. The religion becomes historical in the general sense that it exists over time. But there is a further sense in which a religion may be historical. For the total loving of ultimate concern has the character of a response; it is an answer to a divine initiative. And the divine initiative may be not only the act of creation and conservation but also a personal entrance into human history and a communication of God to his people. Such was the religion of Israel. Such has been Christianity.

Then faith takes on a new dimension. It remains the power of total loving to reveal and uphold all that is good; it remains the bond that unites the religious community in mutual recognition, that directs their common judgments of value, that purifies their beliefs. But it now becomes harkening to the word of Emmanuel, of God-with-us. The history of its origins and developments becomes doctrine as well as narrative; faith is also belief. As a subject grasped by ultimate concern can discern others similarly grasped, so too it can discern God's expression of his total love.

I have been describing faith as the eye of otherworldly love, and doctrinal faith as the recognition of God's own love. Such recognition is on the level of personal encounter. Its formula is Newman's device: *Cor ad cor loquitur*, heart speaketh to heart.[11] It is true that God's word comes to us not immediately but only through the religious community. But the community, as a fellowship of love at the service of mankind, is the sign raised up among the nations, and its members speaking from the heart will speak effectively to those whose hearts the Spirit fills.

Faith, then, subsists and is propagated on a level quite beyond philosophy, or history, or human science; they are the work of Pascal's reason, of experience, understanding, and judgment. But faith is the eye of otherworldly love, and the love itself is God's gift; it is on the level of feelings, values, beliefs, actions, personal encounters, community existence, community action, and community tradition.

However, to say that faith subsists and is propagated on a level beyond experience, understanding, and judgment in no way implies that faith is without experience, understanding, and judgment. The higher levels of man's intentional consciousness do not suppress but presuppose and com-

11 The motto Newman chose on being made a cardinal. See Wilfred Ward, *The Life of John Henry Cardinal Newman*, vol. 2 (London: Longmans, Green, and Co., 1913) 457.

plement the lower.[12] Without experience there is nothing for us to understand; without understanding there is nothing for us to judge; without judgment we do not know, and so we have nothing to love, value, achieve. Inversely,
on the positive side, the many operations come together and cumulatively
regard a single identical object, so that what is experienced is to be understood, what is understood is to be affirmed, what is affirmed is to be evaluated.

However, this continuity has been disregarded or denied in recent decades, and a few clarifications may be in order here, first on the notion of object,
and secondly on intersubjectivity.

First, then, God is not an object among the objects acknowledged by positivists, empiricists, and the like; he is not an object of natural or of human
science; he is not an object in the naive realist sense in which an object is what
is out there and a subject is what is in here. However, he is an object for
intentional and for real self-transcendence, inasmuch as people think of him,
affirm his existence and attributes, fear, worship, love him, speak of him,
praise him. For an object is simply the referred content of an intentional act,
and the enumerated acts of thinking, affirming, worshiping, loving, speaking
are intentional, and they refer to God.[13]

Secondly, besides intending subject and intended object, there is also the
intersubjective relation between two or more intending subjects. So 'I' and
'thou' constitute a 'we' to make *our* plans, do *our* work, develop *our*selves. This
relationship is not subject-to-object but subject-to-subject. Now, there is something similar in total, and so otherworldly, being-in-love, for it puts the existential subject in a personal relationship to God. It is not a relationship to God
as object, for it is prior to all objectification, whether in judgments of value or
beliefs or decisions or words or deeds. It is not similar to human intersubjectivity, for that is between persons with a common horizon; but this being-
in-love determines the horizon of total self-transcendence by grounding the
self and its self-transcendence in the divine lover whose love makes those he

12 Note that Lonergan does not use the term 'sublate' here. That term did
    appear, however, in a lecture delivered just several weeks prior to the
    present lecture, namely, 'The Subject' (3 March 1968). See Bernard
    Lonergan, *A Second Collection*, ed. William F.J. Ryan and Bernard J. Tyrrell
    (latest printing, Toronto: University of Toronto Press, 1996) 80, 84; the latter
    lecture seems to mark its earliest use as applied to the relations among levels
    of consciousness.
13 In the next sentence, there is a gap of about half a minute on both the reel
    and cassette recording. What we have is the following: 'Finally, the possibility
    of God being an object ... place God beyond our horizon would be to deny
    his existence and his goodness.'

loves in love with him, and so with one another. Beyond human intersubjectivity, then, there is a subject-to-subject relationship that is unique and that differs from human intersubjectivity much more than it resembles it.

I have been attempting to characterize Christian faith in a very general fashion. It has not been my present purpose to go into the differences between the Christian churches but rather to suggest a basis for ecumenical dialogue, to point to a horizon common to all Christians and acceptable in some respects to all men of good will.

Question: Why do you use the word 'transcendence'?
Response: In general, transcendence means going beyond, going across and beyond. It is opposed to immanence. There have been philosophies of immanence, particularly since Kant: the impossibility of knowing anything besides your thoughts. You can know what pleases you, what satisfies you, what you like, what you dislike, but you can't know what is good objectively. That is the doctrine of immanence: a relativism with regard to morals, a relativism with regard to value, a relativism with regard to knowledge; not simply a relativism, but there is no such thing as arriving at what is independent of the self, of the subject.

That is the doctrine of immanence; the opposite to it is the doctrine of transcendence, when you assert the possibility of getting beyond yourself. Your horizon is not simply what you can imagine. In other words, you think of persons as being out of their minds if all they can know is what they imagine. To account for getting beyond oneself is, of course, quite a tricky problem in cognitional theory. But the phrase ['transcendence,' 'self-transcendence'] is meant to reject any doctrine of immanence. A doctrine of immanence says all I know is what seems to me, all I know is phenomena, what appears to be good, what appears to be true. To deny that is to say that we know what really is independent of us, what is so whether we say so or not. That is a doctrine of transcendence.

And I divide transcendence into two types: the intentional self-transcendence, namely, knowing what is real, knowing what is so; and real self-transcendence, getting beyond oneself, attending to what is good, not merely to what is good for me but to what is good in itself. If you love a person you do what is good for him or her, not what is good for yourself.

Question: The 'real' also has to do with action, does it not?
Response: It goes on to action. In other words, merely making a judgment of value is a beginning of real self-transcendence but it isn't the completion.

The completion is not merely to make the judgment but also a decision, and not merely to make a decision but also to carry it out.

Question: You mentioned self-transcendence and somehow equated it with authenticity, and I'm associating authenticity with really being oneself, so I'm getting muggy when I put it next to self-transcendence.

Response: Well, your real self, in that sense of really being oneself, is the self-transcending self. Your real self is not backing into childhood narcissism but going beyond yourself, apprehending a world not of fantasy but as it is, apprehending what is worth while objectively, and living according to those apprehensions.

Question: What about the use of drugs as a means of transcendence of psychic difficulties ...

Response: Well, that is a going beyond, and there are cases where it can be defended, but they are very special cases. Involved there is a judgment on youth and on the use of drugs, two very complicated things. The general meaning of the word 'transcend,' in the philosophic context, is to go beyond, which is the meaning I gave. You can use it in other senses, like pulling out of ordinary living by taking drugs. That's a different sense.

Question: What is an objective truth? Is an objective truth for you an objective truth for me?

Response: We both agree that two and two are four.

Question (continued): Let me give you an example. We would regard keeping our older people alive to be an objective good, but the Eskimo might think it is an objective good to bury his ailing parents alive. What about the objective good in the case of the Eskimo burying their parents alive?

Response: I don't say judgments of value are infallible. They also can be mistaken. Again, judgments of value occur within a context, and the context may be more or less developed. For example, one's ethical judgments and one's ethical possibilities depend on the people one is living with. If one is living with very nice people who are very considerate and thoughtful and kind and gentle and so on, it isn't too hard oneself to be thoughtful, considerate, kind, and gentle. But if one is living with a group of thugs and wants to survive, one has to be a bit of a thug oneself. One's moral judgments and one's moral possibilities are conditioned by the milieu in which one lives. They are further conditioned by the development of mankind. And besides developments, there are also deteriorations.

In other words, there are different moral judgments made by different people in different societies. And I say that, as far as moral judgments are concerned, they are objective insofar as the subject is transcending himself in making them, and is a subject who does so habitually. Aristotle put it this way: that the virtuous act is the act that is judged to be virtuous by a man who is virtuous. That leaves room for a great spectrum of moral judgments, and you will have people, on the way and in the process of their development, making the best judgments they can. But you get the objective moral judgment only at the term of the process. Is that meeting your question to some extent? In other words, you are capable of being moral and arriving at moral judgments insofar as you ask the question, Is this worth while? Is this truly good? The good and the uneasy conscience are indications whether your judgment is sound or not. But that alone is not sufficient. You also have to have developed morally, developed your moral feelings, and so on, and that development will be stunted in an inadequate social and cultural milieu.

Question (continued): Can we both be wrong?
Response: Yes. We might both be wrong if we still have to develop morally.

Question [Questioner pursues the direction of the two previous questions.]
Response: People can come fairly quickly, through their praise or blame, through their preferential response, to the determination. I don't think you have any doubt that it is better not to bury your parents in ice. As Aristotle put it, people who discuss ethical questions have to have a considerable experience of life. And he wasn't aware of the experience of different cultures, which is a further qualification we would have to add, like the discussion of moral judgments in the Old Testament: Abraham accepting the idea of offering up his son in sacrifice, and Jacob deceiving his father and getting his father's blessing, and so on. There is such a thing as the development of moral feeling and moral perception.

Question: How does intentional response relate to hope and despair?
Response: Hope and despair are responding to objects. Hope – things look black, but you keep on trying, you have hope. You still see that you might get there. You can have hope that is not merely an abstract judgment; it can be a force that carries you on, it can be towards the attainment of a prospective goal.

Question: What is the motivation?
Response: The motivation is the goodness; it is the objective goodness, the objective excellence, the value, of what you are hoping for. Now in hope there

can be further components, like the ground: why you can hope for something – it may be because of someone else's health, and things like that; or your optimistic outlook; all sorts of things that can contribute to it.

Question: So this is profoundly inside yourself?
Response: It is your moral being. Your moral being has to be something that will get things done, not merely apprehend. It is not only revealing what is good, what is the truly good, but also carrying you to accomplish it.

Question: So you have to take everything in an optimistic view?
Response: Well, I'm not saying that. I say that the reason why a man may be hoping may be his optimism; it may be he is counting on someone else. You hope in God's grace to help you overcome your defects, to overcome temptations to despair; you pray.

Question: How are you using the word 'doctrinal'?
Response: Well, in general, stating that something is true. Now with regard to definitive formulations, do you mean that they are exhaustive? By 'doctrinal,' I simply mean statements of what is true.

Question: What is your definition of truth?
Response: There is the definition of truth and the criterion of truth. The definition of truth is the correspondence between the judgment and the fact. The criterion of truth is reaching a virtually unconditioned in an act of reflective understanding from which the judgment proceeds.

Question: But realizing that you might change your mind next week?
Response: Well, I didn't say that. If the judgment is probable, that's true. If it is a scientific judgment, for example, that's true.

Question: Under what circumstances can a judgment be unconditioned?
Response: The condition for making a judgment is grasping a virtually unconditioned. But the meaning of that I explain in about fifty pages in chapter 10 of *Insight*.

Question: How do you distinguish different kinds of love, especially otherworldly love from this-worldly love?
Response: There is loving God with your whole heart, your whole soul, with all your mind and all your strength. That is from the Old and New Testament. It

is a love without conditions or qualifications or reserve. Insofar as it is without any qualification or condition or reserve, it is something absolute in its character, totally and in every respect. To love any creature in that fashion would be idolatry. It is God's gift to us, St Paul, Romans 5.5: 'The love of God is poured forth in our hearts by the Holy Spirit who is given to us.' Now in that love it is common to distinguish two phases: operative and cooperative. Operative is represented by what you say: St Peter saying at the Last Supper, 'Lord, if everyone should deny you, at least I won't deny you'; and cooperative, when St Peter underwent martyrdom. He not only professed it but he did it.

Question: What do you mean by otherworldly love?
Response: When I say it is otherworldly I mean its object is not some creature, something of this world. I don't say it doesn't occur in this life; I say it does occur in this life. I say it is in anyone in the state of sanctifying grace, though I don't say that anyone in the state of sanctifying grace is skillful enough at psychological introspection to detect it.

Question: Is not conscience being dependent on judgments of value? And if so, how can the criterion of judgments of value be conscience? Is there not a circle here?
Response: There are a lot of circles in it. The fundamental thing is the idea of value, the notion of value, which is an intending and not a knowing. It is the question, Is this worth while? Is it truly good? Is it really important? Asking that question is the first step. There are apprehensions of values, and these occur insofar as one is apprehending things, experiencing, understanding, judging; and further, there is added on to this an intentional response, a feeling that is not just a feeling state like fatigue or hunger or thirst, but a response to an object. It is not simply a response to an object as agreeable or disagreeable, pleasant or unpleasant, but it responds to an object as something good. Take gentleness: you see a person react in a gentle or kind or considerate fashion, and so on. You have a glimpse in that of something that is good in human beings. That is one component. Now, these intentional responses are something in which one develops. One develops in one's sensitivity, so to speak, and one also develops in one's preferences. And there is room there for development. The judgment of value presupposes the question, the development, of this sensitivity towards values. And thirdly, there is knowledge of concrete possibility, knowledge of human reality. If you don't know human reality and you have very fine moral feelings, you go into moral idealism, which is a sort of aberration. And moreover, you have to live in accord with your

judgments of values; otherwise, there is a tendency to rationalization. It is in the morally developed person – his judgments, his self-transcendence when his conscience is good, when he is satisfied with the judgments he makes – that one has the criterion for the judgment of value. The criterion is self-transcendence, getting beyond oneself, when one really is doing that.

Question (continued): How do you define conscience?
Response: Conscience in the sense in which I use it: the sense in which I used it was the fact that just as, for example, when you understand, you are asking for why and you catch on, there is a satisfaction there, isn't there? – the satisfaction of getting the point.

Question (continued): Is it based on your sense of values?
Response: No. It is based on your intelligence. Your intelligence is satisfied, or your intelligence is dissatisfied and you ask further questions; you find that it is satisfactory up to a certain point; you have further questions and you keep on questioning: that ability to be satisfied or keep on questioning on the level of questions for intelligence. On the level of questions for reflection, Is this so, or is it not so? When you grasp the virtually unconditioned you are ready to say, 'That's it.' And thirdly, on the level of questions for deliberation, when you make your judgment of value, there is also involved your moral response, you as a moral being. Are you satisfied or dissatisfied? And that is the good or the uneasy conscience.

Question (continued): So your conscience depends not so much on feelings but on the development of further insights?
Response: It depends on your whole moral development. It depends on your milieu. It depends on insights insofar as morality has to be knowledge of the facts and the real possibilities. It depends upon feelings insofar as it is through feelings as intentional responses to what is objectively good that you have a recognition of values and a capacity to realize them.

Question (continued): How would I know when I have made a judgment of value on an objective good?
Response: There is no simple answer to that question. There is the greater likelihood of your being right according to your knowledge of mankind and of the human situation, in accord with your own moral development, and so on.

Question (continued): Can anyone know an objective good?
Response: Yes, on certain points; but about everything, no one.

Question: What would you say about our present situation?
Response: I would say that any historical situation is a compound of progress and decline. I think we have advanced enormously in knowledge, especially in the natural sciences, and we are having developments in the human sciences. I think that the apprehension of values is something that is being corroded to a great extent. The explanation of the teenage culture is that the young people sense that their elders are not quite convinced of their values, and consequently they can't take them over. They want to make them up for themselves. That is just an opinion on the thing, but it is a straw in the wind. But to make a massive judgment on the whole modern world is just impossible.

Question: I am trying to understand your basis for ecumenical dialogue. [This question was preceded by the questioner's opinion on the matter, including the conviction that both sides would have to free themselves from all ulterior motives and be intent on the one purpose of coming closer to God.]
Response: I didn't attempt to outline all the conditions of a possible dialogue. I was just saying something about the meaning of the word 'faith' in that context. I think what you are saying is fundamentally sound.

Question: Can we compare true human values to morality?
Response: I would say yes. Values are one of the ways in which one approaches the notion of a moral system. There are different ways in which moral systems can be thought out; for example, in terms of natural law, in terms of an ultimate end; in terms of values is another way, and I think that is a sound approach to moral questions. I think it is very close to Aristotle's *Nicomachean Ethics*, though he didn't call it values; he called it *aretê*, virtue or what has been translated as virtue. The word 'morality' is the sort of thing that can be systematized in different ways, and one can discuss at some length the value of the different ways. Is morality conceived as a means to a *summum bonum*, is morality conceived in terms of natural law, or is morality conceived in terms of values? There are different approaches. They are all useful in certain respects. I think that one of the more fruitful ones is the approach through values, and I think that it is through values that one arrives at something true about morality.

3

Faith and Beliefs[1]

In a public lecture at the University of Toronto on 9 January 1968, Professor Wilfred Cantwell Smith began by remarking that much fruitful energy has been devoted to exploring the religious traditions and reconstructing the

1 [A lecture given at the annual meeting of the American Academy of Religion, Newton, MA, on 23 October 1969. Substantially the same lecture was given at other locations in the fall of the same year: at Immaculate Conception Seminary, Darlington, NJ, 18 October; at the Catholic University of America, Washington, DC, 20 November; in part (with the title 'Religious Commitment') at the University of St Michael's College, University of Toronto, 28 November, on the occasion of Lonergan's receiving the honorary degree Doctor of Sacred Letters; with the title 'The Notion of Commitment' at Ignatius College, Guelph, Ontario, 4 December; and at Regis College, Willowdale, ON, date not known. A lecture also entitled 'Faith and Beliefs' was given at Massey College, University of Toronto, 9 January 1973. Again, substantially the same lecture was given at St Peter's College, Jersey City, NJ, on 27 November 1972, but under the title 'Religious Commitment.' Another paper with the title 'Religious Commitment' (longer than the St Michael's lecture of the same name) was delivered at Villanova University in June 1971, and it drew heavily on 'Faith and Beliefs.' The St Michael's lecture on 'Religious Commitment' and the Villanova paper of the same name will be published in the volume of archival materials in the Collected Works.
   An autograph text of 'Faith and Beliefs' can be found in the Lonergan archives, Toronto, file 623. Lonergan's personal corrections and emendations were entered into a more neatly typed copy, likely by another typist, several copies of which are found in the same file in the archives and one copy of which is available in the library of the Lonergan Research Institute, LB 217.1. This second typescript may have been the one that Lonergan used in delivering the lecture. There is a tape recording of the lecture (Institute

history of the overt data of mankind's religious living. Both in detail and in wide compass, the observable forms have been observed and the observations recorded. But Professor Smith went on to claim that a further, a more important, and a more difficult question must be raised. To live religiously is not merely to live in the presence of certain symbols but, he urged, it is to be involved with them or through them in a quite special way – a way that may lead far beyond the symbols, that may demand the totality of a person's response, and may affect his relation not only to the symbols but to everything else: to himself, to his neighbor, and to the stars.[2]

This special involvement, Professor Smith claimed, pleads to be elucidated. And elucidate it he did by naming this involvement, engagement, commitment 'faith' and by distinguishing such faith from the imperatives, rituals, traditions, beliefs that inspire faith or are inspired by faith. So con-

---

Library, TC 537, 1 and 3), and there are only a few variations between the spoken word and the prepared text. There is also a tape recording of the lecture delivered in Guelph. Significant differences between the written text and what appears on the tapes will be indicated in the footnotes below. The editing relies principally on the autograph text and on these two tape recordings.

One of the respondents to the AAR lecture was Professor Wilfred Cantwell Smith. The Newton tape contains Professor Smith's remarks and Lonergan's reply to Smith. Professor Walter Conn of Villanova University forwarded to the Lonergan Research Institute in April 1986 the tape recording of the lecture used here, as well as a second cassette (TC 537, 2) recording Professor Smith's response and part of Lonergan's further comments. Around the same date, Professor William M. Shea, now of St Louis University, sent the Institute a typescript (apparently made by Sister Rose Tadsen) of both the lecture and the response. An edited version of Lonergan's response to Professor Smith is included here. The other respondent to the lecture was Professor Herbert Richardson, but no recording of his response was available at the time of editing.

Lonergan's text had endnotes. These are given here in footnotes, without brackets. Editorial additions to the footnotes are in brackets. Section divisions and titles are Lonergan's.

As several of the notes below will indicate, this paper may be the locus where some of the parts of what became chapter 4 of *Method in Theology* ('Religion') were first written. It is also clear that the precise relation of faith and beliefs is more precisely worked out in *Method in Theology* than it is here.]

2   [Lonergan's own endnote reads: 'I do not know whether this paper has been published. I am going by a typescript sent me by Prof. Smith.' The title of Smith's lecture was 'Faith & Belief, As Seen by a Comparative Religionist.' A copy of the typescript is in an archive file (unnumbered, but following file 675 in Batch XIII) labeled 'Wilfred C. Smith.']

ceived, I think, faith would not be[3] the prerogative of some particular church or religion. It would not be merely ecumenical but universalist. It would be relevant to an understanding of any and every religion. Moreover, its relevance would be of the highest order, for unless one understands what personal involvement in religion is, one can hardly be expected to think or speak very intelligently of religiously committed persons.

No doubt, prior to the Second Vatican Council a universalist view of faith would have been suspect in Roman Catholic circles. But since the Council, since the establishment in Rome both of a Secretariat for Christian Unity and of a Secretariat concerned with non-Christian Religions,[4] it is of the utmost importance for Catholics to think this matter through. Unhesitatingly they grant that God wills all men to be saved. Unhesitatingly they grant that God gives each man sufficient grace for salvation. But what this grace is and how it is related to the phenomena set forth in the history of religions seem shrouded in obscurity.

Accordingly, what profoundly interests Professor Smith as a student of comparative religion also profoundly interests me as a theologian. I propose, then, to raise four questions. First, what is man's capacity for religious involvement? Secondly, in what precisely does such religious involvement consist? Thirdly, in what sense can such involvement be called faith? Fourthly, what is the relation between such faith and religious beliefs?

Such are the questions, and I had best add at once a word about the answers. Obviously they cannot but be sketchy. I cannot present my grounds for my philosophic opinions. I cannot amass the empirical evidence that would be necessary to confirm my views. Accordingly, I must ask you to think of this paper as offering a construct, a model, an ideal type, something that is neither a description of reality nor a hypothesis about reality but just a set of related notions that may prove quite useful to have around when the time does come for forming hypotheses or describing realities.

3 [In both the Newton and the Guelph lectures Lonergan made a somewhat offhand comment at this point distinguishing this notion of faith from that found in the New Testament or in the dogmas. The wording on the Newton tape is not clear. In the Guelph lecture Lonergan said, 'So conceived faith would not be [pause] the notion of faith that you get from a study of the New Testament or the dogmas of the church. Such faith would not be the prerogative ...']

4 [The relevant conciliar document was the 'Declaration on the Relation of the Church to non-Christian Religions,' 28 October 1965; the subsequent Secretariat established was the 'Secretariat for Unbelievers.' In the spoken lecture at Newton, Lonergan added mention of a 'Secretariat for Non-believers' to the two other Secretariats that he named.]

1   Man's Capacity for Religious Involvement

In an essay entitled 'Traum und Existenz' Ludwig Binswanger distinguished dreams of the night and dreams of the morning.[5] In both kinds of dream there is an element of *Existenz*, of being someone, someone conscious, someone within some sort of world, someone somehow dealing with that world or, perhaps, being overwhelmed by it. Any such world, of course, is imaginary, and one's apprehension of it in the dream is symbolic, obscure, fragmentary. But in dreams of the night we are further from our waking state than in dreams of the morning. Dreams of the night respond more to somatic conditions, to the state, say, of one's digestive apparatus. But in dreams of the morning our waking state is being anticipated. Already its problems are dimly sensed. Already the subject is taking a stance with regard to them.

I am not enough of a psychologist to know how well founded Dr Binswanger's distinction is, but at least it provides an introduction to a notion I consider of basic import, the notion of self-transcendence. For in the dream state there is not just the unconscious; however imperfectly, there has emerged a conscious self relating to subjective need or to some sort of 'objective' problem. In dreamless sleep there is neither conscious subject nor intended object. With the dream there is not yet one's full self nor an adequately intended object. But there is the fragmentary recollection or anticipation of both. There have appeared both a self and a self's conscious relation to some other. From that slight beginning we have to mount through four further stages or levels of human consciousness and intentionality if we are to apprehend the self and its capacities.

Most easily identified in our waking states are our sensations, feelings, movements. There is the endless variety of sights to be seen, sounds to be heard, odors to be sniffed, tastes to be palated, shapes and textures to be touched. We feel pleasure and pain, desire and fear, joy and sorrow, and in such feelings there seem to reside the mass and momentum of our lives. We move about in various manners, take now this now that posture, and by the fleeting movements of our facial muscles reveal or betray our emotions.[6]

---

5   [Ludwig Binswanger, 'Traum und Existenz,' *Ausgewählte Vorträge und Aufsätze* (Berne: A. Francke, 1947), vol. 1, pp. 74–97; in English, 'Dream and Existence,' in *Being-in-the-World: Selected Papers of Ludwig Binswanger*, trans. Jacob Needleman (New York: Basic Books, and New York: Harper Torchbooks, 1963) 222–48. Lonergan's endnote refers to the French translation, *Le rêve et l'existence*, with introduction and notes by Michel Foucault (Paris: Desclée, 1954).]

6   [This was Lonergan's wording, in the spoken lecture at Newton, of the last

Still, sensations, feelings, movements reveal no more than the narrow strip of space-time that we immediately experience. One may doubt that man has ever been content with such a world of immediacy. Imagination wants to fill out and round off the picture. Language makes questions possible, and intelligence makes them fascinating. So we ask what and how and what for and why. Our answers extrapolate and serialize and construct and generalize. Memory and tradition and belief put at our disposal the tales of travelers, the stories of nations, the exploits of heroes, the meditations of holy men, the treasures of literature, the discoveries of science, the reflections of philosophers. Each of us has his own little world of immediacy, but all such worlds are just minute strips within a far larger world, a world constructed by imagination and intelligence, mediated by words and meaning,[7] and based largely upon belief.

Now it is that far larger world that is, for each of us, the real world. It is a world unknown to the infant, learned about at home and at school and at work. It is the world in which we live most of our lives.

But you are, I suspect, somewhat uneasy about this larger world that only slightly is 'this sure and firm-set earth on which I tread,'[8] that in the main is constructed by imagination and intelligence, that is mediated by words and meaning, that by and large is based on belief. Such a description, however accurate, is not reassuring. This lack of assurance reveals the presence of a further question and, indeed, a question different in kind from those already considered. The questions already considered were questions for intelligence, asking what x is, and what it is for, and how it is made, and on what principles it works. None of these questions can be answered by a simple yes or no. But whenever any of these questions are answered, the answer itself gives rise to a still further question that can be answered by a simple yes or no. These further questions are questions, not for intelligence, but for reflection. They ask, Is that so? Is that not so? Is it certainly so? Is it only probably so?

---

part of this sentence. The written text has, 'and express our emotions by the fleeting movements of our facial muscles'; the latter is what Lonergan read when he delivered the paper at St Peter's College; and the tape of the Guelph lecture has 'and by the fleeting movements of our facial muscles express our feelings.']

7 [The written texts have only 'mediated by meaning'; the expression 'words and' was added in some of the oral lectures; but see several instances below where the latter expression was given in the written texts themselves.]

8 [The reference is to *Macbeth*, act 2, scene 1, lines 56–57: 'Thou sure and firm-set earth / Hear not my steps, ...' In the Guelph lecture, Lonergan said, '... Macbeth's sure and firm-set earth ...']

Just how such questions can be answered is a very nice problem in cognitional theory. But the fact is that we do answer them. The further fact is that when we affirm that something really and truly is so, then we do not mean that that is what appears, or what we imagine, or what we think, or what seems to be so, or what we are inclined to say. No doubt, very frequently we have to be content with such lesser statements. But the point I would make is that the greater statement is not reducible to the lesser. When we affirm that something really and truly is so, we mean that we somehow have got beyond ourselves, somehow have got hold of what is independent of ourselves, somehow have transcended ourselves.

I have been endeavoring to unfold and clarify the notion of self-transcendence by drawing your attention to a succession of distinct levels of human consciousness. First, I spoke of the subject in his dreams. Secondly, I spoke of the empirical subject awake, sensing, feeling, moving about in his world of immediacy. Thirdly, I spoke of the inquiring subject in a far larger world constructed by imagination and intelligence, mediated by words and meaning, by and large based upon belief. Fourthly, I spoke of the rational subject that reflects, marshals and weighs the evidence, pronounces judgment in the light of the evidence, and by his judgment claims to state something about some part of a world that only to a slight extent is his world of immediacy.

With judgment, then, self-transcendence, insofar as it is cognitional, is complete. But human self-transcendence is not only cognitional; it may also be performative.[9] Beyond questions for intelligence and questions for reflection, there are questions for deliberation. Beyond the pleasures we enjoy and the pains we dread, there are the values to which we may respond with all our being. On the topmost level of human consciousness the subject deliberates, evaluates, decides, controls, acts. He is at once practical and existential: practical, inasmuch as he is concerned with concrete courses of action; existential, inasmuch as control includes self-control, and the possibility of self-control involves responsibility for what he makes of himself.

However, man's self-control can proceed from quite different grounds. It can tend to be mere selfishness. Then the process of deliberation, evaluation, decision is limited to determining what is most to one's advantage, what best

9 [Here occurs the most significant variation between Lonergan's autograph text and the taped lectures. In the autograph text, the adjective used here, and in five succeeding references, is 'real.' With one exception at the same point in both the Newton and Guelph lectures, 'performative' is substituted in the taped lectures (but see the next note and notes 14 and 17). In the 1972 lecture at St Peter's Lonergan had changed the word to 'moral.' 'Performative' is retained here in the edited version.]

serves one's interests, what on the whole yields a maximum of pleasure and a minimum of pain. At the opposite pole, it can tend to be concerned solely with values: with the vital values of health and strength; with the social values enshrined in family and custom, society and education, church or sect, state and law, economy and technology; with the cultural values of religion and art, language and literature, science, philosophy, and history; with the personal value of one that realizes values in oneself and helps realize them in others.

In the measure that one's living, one's aims, one's achievements are a response to values, in that measure a performative self-transcendence[10] is effected. One has got beyond mere selfishness. One has become a principle of benevolence and beneficence, capable of genuine collaboration and of true love. In the measure that real [*sic*] self-transcendence characterizes the members of a society, in that measure their world not only is constructed by imagination and intelligence, mediated by words and meaning, by and large based on belief; it also is a world that is regulated and motivated not by self-seeking but by values, not by what apparently is good but by what truly is good.[11]

I have been attempting to describe man's capacity for self-transcendence, and now I must add two reflections. The first regards the spatial metaphor of speaking of levels of consciousness. To remove this metaphor, I wish to introduce the notion of sublation, not exactly in Hegel's sense, but rather in a sense used by Karl Rahner.[12] Let us distinguish, then, between a sublating set of operations and a sublated set. The sublating set introduces operations that are quite new and distinct; it finds among them a new basis and ground; but so far from stunting or interfering with the sublated set, it preserves them integrally, it vastly extends their relevance, and it perfects their performance.

Now the transition from dreaming to waking is not sublation: waking does not include dreaming but simply puts an end to it.[13] On the other hand, the transitions effected by questions for intelligence, questions for reflection,

---

10 [At this point in the Guelph and St Peter's lectures, Lonergan said, 'a real self-transcendence'; in the Guelph lecture he then corrected himself: 'a performative self-transcendence.']

11 [Thus the wording of the last part of the sentence in the Newton lecture. The written text has simply 'it also is a world that is regulated not by self-seeking but by values, by what truly is good.' The Guelph lecture presents something in between these two: 'a world that is regulated not by self-seeking but by values, not by the apparent good but by what truly is good.' The St Peter's lecture follows what is found in the written lecture.]

12 Karl Rahner, *Hörer des Wortes* (München: Kösel, 1963) 40 [in English, *Hearers of the Word*, trans. Michael Richards (Montreal: Palm Publishers, 1969) 24–25. [On 'sublation,' see above, p. 22, note 12.]

13 [But see below, p. 400, on the symbolic operator.]

questions for deliberation, are sublations. The empirical subject does not vanish when he begins to inquire, to ask what and why and how and what for. On the contrary, he begins to notice what before he had overlooked, to perceive more distinctly, to observe more accurately. Similarly, the empirical and inquiring subject does not vanish when questions for reflection are raised, when he asks whether this or that is or is not so. On the contrary, such questions keep us confronting our insights, explanations, views with ever broader and fuller ranges of data. Finally, the question for deliberation that stops us by asking whether this or that is really worth while introduces the notion of value to complete the cognitional self-transcendence reached through experiencing, understanding, and judging, with the performative[14] self-transcendence of benevolence and beneficence.[15] But this addition and completion in no way dispenses with experiencing, understanding, and judging. One cannot do good without knowing the facts, without knowing what really is possible, without knowing the probable consequences of one's course of action. Just as inquiry directs sense towards knowledge of a universe, just as reflection directs sense and understanding towards truth and reality, so deliberation turns sense and understanding and judgment towards the realization of the good, of values.

My second remark regards the continuity and unity of human consciousness. A faculty psychology divides man up: it distinguishes intellect and will, sense perception and imagination, emotion and conation, only to leave us with unresolved problems of priority and rank. Is sense to be preferred to intellect, or intellect to sense?[16] Is intellect to be preferred to will, or will to intellect? Is one to be a sensist, an intellectualist, or a voluntarist? The questions vanish once one has ceased to think in terms of faculties or powers. What is given to consciousness is a set of interrelated intentional operations. Together they conspire to achieve both cognitional and performative[17] self-transcendence. Such is the basic unity and continuity. No part of the process can be dispensed with, for each has its essential contribution to make. To achieve the good, one has to know the real. To know the real, one has to reach the truth. To reach the truth, one has to understand, to grasp the intelligible.

14 [Here again, in the Guelph lecture, Lonergan corrected himself from 'real' to 'performative.' At St Peter's he said 'moral.']
15 [At St Peter's, Lonergan added 'of wishing well and doing well.']
16 [This last sentence, given in both versions of the autograph, was omitted in the oral presentation of the Newton lecture.]
17 [Again, in the Guelph lecture, Lonergan said 'real' first. At St Peter's he said 'moral' (although the copy of the paper that has been indicated as a possible source has 'real,' uncorrected.)]

To grasp the intelligible, one has to attend to the data. Each successive level of operations presupposes and complements its predecessors. The topmost level is the level of deliberate control and self-control; there consciousness becomes conscience; there operations are authentic in the measure that they are responses to value.

2   What Is Religious Involvement?

I have been speaking of man's capacity for self-transcendence. I have now to ask not about mere capacity but about achievement. Now capacity, I suggest, becomes achievement when one falls in love. Then one's being becomes being-in-love. Such being-in-love has its antecedents, its causes, its conditions, its occasions. But once it has occurred and as long as it lasts, it takes over. It becomes the first principle. From it flow one's desires and fears, one's joys and sorrows, one's discernment of values, one's decisions and deeds.[18]

Being-in-love is of different kinds. There is the love of intimacy, of husband and wife, of parents and children.[19] There is the love of one's fellow men with its fruit in the achievement of human welfare. There is the love of God with one's whole heart and whole soul, with all one's mind and all one's strength (Mark 12.30). It is God's love flooding our hearts through the Holy Spirit given to us (Romans 5.5). It grounds the conviction of St Paul that 'there is nothing in death or life, in the realm of spirits or superhuman powers, in the world as it is or the world as it shall be, in the forces of the universe – nothing in all creation that can separate us from the love of God in Christ Jesus our Lord' (Romans 8.38–39).

Being in love with God, as experienced, is being in love in an unrestricted fashion. All love is self-surrender, but being in love with God is being in love without limits or qualifications or conditions or reservations. It is with one's whole heart and whole soul, with all one's mind and all one's strength. Just as unrestricted questioning is our capacity for self-transcendence, so being in love in an unrestricted fashion is the proper fulfilment of that capacity.

Because that love is the proper fulfilment of our capacity, that fulfilment

18 [There is material in this section that appears later with some changes in *Method in Theology*, at pp. 105–107. While this material was found in the lecture on religion in the institute on Method that Lonergan conducted the previous summer at Regis College, Willowdale, Ontario, still it would seem from the more original autograph copy of the present lecture and the various markings and corrections that Lonergan entered there (see above, note 1) that he was still working out his articulation.]

19 [At St Peter's, Lonergan added 'of brothers and sisters.']

brings a deep-set joy that can remain despite humiliation, privation, pain, betrayal, desertion. Again, that fulfilment brings a radical peace, the peace that the world cannot give (John 14.27). That fulfilment bears fruit in a love of one's neighbor that strives mightily to bring about the kingdom of God on this earth. On the other hand, the absence of that fulfilment opens the way to the trivialization of human life in the pursuit of fun, to the harshness of human life arising from the ruthless exercise of power, to despair about human welfare springing from the conviction that the universe is absurd.

The fulfilment that is being in love with God is not the product of our knowledge and choice. It is God's gift. So far from resulting from our knowledge and choice, it dismantles and abolishes the horizon in which our knowing and choosing went on, and it sets up a new horizon in which the love of God will transvalue our values and the eyes of that love will transform our knowing.

Though not the product of our knowing and choosing, it is a conscious, dynamic state of love, joy, peace, that manifests itself in the harvest of the Spirit, in acts of kindness, goodness, fidelity, gentleness, and self-control (Galatians 5.22).

To say that that dynamic state is conscious is not to say that it is known. What is conscious is, indeed, experienced. But human knowing is not just experiencing. Human knowing includes experiencing but adds to it scrutiny, insight, conception, naming, reflection, checking, judging. The whole problem of cognitional theory is to effect the transition from conscious operations to known operations. A great part of psychiatry is helping people effect the transition from conscious feelings to known feelings. In like manner, the gift of God's love ordinarily is not objectified in knowledge but remains within subjectivity as a dynamic vector, a mysterious undertow, a fateful call to a dreaded holiness.

Because that dynamic state is conscious without being known, it is an experience of mystery. Because it is being in love, the mystery is not merely attractive but fascinating: to it one belongs; by it one is possessed. Because it is an unrestricted, unmeasured being in love, the mystery is other-worldly; it evokes awe. Because it is a love so different from the selfish self that it transcends, it evokes even terror. Of itself, then, inasmuch as it is conscious without being known, the experience of the gift of God's love is an experience of the holy, of Rudolf Otto's *mysterium fascinans et tremendum*.[20] Again, it is

20 Rudolf Otto, *The Idea of the Holy*, trans. John W. Harvey (London: Oxford University Press, 1923; paperback, 1958) [especially chapters 4–6].

what Paul Tillich named a being grasped by ultimate concern.[21] Again, it corresponds to Ignatius Loyola's consolation that has no cause, as interpreted by Karl Rahner.[22]

I have distinguished different levels of consciousness, and now I must add that the gift of God's love is on the topmost level. It is not the consciousness that accompanies acts of seeing, hearing, smelling, tasting, touching. It is not the consciousness that accompanies acts of inquiry, insight, formulation, speaking. It is not the consciousness that accompanies acts of reflecting, marshaling and weighing the evidence, making judgments of fact or possibility. It is the consciousness that also is conscience, that deliberates, evaluates, decides, controls, acts. But it is this consciousness as brought to fulfilment, as having undergone a conversion, as possessing a basis that may be broadened and deepened and heightened and enriched but not superseded, as ever more ready to deliberate and evaluate and decide and act with the easy freedom of those that do all good because they are in love. So the gift of God's love occupies the ground and root of the fourth and highest level of man's waking[23] consciousness. It takes over the peak of the soul, the *apex animae*.

I think many of you will grant that a basic component of religious involvement among Christians is God's gift of his love. But I wish to indicate a reason for thinking that the same may be said[24] of religious involvement in all the world religions, in Christianity, Judaism, Islam, Zoroastrian Mazdaism, Hinduism, Buddhism, Taoism. For Friedrich Heiler has described at some length seven common areas in those religions.[25] While I cannot reproduce here the

21 D.M. Brown, *Ultimate Concern: Tillich in Dialogue* [see above, p. 20, note 10. See also Paul Tillich, *Systematic Theology*, 3 vols. in 1 (Chicago: University of Chicago Press, and New York: Harper & Row, 1967), vol. 1, pp. 10–14, and numerous references in the index.]

22 Karl Rahner, *The Dynamic Element in the Church*, Quaestiones Disputatae 12 (Montreal: Palm Publishers, 1964) 131–37. Rahner takes 'consolation without a cause' to mean 'consolation with a content but without an object.' [In the St Peter's lecture, Lonergan said, 'namely, a consolation that has a content but has not got an intellectually apprehended object.']

23 [In *Method in Theology* the word here is 'intentional.' In the autograph of 'Faith and Beliefs' the word 'intentional' is crossed out, and 'waking' replaces it. See above, p. 12, note 2, regarding the gradual development of the meaning of 'intentional' for Lonergan. In the lecture on religion the previous summer, Lonergan said 'intentional' at this point, and he was to come back to that formulation in the book.]

24 [In the AAR lecture, Lonergan added here the words 'in some sense.']

25 Friedrich Heiler, 'The History of Religions as a Preparation for the Cooperation of Religions,' *The History of Religions, Essays in Methodology*, ed. Mircea

rich texture of his thought, or its nuances, I can at least give a list of the topics he treats, and, from it, draw a conclusion.

The seven common areas are: first, the existence of a transcendent reality; secondly, the immanence of that reality in human hearts; thirdly, the characterization of that reality as supreme beauty, truth, righteousness, goodness; fourthly, the characterization of that reality as love, mercy, compassion; fifthly, our way to that reality is repentance, self-denial, prayer; sixthly, that way is love of one's neighbor, even of one's enemies; seventhly, the way is love of God, so that bliss is conceived as knowledge of God, union with him, or dissolution into him.

Now it is not, I think, difficult to see how these seven common features of the world religions are implicit in the experience of being in love in an unrestricted manner. To be in love is to be in love with someone. To be in love in an unrestricted manner is to be in love with someone transcendent. When someone transcendent is my beloved, the one to whom my being belongs, he is in my heart, real to me from within me. When that love is the fulfilment of my unrestricted thrust to the intelligible, the true, the real, the good, the one that fulfils that thrust must be supreme in intelligence, truth, reality, goodness. Since he comes to me by the gift of his love, he himself must be love. Since my loving him is my transcending of myself, it also is a denial of the self that is transcended. Since loving him means loving attention to him, it is prayer, meditation, contemplation. Since love of him is fruitful, it overflows into love of all those he loves or wishes to love. Finally, from an experience of love focused on mystery there wells forth a longing for knowledge, while love itself

Eliade and Joseph M. Kitagawa (Chicago: University of Chicago Press, 1959) 142–53.

[The following is not in the basic autograph but does appear in one copy of the retyped version (see above, note 1): 'For present purposes it will be best to regard Professor Heiler's position not as an exhaustive empirical statement on the world religions but as an ideal type or model, that is, neither a description nor an hypothesis but a heuristic and expository device open to all the additions and modifications that empirical investigation may dictate. On the nature and proper use of ideal types or models in the present sense, see Henri-Irenée Marrou, *De la connaissance historique* (Paris: Editions du Seuil, 1955) 159–65; in English, *The Meaning of History*, trans. Robert J. Olsen (Baltimore: Helicon, 1966) 167–73.' It is possible that this clarification was prompted by Professor Smith's questions.

Corresponding material may be found in *Method in Theology* at p. 109. Again, it is quite possible to surmise from the autograph that 'Faith and Beliefs' is where this material was first worked out.]

is a longing for union. So for the lover of the unknown beloved, bliss is knowledge of him and union with him, however they may be achieved.

There is, then, a line of reasoning that suggests that a basic component of religious involvement may be the same in members of the world religions.[26] But may one not extend this view to the more elementary forms of religion? Can one not discern in them the harvest of the Spirit that is love, joy, peace, kindness, goodness, fidelity, gentleness, and self-control (Galatians 5.22–23)? As a theologian holding that God gives all men sufficient grace for salvation, I must expect an affirmative answer; but as a mere theologian, I must leave the factual answer to students of the history of religions.

3   Religious Involvement and Faith

Our account of religious involvement or, at least, of a basic component in religious involvement has had one very significant feature. It has outflanked the adage, '*Nihil amatum nisi praecognitum*, Nothing can be loved that is not already known.' The adage is, of course, generally true. For being in love occurs on the fourth level of waking consciousness, and ordinarily this fourth level presupposes and complements the previous levels of experiencing, understanding, and judging. But what ordinarily is so admits exceptions, and such an exception would be what Paul described to the Romans as God's flooding our hearts with his love. Then love would not flow from knowledge but, on the contrary, knowledge would flow from love. It is the knowledge that results from God's gift of his love that, I suggest, constitutes the universalist faith proposed by Professor Smith.

But how can loving generate knowledge? There is the celebrated *pensée* of Blaise Pascal: *Le coeur a ses raisons que la raison ne connaît pas*, The heart has its reasons which reason does not know.[27] Let me indicate what precisely this statement would mean in terms of the analysis of human consciousness already presented.

First, by the heart is meant the subject in love, the subject attaining performative self-transcendence on the fourth level of waking consciousness.

Secondly, by reason is meant the subject on the first three levels of waking consciousness, the subject as attaining cognitional self-transcendence through experiencing, understanding, and judging.

26 [In the AAR lecture, Lonergan said simply, 'may be the same in the world religions.']
27 [See above, p. 19, note 9.]

Thirdly, by the reasons known to the heart and unknown to reason are meant the subject's responses to values – vital, social, cultural, personal – as distinct from his desires for pleasure and his fears of pain.

Fourthly, while values attract and disvalues repel us spontaneously, still it is when we are in love, and in the measure that we are in love, that we discern values and disvalues clearly, finely, delicately, fully, and that we respond to them firmly and powerfully. There is, then, a knowledge that is born of love. It is a knowledge of values and disvalues, of good and evil. It is a knowledge that consists in one's response to the values and disvalues and, more specifically, in the development, strength, fullness, refinement of one's responding.

By a universalist faith, then, I would understand the transvaluation of values that results from God's gift of his love. Just as the gift of that love, so too the consequent transvaluation of values is, in some sense, a constant. It does not presuppose any specific set of historical conditions. It can be bestowed on the members of any culture at any stage in its development. The values that are transvalued may vary, but the process of transvaluation has its constant ground in God's gift of his love.

4   Religious Beliefs

Religious involvement is intensely personal, but it is not so private as to be solitary. It can occur in many. They can discover the common orientation in their lives, encourage and support one another, find ways of expressing their deepest concern and of integrating it within the matrix of their social and cultural forms.

Already I have indicated how experience of the mystery of love and awe can lead, on the cultural level of the world religions, to acknowledgment of a transcendent reality immanent in human hearts, supreme in beauty, intelligence, truth, reality, goodness, characterized by love, mercy, compassion, to be approached through self-denial and prayer, through love of one's neighbor, and through love of God above all.

But the same experience, in an earlier cultural period, will give rise to hierophanies. For early expression results from insight into sensible presentations.[28] So it is easy, then, to express the spatial but not the temporal, the specific but not the generic, the external but not the internal, the human but

28   Ernst Cassirer, *The Philosophy of Symbolic Forms*, trans. Ralph Manheim, vol. 1: *Language* (New Haven: Yale University Press, 1953) 198–215. [For some of this material, compare *Method in Theology* 108.]

not the divine. Only insofar as the temporal, the generic, the internal, the divine can somehow be associated with or, as is said, projected upon the spatial, specific, external, human can an insight be had and expression result. So it is that, by associating religious experience with its outward occasion, the experience becomes expressed and thereby something determinate and distinct for human consciousness.

Such outward occasions, called hierophanies, are many. When each of the many is something distinct and unrelated to the others, there arise the gods of the moment. When they are many but recognized as possessing a family resemblance, then there is a living polytheism represented today by the 800,000 gods of Shintoism.[29] When distinct religious experiences are associated with a single place, there is the god of this or that place. When they are the experiences of a single person and united by the unity of that person, then there is the god of the person, such as was the God of Jacob or the God of Laban.[30] Finally, when the unification is social there result the god or gods of the group.

In brief, similar religious experiences become objectified differently at different stages of human development.[31] But there is a still further source of difference. We have conceived religious experience in terms of self-transcendence, and we must remember that human self-transcendence is ever precarious. Self-transcendence involves a tension between the self as transcending and the self as transcended. It follows that human authenticity never is some pure and serene and secure possession. It is ever a withdrawal from unauthenticity, and every successful withdrawal only brings to light the need for still further withdrawals. Our advance in understanding is also the elimination of oversights and misunderstandings. Our advance in truth is also the correction of mistakes and errors. Our moral development is through repentance for our sins. Genuine religion is discovered and realized by redemption from the many traps of religious aberration. So we are bid to watch and pray, to make our way in fear and trembling. And it is the greatest saints that proclaim themselves the greatest sinners, though their sins may seem slight indeed to less holy folk that lack their discernment and their love.

This dialectical character of self-transcendence explains why almost any characteristic of religion can be matched in the history of religions by its

29 Ernst Benz, 'On Understanding Non-Christian Religions,' *The History of Religions* (see above, note 25) 121–24.
30 On biblical apprehensions, see Norbert Lohfink, *Bibelauslegung im Wandel* (Frankfurt am Main: J. Knecht, 1967) 107–28.
31 [For this material, compare *Method in Theology* 110.]

opposite. Being in love, we said, is being in love with someone. It has a personal dimension. But this can be overlooked in a school of prayer and asceticism that stresses the orientation of religious experience to transcendent mystery. The transcendent is nothing in this world. Mystery is the unknown. Without formulating a transcendental notion of being as not merely the known but also the asked about, transcendent mystery can come to be named nothing at all.[32]

At a far earlier stage, transcendence can be overemphasized and immanence overlooked. Then God becomes remote, irrelevant, almost forgotten.[33] Inversely, immanence can be overemphasized and transcendence overlooked. Then the loss of reference to the transcendent will rob symbol, ritual, recital of their proper meaning to leave them merely idol and magic and myth. Then too the divine may be identified with life as universal process – a process in which individual and group are part, and of which they participate.[34]

I have conceived religious experience as an ultimate fulfilment of man's capacity for self-transcendence, and this view of religion is sustained when God is conceived as the supreme realization of the transcendental notions of intelligence, truth, goodness. Inversely, when religious experience is not strictly associated with self-transcendence, then too easily the love of God seeks reinforcement in the erotic, the sexual, the orgiastic. On the other hand, religious experience involves not only love but also awe and, in the sinner, even terror. Unless religion is totally directed to what is good, to a genuine love of one's neighbor and to a self-denial that is subordinated to a fuller goodness in oneself, then the cult of a God that is terrifying can slip over into the demonic, into an exultant destructiveness of oneself and of others.[35]

I have been deriving religious beliefs from the experience of the mystery of love and awe and, as well, deriving religious aberrations from misinterpretations and distortions of the same experience. However, religious beliefs

32 See Benz (above, note 29) 120–21, 124–26; also Heiler (above, note 25) 138–39.
33 [The following note appears in Lonergan's endnotes, without a corresponding index in the autograph text. *Method in Theology* 110 indicates that this is the appropriate place for it. On the other hand, archive item A2462, file 623 (see above, note 1) places it at the end of this paragraph, but obviously as a second thought.] On 'The Distant God' and on 'Cosmo-biology and Mystery' see F.M. Bergounioux and J. Goetz, *Prehistoric and Primitive Religions* (London: Burns and Oates, 1965) 82–91, 117–26.
34 [*Sic* in the autograph text. *Method in Theology* 111 changes this to 'of which the individual and the group are part and in which they participate.']
35 See Antoine Vergote, *Psychologie religieuse* (Bruxelles: Dessart, 1966) 55–57.

usually are a great deal more than the objectification of personal experience. They play a major role in one's *Weltanschauung*, one's total outlook, one's already mentioned real world constructed by imagination and intelligence, mediated by words and meaning, based by and large on belief, and hopefully regulated by values. As sociologists insist, such a world is constructed not individually but socially.[36] As theorists of historicity would add, it is the work not of a generation but of the ages.[37] Now religious experience makes two contributions to the construction of reality. Because it is an experience of mystery, it gives rise to inquiries and investigations that otherwise would not be undertaken. Because it is a dynamic state of being in love, it opens one's eyes to values and disvalues that otherwise would not be recognized, and it gives the power to do the good that otherwise would not be attempted. There results a transvaluation of values and, consequently, a transformation of the dynamics of one's world. So religious people live in a world transfused by religious experience, informed by the investigations to which the experience gives rise, and motivated by the evaluations which it grounds.

5   Use of the Model

It was my hope to sketch a construct, a model, an ideal type containing a systematic distinction between a faith born of otherworldly love and possibly common to all genuine religions, and, on the other hand, the many diverse and often opposed beliefs to which religious people subscribe.

But in concluding I must point out that my model is just a skeleton. To apply it to any particular religion further parts may need to be added. Moreover, because religions can differ in fundamental ways, one must have different sets of parts to add, and even one may have to add them in quite different ways.

Let me illustrate this with an example. My account of religious beliefs does not imply that they are more than objectifications of religious experience. It is a view quite acceptable to the nineteenth-century liberal Protestant or to the

---

36 Peter L. Berger and Thomas Luckmann, *The Social Construction of Reality, A Treatise in the Sociology of Knowledge* (Garden City: Doubleday, 1966) [especially pp. 149–82.]

37 Hans-Georg Gadamer, *Wahrheit und Methode* (Tübingen: J.C.B. Mohr [Paul Siebeck], 1960) 261. The assumptions of the individual are not so much his judgments as the historicity of his cultural being. [In English, see *Truth and Method*, trans. Joel Weinsheimer and Donald G. Marshall (New York: Crossroad, 1989) 293–94.]

twentieth-century Catholic modernist.[38] But it is unacceptable to most of the traditional forms of Christianity, in which religious beliefs are believed to have their origin in charism, prophecy, inspiration, revelation, the word of God, the life, death, and resurrection of Christ. Obviously, to be applicable to this traditional type of religious belief, the skeleton model needs to be fleshed out, and fleshing it out calls for creativity.

Let us begin, then, from a human analogy. If a man and a woman were to love each other yet never avow their love, there would be lacking to their love an interpersonal component, a mutual presence of self-donation. Without that interpersonal component, their love would not have the opportunity to grow. There would not be the steady increase in knowledge of each other. There would not be the constant flow of favors given and received that would make love conscious of its reality, its strength, its durability, aware it could always be counted on.

Now if there is this interpersonal element to human love, if that element is a distinct and important factor in its emergence and in its growth, something somehow similar could also be thought of religious love. But, then, we should not solely have the gift of God's love flooding our hearts. We should not solely believe what results from the objectification of that love. Besides completing our personal self-transcendence in the secrecy of our hearts, God would also address his people as a people, announce to them his intentions, send to them his prophets, his Messiah, his apostles. In that case religious beliefs would be objectifications not only of internal experience but also of the externally uttered word of God.

To conclude, I suggest, first, that there is a construct, model, ideal type grounding a systematic distinction between faith and beliefs[39] but, secondly, to be applied to disparate religious positions, the model has to admit additions and transformations that radically modify perspectives and meaning.

Response to Wilfred Cantwell Smith

[As indicated above in note 1, Wilfred Cantwell Smith was one of the respondents when Lonergan delivered this paper at the American Academy of Religion. His response was quite favorable and complimentary. He posed two

38 [In his oral delivery at Newton and Guelph (but not at St Peter's), Lonergan omitted 'Protestant' and 'Catholic': 'It is a view quite acceptable to the nineteenth-century liberals or to the twentieth-century modernists.']

39 [The Newton lecture has '... a systematic distinction between *a universalist* faith and beliefs.']

questions, which can be put simply in the following terms. First, why is the achievement of self-transcendence at its highest level in love not itself called 'faith'? And second, why is faith called a knowledge? Lonergan responded as follows.]

I wish to thank Dr Smith for his comments on my paper. In answer to his question, I really don't know what I can do. On the notion of faith, we come from different religious backgrounds. I think I more naturally tend to connect faith with some sort of judgment, in this case, with moral judgment. Anyone who has been influenced by the Reformers, and especially by Luther's *fides fiducialis*, has an entirely different approach to the notion of faith. Among different Christian groups there are quite different interpretations of faith, and I think that that element in my background led me to speak the way I did.

Fundamentally, as you [Professor Smith] conceive faith, involvement itself can be called faith. One of the points or difficulties you raise is that I said faith was not usually objectified. By that I mean that the average ... [pause in the tape for about ten seconds] ... because I was interested in some sort of an intellectualist notion of faith because of my tradition, without reflecting on the difficulties that could be raised; and certainly I have no desire to go into any discussions about what different parts of scripture might mean. That would be beyond my present context.

I did use that saying of Pascal to show how love can be a source of knowledge that otherwise we do not have, simply because your interests are other, your values are different. I don't think that we have any real difference of opinion here. I am quite willing to admit that faith, as it is understood by Professor Smith in the paper to which I have alluded, would very well be represented by the involvement itself, by the being in love.

4

Merging Horizons: System, Common Sense, Scholarship[1]

1   Systematic Understanding

The study of logic, of mathematics, of the natural sciences, of the generalizing human sciences such as economics, psychology, sociology all have accustomed us to a style and mode of thought in which controls are constantly and explicitly applied. Terms are defined, assumptions are expressed and acknowledged, hypotheses are formulated and verified, conclusions are drawn in accord with logical paradigms. Such constant and explicit control has made

---

1 A lecture given at University College of the University of Toronto on 4 November 1970, and repeated both at Campion College on the Regina Campus of the University of Saskatchewan on 2 February 1971 and at St Paul's College of the University of Manitoba on 4 February 1971.

   The lecture was subsequently published in *Cultural Hermeneutics* 1:1 (April 1973) 87–99. (This periodical was later renamed *Philosophy and Social Criticism,* beginning with volume 5 in 1978; under both titles, Lonergan was listed as one of the consulting editors.)

   Both at Campion College and at St Paul's College, the lecture was taped (Lonergan Research Institute Archives, Toronto, tapes 631 and 631a). These recordings closely match the published lecture, except for varied introductions to different audiences, and the inclusion of brief summaries of the principal sections of the lecture.

   File 513 in the Lonergan Research Institute Archives contains the following: (1) an autograph typescript of the lecture with Lonergan's corrections; (2) a carbon copy of the manuscript (with additional corrections) sent to D. Reidel Publishing Company, Dordrecht, The Netherlands, for publication in *Cultural Hermeneutics;* and (3) an author's proof copy from this publisher with minor textual corrections by Lonergan.

this type of thought quite well known, quite easily objectified, quite readily spoken about. Let us name it the systematic type, and let us go on to consider two further types of intellectual development that exist and function but easily are overlooked;[2] I refer to the commonsense type and the scholarly.

The editing here relies principally on the published version in *Cultural Hermeneutics*, but the autograph and the tape recordings were consulted, and changes from the published text, whether signaled here or not, are based on those sources.

The autograph contains evidence that Lonergan originally thought of the title of the lecture as 'Merging Horizons and Insight.' This title is crossed out at the top of page 1, and the title that appears here is typed in above it. However, the running head on each page of the autograph has 'MHI.'

Section divisions and titles are editorial, as are all footnotes.

Lonergan began the Campion College lecture with the following. 'Human understanding develops in quite different manners. I want to say something on the intellectual development of the scholar, the man of letters, the linguist, the exegete. I shall speak not only of the scholar. I shall speak very briefly of the systematic type of knowing, and a little more fully about common sense. You all have common sense. You have had it for a long time. But it is one thing to be a person of common sense, and it is another thing to know precisely what that means, to thematize it, as the phenomenologists say. Then I will speak on the understanding of the scholar, his development of understanding, under four main headings, namely, understanding the thing, understanding the words, understanding the author, and at times understanding oneself. And finally, I will speak on the truth of one's understanding. How does one know that one's understanding is true?' In the St Paul's lecture, he began as follows (with the ellipse in the transcription marking an indistinct spot on the tape). 'I wish to speak to you about different ways in which human understanding develops. I will speak of three ways: the systematic type of development, the commonsense type of development, and the scholarly type. I will be very brief on the systematic, a bit longer on the commonsense, most of all on the scholarly type of development. The word ... all three: merging horizons. The different types of development give rise to different approaches. Different approaches give rise to different fields, areas, in which one operates, called "horizons." The approach and the field make the horizon, and merging horizons are to combine [*sic*] two or more different horizons. One can combine the scholarly and the scientific types of horizon, as when you use a modern science such as economics to understand the workings of an ancient empire (the scholarly). You can combine the commonsense and the scientific, as when the technician not only knows a theory but also knows how to handle it in the concrete. The commonsense and the scholarly are the merging horizons that need most elucidation, so I will spend most of my time on them. First, then, on the systematic, on which I'm just giving you a paragraph.'

2 In the Campion College lecture, Lonergan added, 'they have not got this explicit, formal, objectifiable type of control.'

2   Commonsense Understanding

Commonsense intelligence is marked by spontaneity. There is spontaneous inquiry: the cascade of questions from the child, the alert wonder of the boy, the sharp-eyed attention of the adult. There is the spontaneous accumulation of insights: an answer to one question only generates more questions; to speak or act on the basis of what we have understood often reveals to us the inadequacy of our insights,[3] and that revelation leads to further inquiry and fuller insight. There is the spontaneous process of teaching and learning. Not only are we born with a natural desire to inquire and understand, but also we are born into a community with an accumulated common fund of tested answers. So we watch others do things, try to do as much ourselves, fail, watch again and try again, until practice makes perfect.[4]

But if one asks what is the content of that common accumulation and common store, one must not expect an answer in terms of definitions, postulates, and inferences.[5] The Athenians depicted in Plato's early dialogues knew quite well what they meant by courage, sobriety, justice, knowledge. But neither they nor Socrates were able to arrive at universally valid definitions. And when eventually definitions were achieved, as in Aristotle's *Nicomachean Ethics,* thought had shifted from the commonsense into the systematic mode. Again, common sense does not express itself in universally valid propositions. Its accumulated wisdom is set forth in proverbs, and proverbs are not universal rules but rather pieces of advice that commonly it is well to bear in mind. Like the rules of grammar, proverbs admit exceptions, and, often enough, the existence of exceptions is marked by a contrary proverb. 'Strike the iron while it is hot' and 'He who hesitates is lost' say more or less the same thing. But they are completed[6] rather than opposed by the contrary proverb, 'Look before you

3 The formulation here is taken from the Campion College lecture. The published lecture had simply '... reveals the inadequacy of our insights ...' The wording in the St Paul's lecture was '... will bring to light the inadequacy of our understanding.'

4 In the Campion College lecture, Lonergan added, 'There is, then, a triple spontaneity of common sense: spontaneous inquiry, spontaneous accumulations of insight, spontaneous processes of teaching and learning.' In the St Paul's lecture, he said, 'Therefore common sense is characterized by a triple spontaneity: spontaneity in asking questions, wondering ...; spontaneity in the accumulation of insights – one insight leads to a further question, and that to still more questions; and a spontaneous process of teaching and learning.'

5 In the St Paul's lecture, Lonergan added, 'That pertains to the systematic type.'

6 'Completed' is the word given in all the sources for this lecture. Elsewhere, as

leap.'[7] Again, it has been thought that common sense proceeds by analogy. But its analogies resemble, not the logicians' argument from analogy, but rather Jean Piaget's adaptation, which consists of two parts: first, an assimilation that brings into play operations that were successful in a somewhat similar case and, secondly, an adjustment that takes into account the differences between the earlier and the present task.[8]

Indeed, Piaget's conception of learning as the accumulation and grouping of adaptations brings to light a basic characteristic of common sense. It is open-ended, ongoing, ever adding further adjustments. For it is the specialization of human intelligence in the realm of the particular and the concrete. The particular and the concrete are almost endlessly variable. The man of common sense is the man that sizes up each new situation and, if it differs significantly, adds the insight that will guide the right adjustment to acquired routines.

Further, it is this open-ended, ongoing character of commonsense intelligence that differentiates it from systematic intelligence. Knowledge that can be packaged in definitions, postulates, and deductions is knowledge that is rounded-off, complete, finished. To insert further insights in a system really is to scrap the system and replace it by a new systematization. But commonsense intelligence is a habitual accumulation of insights that provides only a nucleus or core to which further insights must be added before one speaks or acts. And that nucleus is not some system of general truths. Rather it is like some multiple-purpose and multiply-adjustable tool that can be employed in all sorts of ways but never is actually to be employed without the appropriate adjustment being made.

Finally, common sense is not some one thing common to all mankind. It is endlessly variable. Each region, each locality, each language, each class, each

---

in 'Doctrinal Pluralism' (see below, p. 79), the word used here is 'complemented.'

7 The wording of the last two sentences is taken from the oral lectures rather than from the published version.

8 In the St Paul's lecture, Lonergan summed up at this point as follows: 'Therefore, common sense is not expressible in definitions, universal propositions, inferences. It has its own way of going about things. As the linguistic analysts say, you know the meaning of a word when you know how to use it, not when you're able to define it. That could consist of nothing. The definition may be faulty. And it hasn't got universal propositions; it uses proverbs, pieces of advice. And it doesn't deduce in accord with a logical paradigm; it proceeds more in the way described by Jean Piaget in his celebrated work on child development.'

occupation, each generation tends to develop its own brand. The man of common sense is ready to speak and act appropriately in any of the situations that commonly arise in his milieu. But he also knows that others do not share all his ideas, and he comes to know how they will speak and act in the situations in which they find themselves. If into his circle of acquaintances there comes a stranger, then the stranger is strange because his ways of speaking and acting are governed by another, unfamiliar brand of common sense. Inversely, when one migrates from one's original milieu, moves to another city, takes a new job, enters a new circle of acquaintances, then one must be ready to do in Rome what the Romans do. One has to remodel one's common sense, and, to do so, one must move slowly, be ever on the alert, discover what has to be done to remove the strangeness others sense, the surprise they feel, the impression they have that this is odd, that out of place, and the other inept.[9]

3   Scholarly Understanding

Let us now turn from the commonsense to the scholarly type of intellectual development, the development characteristic of the man of letters, the linguist, the exegete, the interpreter, the historian. Like the systematic thinker, the scholar moves out of his immediate environment and is concerned with matters that ostensibly are of no practical interest. But unlike the systematic thinker and like the man of common sense, the scholar does not aim at knowledge that can be packaged in definitions, postulates, and inferences. Rather he is concerned to enter the milieu and to understand the ways of thinking, speaking, acting, of another real or fictitious place and time. To use the language of Professor Gadamer in his great work *Wahrheit und Methode*,[10] scholarship is a matter of *Horizontsverschmelzung*, of merging or fusing horizons. It is a matter of retaining the common sense that guides one's own speaking and acting and that interprets the words and deeds of other people in one's milieu, and nonetheless acquiring the ability to interpret the words and deeds of other people, real or fictitious, of another, often remote place and

---

9 In both the Campion College lecture and the St Paul's lecture, Lonergan added a rather informal summary of his comments on common sense (slightly different in each lecture). Since the summaries simply repeated much of the text, they are omitted here.

10 Hans-Georg Gadamer, *Wahrheit und Methode* (see above, p. 46, note 37) 286–90, 356–60; in the English translation cited in the same note (*Truth and Method*) see the index under Fusion of horizons.

time. For the scholar, as it were, lives in two worlds, possesses two horizons. He is not an anachronist reading contemporary common sense into the past; and he is not an archaist employing an ancient common sense in contemporary speech and action.[11] To be neither an anachronist nor an archaist, he must both retain the common sense of his own place and time and, as well, develop the common sense of another place and time.

Now the merging or fusing of a commonsense and a scholarly horizon is not the only case of such merging. Commonsense and scientific understanding can merge to give us technicians. Scholarly and scientific understanding can merge to apply modern economics to the understanding of ancient empires. But it is the merging of commonsense and scholarly horizons that, I think, stands most in need of elucidation. So I propose to select one of the scholar's tasks, that of interpretation, of exegesis, of correctly understanding an author's meaning. On the general character of documents to be interpreted I shall be brief. I shall speak more fully on the process of coming to understand what the author was treating, what precisely his words meant, what his cast of mind and outlook were, what finally in the interpreter himself may have been blocking his understanding. I shall close with some account of the proximate and the remote criteria that guide one's judgment on the accuracy of one's interpretation.[12]

First, then, the documents to be interpreted are, in general, not expressions of systematic thought. There is an abundant exegetical literature on the simple Gospels but, as Professor Castelli has pointed out, there is little or none on Euclid's *Elements*.[13] The reason for this is not hard to fathom. A systematic work defines its terms, sets forth explicitly its assumptions, and draws its conclusions in accord with logical rules. Insofar as the systematic ideal is realized, there can be problems of learning, of coming to understand

---

11 In the St Paul's lecture, Lonergan added, 'He doesn't think the fifth-century Athenians were twentieth-century modernists, and he doesn't carry on in the modern world like a fifth-century Athenian.'

12 In the St Paul's lecture, Lonergan added, 'From now on, then, on interpretation.' Compare the remainder of this lecture with related elements from chapter 7 in *Method in Theology*.

13 The reference to Castelli is uncertain. The same example is given in *Method in Theology* 153, but there is no reference to Castelli. In the St Paul's lecture, Lonergan added, 'Euclid's *Elements* were written about 300 years before the Gospels, but there is no need for interpretation. There are no commentaries written on Euclid's *Elements*. It's difficult understanding them perhaps, and you may need a teacher to come to understand them, but there are no ambiguities there.'

what the system propounds, but there are not the problems of interpretation, problems that spring from obscure passages in which little meaning is apparent, and from ambiguous passages for which more than one meaning comes to mind.[14]

Next, there are four ways in which the interpreter has to develop his understanding: he has to understand the thing with which the document deals; he has to understand the words that the document employs; he has to understand the author that composed the document; and finally he may have to understand himself.

3.1 Understanding the Thing

The interpreter, then, has to understand the thing treated in the text. Commonly he will possess such an understanding before considering the text, for he presumably will know the language in which the text is written and the things to which the words of that language refer. Still, such knowledge is only general and potential. It will become particular and actual only through a study of the text. And the point to be stressed here is that the greater the interpreter's experience, the more cultivated his understanding, the better balanced his judgment, and the more delicate his conscience, the greater will be the likelihood that he will hit upon the meaning intended by the author.

In saying this I am, of course, rejecting a well-known and frequently repeated principle – the principle of the empty head. According to this principle, if one is to practice not eisegesis but exegesis, if one is not to read into the text what is not there, if one is not to settle in a priori fashion what the text must mean no matter what it says, then one must just drop all preconceptions of every kind, attend simply to the text, see all that is there and nothing that is not there, allow the author to speak for himself, allow him to be his own interpreter.

Now such contentions are both right and wrong. They are right insofar as they impugn a well-known evil: interpreters very easily impute to authors opinions that the authors never entertained. But they are wrong in the remedy they propose, for they take it for granted that the interpreter has only to take a good look at a text and he will see what is there. That is quite mistaken. It rests on a naive intuitionism. So far from tackling the complex

14 In the St Paul's lecture Lonergan added, 'So much for the type of document that needs interpretation. In general it's not systematic writing, it's common-sense writing.'

task of coming to understand the thing, the words, the author, and oneself, the principle of the empty head bids interpreters to forget their own views and attend to what is out there. But all that is out there is a series of black marks on a white background. Anything over and above a reissue of the same marks in the same order will be mediated by the experience, the understanding, the judgment, and the responsibility of the interpreter. The narrower his experience, the less cultivated his understanding, the poorer his judgment, the more careless he is about his responsibilities, then the greater the likelihood that he will impute to the author an opinion the author never entertained. On the other hand, the broader his experience, the more developed his understanding, the better balanced his judgment, the keener his sense of responsibility, then the greater the likelihood that he will envisage all possible interpretations and assign to each its appropriate degree of probability.

Interpretation, then, is not just a matter of looking at signs. It is a matter of being guided by the signs in a process that moves from one's antecedent general and potential knowledge to the consequent actual knowledge of what a particular author meant in a given sentence, paragraph, chapter, or book. The greater one's initial resources, the greater the likelihood that one will have the requisite general and potential knowledge.

3.2 Understanding the Words

Besides understanding the thing, the interpreter must understand the words. Now it does happen that, when the writer meant P, the reader thinks of Q. But in that case, sooner or later, difficulty will arise. Not all that is true of P is also true of Q, and so the author will appear to be saying what is false or even absurd.

At this point there comes to light the difference between the interpreter and the controversialist. The latter will assume that his misunderstanding yields a correct interpretation, and he will proceed to demonstrate the author's numerous errors and absurdities. But the interpreter will consider the possibility that he himself is at fault. He reads further. He rereads. Eventually he stumbles on the possibility that the writer was thinking not of Q but of P, and with that correction the meaning of the text becomes plain.[15]

Now this process can occur any number of times. It is the self-correcting process of learning. Data give rise to questions. Insights suggest answers.

15 In the St Paul's lecture Lonergan added, 'and the absurdities disappear.'

Answers give rise to still further questions. Gradually there is built up an accumulation of insights that correct and complement one another and that together fit the data like a glove fits a hand. Such insights constitute one's understanding of the text, one's *Verstehen*. They are distinct from the expression of that understanding, which is one's interpretation of the text, one's *Auslegen*. Finally, both the understanding and the interpretation are distinct from the judgment that one's understanding and interpretation are correct.[16]

Now it is understanding that surmounts what is called the hermeneutic circle. The meaning of a text is an intentional entity. It is a unity that is unfolded through parts, sections, chapters, paragraphs, sentences,[17] words. We can grasp the unity, the whole, only through grasping the parts. But at the same time the parts are determined in their meaning by the whole which each part partially reveals. Such is the hermeneutic circle. Logically this reciprocal dependence would constitute a vicious circle. But logic has to do with concepts and propositions, words and sentences. Understanding is prelogical, preconceptual, prepropositional. One comes to understand not by deducing but by a self-correcting process of learning that spirals into the meaning of the whole by using each new part to fill out and qualify and correct the understanding reached in reading the earlier parts.

Rules of hermeneutics or exegesis list the points worth considering in one's effort to arrive at an understanding of a text. Such are an analysis of the composition of the text, the determination of the author's purpose in writing, knowledge of the people for whom he wrote, of the occasion on which he wrote, of the nature of the linguistic, grammatical, stylistic means he employed. However, the main point about all such rules is that one does not understand the text because one has observed the rules, but one observes the rules to arrive at an understanding of the text. Observing the rules can be no more than the pedantry of the obtuse. The essential observance is to note one's every failure to understand clearly and exactly, and to sustain one's reading and rereading until one's inventiveness or good luck have eliminated all one's failures in comprehension.[18]

16 In the St Paul's lecture Lonergan added, 'or probable.'
17 The word 'sentences' does not appear in the autograph or in the published text in *Cultural Hermeneutics*. But Lonergan included it in the Campion College lecture; and see *Method in Theology* 159.
18 In the Campion College lecture, Lonergan adds here, 'One observes the rules in order to come to understanding, but the rules are not an infallible guide to the understanding. That is the self-correcting process of learning that [washes out?] what is not clear, and finally gets it clear.'

3.3 Understanding the Author

Besides understanding the thing and the words, one may have the task of understanding the author. When the meaning of a text is plain, then *with* the author and *by* his words we understand the thing to which his words refer. When a simple misunderstanding occurs, as when the reader thinks of *Q* when the author meant *P*, then the correction is effected by sustained rereading and inventiveness. But there are more difficult cases. Then a first reading yields a little understanding and a host of puzzles. A second reading yields very little more understanding and a far greater number of puzzles. There has emerged the problem of understanding not only the thing and the words but also the author himself, his nation, language, time, culture, way of life, and cast of mind.

Now the self-correcting process of learning, the process of questions leading to insights and answers, and answers leading to still further questions, is the manner in which we acquire not only the understanding that informs our own speaking and acting but also the understanding that apprehends the different ways in which others speak and act. Even with our contemporaries with the same language, culture, and station in life, we not only understand things with them but also understand things in our own way and, at the same time, their different way of understanding the same things. We can remark that a phrase or an action is 'Just like you.' By that we mean that the phrase or action fits in, not with our own way of understanding things, but with our own way of understanding the way others understand. But just as we can come to an understanding of our fellows' understanding, a commonsense grasp of the ways we understand not with them but them, so too the same process can be pushed to a far fuller development, and then the self-correcting process takes us out of our milieu and brings us to some understanding of the common sense of another place and time, another culture and cast of mind. But in this case the process of questions leading to insights and answers, and of answers generating ever more questions, is the almost life-long business of becoming a scholar, of becoming a person in whom two horizons merge, the horizon of contemporary common sense opened out and extended to include without confusion the horizon of the common sense of another place and time.

3.4 Understanding Oneself

Besides understanding the thing, the words, and the author, an interpreter may be challenged to an understanding of himself. For the major texts, the classics, in letters, in history, in philosophy, in religion, in theology, not only are beyond the initial horizon of their interpreters but also may demand of the interpreters an intellectual, or moral, or religious conversion.

In such a case the interpreter's initial knowledge of the thing, the object, treated in the document is just inadequate. He will come to know it only by pushing the self-correcting process of learning to a revolution in his own outlook. He can succeed in finding an author's wavelength and locking on to it only by effecting a radical change in himself. It is not so much that his previous understanding of himself was mistaken as that he has to give himself a new self to be understood.

This is the existential dimension in the hermeneutical problem. It lies at the very root of the perennial divisions of mankind in their views on reality, morality, religion. Moreover, insofar as conversion is only the basic step, insofar as there remains the labor of thinking out everything from the new and profounder viewpoint, there results the characteristic of the classic set forth by Friedrich Schlegel and quoted by Professor Gadamer: 'A classic is a writing that is never fully understood. But the educated that keep educating themselves always want to learn more from it.'[19]

From this existential dimension there results a further aspect of the problems centering in hermeneutics. The classics ground a tradition. They create the milieu in which they are studied and interpreted. They produce in the reader through the cultural tradition the mentality, the *Vorverständnis*, from which they will be read, studied, interpreted. Now such a tradition may be genuine, authentic, a long accumulation of insights, adjustments, re-interpretations, that repeats the original message afresh for each age. In that case the reader will exclaim, as did the disciples on the way to Emmaus in the Gospel of Luke: 'Did not our hearts burn within us, when he spoke on the way and opened to us the scriptures?' (Luke 24.32). On the other hand, the tradition may be unauthentic. It may consist in a watering-down of the original message, in recasting it into terms and meanings that fit into the assumptions and convictions of those that have dodged the issue of radical conversion. In that case a genuine interpretation will be met with incredulity and ridicule, as was St Paul when he preached in Rome and was led to quote Isaiah: 'Go to this people and say: you will hear and hear but never understand; you will look and look but never see' (Acts 28.26).

19 See Gadamer, *Truth and Method* 290, note 218. The translation in the text is Lonergan's own. Lonergan's reference, as in *Method in Theology*, is to the German (see above, p. 46, note 37) 274, note 2.

I have presented my thought in terms of a sharp antithesis. Reality is more complex. A cultural tradition will contain very many things, and each of them may be authentic in some ways and unauthentic in others. Still, this complexity is not the main issue. That lies in the fact that merging horizons are a matter not only of the present moving into the past but also of the past becoming alive in the present and challenging the assumptions both of the individual scholar and of the tradition that has nurtured him.[20]

4   The Truth of Interpretation

We have considered the work of interpretation as coming to understand the thing, the words, the author, and oneself. We now must ask how one can tell whether or not one's interpretation is correct. Here one must distinguish between the proximate and the remote criteria of truth, and we shall begin from the proximate.

20 In the Campion College lecture, Lonergan adds the following. 'So much for the question of the development of understanding in the interpreter. What is to be interpreted, in general, is not systematic thinking, thinking that can be packaged in definitions, postulates, and deductions. It's more the literary type of thing. Again, there are four components to the development of understanding in the interpreter: his understanding of the thing – in other words, the principle of the empty head is too simple; it's not simply a matter of having no preconceptions; the more he has in his head, the better. Secondly, understand the words – the difference between the controversialist who thinks his misunderstanding is the correct interpretation and the interpreter who, when he finds something odd about an author, starts reading and rereading until he comes to see what the author really meant; the hermeneutic circle – if you want to express the work of the exegete in logical terms, you're going to be expressing a vicious circle, but the question is not a logical problem, it's a problem of developing understanding that can keep correcting itself as one reads and finally gets the whole view. Finally, the significance of rules of interpretation: they don't guarantee that you'll understand; they help you to understand, supply you with questions, but the real thing to do to develop in understanding, to get the correct understanding of the text, is to notice every instance which doesn't seem quite clear, doesn't seem to jell, and ask further questions there. Thirdly, understanding the author is not a different kind of process, but it's a much more elaborate matter of development. And finally, understanding oneself, the existential component in interpreting really first-class works, namely, *you* have to grow.' A similar summary was given in the St Paul's lecture at the end of the first sentence of the next section, and the matter of 'understanding oneself' received slightly more attention: 'Finally, understanding oneself, giving oneself a new self to be understood, is a very fundamental thing, and the existential aspect of the matter is the root of constant, perennial divisions about reality, morality, and religion.'

The proximate criterion of the truth of an interpretation is that no further relevant questions arise. If there are no further relevant questions, then there is no opportunity for further insights arising, and if there is no opportunity for further insights arising, then there is no opportunity for effecting a correction of the understanding already attained.

However, the relevant questions usually are not the questions that inspired the investigation. One begins from one's own viewpoint, from the interests, concerns, purposes one had prior to one's study of the text. But the study itself is a process of learning. As one learns, one discovers more and more the questions that concerned the author, the issues that confronted him, the problems he was trying to solve, the material and methodical resources at his disposal for solving them. So bit by bit one comes to set aside one's own initial interests and concerns, to share ever more fully the interests and concerns of the author, to reconstruct the context of his thought and speech.

But what precisely is meant by the word 'context'? There are two meanings. There is the heuristic meaning the word has at the beginning of an investigation, and it tells where to look to find the context. There is the actual meaning the word acquires as one moves out of one's initial horizon and into the fuller view that includes a significant part of the author's.

Initially, then, and heuristically, the context of the word is the sentence. The context of the sentence is the paragraph. The context of the paragraph is the chapter. The context of the chapter is the book. The context of the book is the author's *opera omnia*, his life and times, the state of the question in his day, his problems, prospective readers, scope, and aim.

Actually, however, and eventually, context is the interweaving of questions and answers in limited groups. To answer any one question will give rise to further questions. To answer them will give rise to still more. But while this process can recur a number of times, while it would go on indefinitely if one kept changing the topic, still it does not go on indefinitely on one and the same topic. Context, then, is a nest of interlocked or interwoven questions and answers. It is limited inasmuch as all the questions and answers have a bearing, direct or indirect, upon a single topic. Finally, because the context is limited, there comes a point when no further relevant questions arise, and then there emerges the possibility of judgment. For when there are no further relevant questions, there also is no opportunity for further insights to occur and thereby correct, qualify, complement the insights already attained.

Still, what is this single topic that limits the set of relevant questions and answers? As the distinction between the heuristic or initial and the actual or eventual context makes plain, this topic is something to be discovered in the course of the investigation. By persistence or good luck or both, one hits upon some element in the interwoven set of questions and answers. One follows up one's discovery by further questions. Sooner or later one hits upon some other element, then several more. There is a period in which insights multiply at a great rate, when one's perspectives are constantly being reviewed, enlarged, qualified, refined. One reaches a point where the overall view emerges, when other components fit into the picture in a subordinate manner, when further questions yield ever diminishing returns, when one can say just what was going forward and back up one's statement with multitudinous evidence.

The single topic, then, is something that can be indicated generally in a phrase or two yet unfolded in an often enormously complex set of subordinate and interconnected questions and answers. One reaches that set by striving persistently to understand the object, to understand the words, to understand the author, and to understand oneself. The key to success is to keep adverting to what as yet has not been understood, for there lies the source of further questions, and to hit upon the questions directs attention to the parts of the text where answers may be found. So R.G. Collingwood has praised the famous advice of Lord Acton, 'Study problems, not periods.'[21] So Professor Gadamer has praised Collingwood's insistence that knowledge consists, not just in propositions, but in answers to questions, so that to understand the answers one must know the questions as well.[22] My own point, however, is not simply the interconnection of questions and answers but rather the fact that such interconnection comes in limited blocks, that one arrives at a margin where there are no further questions relevant to a specific given topic, that at that margin one can recognize one's task as completed and pronounce one's interpretation as probable, or as highly probable, or in some respects, perhaps, as certain.

In general, an interpreter's judgment will be nuanced. If really there were no further relevant questions on any aspect of the matter, then his judgment would be certain. But it can be that further relevant questions exist to which he does not advert, and this possibility counsels modesty. Again, it can happen that he does advert to further relevant questions but has failed to find answers to them, and in this case the further questions may be few or many, of central interest or of peripheral concern. It is this range of possibilities that leads interpreters to speak with greater or less confidence and with many

21 R.G. Collingwood, *The Idea of History* (Oxford: Clarendon, 1946) 281.
22 Gadamer, *Wahrheit und Methode* 351–60; *Truth and Method* 369–79.

careful distinctions between the more probable and the less probable elements in their interpretation.

So much for the proximate criterion of the truth of an interpretation.[23] There remains the remote criterion, a matter on which we have already touched when speaking of the existential component in the interpreter's understanding. But to treat the matter a little more fully, let us go back to our initial contrast between the systematic, the commonsense, and the scholarly development of understanding.

Now the systematic type, precisely in the measure that it succeeds in getting all assumptions out in the open and all procedures under control, achieves a detached and impersonal character. What is supposed does not depend on what so-and-so's teachers taught him or on what he thinks they taught him. What is done is not subject to the bias that would be imposed by the past development, the values, the goals, the feelings of this or that individual. In brief, when a system errs, it does so not accidentally but systematically.[24]

In contrast, the commonsense type of development is one's project in living, one's making oneself what one is to be. It is cognitive of one's world, in communication with one's fellows, practical. Through it one is sharing and adapting a cultural tradition that was built up over the millennia. Of that tradition one has no full and precise inventory of its store. With respect to it one has no mode of control over and above the commonsense process of spontaneous inquiry, spontaneously accumulating insights, spontaneously teaching and learning. In that spontaneous development each new advance

23 In the Campion College lecture, Lonergan adds the following: 'In general it is, Are there further relevant questions? What do you mean by "relevant"? I mean relevant in terms of context, in terms of an interlocking set of questions and answers that arise right out of the data. And when you've got hold of that, you know it isn't obscure. You see this much at least pinned right down. What keeps this context limited is that it is all centered upon some single topic, and that ... has to fit right on to the data. Finally, the judgment will be in general nuanced. If there really are no further questions, the interpretation is certain, but it may be that there are further questions that the interpreter has not adverted to, and that's why you say, "Well, I think this is it." You speak modestly. Again, he may know of further questions that he is unable to answer, and these further questions may be few or many, central or peripheral, and this gives you a great deal of room for giving qualified answers.' A similar summary was given at this same point in the St Paul's lecture.

24 In the St Paul's lecture Lonergan added, '... because a systematic error can be spotted, ferreted out. You have the type of security with the system that you don't have in the other.'

is a function, not of precise assumptions and procedures, but rather of the total apperceptive mass that has resulted from all previous acquisitions of insight. Since the errors of system are systematic, a case can be made for the use of Cartesian methodic doubt in the construction of a philosophic or scientific system. But the controls of common sense are not explicit but implicit; they are immanent and operative in our being attentive, intelligent, reasonable, responsible. If we have gone astray, if the tradition we have inherited has gone astray, doubting everything is no solution, for that would only reduce us to a second childhood. We have no choice but to follow the advice of John Henry Newman – to accept ourselves as we are, and by dint of constant and persevering attention, intelligence, reasonableness, responsibility strive to expand what is true and force out what is mistaken in views that we have inherited or spontaneously developed.

There remains the third development of human intelligence, the scholarly. In its essentials this development resembles not the systematic but the commonsense type. But if it is concerned with the words and deeds of individuals or groups, if it aims at an understanding of the particular and concrete, if it leaves to the systematizers to proclaim any universal truths for which scholarship provides the evidence, still it is withdrawn from the hurly-burly of everyday living, it can forget the passions of the present without entering into the passions of the past, and the results reached by any scholar will be checked not only by his peers but also, if the results survive, by their successors. Besides the systematic tradition and the commonsense tradition, there is also the scholarly. All three can suffer decadence and decay. But it is the scholarly that can migrate to earlier times, that can discern their truth and error, their values and aberrations, that can be challenged by the past to criticize the present and, through that criticism, provoke a renewal. It is through such renewals that is to be met the remote criterion of truth, the criterion that consists in the twofold authenticity – the authenticity of the tradition one has inherited and the authenticity of one's own assimilation of it.[25]

25 Lonergan concluded the Campion College lecture as follows: 'The remote criterion, then, is concerned with one's overall development. If one's thought is systematic, it becomes impersonal, and problems that exist in commonsense intelligence and scholarly intelligence are eliminated. But still, the commonsense world is run by common sense, not by scientists, and the correction of commonsense error is to keep on, hoping that the truth one has will eliminate the errors that one has fallen into. The scholarly approach enables one to seize the truths grasped and the values appreciated in the

Questions after the Campion College Lecture

Question: Wouldn't you say that the picture of the scientist that you have drawn is idealized and unrealistic?

Response: I agree. I wouldn't attempt tonight to talk about the sciences here. I just dropped them in by way of a contrast, as a different type of understanding, in which an impersonal approach is achieved, a collective approach. Science can be beautifully wrong on fundamental things. Up to 1926 most physicists considered it scientific to affirm a mechanist determinism, and quantum theory just shot that right down ... But the individual scientist also has to be a man of common sense, or he won't know enough to come in out of the rain. And he should be a scholar, at least in his own field.

Question: [Question unclear on tape.]

Response: Conceptualists conceive understanding as something that results from concepts, and concepts result from some sort of an intellectual look. So you have development on that showing only when *things* change, when things develop. But Aristotelians and Thomists hold that understanding is with respect to sensible data, and it expresses itself in concepts, with the result that the more you understand, and the more accurately you understand, your concepts keep moving. And that's the priority of understanding to concepts, consequently to the propositions, and to the rules of logic that govern concepts and propositions: an intellectualist position. It's what *Insight* is about, and also my *verbum* articles on St Thomas.[26]

---

past and use them for a critique of one's own place and time and thereby provoke a renewal. I thank you.' The corresponding summary in the St Paul's lecture is as follows: 'I have spoken, then, of the remote criterion in systematic thinking, which becomes impersonal simply because the systematic ... is not subject to feelings, and so on. In the commonsense type, the remote control is the good life, and study. And in the scholarly, you have more control because you have many scholars and they can criticize one another, and also the scholarly makes possible the criticism of the present from the life [or, in the light] of the past. I thank you.'

26 Bernard Lonergan, 'The Concept of *Verbum* in the Writings of St Thomas Aquinas,' *Theological Studies* 7 (1946) 349–92; 8 (1947) 35–79; 404–44; 10 (1949) 3–40; 359–93. Now available as *Verbum: Word and Idea in Aquinas*, vol. 2 in Collected Works of Bernard Lonergan, ed. Frederick E. Crowe and Robert M. Doran (Toronto: University of Toronto Press, 1997).

Question: [Question unclear, but it had to do with the relation of insight and concepts.]

Response: That's true: unless you've expressed your understanding in concepts, you won't be able to say what you've understood. It will be just a bright theory you had. You need both, but it makes a big difference which is more fundamental, because you will exclude the possibility of a theory of development if you put concepts prior. It's not an easy matter, but the simplest way to establish it is diagrams. If you get the diagram you can solve the problem, and if you don't you can't. The massive proof of it is Euclid's *Elements*. Euclid's *Elements* are not logically satisfactory. In other words, he uses unformulated insights, and this occurs frequently, and a statement of Euclidean geometry that is satisfactory to the contemporary logician needs postulates that Euclid can't express. In other words, you start bringing in postulates of the type of inclusion, or betweenness, or something like that. Now, how was it that this correct geometry, which is not logically satisfactory, was arrived at? It wasn't through logical procedures, because its logic is faulty. It's because they understood. And that they understood is the sort of thing you can illustrate with diagrams.[27] What is meant by this priority of understanding is that intelligence operates with respect to symbols of one kind or another. The mathematician can be doing the most abstruse stuff, but he has that image in his symbols.

Questions after the St Paul's Lecture

Question: I have a difficulty in seeing how the systematic can be brought to bear on the scholarly.

Response: [The response began by mentioning Fustel de Coulange's book *La cité antique*,[28] which Lonergan described as a systematic social study. This study] is probably least applicable to Sparta, but it's most helpful in studying the Spartans, the city of Sparta and its history, simply because it provokes all

27 Lonergan then proceeded to give his usual example of the first proposition in the first book of the *Elements*: the problem of constructing an equilateral triangle on a given base in a given plane. See *Topics in Education* (see above, p. 15, note 5) 111–12.

28 Numa Denis Fustel de Coulanges, *La cité antique* (Paris: Librairie Hachette, 1864, 1876, 1912); a translation by Willard Small, *The Ancient City: A Study on the Religion, Laws, and Institutions of Greece and Rome* (Boston: Lee and Sheppard, 1873), has been published in Doubleday Anchor Books (Garden City, NY: Doubleday, 1956, 1980).

sorts of questions to which you get negative answers, and the fact that you're asking questions and finding out what really is relevant to Sparta. That's one example. Another way: set up an economic model of an ongoing depression in an economy, and use that for the study of the breakdown of the Roman Empire. That's the sort of thing I think has been done, the economic history of the Roman Empire. The name of the author escapes me at the moment.[29] It's that sort of thing in which you bring the two together. It's like the troubleshooter, the man with a fine theoretical knowledge of the concrete situation. If you find that the concrete situation is a mess, well, you have to have a first-class history before you can start doing anything. The scientific component won't do history for you, but it can stimulate your history, and at the same time the theoretical side will illuminate it.

Question: What makes a question relevant?
Response: What makes a question relevant is this business of context, formally understood. You can build up a limited context, and that provides a basis of what's relevant. For example, my doctoral thesis was on operative grace in St Thomas. It was a topic on which Thomas changed his mind about every year, and he changed his mind on about ten related topics as well. When you get Thomas saying different things on ten topics year after year, you have a much better blocking together of material than if he had said the same thing day after day, year after year: ... that ongoing set of questions and answers that Thomas was considering when he was treating operative grace. Now that's my central context. To handle that there are subordinate contexts, such as operation, liberty, God's action on the will, and so on and so forth. The further subordinate contexts were needed to understand the main context. I was much surer of that main context than of those subordinate contexts. I was surer of them when I could get a development where I could clear up terminological ambiguities, and so on. The more you have refinements, the better you can pin things down. [The last sentence gives the sense of a very rapidly delivered sentence that is difficult to decipher.] And the way these questions and answers will tie together under the overall leading topic is what provides your criterion of relevance.

A very simple illustration of relevance: a man leaves his perfectly ordered home in the morning; he comes back at night, and he finds the windows

29 Elsewhere Lonergan mentions Mikhael Ivanovich Rostovtzeff, *The Social and Economic History of the Roman Empire* (Oxford: The Clarendon Press, 1926). See *Topics in Education* 15, note 47.

broken, water on the floor and dripping from the walls, smoke in the air. Well, he shouldn't leap to the judgment that there was a fire ..., but if he says, 'Something happened,' he's saying something that he's certain of. If he goes on and says, 'Where's my wife?' well, that isn't relevant to that first statement. It's relevant to him, but not to that first question, What happened?

Question: Is the determination of relevance anything more than a personal decision?
Response: It's more than a personal decision, yes. To go back to my doctoral thesis, I started out a Molinist. At the end of two months I was sure that was irrelevant to the understanding of Thomas. There were studies of everything that was written on both grace and liberty from Anselm to Thomas, and there were monographs on the bigger figures. I was able through that to pinpoint just where Thomas started out from, and what led to the problems that he successfully solved. It's all a matter of what you discover in your investigations that pins things down, not anything previous, which can go by the board as you proceed.

Question: [A long question, indistinct on tape, seemed to question whether models taken from the sciences were not too static to study historical development.]
Response: There are models that are dynamic, and over time, like progress-decline-redemption. There is Piaget's operational development in terms of learning as a process of adapting to new objects and new situations, and these adaptations form groups, and a certain group will represent the boy of seven, and another group the same person at an older age, and so on. You can have that dynamic type of model. But in general the model is not something that 'hits on'; it's a source of questions and answers with respect to more concrete matter. You have to decide what you want to do. If you want to do just straight history, then you use your models just as a source of questions and perhaps of explanations, but very, very carefully. Marrou, *The Meaning of History*,[30] discusses the use of models and gives all the warnings about the dangers connected with them.

Question: You started without the Cartesian framework of doubt, but is your position Kantian?

30 Henri-Irenée Marrou, *The Meaning of History*, trans. Robert J. Olsen (Baltimore and Dublin: Helicon, 1966). See below, p. 333, note 3.

Response: No. The basis of philosophical system for me is cognitional theory, and the basis of cognitional theory is performing cognitional operations and working at what's going on. Just as clinical psychology, to a great extent (not entirely), is enamored of helping people to identify and name the feelings that they feel but have no name for, don't identify, don't recognize, so there are cognitional events that can be acknowledged and named. Seeing: all you have to do is open and close your eyes. Hearing: well, you're always hearing unless you're in a soundproof room. You're always touching something; you can just increase or decrease the amount of touching you're doing. Those experiences are quite easy to pick up. Insight is a different matter. You have to have one insight coming after another. You have to keep reproducing them. It's a matter of catching on. To give you an experience of it, Euclid's first proposition is logically unsatisfactory. [Again, Lonergan presents the problem.] There is no possibility of proving, on Euclid's definitions and postulates, that the two circles will intersect at some point *C.* But you can see it's so, and the modern cult of logic means that Euclid has to be rewritten and has been rewritten. This sort of thing is occurring all the time in Euclid: the unacknowledged insight. To be logically satisfying you have to acknowledge all the insights that are relevant to your results. The mathematicians discovered that they were operating with unacknowledged insights. Now, that's just one instance of an insight. Recognizing all the different ways in which insights occur is the experience on which you can appropriate what your own understanding is. And again, my book *Insight*: the first chapter, examples from mathematics; the next four chapters, examples from physics; the next three chapters, examples from commonsense understanding. I wrote the book to give people the opportunity to experience their own understanding, their own ability to get the point, and so to be able to stand on their own feet. A former pupil said to me, 'We don't depend on you. You showed us how to depend on ourselves.' That's my basis. Cognitional theory depends on your own experience of your own knowing. Epistemology depends on cognitional theory. Metaphysics comes out of both. What are you doing when you are knowing? Why is doing that knowing? What do you know when you do it? These are the three fundamental philosophical questions.

5

Doctrinal Pluralism[1]

A discussion of a pluralism in church doctrines needs a rather broad context. Accordingly my remarks will come under the following series of headings:

1 [The Pere Marquette Theology Lecture delivered at the Performing Arts Center, Milwaukee, Wisconsin, 3 April 1971. It was published the same year by Marquette University Press, and given a second printing in paperback by the same Press in 1972.

Three distinct typed versions of this paper, each with two copies, can be found at the Lonergan Research Institute. The library has two photocopies (LB 225 and file 629) of a paper typed by Lonergan with the title 'Doctrinal Pluralism' but with a running head 'SAP' on every page but the first (here 'SAP 1'). It consists of thirty-seven pages of text and two pages of endnotes. A note by Frederick Crowe in LB 225 indicates that 'SAP' means 'Some Aspects of Pluralism.' SAP 1 was used for a presentation at a Faculty Seminar, Regis College, Toronto, on 16 November 1970.

Next, file 617 in the archives has two photocopies of another, somewhat longer, and clearly later version, again with the title 'Doctrinal Pluralism' and the running head 'SAP' (here 'SAP 2'). The first twenty-three pages of SAP 2 (for all practical purposes, the first six sections) are simply photocopied from SAP 1, but a number of changes in these sections are pasted over the earlier version. Section 7 was substantially rewritten in SAP 2, and what appears there is retained in the final version. Section 8 is exactly the same in the two SAP documents, except for its last paragraph. Sections 9 and 10 are rewritten in SAP 2, and section 11, which did not appear in SAP 1 (though its topic, demythologization, is very briefly addressed there in section 9) is added.

Finally, the same archive file contains two copies (one carbon and one photocopy) of what seems to be the autograph of the completed lecture (here 'the autograph'). And even here, at least the first page of the carbon is not the same typed page that was photocopied, though the two are identical

1 Pluralism and Communications
2 Pluralism and Classicist Culture
3 Pluralism and Relativism
4 Undifferentiated and Differentiated Consciousness
5 Pluralism and Theological Doctrines
6 Pluralism and Conversion
7 Pluralism and Church Doctrines: The First Vatican Council
8 Pluralism and Church Doctrines: The Ongoing Context
9 The Permanence and Historicity of Dogma
10 Pluralism and the Unity of Faith
11 The Permanence of Dogma and Demythologization[2]

---

in their words. Clearly, SAP 2 was assembled in proximate preparation for the autograph, but further changes are made by hand in the autograph, and in fact each of the copies of the autograph has distinct changes written in the margins.

Editing here proceeded, first, by comparing the Marquette University text with the autograph and comparing sections 1 through 6 of that text with each of the SAP documents. Then attention was paid to the changes that appear in the SAP 2 version of section 7. The composition of section 8 is fairly straightforward, but more work had to be done again on sections 9, 10, and 11. Also significant is the fact that Lonergan acknowledges in *Method in Theology* (p. x, note 1) that 'Chapter Twelve [Doctrines] contributed much to *Doctrinal Pluralism*, The Pere Marquette Lecture for 1971, published by the Marquette University Press.' Comparisons with that chapter are instructive, and some will be noted here. In fact, the influence seems to go both ways: there are items that appear in chapter 12 of *Method in Theology* that seem to have been written originally for 'Doctrinal Pluralism.'

Subsequent to the Pere Marquette Lecture, Lonergan led a discussion seminar on 'Doctrinal Pluralism' at the Twenty-Sixth Annual Convention of the Catholic Theological Society of America, 17 July 1971, in Baltimore, Maryland. But he did not deliver a paper on that occasion. An Italian translation of the lecture by Giovanni Sala, *Il Pluralismo dottrinale* (Catania: Edizioni Paoline), was published in 1977.

Bracketed footnotes in the current edition are editorial. The other footnotes are Lonergan's, with a few editorial additions (for example, English translations of books that he cited in the original).]

2 [Several notes are in order on this list. First, see below, p. 77, where section 4 is entitled 'Undifferentiated and Variously Differentiated Consciousness.' The word 'Variously' does not appear in this initial list in any of the typescripts, but it is present even in the SAP documents when the text comes to section 4. However, in the SAP documents the subtitle 'Undifferentiated and Variously Differentiated Consciousness' is substituted for an original subtitle, 'Pluralism and Theological Doctrines,' that is, the subtitle of the next section. It is likely that Lonergan made that mistake while typing this initial list and then corrected it.

1   Pluralism and Communications

In the final paragraph of the Gospel according to Matthew, our Lord bid the Eleven to go forth and make all nations his disciples. This command has always stood at the basis of the church's mission, but in our age it has taken on a special significance. On the one hand, anthropological and historical research has made us aware of the enormous variety of human mentalities, cultures, and social arrangements. On the other hand, even a brief experience of historical investigation makes one aware how diligently yet how circumspectly one must proceed if one is to hope to reconstruct the meanings and intentions of another people, another time, another place. So it is that now we can know so much more about all nations and about the differences among them. So too it is that now we can understand the vastness and the complexity of the task of preaching the gospel to all nations.

This fact of diversity entails a pluralism, not yet of doctrines but at least of communications. If one doctrine is to be preached to all, still it is not to be preached in the same manner to all.[3] If one is to communicate with those of another culture, one must employ the resources of their culture. To employ simply the resources of one's own culture is not to communicate with the other but to remain locked up in one's own. On the other hand, it is not enough simply to employ the resources of the other culture; one must do so creatively. Merely to employ the resources of the other culture would be to fail to communicate the Christian message. But creative employment of those resources makes it possible to say in that culture what as yet had not been said.

There is a further point. Once Christian doctrine has been introduced

---

Second, regarding the ninth item, SAP 1 has 'Immutability' rather than 'Permanence.' So does SAP 2, but there it is crossed out by hand, and 'Permanence' is typed in the margin. And in section 7, as rewritten for SAP 2 and retained in the final version, we find Lonergan saying, '... it seems better to speak of the permanence of the meaning of dogmas rather than of the immutability of that meaning.' See below, p. 92. Even in SAP 1, p. 26, Lonergan corrects himself: he had written 'the meaning of dogma is claimed to be ever the same,' but 'ever the same' is crossed out and above this phrase there is typed, 'a permanent acquisition.' See also *Method in Theology* 323 (quoted below, note 30), where evidence is provided that the position on this issue found in *Method in Theology* was probably worked out while Lonergan was writing and rewriting 'Doctrinal Pluralism.'

Third, as indicated in note 1, SAP 1 does not contain section 11.]

3 This distinction was drawn by Pope John XXIII in his opening address, 'Gaudet Mater Ecclesia,' at Vatican II; see *Acta Apostolicae Sedis* 54 (1962) 792 lines 9–15.

successfully within a culture, it will proceed to develop along the lines of that culture. So it was that the gospel first preached in Palestine developed into a Judaic Christianity that employed the thought forms and stylistic genera of *Spätjudentum* in its apprehension of the Christian mysteries.[4] So too down the ages there have developed the idiosyncrasies of many local or national churches. Nor do these ongoing differences, once they are understood and explained, threaten the unity of faith. Rather, they testify to its vitality. For, as once was said, *quidquid recipitur ad modum recipientis recipitur,* while the absence of varying modalities would seem to prove an absence of genuine assimilation and the presence of only a perfunctory acceptance.

2   Pluralism and Classicist Culture

The contemporary notion of culture is empirical. A culture is a set of meanings and values informing a common way of life, and there are as many cultures as there are distinct sets of such meanings and values.

But this manner of conceiving culture is relatively recent. It is a product of empirical human studies. Within less than one hundred years, it has replaced an older, classicist view that had flourished for over two millennia. On the older view, culture was conceived normatively. It was the opposite of barbarism. It was a matter of acquiring and assimilating the tastes and skills, the ideals, virtues, and ideas that were pressed upon one in a good home and through a curriculum in the liberal arts. It stressed not facts but values. It could not but claim to be universalist. Its classics were immortal works of art, its philosophy was the perennial philosophy, its laws and structures were the deposit of the prudence and the wisdom of mankind. Classicist education was a matter of models to be imitated, of ideal characters to be emulated, of eternal verities and universally valid laws. It sought to produce, not the mere specialist but the *uomo universale* that could turn his hand to anything and do it brilliantly.

The classicist is not a pluralist. He knows that circumstances alter cases but he is far more deeply convinced that circumstances are accidental and that, beyond them, there is some substance or kernel or root that fits in with

4 See, for example, Jean Daniélou, *Théologie du judéo-christianisme* (Tournai and Paris: Desclée, 1959), in English, *The Theology of Jewish Christianity*, trans. & ed. John A. Baker (London: Darton, Longman & Todd, 1964); *Les symboles chrétiens primitifs* (Paris: Editions du Seuil, 1961), in English, *Primitive Christian Symbols*, trans. Donald Attwater (London: Burns & Oates, and Baltimore: Helicon, 1964); *Etudes d'exégèse judéo-chrétienne* (Paris: Beauchesne, 1966).

classicist assumptions of stability, immutability, fixity. Things have their specific natures; these natures, at least in principle, are to be known exhaustively
through the properties they possess and the laws they obey; and over and
above the specific nature there is only individuation by matter, so that knowledge of one instance of a species automatically is knowledge of any instance.
What is true of species in general, also is true of the human species, of the one
faith coming through Jesus Christ, of the one charity given through the gift of
the Holy Spirit. It follows that the diversities of peoples, cultures, social
arrangements can involve only a difference in the dress in which church
doctrine is expressed, but cannot involve any diversity in church doctrine
itself. That is *semper idem.*

The pluralist begs to differ.[5] He insists that human concepts are products
and expressions of human understanding, that human understanding develops over time, and that it develops differently in different places and in
different times. Again, he would claim that a human action determined solely
by abstract properties, abstract principles, abstract laws would be not only
abstract but also inhumanly inept on every concrete occasion. For possible
courses of human action are the discoveries of human intelligence, perhaps
remotely guided by principles and laws, but certainly grasped by insight into
concrete situations. Moreover, it is by further insight that the probable results
of each possible course of action are determined, and that determination, so
far from settling the issue, stands in need of a free and hopefully responsible
choice before action can ensue. Finally, insofar as a situation or a course of
action is intelligible, it can recur; but the less intelligent people are, the less
they learn from the defects of previous acts, and the more likely they are to
settle into some routine that keeps repeating the same mistakes to make their
situation ever worse. On the other hand, the more intelligent they are, the
more they can learn from previous mistakes, and the more they will keep
changing their course of action and, as well, keep changing their situation
and so necessitating still further changes in their courses of action.[6]

The pluralist, then, differs from the classicist inasmuch as he acknowledges human historicity both in principle and in fact. Historicity means – very
briefly – that human living is informed by meanings, that meanings are the

5 [The sap documents have here the sentence, 'He refuses to grant that
   human concepts resemble Plato's immutable forms.' The sentence is crossed
   out by hand in sap 2.]
6 [The wording is taken from the sap documents. In the typing of the autograph a line was missed: the autograph and the Marquette text read, '... and
   the more they will keep changing their situation and so necessitating ...']

product of intelligence, that human intelligence develops cumulatively over time, and that such cumulative development differs in different histories.

Classicism itself is one very notable and, indeed, very noble instance of such cumulative development. It is not mistaken in its assumption that there is something substantial and common to human nature and human activity. Its oversight is its failure to grasp that that something substantial and common also is something quite open. It may be expressed in the four transcendental precepts: Be attentive, Be intelligent, Be reasonable, Be responsible. But there is an almost endless manifold of situations to which men successively attend. There vary enormously the type and degree of intellectual and moral development brought to deal with situations. The standard both for human reasonableness and for the strength and delicacy of a man's conscience is satisfied only by a complete and lifelong devotion to human authenticity.

I have been outlining the theoretic objections to classicist thought. Far more massive are the factual objections. For a century and a half there have been developing highly refined methods in hermeneutics and history, and there have been multiplying not only new modes of studying scripture, the Fathers, the Scholastics, the Renaissance and Reformation, and subsequent periods, but also there have emerged numerous historically-minded philosophies. To confine the Catholic Church to a classicist mentality is to keep the Catholic Church out of the modern world and to prolong the already too long prolonged crisis within the Church.

3   Pluralism and Relativism

As the breakdown of Scholasticism has left many Catholics without any philosophy, so the rejection of the classicist outlook leaves many without even a *Weltanschauung*. In this state of almost complete disorientation, they feel confronted with an endless relativism when they are told that no one in this life can aspire to a knowledge of all mathematics, or all physics, or all chemistry, or all biology, or the whole of human studies, or of all the philosophies, or even of the whole of theology.

What is worse is that usually they are not equipped to deal effectively and successfully with the premises set forth by relativists. These premises are: (1) the meaning of any statement is relative to its context; (2) every context is subject to change; it stands within a process of development and/or decay; and (3) it is not possible to predict what the future context will be.

The trouble is twofold. On the one hand, these premises, as far as they go, are true. On the other hand, the complement they need does not consist primarily in further propositions. It is to be found only by unveiling the invariant structure of man's conscious and intentional acts; and that unveiling is a long and difficult task.[7] That task cannot be even outlined here, and so we have to be content to indicate briefly the type of qualification that can and should be added to the premises of relativism.

It is true that the meaning of any statement is relative to its context. But it does not follow that the context is unknown or, if it is unknown, that it cannot be discovered.[8] Still less does it follow that the statement understood within its context is mistaken or false. On the contrary, there are many true statements whose context is easily ascertained.

It is true that contexts change, and it can happen that a statement that was true in its own context ceases to be adequate in another context. It remains that it was true in its original context, that sound historical and exegetical procedures can reconstitute the original context with greater or less success and, in the same measure, arrive at an apprehension of the original truth.[9]

It is true that one cannot predict in detail what future changes of context will occur. But one can predict, for example, that the contexts of descriptive statements are less subject to change than the contexts of explanatory statements. Again, with regard to explanatory statements, one can predict that a theory that radically revised the periodic table of chemical elements would account not only for all the data accounted for by the periodic table but also for a substantial range of data for which the periodic table does not account.

Finally, as already remarked, if one wishes a more solid and searching treatment of the issue, one has to undertake a thorough exploration of the three basic issues in philosophy, namely, What am I doing when I am knowing (cognitional theory)? Why is doing that knowing (epistemology)? and What do I know when I do it (metaphysics)?

7 For a sketch of the task, see the essay 'Cognitional Structure,' in *Collection: Papers by Bernard Lonergan*, ed. Frederick E. Crowe (New York: Herder & Herder, and London: Darton, Longman & Todd, 1967) 221–39; 2nd ed., vol. 4 in Collected Works of Bernard Lonergan, ed. Frederick E. Crowe and Robert M. Doran (Toronto: University of Toronto Press, 1988; paperback ed., 1993) 205–21. Further references are to the Collected Works edition.

8 On the relativist contention that context is infinite, see Bernard Lonergan, *Insight* (see above, p. 3, note 2) 366–71 in the Collected Works edition.

9 [SAP 1 has 'It remains that it was true in its original context, that that truth can be reformulated in the present context, and that sound exegetical and historical procedures can reconstitute the original context.' In SAP 2, the altered sentence is pasted over the original one.]

4   Undifferentiated and Variously Differentiated Consciousness[10]

For centuries theologians were divided into schools. The schools differed
from one another on most points in systematic theology. But they all shared a
common origin in medieval Scholasticism and so they were able to understand one another and could attempt, if not dialogue, at least refutation. But
with the breakdown of Scholasticism, that common ancestry is no longer a
bond. The widest divergences in doctrine are being expressed by Catholic
theologians. If each abounds in his wisdom, he also tends to be mystified by
the existence of views other than his own.

If one is to understand this enormous diversity, one must, I believe, advert
to the sundry differentiations of human consciousness. A first differentiation
arises in the process of growing up. The infant lives in a world of immediacy.
The child moves towards a world mediated by meaning. For the adult the real
world is the world mediated by meaning, and his philosophic doubts about
the reality of that world arise from the fact that he has failed to advert to the
difference between the criteria for a world of immediacy and, on the other
hand, the criteria for the world mediated by meaning.

Such inadvertence seems to be the root of the confusion concerning
objects and objectivity that has obtained in Western thought since Kant
published his *Critique of Pure Reason*.[11] In the world of immediacy the only
objects are objects of experience, where 'experience' is understood in the
narrow sense and denotes either the outer experience of sense or the inner
experience of consciousness. But in the world mediated by meaning – that is,
mediated by experiencing, understanding, and judging – objects are what are
intended by questions and known by intelligent, correct, conscientious answers. It is by his questions for intelligence (*quid sit? cur ita sit?*), for reflection
(*an sit?*), for moral deliberation (*an honestum sit?*) that man intends without yet
knowing the intelligible, the true, the real, and the good. By that intending
man is immediately related to the objects that he will come to know when he
elicits correct acts of meaning. Accordingly, naive realism arises from the
assumption that the world mediated by meaning is known by taking a look.
Empiricism arises when the world mediated by meaning is emptied of everything except what can be seen, heard, felt. Idealism retains the empiricist
notion of reality, insists that human knowledge consists in raising and answer-

10 [See above, note 2.]
11 On the Kantian notion of object, see, briefly, *Collection* 193–94; at length,
Jacques Colette et al., *Procès de l'objectivité de Dieu* (Paris: Editions du Cerf,
1969).

ing questions, and concludes that human knowledge is not of the real but of
the ideal. Finally, a critical realism claims that adult human knowledge of
reality consists, not in experiencing alone but in experiencing, understanding, and judging.[12]

Besides the differentiation of consciousness involved in growing up, further differentiations occur with respect to the world mediated by meaning.
Here the best known is the differentiation of commonsense meaning and
scientific meaning. Its origins are celebrated in Plato's early dialogues, in
which Socrates explains what he means by a definition that applies *omni et soli*,
seeks definitions of courage, sobriety, justice, and the like, shows the inadequacy of any proposed definition, admits that he himself is unable to answer
his own questions. But a generation or so later in Aristotle's *Nicomachean
Ethics*, we find not only general definitions of virtue and vice but also definitions of an array of specific virtues, each one flanked by vices that sin by excess
or by defect. However, Aristotle not merely answered Socrates' questions but
also set up the possibility of answering them by a sustained scrutiny of linguistic usage, by selecting the precise meaning he assigned to the terms he
employed, by constructing sets of interrelated terms, and by employing such
sets to systematize whole regions of inquiry.

Thereby was effected the differentiation of commonsense meaning and
scientific meaning. Socrates and his friends knew perfectly well what they
meant by courage, sobriety, justice. But such knowledge does not consist in
universal definitions. It consists simply in understanding when the term may
be used appropriately, and such understanding is developed by adverting to
the response others give to one's statements. As it does not define, so too
common sense does not enounce universal principles. It offers proverbs, that
is, pieces of advice it may be well to bear in mind when the occasion arises;
hence 'Strike the iron while it is hot' and 'He who hesitates is lost' are not so

---

12 [Beginning with 'By that intending' (mid-paragraph) SAP 1 has, 'By that
    intending man is immediately related to the objects in the world mediated by
    meaning; answers only mediately are related to such objects, i.e., only inas-
    much as they are answers to questions. On this showing the tendency to an
    empiricism arises when one applies the criteria of the world of immediacy to
    activities with respect to the world mediated by meaning. The tendency to
    idealism accepts the empiricist notion of reality, insists that human cogni-
    tional activity consists in raising and answering questions, mistakenly grants
    that such activity is concerned with merely ideal objects. Finally, a critical
    realism asserts that adult human knowledge of reality is a matter not solely of
    experiencing but of experiencing, understanding, and judging.' In SAP 2 the
    wording that appears in the text here is pasted over this earlier wording.]

much contradicted as complemented[13] by 'Look before you leap.' Finally, common sense does not syllogize; it argues from analogy. But its analogies resemble, not those constructed by logicians, in which the analogue partly is similar and partly dissimilar, but rather Piaget's adaptations, which consist in two parts: an assimilation that calls on the insights relevant to somewhat similar situations, and an adjustment that adds insights relevant to the peculiarities of the present situation.

But besides the world mediated by commonsense meanings, there is another world mediated by scientific meanings, where terms are defined, systematic relationships are sought, procedures are governed by logics and methods. This second world was intuited by Plato's distinction between the flux of phenomena and the immutable Forms. It was affirmed more soberly in Aristotle's distinction between the *priora quoad nos* and the *priora quoad se*. It has reappeared in Eddington's two tables: one brown, solid, heavy; the other colorless, mostly empty space, with here and there an unimaginable wavicle.[14] So it is that scientists live in two worlds: at one moment they are with the rest of us in the world of common sense; at another they are apart from us and by themselves with a technical and controlled language of their own and with reflectively constructed and controlled cognitional procedures.

Besides the scientific, there is a religious differentiation of consciousness. It begins with asceticism and culminates in mysticism. Both asceticism and mysticism, when genuine, have a common ground. That ground was described by St Paul when he exclaimed: '... God's love has flooded our inmost heart through the Holy Spirit he has given us' (Romans 5.5). That ground can bear fruit in a consciousness that lives in a world mediated by meaning. But it can also set up a different type of consciousness by withdrawing one from the world mediated by meaning into a cloud of unknowing.[15] Then one is for God, belongs to him, gives oneself to him, not by using images, concepts, words, but in a silent, joyous, peaceful surrender to his initiative.[16]

---

13 [See above, pp. 51–52, note 6.]
14 Sir Arthur Eddington, *The Nature of the Physical World* (Cambridge: Cambridge University Press, 1928); see Introduction, xi–xv.
15 See William Johnston, *The Mysticism of the Cloud of Unknowing* (New York, Rome, Tournai, Paris: Desclée, 1967); also his *The Still Point: Reflections on Zen and Christian Mysticism* (New York: Fordham University Press, 1970) 27–41. See also Karl Rahner, *The Dynamic Element in the Church* (see above, p. 40, note 22) 129–42.
16 [In SAP 1 we find, 'That ground can bear fruit in a consciousness that lives in a world mediated by meaning. But it can also withdraw one for a time from

Ordinarily the scientific and the religious differentiations of conscious-ness occur in different individuals. But they can be found in the same individual as was the case with Thomas of Aquin. At the end of his life, his prayer was so intense that it interfered with his theological activity. But earlier there could have been an intermittent religious differentiation of conscious-ness, while later still further development might have enabled him to com-bine prayer and theology as Teresa of Avila combined prayer and business.

Besides the scientific and the religious, there is the scholarly differentia-tion of consciousness. It combines the common sense of one's own place and time with a detailed understanding of the common sense of another place and time. It is a specifically modern achievement and it results only from a lifetime of study.

Besides the scientific, the religious, and the scholarly, there is the modern philosophic differentiation. Ancient and medieval philosophers were princi-pally concerned with objects. If they attained any differentiation, that did not differ from the scientific. But in modern philosophy there has been a sus-tained tendency to begin, not from the objects in the world mediated by meaning but from the immediate data of consciousness. In a first phase, from Descartes to Kant, the primary focus of attention was cognitional activity. But after the transition provided by German idealism, there was a notable shift in emphasis. Schopenhauer wrote on *Die Welt als Wille und Vorstellung;* Kierkegaard took his stand on faith; Newman took his on conscience; Nietzsche extolled the will to power; Dilthey aimed at a *Lebensphilosophie;* Blondel at a philosophy of action; Scheler was abundant on feeling; and similar tendencies, reminis-cent of Kant's emphasis on practical reason, have been maintained by the personalists and the existentialists.

We have distinguished four differentiations of consciousness: the scien-tific, the religious, the scholarly, and the modern philosophic. We have noted the possibility of one compound differentiation in which the scientific and the religious were combined in a single individual. But there are five other possibilities of twofold differentiation,[17] and there are four possibilities of

---

the world mediated by meaning into the cloud of unknowing, and then one is for God, belongs to him, gives oneself to him, not by one's own initiative but in a silent, joyous, peaceful surrender to his initiative.' And the footnote reference to Johnston and Rahner occurs at the very end, at 'initiative.' The changes are pasted into SAP 2.]

17 The five are: scientific and scholarly; scientific and philosophic; religious and scholarly; religious and philosophic; scholarly and philosophic.

threefold differentiation.[18] Further, there is one case of fourfold differentiation, in which scientific, religious, scholarly, and philosophic differentiations are combined. Finally, there is also one case of undifferentiated consciousness, which is at home only in the realm of common sense: it shares Heidegger's affection for the pre-Socratics, the linguistic analyst's insistence on ordinary as opposed to technical language, and the strident devotion to the Bible of those that want no dogmas.

There are, then, on this analysis, sixteen different types of consciousness, and from them result sixteen different worlds mediated by meaning.[19] Still, this division is highly schematic. Further differences arise when one considers the degree to which consciousness has developed, the measure in which differentiated consciousness is integrated, the obnubilation imposed upon a consciousness that is less differentiated than its place and time demand, and the frustration imposed upon a consciousness that has achieved a greater differentiation than most other people in its social circle.

5   Pluralism and Theological Doctrines

We have been considering diverse differentiations of human consciousness. Our aim has been to gain an insight into contemporary theological pluralism. It is time for us to set about applying the distinctions that have been drawn.

In general, the more differentiated consciousness is quite beyond the horizon of the less or the differently differentiated consciousness. Inversely, the less differentiated consciousness can easily be understood by the more differentiated, insofar as the former is included in the latter.

Undifferentiated consciousness is the most common type. To this type will always belong the vast majority of the faithful. As a type it can be understood by everyone. But it itself is only mystified by the subtleties of scientifically differentiated consciousness, by the oracles of religiously differentiated consciousness, by the strangeness of scholarly differentiated consciousness, by the profundities of the modern philosophic differentiation. One can preach to it and teach it only by using its own language, its own procedures, its own resources. These are not uniform. There are as many brands of common sense as there are languages, sociocultural differences, almost differences of place

18 The four are: scientific, religious, and scholarly; scientific, religious, and philosophic; scientific, scholarly, and philosophic; religious, scholarly, and philosophic.

19 [Below, p. 98, Lonergan will add the aesthetic and say there are thirty-two different ways that consciousness may be structured.]

and time. The stranger is strange because he comes from another place. Hence to preach the gospel to all men calls for at least as many men as there are different places and times, and it requires each of them to get to know the people to whom he is sent, their manners and style and ways of thought and speech. There follows a manifold pluralism. Primarily it is a pluralism, not of doctrine but of communications. But within the realm of undifferentiated consciousness there is no communication of doctrine except through the available rituals, narratives, titles, parables, metaphors, modes of praise and blame, command and prohibition, promise and threat.

An exception to this last statement must be noted. The educated classes in a society such as was the Hellenistic normally are instances of undifferentiated consciousness. But their education had among its sources works of genuine philosophers, so that they could be familiar with logical principles and take propositions as the objects on which they reflected and operated. In this fashion the meaning of *homoousion* for Athanasius was contained in a rule concerning propositions about the Father and the Son: *eadem de Filio, quae de Patre dicuntur, excepto Patris nomine.*[20] Again, the meaning of the one person and two natures mentioned in the second paragraph of the decree of Chalcedon stands forth in the repeated affirmation of the first paragraph that it is one and the same Son our Lord Jesus Christ that is perfect in divinity and the same perfect in humanity, truly God and the same truly man, consubstantial with the Father in his divinity, and the same consubstantial with us in his humanity, born of the Father before the ages in his divinity, and these last days the same ... born of the Virgin Mary in his humanity.[21] Now the meaning of the first paragraph can be communicated without any new technical terms. However, logical reflection on the first paragraph will give rise to questions. Is the humanity the same as the divinity? If not, how can the same be both God and man? It is only after these questions have arisen in the mind of the inquirer that it is relevant to explain that a distinction can be drawn between person and nature, that divinity and humanity denote two natures, that it is one and the same person that is both God and man. Such logical clarification is within the meaning of the decree. But if one goes on to raise metaphysical questions, such as the reality of the distinction between person and nature, one moves not only beyond the questions explicitly envisaged by the decree but also beyond the horizon of undifferentiated consciousness.

20 [the same things are predicated of the Son as of the Father, except the name 'Father'] Athanasius, *Oratio III contra Arianos*, 4, in PG 26, 329 A.
21 DS 301–302.

Turning now to religiously differentiated consciousness, we observe that it can be content with the negations of an apophatic theology. For it is in love, and on its love there are not any reservations or conditions or qualifications. It is with one's whole heart and whole soul and all one's mind and all one's strength. By such love a person is orientated positively to what is transcendent in lovableness. Such a positive orientation and the consequent self-surrender, as long as they are operative, enable one to dispense with any intellectually apprehended object;[22] and when they cease to be operative, the memory of them enables one to be content with enumerations of what God is not.

It may be objected that *nihil amatum nisi praecognitum*. But while that is true of other human love, it does not seem to be true of the love with which God floods our inmost hearts through the Holy Spirit given to us. That grace is the finding that grounds our seeking God through natural reason[23] and through positive religion. That grace is the touchstone by which we judge whether it is really God that natural reason reaches or positive religion preaches. That grace would be the grace sufficient for salvation that God offers all men, that underpins what is good in all the religions of mankind, that explains how those that never heard the gospel can be saved. That grace is what enables the simple faithful to pray to their heavenly Father in secret even though their religious apprehensions are faulty. That grace is what replaces doctrine as the *unum necessarium* in religions generally. That grace indicates the theological justification of Catholic dialogue with Christians, with non-Christians, and even with atheists, who may love God in their hearts without knowing him with their heads.

However, what is true of religions generally is not true of the Christian religion. For it knows God not only through the grace in its heart but also through the revelation of God's love in Christ Jesus and the witness to that revelation down the ages through the church. Christian love of God is not just a state of mind and heart; essential to it is the intersubjective, interpersonal component in which God reveals his love and asks ours in return. It is at this point that there emerges the function of church doctrines and of theological doctrines. For that function is to explain and to defend the authenticity of the church's witness to the revelation in Christ Jesus.

22 See Johnston or Rahner cited above, note 15.

23 On the transition from Vatican I to the contemporary context on natural knowledge of God, see my paper, 'Natural Knowledge of God,' *Proceedings of the Twenty-Third Annual Convention*, Catholic Theological Society of America 23 (1968) 54–69; in *A Second Collection* (see above, p. 22, note 12) 117–33.

As already explained, there was a slight tincture of scientifically differentiated consciousness in the Greek councils. In the medieval period there was
undertaken the systematic and collaborative task of reconciling all that had
been handed down by the church from the past. A first step was Abelard's *Sic
et non*, in which some one hundred and fifty-eight propositions were both
proved and disproved by arguments from scripture, the Fathers, the councils,
and reason.[24] In a second step there was developed the technique of the
quaestio: Abelard's *non* became *videtur quod non* and his *sic* became *sed contra est.*
To these were added a general response, in which principles of solution were
set forth, and specific responses, in which the principles were applied to the
conflicting evidence. A third step was the composition of books of Sentences
that collected and classified relevant passages from scripture and subsequent
tradition. A fourth step were the commentaries on the books of Sentences in
which the technique of the *quaestio* was applied to these richer collections of
materials. The fifth step was to obtain a conceptual system that would enable
the theologian to give coherent answers to all the questions he raised; and this
was obtained partly by adopting and partly by adapting the Aristotelian corpus.

Scholastic theology was a monumental achievement. Its influence on the
church has been profound and enduring. Up to Vatican II, which preferred a
more biblical turn of speech, it has provided much of the background whence
proceeded pontifical documents and conciliar decrees. Yet today by and
large it is abandoned, and that abandonment leaves the documents and
decrees that relied on it almost mute and ineffectual. Such is the contemporary crisis in Catholicism. It is important to indicate why it exists and how it can
be overcome.

The Scholastic aim of reconciling all the documents of the Christian
tradition had one grave defect: it was content with a logically and metaphysi-
cally satisfying reconciliation; it did not realize how much of the multiplicity
in the inheritance constituted not a logical or metaphysical but basically a
historical problem.

Secondly, the Aristotelian corpus, on which Scholasticism drew for the
framework of its solutions, suffers from a number of defects. The *Posterior
Analytics* set forth an ideal of science in which the key element is the notion of
necessity, of what cannot be otherwise. On this basis, science is said to be of the
necessary, while opinion regards the contingent; similarly, wisdom is concerned with first principles, while prudence regards contingent human

24 *PL* 178, 1339–1610.

affairs. There follows the primacy of speculative intellect, and this is buttressed by a verbalism that attributes to common names the properties of scientific terms. Finally, while man is acknowledged to be a political animal, the historicity of the meanings that inform human living is not grasped, and much less is there understood the fact that historical meaning is to be presented not by poets but by historians.

In contrast, modern mathematics is fully aware that its axioms are not necessary truths but only freely chosen and no more than probably consistent postulates. The modern sciences ascertain, not what must be so but only what is in itself hypothetical and so in need of verification. First principles in philosophy are not verbal propositions but the de facto invariants of human conscious intentionality. What was named speculative intellect now is merely the operations of experiencing, understanding, and judging, performed under the guidance of the moral deliberation, evaluation, decision that selects a method and sees to it that the method is observed. The primacy now belongs to practical intellect, and, perforce, philosophy ultimately becomes a philosophy of action. Finally, it is only on the basis of intentionality analysis that it is possible either to understand human historicity or to set forth the foundations and criticize the practice of contemporary hermeneutics and critical history.

The defects of Scholasticism, then, were the defects of its time. It could not inspect the methods of modern history and thereby learn the importance of history in theology. It could not inspect modern science and thereby correct the mistakes in Aristotle's conceptual system. But if we cannot blame the Scholastics for their shortcomings, we must undertake the task of remedying them. A theology is the product not only of a faith but also of a culture. It is cultural change that has made Scholasticism no longer relevant and that demands the development of a new theological method and style, continuous indeed with the old, yet meeting all the genuine exigences both of the Christian religion and of up-to-date philosophy, science, and scholarship.

Until that need is met, pluralism will obtain. Undifferentiated consciousness will continue its ban on technical theology. Scientifically differentiated consciousness will ally itself with secularism. Religiously differentiated consciousness will know that the main issue is in the heart and not the head. Scholarly differentiated consciousness will continue to pour forth the fruits of its research in interpretations and histories. Philosophically differentiated consciousness will continue to twist and turn in its efforts to break loose from Kant's grasp. But the worthy successor to thirteenth-century achievement will be the fruit of a fourfold differentiated consciousness, in which the workings of common sense, science, scholarship, intentionality analysis, and the life of prayer have been integrated.

6   Pluralism and Conversion

Conversion involves a new understanding of oneself because, more fundamentally, it brings about a new self to be understood. It is putting off the old man and putting on the new. It is not just a development but the beginning of a new mode of developing. Hence, besides the beginning, there is to be considered the consequent development. This may be great or average or small. It may be marred by few or by many relapses. The relapses may have been corrected fully, or they may still leave their traces in a bias that may be grave or venial.

Conversion is three-dimensional. It is intellectual inasmuch as it regards our orientation to the intelligible and the true. It is moral inasmuch as it regards our orientation to the good. It is religious inasmuch as it regards our orientation to God. The three dimensions are distinct, so that conversion can occur in one dimension without occurring in the other two, or in two dimensions without occurring in the other one. At the same time, the three dimensions are solidary. Conversion in one leads to conversion in the other dimensions, and relapse from one prepares for relapse from the others.

By intellectual conversion a person frees himself from confusing the criteria of the world of immediacy with the criteria of the world mediated by meaning. By moral conversion he becomes motivated primarily, not by satisfactions but by values. By religious conversion he comes to love God with his whole heart and his whole soul and all his mind and all his strength; and in consequence he loves his neighbor as himself.

The authentic Christian strives for the fullness of intellectual, moral, and religious conversion. Without intellectual conversion he tends to misapprehend not only the world mediated by meaning but also the word God has spoken within that world. Without moral conversion he tends to pursue not what truly is good but what only apparently is good. Without religious conversion he is radically desolate: in the world without hope and without God (Ephesians 2.12).

While the importance of moral and religious conversion will readily be granted, hesitation will be felt by many when it comes to intellectual conversion. They will feel that it is a philosophic issue and that it is not up to theologians to solve it. But while these contentions are true, they are not decisive. The issue is also existential and methodical. Theologians have minds. They have always used them. They may use them properly and they may use them improperly. Unless they find out the difference for themselves or learn about it from someone else, they will be countenancing a greater pluralism than can be tolerated.

Indeed, in my opinion, intellectual conversion is essentially simple. It occurs spontaneously when one reaches the age of reason, implicitly drops earlier criteria of reality (are you awake? do you see it? is it heavy? and so forth), and proceeds to operate on the criteria of sufficient evidence or sufficient reason. But this spontaneous conversion is insecure. The use of the earlier criteria can recur. It is particularly likely to recur when one gets involved in philosophic issues. For then the objectification of what is meant by sufficient evidence or sufficient reason is exceedingly complex while the objectification of taking a good look is simplicity itself. So one becomes a naive realist, or an empiricist, or an idealist, or a pragmatist, or a phenomenologist, and so on.

Now, in any individual, conversion can be present or absent. In the former case it can be present in one dimension or in two or in all three; it can be enriched by development, or distorted by aberration, and the development and aberration may be great or small. Such differences give rise to another variety of pluralism. Besides the pluralism implicit in the transition from classicist to modern culture, besides the pluralism implicit in the coexistence of undifferentiated and variously differentiated consciousness, there is the more radical pluralism that arises when all are not authentically human and authentically Christian.

Unauthenticity may be open-eyed and thoroughgoing, and then it heads for a loss of faith. But the unconverted may have no real apprehension of what it is to be converted. Sociologically they are Catholics, but on a number of points they deviate from the norm. Moreover, they commonly will not have an appropriate language for expressing what they really are, and so they will use the language of the group with which they identify socially. There will result an inflation of language and so of doctrine. Terms that denote what one is not will be stretched to denote what one is. Doctrines that are embarrassing will not be mentioned. Unacceptable conclusions will not be drawn. So unauthenticity can spread and become a tradition, and, for those born into such a tradition, becoming authentic human beings will be a matter of purifying the tradition in which they were brought up.[25]

25 [The SAP documents reveal two earlier attempts at this paragraph:
   (1) 'Unauthenticity may be open-eyed and thoroughgoing, and then it leads to a loss of faith. But also it may lack clear self-awareness, and what

Quite by itself, the pluralism resulting from a lack of conversion can be perilous. But the dangers are multiplied many times when the lack of conversion combines with other modes of pluralism. The transition from classicist culture to modern historical mindedness, if combined with lack of conversion, can amount to a watering down of the faith. Undifferentiated consciousness, combined with defective conversion, will opt for the Gospels and drop the dogmas. Religiously differentiated consciousness without intellectual conversion will deprecate insistence on doctrines. Scholarly differentiated consciousness can unleash floods of information in which origins are ever obscurer and continuity hard to discern. The modern philosophic differentiation of consciousness can prove a trap that confines one in a subjectivism and a relativism.

7   Pluralism and Church Doctrines: The First Vatican Council[26]

On pluralism and church doctrines there is an important pronouncement made in the constitution, *Dei Filius*, promulgated by the First Vatican Council. It occurs in the last paragraph of the fourth and final chapter of the decree (DS 3020) and in the appended canon (DS 3043). It is to the effect that there

happens then has been studied somewhere by Karl Jaspers. On a number of points the person will be what a Christian is supposed to be, but on another number of points he will not be what he is supposed to be. Moreover, this discrepancy will lead to a devaluation of Christian language. Terms that denote what one is not will be broadened to cover what one is. Doctrines that are embarrassing will not be mentioned. Conclusions that would not be accepted are not drawn.' (Crossed out on p. 23 of SAP 1.)

(2) 'Unauthenticity may be open-eyed and thoroughgoing, and then it heads for a loss of faith. But the unconverted need have no clear idea what it is to be converted. They can be unaware of what they are. On a number of points they will be Catholic, but on a number of other points they will not be. There will result a devaluation, an inflation, of language and of doctrine. Terms that denote what one is not will be broadened to cover what one is. Doctrines that are embarrassing will not be mentioned. Unacceptable conclusions will not be drawn.' (Typed on p. 23 of SAP 1, pasted over in SAP 2 by the version given in the text above.)

26 [As indicated above, this section was completely rewritten for SAP 2. SAP 1 introduces the question treated in the section as having to do with 'the immutability of faith' and 'the distinction between faith and reason' as these were viewed in the writings of Anton Günther and Jakob Frohschammer. It is in section 7 of SAP 2 that Lonergan explicitly states that 'permanence' rather than 'immutability' of meaning is what Vatican I means in addressing the question in *Dei Filius* (but see above, note 2, for an anticipation of this in a correction made in SAP 1). That he was still thinking more in terms of

is ever to be retained that meaning of a dogma that was once declared by the church, and that there is to be no departure from it on the pretext of some profounder understanding (DS 3020). Moreover, this pronouncement at least historically has a reference to pluralism. For earlier the Holy See had condemned the thoroughgoing pluralism of Anton Günther (DS 2828–2831) and of Jakob Frohschammer (DS 2850–2861; also, 2908–2909), and Cardinal Franzelin had pursued the matter further both in the *votum* he presented to the preconciliar committee[27] and in his schema, *Contra errores ex rationalismo derivatos,* presented for discussion in the early days of Vatican I.[28]

In true classicist style, however, the fourth chapter is proceeding, not against historical persons but against errors. The main thrust of chapter 4, as appears from the three appended canons (DS 3041–3043), is against a rationalism that considers mysteries nonexistent, that proposes to demonstrate the

---

immutability in SAP 1 can be surmised from the title of that document's section 9. Again, see above, note 2. A large part of section 7 in SAP 1 is devoted simply to quoting paragraphs from *Dei Filius* and making a few comments on them, in order to throw light on the last paragraph of the fourth chapter of that document (DS 3020) and on an appended canon (DS 3043). The relevant section of that paragraph from *Dei Filius* reads (in Lonergan's translation in SAP 1, p. 29): 'For the doctrine of faith, which God has revealed, has not been proposed as some sort of philosophic discovery to be perfected by the talent of man. It is a divine deposit, given to the Spouse of Christ, to be guarded faithfully and to be declared infallibly. Hence there is ever to be retained that meaning of the sacred dogmas that once was declared by holy mother church. From that meaning there is to be no departure under the pretext of some higher understanding.' Lonergan says of the canon (SAP 1, p. 28), '[It] condemns those that affirm that with the advance of science it is possible to attribute to the dogmas propounded by the church a meaning other than that which the church has understood and still understands.' In SAP 2 the material is more organized, perhaps because Lonergan came to see more clearly that 'the exact meaning of this paragraph and canon' (SAP 1, on a page numbered '24 and 25') has to do with 'permanence of meaning' rather than 'immutability of meaning.']

27 The *votum* has been published in an appendix to the work of Hermann-Josef Pottmeyer, *Der Glaube vor dem Anspruch der Wissenschaft* (Freiburg im Breisgau: Herder, 1968); see especially *Anhang,* pp. 50*, 51*, 54*, 55*. The author, to whom we are indebted, has some twenty-five pages [431–56] on the passage with which we are concerned. [There is a copy of this book in the Lonergan Archives. Lonergan has underlined and sidelined a number of items in these twenty-five pages.]

28 See chapters V, VI, XI, XII, and XIV of the schema, in Johannes Dominicus Mansi, *Sacrorum conciliorum nova et amplissima collectio* (Graz: Akademische Druck-u. Verlagsanstallt, 1960–1961), vol. 50, cols. 62–69, and the abundant annotations, ibid. columns 83–108.

dogmas, that defends scientific conclusions even though opposed to church doctrines, that claims the church to have no right to condemn scientific views, and that grants science the competence to reinterpret the church's dogmas.

Against such rationalism the council had distinguished (1) the natural light of reason, (2) faith, (3) reason illumined by faith, and (4) reason operating beyond its proper limits.'

Reason, then, or the natural light of reason, has a range of objects within its reach (DS 3015). It can know with certitude the existence of God (DS 3004), and it can know some though not all of the truths revealed by God (DS 3005, 3015). It must submit to divine revelation (DS 3008) and such submission is in harmony with its nature (DS 3009). In no way does the church prohibit human disciplines from using their proper principles and methods within their own fields (DS 3019).

Faith is a supernatural virtue by which we believe to be true what God has revealed, not because we apprehend the intrinsic truth of what has been revealed but because of the authority of God who reveals and can neither deceive nor be deceived (DS 3008). By divine and catholic faith are to be believed all that is both revealed by God in scripture or tradition and, as well, has been proposed to be believed as revealed[29] either in a solemn pronouncement by the church or in the exercise of its ordinary and universal teaching office (DS 3011). Among the principal objects of faith are the mysteries hidden in God which, were they not revealed, could not be known by us (DS 3015, see 3005).

Reason illumined by faith, when it inquires diligently, piously, soberly, reaches with God's help some extremely fruitful understanding of the mysteries both in virtue of the analogy of things it knows naturally and in virtue of the interconnection of the mysteries with one another and with man's last end. But it never becomes capable of grasping them after the fashion it grasps the truths that lie within its proper range. For the divine mysteries by their very nature so exceed created intellect that, even when given by revelation and accepted by faith, still by the veil of faith itself they remain as it were covered over by some sort of cloud (DS 3016). It would seem to be the understanding attained by reason illumined by faith that is praised in the quotation from Vincent of Lerins (DS 3020). For this understanding regards, not some human invention but the mysteries revealed by God and accepted on faith; and

29 [There was an omission in the Marquette University text, which reads, '… has been proposed to be revealed …']

so from the nature of the case it will be '... *in suo dumtaxat genere, in eodem scilicet dogmate, eodem sensu eademque sententia*'[30] (DS 3020).

Finally, there is reason that steps beyond its proper bounds to invade and disturb the realm of faith (DS 3019). For the doctrine of faith, which God has revealed, has not been proposed as some sort of philosophic discovery to be perfected by human talent. It is a divine deposit, given to the spouse of Christ, to be guarded faithfully and to be declared infallibly. Hence there is ever to be retained that meaning of the sacred dogmas that once was declared by holy mother church; and from that meaning there is to be no departure under the pretext of some profounder understanding (DS 3020).

In this passage a definite limit is placed on doctrinal pluralism. Similarly, in the corresponding canon, there is condemned anyone that says it is possible that eventually with the progress of science there may have to be given to the dogmas propounded by the church a meaning other than that which the church understood and understands (DS 3043).

First, then, there is affirmed a permanence of meaning: '... *is sensus perpetuo est retinendus ... nec umquam ab eo recedendum ...*'; '*in eodem scilicet dogmate, eodem sensu eademque sententia*' (DS 3020);[31] '*... sensus tribuendus sit alius ...*' (DS 3043).[32]

Secondly, the permanent meaning is the meaning declared by the church (DS 3020), the meaning which the church understood and understands (DS 3043).

Thirdly, this permanent meaning is the meaning of dogmas (DS 3020, 3043). But from the context of the paragraph the meaning of dogmas has this permanence because it conveys the doctrine of faith, revealed by God, which was not proposed as a philosophic invention to be perfected by human talent.

Now God reveals both truths that lie within the range of human intelligence and divine mysteries, hidden in God, that could not be known unless they were revealed (DS 3015, 3005). It would seem that it is the mysteries that transcend the intelligence of the human mind (DS 3005) and by their very nature stand beyond created intellect (DS 3016) that are not mere philo-

---

30 [... within the same genus, within the same dogma, within the same meaning and view (thus Lonergan's own translation in SAP 1, p. 27). But see also *Method in Theology* 323: 'Again, it is permanence rather than immutability that is meant when there is desired an ever better understanding of the same dogma, the same meaning, the same pronouncement.'].

31 [there is ever to be retained that meaning ... and from that meaning there is to be no departure ... in the same dogma, the same meaning, and the same pronouncement]

32 [that another meaning is to be attributed]

sophic inventions that human talent could perfect. On the other hand, truths that naturally are knowable would seem capable of being known more accurately with the progress of science (DS 3043).

It would seem, then, that dogmas refer to the church's declaration of revealed mysteries.[33]

Fourthly, the meaning of the dogma is not apart from a verbal formulation, for it is a meaning declared by the church. However, the permanence attaches to the meaning and not to the formula. To retain the same formula and give it a new meaning is precisely what the third canon excludes (DS 3043).

Fifthly, it seems better to speak of the permanence of the meaning of dogmas rather than of the immutability of that meaning. For permanence is what is implied by *retinendus, non recedendum, non ... alius tribuendus.* Again, it is permanence rather than immutability that is meant when there is asserted a growth and advance in understanding, knowledge, wisdom with respect to the same dogma and the same meaning (DS 3020).

Finally, let us ask why the meaning of dogmas is permanent. There are two answers. The first assigns the *causa cognoscendi*, the reason why we know it to be permanent. The second assigns the *causa essendi*, the reason why it has to be permanent.

First, the *causa cognoscendi*. What God reveals, what the church infallibly declares, is true. What is true is permanent. The meaning it had in its own context can never truthfully be denied.

Secondly, the *causa essendi*. The mysteries lie beyond the range of human intelligence (DS 3005), created intellect (DS 3016). They could not be known by us unless they were revealed (DS 3015). They are known by us, not because their intrinsic truth is grasped but because of God's authority (DS 3008). Our understanding of them can increase when reason is illumined by faith; but it is an understanding of the revealed mystery – *in eodem dogmate* – and not of some human substitute for the mystery (DS 3016, 3020). It would be to

---

33 [This position, found also in *Method in Theology*, is not as clear at this point in SAP 1; rather (quoting from a page numbered '25 and 26'), 'dogmas' in the sense of Vatican I '... would seem to coincide with the truths to be believed by divine and catholic faith,' and those truths include 'all (1) that is contained in scripture and tradition and (2) that has been proposed to be believed as divinely revealed either in a solemn pronouncement by the church or in its ordinary and universal teaching office.' Later, however, in section 9 of SAP 1 there can be found the statement that dogmas are immutable 'because they refer to mysteries hidden in God that, unless revealed, could not be known.' The formulation is in process of being worked out.]

disregard divine transcendence if one handed the mysteries over to philosophic or scientific reinterpretation.

Such, it seems to me, is the meaning of the pronouncement of the constitution *Dei Filius* with respect to the permanence of the meaning of the dogmas. But since the First Vatican Council there have occurred further developments. While Anton Günther and Jakob Frohschammer were concerned with human historicity, the council was content simply to point out where their views were unacceptable. It did not attempt to integrate its contentions with what is true in the affirmation of human historicity. To this topic we must now attend.

8   Pluralism and Church Doctrines: The Ongoing[34] Context

A statement has a meaning in a context. If one already knows the context, the meaning of the statement is plain. If one does not know the context, one discovers it by asking questions. The answer to a first question may suggest two further questions. The answers to them suggest still more. Gradually there is woven together an interlocking set of questions and answers, and, sooner or later, there is reached a point where further questions have less and less relevance to the matter in hand. One could ask about this and that and the other, but the answers would not help one to understand better the meaning of the original statement. In brief, there is a limit to useful questioning, and when that is reached the context is known.

Such is the prior context, the context within which the original statement was made and through which the original meaning of the statement is determined. But besides the prior context, there is also the subsequent context. For a statement may intend to settle one issue and to prescind from other issues. But settling the one does not burke the others. Usually it contributes to a clearer grasp of the others and a more urgent pressure for their solution. According to Athanasius, the Council of Nicea used a nonscriptural term in a confession of faith, not to set a precedent but to meet an emergency. But the emergency lasted for thirty-five years, and, some twenty years after it had subsided, the First Council of Constantinople felt it necessary to answer the question whether only the Son or also the Holy Spirit was consubstantial with the Father. Fifty years later at Ephesus, it was necessary to clarify Nicea by affirming that it was one and the same that was born of the Father and born of the Virgin Mary. Twenty-one years later it was necessary to add that one and the

---

34 [In the SAP documents, 'Expanding' was typed, then replaced by 'Ongoing.']

same could be both eternal and temporal, both immortal and mortal, because he had two natures. Over two centuries later there was added the further clarification that the divine person that had two natures also had two operations and two wills. Within this matrix there arose a series of questions about Christ as man. Could he sin? Did he feel concupiscence? Was he in any way ignorant? Did he have sanctifying grace? To what extent? Did he have immediate knowledge of God? Did he know everything pertaining to his mission? Such is the Christological context that did not exist prior to Nicea but, bit by bit, came into existence subsequently to Nicea. It does not state what was intended at Nicea. It does state what resulted from Nicea and what became in fact the context within which Nicea was to be understood.

As one may distinguish prior and subsequent stages[35] in an ongoing context, so one ongoing context may be related to another. Of these relations the commonest are derivation and interaction. The Christological context that was built up by answering questions that stemmed from the decision at Nicea was itself derived from the earlier tradition expressed in the New Testament, by the Apostolic Fathers, by orthodox Judaic Christianity, by the Christian apologists, and by the later ante-Nicene Fathers. Again, out of the whole of earlier Christian thought there was derived the ongoing context of medieval theology, and this ongoing context interacted with subsequently developed church doctrines, as is clear from the dependence of theologians on church authority and, inversely, from Scholastic influence on pontifical and conciliar statements up to the Second Vatican Council.

Now such ongoing contexts are subject to many influences. They are distorted by the totally or partly unconverted that usually are unaware of the imperfections of their outlook. They are divided by the presence of people with undifferentiated or differently differentiated consciousness. They are separated because members of different cultures construct different contexts by finding different questions relevant and different answers intelligible.

Such differences give rise to a pluralism, and the pluralism gives rise to incomprehension and exasperation. The unconverted cannot understand the converted, and the partly converted cannot understand the totally converted. Inversely, because they are misunderstood, the converted are exasperated by the unconverted. Again, undifferentiated consciousness does not understand differentiated consciousness, and partially differentiated consciousness does not understand a fourfold differentiated consciousness.

35 [The Marquette University text has 'ages,' but the typescripts and *Method in Theology* 314 indicate that the word should be 'stages.']

Inversely, because it is met with incomprehension, more adequately differentiated consciousness is exasperated by less adequately differentiated consciousness. Finally, our historically-minded contemporaries have no difficulty understanding the ghettos in which a classicist mentality still reigns, but the people in the classicist ghettos not only have no experience of serious historical investigation but also are quite unaware of the historicity of their own assumptions.

There exists, then, a stubborn fact of pluralism. It is grounded in cultural difference, in greater or less differentiation of consciousness, and in the presence and absence of religious, moral, and intellectual conversion. How such pluralism is to be met within the unity of faith is a question yet to be considered. But first we must attempt to indicate how to reconcile the permanence with the historicity of the dogmas.[36]

9 The Permanence and the Historicity of Dogma[37]

The meaning of the dogmas is permanent because that meaning is not a datum but a truth, and that truth is not human but divine. The data of sense are merely given. As merely given, they are not yet understood, and much less is there any understanding verified as probably true. Even when they are

36 [This paragraph replaces the following one found in SAP 1: 'Such pluralism is a stubborn fact. Those that understand are far outnumbered by those that do not, and the majority has no intention of learning from the minority. The classicist can rightly argue that classical culture is morally superior to its modern successor. Undifferentiated consciousness has no notion of what is meant by differentiated consciousness, and it will have no notion of it until it ceases to be undifferentiated and becomes differentiated; indeed, it will have no adequate notion until it attains the fourfold differentiation. Finally, the unconverted or partially converted can appeal to the parable of the cockle (Mt 13.24–30) and that appeal can more readily be granted if they do not insist on governing the church or teaching in it.' See below, p. 102, for mention of 'lack of conversion' in 'those that govern the church or teach in the church.' See also *Method in Theology* 330.]

37 [On the subtitle, see above, notes 2 and 26. This section was completely rewritten for SAP 2. In SAP 1, its first paragraph reads, 'What we have learned from our study of the constitution *Dei Filius* has now to be placed in its ongoing context. First, then, we ask in what respect a dogma is immutable. Secondly, how is it known (*causa cognoscendi*) to be immutable. Thirdly, why is it immutable (*causa essendi*). Fourthly, we ask whether the immutability of dogma excludes demythologization. Fifthly and finally we ask whether immutability excludes historicity.' In response to the first question, Lonergan writes, 'It is immutable in its meaning, in the meaning declared by the church, in the meaning from which one is not to depart under the pretext

understood and when the understanding is probably verified, there ever remains the possibility of the discovery of still further relevant data that may compel a revision of earlier views. But the dogmas are not data but truths, and the truths proceed, not from human understanding and verification, but from God's understanding of himself in his transcendence. There is no possibility of man in this life improving on God's revelation of the mysteries hidden in God, and so the meaning of the dogmas, because it is true, is permanent, and because it is concerned with the divine mysteries, it is not subject to human revision.

---

of a deeper understanding, in the meaning which the church has understood and understands.' Again, 'What is immutable, then, is a meaning and not a verbal formula ... Again, it is not the same verbal formula but the same meaning that can be discerned in the *verbis et rebus* of divine revelation, in the words of scripture, in the councils of the church, and in the explanations of theologians.' The change of 'immutability' in SAP 2 to 'permanence' seems to have dictated the other changes in the manuscript between SAP 1 and SAP 2.

The question of demythologization was removed from this section when the section was rewritten, and moved to the final section, § 11, where the treatment and indeed even the very notion of demythologization are greatly developed. In SAP 1, the issue receives only one paragraph: 'Fourthly, does the immutability of the dogmas exclude demythologization? Demythologization may be mistaken or correct. The immutability of the dogmas excludes mistaken demythologization. But it does not exclude correct demythologization. Since the end of the second century there has been in the church a philosophic demythologization of the anthropomorphisms of scripture and the creeds. The Father has no right hand at which the Son might sit. Whether there exists a correct historical demythologization over and above the philosophic demythologization is a further question that cannot here be considered. We must be content with the general principle that, if a meaning has been revealed by God, then it cannot be the object of correct demythologization, and if it has not been revealed by God, then it cannot be an immutable dogma.' As for the historicity question, it is the subject of the entire rewritten section 9, whereas in SAP 1 it too receives only one paragraph: 'Finally, does immutability exclude historicity? Historicity pertains, not to the meaning revealed by God, but to the various contexts within which in the course of time that meaning has been expressed and communicated. Such contexts are many. There are, if we prescind from lesser differences, the context of the *res et verba* through which revelation occurred, the context of Palestinian and Hellenist preaching by the apostles, the context of the New Testament, the context of early Christian writers and the ante-Nicene Fathers, the ongoing context of the councils, the context of medieval Scholasticism, of the Counter Reformation, of the theological manuals, of the present day when classicism and Scholasticism have been largely repudiated.']

However, meaning can be grasped only by grasping its context. The meaning of a dogma is the meaning of a declaration made by the church at a particular place and time and within the context of that occasion. Only through the historical study of that occasion and the exegetical study of that declaration can one arrive at the proper meaning of the dogma.

Now this historicity of dogma has been obscured by the massive continuity that the church has been able to build up and maintain. The dogmas clustered into a single ongoing context. That context merged into a static, classicist culture, to influence it profoundly. There was developed a theoretical theology that integrated both the dogmas and the theology with a philosophic view of the cosmos. The philosophic view was derived from one main source, and its unity was further strengthened by the dogmas. Finally, the scholarly differentiation of consciousness was rarely attained, so that cultural and other differences tended to be overlooked.

Today, however, classicist culture has yielded place to modern culture with its dynamism and its worldwide pluralism. The sciences seek to occupy the whole realm of theory, and philosophy is driven to migrate to the realm of interiority, or of religion, or of art, or of the undifferentiated consciousness of some brand of common sense. Such philosophic pluralism is radical. Further, scholars have become a large, collaborative, methodical group with an enormous output that only specialists can follow. Theologians can be tempted to desert theology for scholarship. Theologians and scholars can regard recourse to philosophy as foolhardy. Religiously differentiated consciousness can remain assured that religion is a matter not for the head but for the heart.

Such, by and large, is the contemporary situation. For many, to whom the meaning of the word 'truth' is obscure, it is not enough to say that the dogmas are permanent because they are true. They want to know whether the dogmas are permanently relevant.

10   Pluralism and the Unity of Faith[38]

There are three sources of pluralism. First, linguistic, social, and cultural differences give rise to different brands of common sense. Secondly, con-

---

38 [This section is considerably shorter in SAP 1. Some of the paragraphs are quite similar, but even these show some differences. The section as in SAP 1, which ended that document, reads as follows.

'The root and ground of unity is charity, agape, the fact that God's love has flooded our hearts through the Holy Spirit he has given us. The accept-

sciousness may be undifferentiated or it may differentiate to deal effectively with such realms as those of common sense, transcendence, theory, scholarship, interiority. Such differentiations may be single or they may combine so that, mathematically, there are sixteen different ways (thirty-two if the realm of the aesthetic is added) in which consciousness may be structured and so envisage its world. Thirdly, in any individual at any time there may be the mere beginnings, or greater or less progress, or the high development, of intellectual, of moral, and of religious conversion. Finally, the foregoing sets of differences are cumulative. One is born in a given linguistic, social, and cultural milieu. One's consciousness remains undifferentiated or it differentiates in any of a number of manners. One may fail to attain any type of conversion; one may attain conversion in one or two or all three manners; and the conversion attained may be followed up by greater or less development.

Pluralism is not something new. But in the past a number of devices served either to eliminate it or to cover over its existence. Culture was conceived normatively. What is normative also is universal, if not de facto then at least de jure. Though there did exist the simple faithful, the people, the natives, the barbarians, still career was open to talent. One entered upon it by diligent study of the ancient Latin and Greek authors. One pursued it by learning Scholastic philosophy and theology and canon law. One exercised it by one's

----

ance of that gift constitutes religious conversion and leads to both moral and intellectual conversion.

'However, religious conversion, if it is Christian, is not just a state of mind and heart. Essential to it is an intersubjective, interpersonal component. Besides the gift of the Spirit within, there is the outward challenge of Christian witness, which recalls the fact that of old in many ways God has spoken to us through the prophets but in this latest age through his Son (Hebrews 1.1–2).

'The function of church doctrines lies within the function of bearing witness. For there are mysteries revealed by God and infallibly declared by the church (DS 3016, 3020). Their meaning is independent of human historical process. But the contexts within which such meaning is grasped and expressed vary both with cultural differences and with the measure in which consciousness is differentiated.

'Such variations of context, so far from violating the unity of faith, manifest its richness and its vitality. What is opposed to the unity of faith is the absence of conversion: opposed to faith itself is the absence of religious conversion; opposed to the unity of faith is the absence of moral or of intellectual conversion.

'Also opposed to the unity of faith is the bigotry that seeks to impose its own culture or its own type of consciousness on those with a different culture or a different type of consciousness.']

fluent teaching or conduct of affairs in the Latin tongue. It was quite a system in its day, but now its day is over. We have to call on other resources.[39]

First, then, the root and ground of unity is being in love with God, the fact that God's love has flooded our hearts through the Holy Spirit he has given us (Romans 5.5). The acceptance of that gift constitutes religious conversion and leads to moral and to intellectual conversion.

Secondly, religious conversion, if it is Christian, is not just a state of mind and heart. Essential to it is an intersubjective, interpersonal component. Besides the gift of the Spirit within, there is the outward encounter with Christian witness. That witness recalls the fact that of old in many ways God has spoken to us through the prophets but in this latest age through his Son (Hebrews 1.1–2).

Thirdly, the function of church doctrines lies within the function of witness. For the witness is to the mysteries revealed by God and, for Catholics, infallibly declared by the church. Their meaning is beyond the vicissitudes of human historical process. But the contexts within which such meaning is grasped and expressed vary both with cultural differences and with the measure in which consciousness is differentiated.

Such variation is familiar to us from the past. According to Vatican II, revelation occurred not through words alone but through deeds and words. The apostolic preaching was addressed not only to Jews in the thought forms of *Spätjudentum* but also to Greeks in their language and idiom. The New Testament writings spoke more to the heart than the head, but the Christological councils aimed solely at formulating truth to guide one's mind and lips. When Scholastic theology recast Christian belief into a mold derived from Aristotle, it was deserting neither divine revelation nor scripture nor the councils. And if modern theologians were to transpose medieval theory into terms derived from modern interiority and its real correlatives, they would do for our age what the Scholastics did for theirs.

There has existed, then, a notable pluralism of expression. Currently in the church there is quietly disappearing the old classicist insistence on worldwide uniformity, and there is emerging a pluralism of the manners in which Christian meaning and Christian values are communicated. To preach

---

39 [This description of the pursuit of career, which SAP 2 (p. 35) indicates may have first been written for this paper, is related in *Method in Theology* (p. 327) to 'the unity of faith' conceived as 'a matter of everyone subscribing to the correct formulae'; and such classicism is there called 'the shabby shell of Catholicism.']

the gospel to all nations is to preach it to every class in every culture in the manner that accords with the assimilative powers of that class and culture.

For the most part, such preaching will be to undifferentiated consciousness, and so it will have to be as multiform as are the diverse brands of common sense generated by the many languages, social forms, and cultural meanings and values of mankind. In each case the preacher will have to know the brand of common sense to which he speaks, and he will have ever to keep in mind the fact that, in undifferentiated consciousness, coming to know does not occur apart from acting.

But if the faith is to be nourished in those whose consciousness is undifferentiated, those with differentiated consciousness are not to be neglected. Now just as the only way to understand another's brand of common sense is to come to understand the way he or she would understand, speak, act in any of the series of situations that commonly arise, so too the only way to understand another's differentiation of consciousness is to bring about that differentiation in oneself.

Now each differentiation of consciousness involves a certain remodeling of common sense. Initially common sense assumes its own omnicompetence because it just cannot know better. But as successive differentiations of consciousness occur, more and more realms are entered in the appropriate fashion and so are removed from the competence of common sense. Clarity and adequacy increase by bounds. One's initial common sense is purged of its simplifications, its metaphors, its myths, its mystifications. With the attainment of full differentiation, common sense is confined entirely to its proper field of the immediate, the particular, the concrete.

However, there are many routes to full attainment and many varieties of partial attainment. Preaching the gospel to all means preaching it in the manner appropriate to each of the varieties of partial attainment and, no less, to full attainment. It was to meet the exigences proper to the beginnings of theoretically differentiated consciousness that Clement of Alexandria denied that the anthropomorphisms of scripture were to be interpreted literally.[40] It was to meet the exigences proper to the full theoretical differentiation of consciousness that medieval Scholasticism sought a coherent account of all the truths of faith and reason. It was to meet the exigences of a scholarly differentiation of consciousness that the Second Vatican Council decreed

---

40 Clement of Alexandria, *Stromata* v, c. 11, 68, 3; in *PG* 9, 103 B; and in Clemens Alexandrinus, Zweiter Band, Stromata Buch I–VI, ed. Otto Stählin (Leipzig: J.C. Hinrichs, 1906) 371, lines 18–22; also v, c. 11, 71, 4; *PG* 9, 110 A; Stählin 374, line 15.

that the interpreter of scripture had to determine the meaning intended by the biblical writer and accordingly had to do so by understanding the literary conventions and cultural conditions of his place and time.[41]

The church, then, following the example of St Paul, becomes all things to all men (1 Corinthians 9.22). It communicates what God has revealed both in the manner appropriate to the various differentiations of consciousness and, above all, in the manner appropriate to each of the almost endless brands of common sense, especially of undifferentiated consciousness. But these many modes of speech constitute no more than a pluralism of communications, for all can be *in eodem dumtaxat genere, in eodem scilicet dogmate, eodem sensu eademque sententia.*[42]

Still, becoming all to all, even though it involves no more than a pluralism of communications, nonetheless is not without its difficulties. On the one hand, it demands a many-sided development in those that teach and preach. On the other hand, every achievement is apt to be challenged by those that fail to achieve. Those that are not scholars can urge that attending to the literary genre of biblical writings is just a fraudulent device for rejecting the plain meaning of scripture. While theorists insist that one must feel compunction before attempting to define it, nontheorists suggest the contrary by asserting that it is better to feel compunction than to define it. Those whose undifferentiated consciousness is unmitigated by any tincture of theory will not grasp the meaning of dogmas such as that of Nicea, and they may leap gaily to the conclusion that what has no meaning for them is just meaningless.

Such difficulties suggest such rules as the following. First, because the gospel is to be preached to all, there must be sought the modes of representation and expression appropriate to communicating revealed truth both to every brand of common sense and to every differentiation of consciousness. Secondly, no one simply because of his faith is obliged to attain one or more differentiations of consciousness. Thirdly, no one simply because of his faith is obliged to refrain from attaining an ever more differentiated consciousness. Fourthly, anyone may strive to express his faith in the manner appropriate to his differentiation of consciousness. Fifthly, no one should pass judgment on matters he does not understand, and the statements of a more differentiated consciousness are not going to be understood by persons with a less or a differently differentiated consciousness.

41 Dogmatic Constitution on Divine Revelation ('Dei Verbum'), chapter 3, § 12, in *Vatican Council II: The Conciliar and Post Conciliar Documents*, vol.1, ed. Austin Flannery, O.P. (Northport, NY: Costello Publishing Co., new revised ed., 1992) 757–58.
42 [See above, note 30, for translation.]

Finally, there is the type of pluralism that results from the presence or absence of intellectual, of moral, or of religious conversion. It is this type of pluralism that is perilous to unity in the faith especially when a lack of conversion exists in those that govern the church or teach in the church. Moreover, the dangers are multiplied when, as at present, there is going forward in the church a movement out of classicist culture and into modern culture, when persons with differently[43] differentiated consciousness not only do not understand one another but so extol either advanced prayer, or theory, or scholarship, or interiority, as to exclude development and set aside achievement in the other three.

11   The Permanence of Dogma and Demythologization

Cosmogonies, myths, sagas, legends, apocalypses arise at a time when distinct functions of meaning are not distinguished.[44] Meaning is not only communicative. It is a constitutive element in human living, knowing, and doing. But this constitutive function is overextended when it is employed to constitute not only man's being in the world but also the world man is in.

To demythologize is to confine constitutive meaning within its proper bounds.[45] This is a very long task and so different stages in the process have to be distinguished.[46]

The earliest stage is the reinterpretation of myth. Thought is still prephilosophic and prescientific, and so there still occur the types of expression that philosophy and science will eliminate. Nonetheless, older myth is being purified. In the Old Testament there is no primeval battle of gods, no divine generation of kings or chosen peoples, no cult of the stars or of sexuality, no sacralization of the fruitfulness of nature. God's action is his action in a history of salvation, and the account of creation in Genesis is the

---

43 [The word 'differently' was left out of the typing of the autograph, and so did not appear in the Marquette University text. It is restored from SAP 2.]
44 [On the functions of meaning, see *Method in Theology* 76–81.]
45 [This is the developed notion of demythologization referred to above in note 39.]
46 One instance of the process has been convincingly described by Bruno Snell, *The Discovery of the Mind in Greek Philosophy and Literature*, trans. T.G. Rosenmeyer (New York: Harper Torchbooks, 1960, and New York: Dover Publications, 1982). This translation contains a chapter, 'Human Knowledge and Divine Knowledge among the Early Greeks,' pp. 136–52, not found in the original, *Die Entdeckung des Geistes* (Hamburg: Claassen und Goverts, 1948).

opening of the story. Similarly, in the New Testament the faith of the community is directed towards God's saving acts in an earthly history. Elements of apocalyptic and gnostic mythology are employed only to facilitate the expression of the faith, and when they fail to do so they are rigorously excluded.[47]

A second stage is philosophic. It begins, perhaps, with Xenophanes, who noticed that the gods of the Ethiopians look like Ethiopians while the gods of the Thracians look like Thracians. He also contended that if lions and horses and oxen had hands and could do such works as men do, then the gods of the lions would resemble lions, the gods of the horses would resemble horses, and the gods of the oxen would resemble oxen. The point was picked up by Clement of Alexandria, who taught that the anthropomorphisms of the Bible were not to be taken literally, and thereby started the centuries-long efforts of Christians to conceive God on the analogy of spirit rather than of matter.[48]

A third stage is theological. If God is to be conceived on the analogy of spirit, then in God there can be Father and Son only if there can be some sort of spiritual generation. So Origen conceived the Son to proceed from the Father as an act of will from the mind, Augustine found his analogy in the origin of inner word from true knowledge, while Aquinas showed how the origin of concept from understanding could be named a generation.[49] In similar fashion systematic theologians down the ages have sought analogies that yielded some fruitful understanding of the mysteries.

A fourth stage is scientific. Copernicus gave the first thrust towards a transformation of man's image of the universe, Darwin did as much for a transformation of man's notion of the origin of his body, Freud invaded the secrets of his soul. While neither Copernicus nor Darwin nor Freud have uttered the last word in their respective fields, still we no longer argue from the Bible against them.

A fifth stage is scholarly. Hermeneutics and critical history have disrupted the classicist dream of a single standardized culture with the consequence of a standardized man. There has been discovered human historicity – the fact

47 I am summarizing Kurt Frör, *Biblische Hermeneutik, Zur Schriftauslegung in Predigt und Unterricht* (München: Kaiser, 1967). [The margin of SAP 2 has 'kf71ff,' and the relevant pages are 71–78.]

48 See note 42 for the reference to Clement.

49 Origen, *De principiis*, Book 1, chapter 2, § 6. [Lonergan refers to 'Koetschau 35, 40'; there is an English translation of Paul Koetschau's text of the *De principiis* by G.W. Butterworth (New York: Harper Torchbooks, 1966); the relevant reference is on p. 19.] See also Augustine, *De trinitate*, xv, xii, 22, in *PL* 42, 1075; Aquinas, *Summa theologiae*, 1, q. 27, a.2.

that, while abstract concepts are immutable in virtue of their abstractness, nonetheless human understanding keeps developing to express itself in ever different images and slogans and to replace earlier by later abstractions.

A sixth stage is post-Scholastic theology. It has to comprehend the previous five stages. It has to discover the invariants of human development. It has to take its stand both on inner religious experience and on the historicity of personal development within the Christian community.

So understood, demythologization is simply the ongoing growth and advance of understanding, knowledge, and wisdom desired by the First Vatican Council (DS 3020). It can eliminate misconceptions of what God did reveal. But it is powerless against anything that God really did reveal and the church infallibly has declared.

Finally, let me note that demythologization in the foregoing sense is quite different from Rudolf Bultmann's *Entmythologisierung*. The latter's views arise in a quite peculiar context. Modern scholarship derives from the German historical school of the early nineteenth century. While it expressed a reaction against Hegel's apriorist views on the meaning of history, it was far from resembling strict empirical science, in which there is added to the data only an understanding that arises from the data. As Wilhelm Dilthey discovered, the historical school was full of ideas derived from the Enlightenment and even from Hegel.[50] What eliminated from historical scholarship such alien influences was simply a positivist empiricism that ruled out other presuppositions and postulated that human history be a closed field of causally interconnected events.[51] Such a view of history has been rejected by such historians as Carl Becker in the United States, R.G. Collingwood in England, H.-I. Marrou in France. But the outstanding theological reaction was effected by Karl Barth and Rudolf Bultmann. They took their stand on moral and religious conversion. But they did not advert to the fact that besides moral and religious conversion there also is intellectual conversion. Accordingly, they were incapable of effecting any serious criticism of the philosophic presuppositions of the historicism in vogue at the beginning of this century. Very summarily, Barth was content with a fideist affirmation of Christian truth. Bultmann did 'scientific' work on the New Testament, while his morally and religiously converted being assented to the locally preached kerygma of the fact of God's self-revelation in Christ Jesus.

50 See Hans-Georg Gadamer, *Wahrheit und Methode* 185–86; *Truth and Method* 197–99.
51 Frör, *Biblische Hermeneutik* 28–29.

LECTURES AT MASSACHUSETTS INSTITUTE OF TECHNOLOGY

6

The World Mediated by Meaning[1]

I am not attempting to define the meaning of the word 'meaning.' Indeed, several years ago there was published a book with the title *The Meaning of Meaning*,[2] but so far from finding some one meaning of the word 'meaning,' it concluded that there were several hundred.

The lack of definition, however, is no obstacle to sufficient clarity. Socrates sought universal definitions, but he had to admit that not only the Athenian public but also he himself was unable to produce them. A current philosophy maintains that one reveals the meaning of a word, not by offering a universal definition, but by ascertaining how it is used appropriately.

1   The first of three lectures that Lonergan delivered in a seminar on Technology and Culture at the Massachusetts Institute of Technology. This lecture was delivered on 24 April 1972; two other lectures, 'Is It Real?' and 'What Are Judgments of Value?' were delivered on 1 May and 8 May, respectively, and follow in this volume immediately after the present selection. In 1971–72, Lonergan was Stillman Professor at the Harvard Divinity School.

  There are tape recordings of the second and third lectures, but none of this first lecture. The archives of the Lonergan Research Institute, Toronto, have a typescript of the notes that Lonergan used in delivering the lecture: File 508, item A2343. That typescript is the only source used for editing the lecture here. In a few places, especially toward the beginning, words had to be added to supplement the sketchy character of the notes. It will be noted that some passages in the notes are similar to the corresponding treatment in *Method in Theology*. All divisions of the text and all footnotes are editorial.

2   The reference here may be to Charles Kay Ogden, *The Meaning of Meaning: A Study of the Influence of Language upon Thought, and of the Science of Symbolism* (London: Routledge & Paul, 1949, 10th ed.).

I shall begin by indicating what meaning does, what are its functions. These will be said to be cognitive, effective, constitutive, and communicative. A second topic will be the carriers of meaning, and then we shall advert to the fact that meaning is expressed not only by language but also by intersubjectivity, by art, by symbols, and by an individual's or a people's character, achievement, stand. A third topic will be the differentiation of the worlds mediated by meaning, and finally we shall say something on the control over meaning.[3] Our purpose is to advert to the world mediated by meaning and to comment on its diversity and its problems.

1   Functions of Meaning

1.1   The Cognitive Function

Prior to the world mediated by meaning, there is a world of immediacy, the world of the infant.

Jean Piaget has described the developing, differentiating, and combining of operations of the infant – of head and neck, eyes and hands, maintaining balance, walking.[4] When hearing and speaking first develop, words denote things immediate to the infant – no transition has as yet begun.

As the command and use of language grow, the transition is made to the absent, the far away, the future, the ideal, the fantastic, the memories of other men, the common sense of the community, the pages of literature, the labors of scholars, the investigations of scientists, the experience of saints, the meditations of philosophers and theologians.

The larger world, mediated by meaning, does not lie within anyone's immediate experience; it is not the integral sum of all the worlds of immediate experience. It involves an addition to experience through acts of understanding, formulation, reflection, and judgment.

These additions give the mediated world its order, its structure, its unity; they make it an orderly whole of almost endless differences, partly known and familiar, partly in a surrounding penumbra of things we know about but never have examined and explored, partly an unmeasured region of the things we know nothing about.

3 At this point in the notes, there is the one line, 'Functions, carriers, differentiations, controls.'
4 Jean Piaget, *La naissance de l'intelligence chez l'enfant* (Neuchâtel, Paris: Delacheux et Niestlé, 1936); in English, *The Origins of Intelligence in Infants*, trans. Margaret Cook (New York: International Universities Press, 1952).

It is this larger world that for us is the real world; within it there are unnumbered instances of narrow strips of space and time that make up the tiny worlds of the immediate experience of mankind.

Though the larger world is the real world, still it is insecure, for meaning is insecure. There is truth but also error, fact but also fiction, honesty but also deceit, science but also myth.

So much for the cognitive function of meaning. Next, its effective function.

1.2   The Effective Function

Besides the world that we know about, there is the further world that we make. What we make, we first intend. We imagine and plan, investigate possibilities, weigh pros and cons, enter into contracts, have orders given and executed.

It is not enough to mean; one also has to do; but our technological society is aware that the intervention of meaning, of science and of technical inventions, vastly increases man's power of doing.

Next we turn from the effective function to the constitutive function.

1.3   The Constitutive Function

The constitutive function of meaning involves the transformation of nature and the transformation of man himself.

The movement from the child entering kindergarten to the student completing a doctoral dissertation is a recapitulation of the vastly longer process of the education of mankind.

Religions and art forms, languages and literatures, sciences, philosophy, history, all had their rude beginnings, their flowering, their decline, their renascence.

What is true of cultural achievements, is true also of social institutions. The family, the state, the law, the economy are not fixed and immutable entities. They adapt to changing circumstances, they can be reconceived in the light of new ideas, they can be subjected to revolutionary change.

All such change essentially is a change of meaning – a change of idea or concept, of judgment or evaluation, of order or request. The state can be changed by rewriting the constitution; more subtly it can be changed by reinterpreting the constitution or, again, by working on men's minds and hearts to change the objects that command their respect, hold their allegiance, fire their loyalty.

1.4 The Constitutive and Communicative Functions

Community is a matter of a common field of experience, and without that people get out of touch. It is a matter of a common understanding, and without that there arises misunderstanding, distrust, suspicion, fear, hatred, violence. It is a matter of common judgments, and without them people live in different worlds. It is a matter of common consent on values and goals, and without that people work at cross-purposes.

Such community is the source of common meaning, and such common meaning is the act and form that finds expression in polity and family, in the legal and the economic system, in customary morals and educational arrangements, in language and literature, art and religion, philosophy, science, and history.

Much more could be said about constitutive meaning. It is here where man's freedom reaches its high point, here that his responsibility is greatest, here that there emerges the existential subject who discovers for himself that he has to decide for himself what he is to make of himself. But I must move on to my second topic, carriers of meaning.

2   Carriers of Meaning

2.1 Language

The most conspicuous, the most refined, the most far-reaching, the most versatile carrier of meaning is language. There is the everyday language of home and office, work and play, the technical language of craftsmen and specialists of all kinds, and the literary language of the permanent work, the *opus*, the *poiêma*.

But there are other carriers of meaning.

2.2 Intersubjectivity

By intersubjectivity is meant that human persons spontaneously take care of one another. Just as one spontaneously raises one's arm to ward off a blow to one's head, so with equal spontaneity one reaches out to save another from falling. Perception, feeling, and bodily movement are involved, but the help given another is not deliberate but spontaneous. One adverts to it, not before it occurs, but while it is occurring. It is as if 'we' were members of one another prior to our distinctions of each from the others.

Besides the intersubjectivity of action and feeling, there also are intersubjective communications of meaning. Such communications are, I suspect, extremely numerous. But my present purpose is to illustrate a genre, and so I shall attempt a brief phenomenology of a smile.[5]

First, a smile has a meaning. It is not just a certain combination of movements of lips, facial muscles, eyes. It is a combination with a meaning, and so it is distinguished from the meaning of a frown or a scowl, or a stare, a glare, a snicker, a laugh. We all know about this meaning, and so we do not go about the streets smiling at everyone we meet. We know we should be misunderstood.

Next, a smile is highly perceptible. For our perceiving is not just a function of the impressions made on our senses. It has an orientation of its own, and it selects, out of a myriad of others, just those impressions that can be constructed into a pattern with meaning. So one can converse with a friend on a noisy street, unattentive to the surrounding tumult, and select just the low sounds with meaning.

Further, because of its meaning, a smile is easily perceived. Smiles occur in an enormous range of variations of facial movements, lighting, and angle of vision. But even an incipient and suppressed smile is not missed.

Where linguistic meaning tends to be univocal, smiles have many meanings: recognition, welcome, friendliness, friendship, love, joy, delight, contentment, satisfaction, amusement, rejection, contempt.

The meaning of the smile resides in the manner in which it modifies the intersubjective situation. It supposes the interpersonal situation with its antecedents in previous encounters. It is a determinant in the present situation both at its opening and as it unfolds. Moreover, that meaning is not about some object. Rather, it reveals or even betrays the one that smiles, and the revelation is immediate. I do not see the smile and infer its meaning. Rather, the revelation occurs inasmuch as the smile affects my feelings, attitudes, response.

2.3 Images, Art, Incarnate Meaning

Besides language and intersubjectivity, there are other carriers of meaning. There is the meaning of symbolic images and representations that call forth

5 For other references to this common theme in Lonergan's writings, see
   Philosophical and Theological Papers 1958–1964, ed. Robert C. Croken,
   Frederick E. Crowe, and Robert M. Doran (Toronto: University of Toronto
   Press, 1996) 97–98 & n.4.

feelings or, inversely, are evoked by feelings. Such meaning has received great attention in our century not only from the pioneering psychotherapists but also from the later anthropologists that studied symbols outside any therapeutic context.

Again, there is the meaning embodied in works of art: in music, song, or dance, in paintings, mosaics, sculpture, in architecture, in epic and lyric, in tragedy and comedy.

Finally, there is what I would call incarnate meaning. It is the meaning inherent in noble, heroic, or traitorous and repulsive deeds: the meaning of Marathon or Thermopylae, of Socrates or Jesus, of Judas Iscariot or a Don Juan.

3   Differentiations of Consciousness

We have adverted to functions and to carriers of meaning; we have now to turn to differentiations of human consciousness, to the quite different manners in which men go about constructing their worlds mediated by meaning. We shall mention several such differentiations: the linguistic, the religious, the literary, the systematic, the scientific, the scholarly, and what perhaps may be named the modern philosophic.

3.1   The Linguistic Differentiation

The linguistic differentiation of consciousness has already been described: it is the transition from the world of immediacy of the infant in the nursery to the fully human world, the world mediated by meaning.

It is well known how much names, words, speech are prized by primitive peoples, and the significance of that esteem may best be sensed in the story of Helen Keller. Cold water from a pump over a well was gushing over her hands. Her teacher then made the sign for the word 'water' on her hand. That was the occasion when first she discovered that such a touch was a name, that it meant the water she had just felt. She was overcome with emotion, knelt down and touched the earth, and made known her desire to learn its name. Within a short space of time she had learnt about twenty names.[6]

Another indication of the significance of language comes in a study by Ernst Cassirer, *The Philosophy of Symbolic Forms*, in which there is indicated

6   Helen A. Keller, *The Story of My Life* (New York: Doubleday, 1954). For the passage on 'water,' see pp. 36–37.

the evidence for the concomitance of aphasia, agnosia, and apraxia. Trouble with speech is accompanied by trouble with knowledge and trouble with action.[7]

3.2 The Religious Differentiation

Speech is an almost universal human phenomenon. Almost as universal until this century has been the religious differentiation of consciousness. Endless in its variations, it commonly is marked by an intermittent withdrawal from everyday activities and concerns. It can be gregarious, but its more intense moments are often solitary and silent. Mircea Eliade has written a book on Shamanism with the subtitle *Archaic Techniques of Ecstasy*.[8] So down the ages there have been people devoting their lives to a growth in holiness, and such ascetics and mystics develop a type of consciousness expressed by the peace and joy on the countenance of a statue of the seated Buddha.

3.3 The Literary Differentiation

A third differentiation of consciousness is the literary. Early language has little difficulty developing words that denote what is spatial, external, specific, human – in brief, what can be found interesting, inspected, pointed out, named. But it has difficulty with the temporal, the internal, the generic, the divine. The tenses of its verbs refer not to different times but to different kinds of action. Possessive pronouns develop before personal pronouns: what a person has or owns is more manageable than the person himself. Homer is said to have countless words for such things as peering, staring, glaring, peeking, but no generic word to denote seeing. Finally, the divine is mediated by the hierophany, by the outward event or place or thing that was the occasion of a religious experience.

Now the development of a literature is the means for effecting the transition from the limitations of early language to the full articulateness of later expression. The matter is beautifully illustrated by Bruno Snell in his book

---

7 Ernst Cassirer, *The Philosophy of Symbolic Forms*, trans. Ralph Manheim, 3 vols. (New Haven, CT: Yale University Press, 1953, 1955, 1957); see vol. 3, *The Phenomenology of Knowledge* 205–77.
8 Mircea Eliade, *Le Chamanisme et les techniques archaïques de l'extase* (Paris: Librairie Payot, 1951); in English, *Shamanism: Archaic Techniques of Ecstasy*, trans. Willard R. Trask (Princeton: Princeton University Press, 1972).

The Discovery of the Mind.[9] By his protracted similes, Homer was able to describe and so objectify the characters of his heroes: a lion never retreats, Hector is a lion. Then the lyric poets objectified intense personal feelings. The tragedians objectified decisions, their consequences, and the conflicts that ensued. As the literature develops, reflections on human knowledge multiply. For Homer, the Muses were omnipresent and saw everything; that is why the bard is able to narrate events as though he were an eyewitness. For Hesiod, the Muses do not inspire but teach. They may teach the truth but they may also teach plausible falsehood. Hesiod had been singled out by them and taught not to repeat the folly and the lies of his predecessors but to tell the truth about the struggle in which man ekes out his livelihood.

Xenophanes was still more critical. He rejected the multitude of anthropomorphic gods and maintained that god is unity, perfect in wisdom, operating without toil, bringing things about merely by the thought of his mind.

For Hecataeus, the stories of the Greeks were many and foolish. Man's knowledge is not a gift of the gods; stories about the past are to be judged by everyday experience; advance in knowledge is by inquiry and search, and the search has to be deliberate and planned, and not just a series of accidents, such as happened to Odysseus.

The empirical interest lived on in Herodotus, in the physicians, in the physicists. But a new turn emerged with Heraclitus. He maintained that the mere amassing of information did not make men grow in intelligence. Where his predecessors were opposed to ignorance, he was opposed to folly. He prized eyes and ears but thought them bad witnesses for men with barbarian souls. There is an intelligence, a *logos*, that steers through all things; it is found in god and man and beast, the same in all though in different degrees. To know it is wisdom.

Parmenides discovered argument. His arguments were not good, but they had the effect of revealing a component in human knowledge that could run contradictory to what seemed evident to sense. In a vague anticipation of the principle of excluded middle, he denied the occurrence of becoming, the existence of something intermediate between being and nonbeing. In another vague anticipation of the principle of identity, he concluded that there could be only one being.

The stage was set for the emergence of the Sophists, of Platonists, Aristotelians, Stoics, Epicureans. There developed the classical culture that reigned in the West up to the present century.

9 See above, p. 102, note 46.

3.4 The Systematic Differentiation

So there arises the systematic differentiation of consciousness. Man objectifies his thinking processes in logic: the spontaneous process of ascertaining the meaning of words by learning correct or at least appropriate usage is supplemented by definitions; proverbs, the sage bits of advice that it is well to bear in mind on various occasions, give way to the formulation of principles; definitions and principles are so chosen that they cohere and form systems of interconnected terms; systems, finally, can be related to one another and, between them, organize the whole range of objects of human knowledge. Such was the achievement of the Aristotelian corpus, and the aim of the medieval theologian Thomas of Aquin was to adapt Aristotle to Christian living.

3.5 The Scientific Differentiation

By the scientific differentiation of consciousness, I refer of course to modern science. The aim of an Aristotle or an Aquinas was to ascertain and state what was true. Their systems were intended to be permanent achievements. But modern science, while it intends truth, intends it only as an ultimate goal. Its proximate aim is an ever better understanding of the data of experience and, no less, the data accessible through experiment. What the modern scientist refutes, he will consider certainly mistaken. But what he positively advances, he will pronounce no more than probable, the best available opinion. So modern science is an ongoing process. As it advances in understanding, it is drawing nearer to truth. But until there are no unexplained phenomena, modern science cannot settle down in some permanent abode.

3.6 The Scholarly Differentiation

To speak of the scholarly differentiation of consciousness, I first must say something about the universal and spontaneous procedure of developing intelligence. This procedure is neither that of an Aristotle nor that of modern science. It is a spontaneous and interlocking accumulation of insights. They are acquired in a spontaneous process of teaching and learning that constantly goes forward in the individuals within a group. And this process is most pronounced in the new arrivals, in children learning from their parents and their peers, in newcomers gradually catching on to the ways of speech and action in a new community.

Now while human intelligence everywhere develops in this spontaneous fashion, still the same fashion has different results in different communities. A person from the next village is strange because he speaks and acts in a different fashion. A person from another state is stranger still. A person from another country is not only strange but also foreign. To move to another country involves learning a new language and adapting to a new style.

So we come to the scholarly differentiation of consciousness: it is a matter of coming to understand the ways of thought and speech and action of another people, or of one's own people at an earlier time. Such knowledge is not systematic, a matter of definitions and postulates. It is not scientific, a matter of hypotheses and theories that can be verified in endless instances. Its structure is like the structure of common sense – a gradual accumulation of insights that, with the addition of a few more insights into some particular matter in hand, will grasp what was meant by a statement, what was the aim of an action, what was done at a town meeting or a court or a school, in some strange and distant land. As common sense is the way our intelligence deals with the concrete and particular in the present, so too scholarship is a specialization of intelligence that grasps the manner in which people with a different brand of common sense dealt with the concrete and particular in their place and time.

3.7   The Modern Philosophic Differentiation

Finally, there is what I should name the modern philosophic differentiation of consciousness. Just as clinical psychology, among other concerns, also aims at helping people advert to feelings they have and experience but have not identified, objectified, named, brought out into the open, so too the cognitional theorist may direct his efforts to helping people advert to their mental operations, distinguish them from one another, name them precisely, relate them to one another, combine them in various groups, come to grasp the procedures of common sense, of systematizers, of modern science, of scholarship. Next, on the basis of knowing what one is doing when one is knowing, one can go on to explain why doing that is knowing, and finally to outline what one knows when one does it.

I have spoken of the four different functions of meaning – cognitive, effective, constitutive, communicative; of its different carriers – language, intersubjectivity, symbols, art, and incarnate meaning; of several differentiations of consciousness – linguistic, religious, literary, systematic, scientific, scholarly, and modern philosophic. Now I shall have to say something about the control of meaning.

4   The Control of Meaning

First, it seems agreed among anthropologists that the members of primitive cultures, while quite intelligent and rational in everyday affairs, nonetheless live in a world shot through with myth and magic. As our own being is being in a world mediated by meaning, so too theirs also is being in a world mediated by meaning. But while we have a fairly clear distinction between the cognitive, effective, and constitutive functions of meaning, they have not. In myth, the constitutive function of meaning is not limited to constituting the subject but is extended into the constitution of the world in which he lives. In magic, the effective function of meaning is not limited to directing human activity but is extended to bringing about results beyond the range of human power.

Many factors contribute to the control of meaning that eliminates or at least neutralizes myth and magic: the multiplication and differentiation of arts and crafts, the growth of cities, the flourishing of trade, the concentration of power and, with its breakdown, the emergence of a new individualism, and, if last not least, reflection on human language and human knowledge. Alphabets make words visible, grammars schematize their morphology and syntax, dictionaries indicate their meanings, logics foster clarity, coherence, and rigor, hermeneutics explores different worlds mediated by meaning, philosophies ask whether the worlds we happen to mean really exist.

Perhaps the most venerable of the controls of meaning lies in the classical culture that took its rise in ancient Greece and Rome, came to new life well before the middle of the present millennium, and, in many places, lasted right into this century. Its beliefs were regarded as eternal verities, its art and literature were praised as immortal, its laws and institutions were the deposit of the prudence and the wisdom of mankind. Change was never more than accidental; the substance of human living was ever the same. There were the educated and the uneducated, but all genuine education had but a single goal: culture.

This normative notion of culture no longer obtains. Today we think of culture empirically. It is the set of meanings and values immanent in a way of life. There have always been many such sets. They may remain unchanged for ages. They may be in a process of rapid development. They may be in decline.

Contemporary acceptance[10] of an empirical notion of culture can be unsettling. It can lead to the mistaken conclusion that there exist no cultural

---

10 This and the next paragraph appear on a separate page. They would seem to belong here, before the final paragraph.

norms, when all that follows is that such norms must be flexible. It is always right to be attentive, to be intelligent, to be reasonable, to be responsible. But one observes such general precepts in many different ways, in accord with differing circumstances, differing educational opportunities, different ways of life.

To reflect on the world mediated by meaning is to come to appreciate the importance of language, to discern that it fulfils cognitive and effective and constitutive functions as well as the obvious function of communicating, to learn that there are radically different techniques in which human conscious-ness operates, to understand that to master all these techniques calls for an almost lifelong educational program, to comprehend, finally, the great variety of human mentalities that have developed down the ages and coexist at the present time.

In conclusion, I may perhaps say that I have been indicating a context in which the topics of this seminar may be set together.[11] For I have spoken of cognitive, effective, and constitutive meaning. Technology is an instance of the embodiment of effective meaning. Culture is an instance of constitutive meaning. Finally, the differentiations of human consciousness – linguistic, religious, literary, systematic, scientific, scholarly, and modern philosophic – offer an introductory scale on which different cultures may be compared.

11 See above, n.1, p. 107.

7

Is It Real?[1]

In a valuable paper presented at the twenty-third annual convention of the Catholic Theological Society of America Professor Edward MacKinnon explained:

> Since the publication of Wittgenstein's *Philosophical Investigations* there has been a growing consensus that the meaningfulness of language is essentially public and only derivatively private. Unless this were so language could not serve as a vehicle for intersubjective communication. The meaning of a term, accordingly, is explained chiefly by clarifying its use, or the family of usages associated with it. This requires an analysis both of the way terms function within language, or

---

1 The second lecture, delivered on 1 May 1972, in the 'Technology and Culture Seminar' at the Massachusetts Institute of Technology; see above, p. 107, note 1.

    Lonergan's typescript of the lecture is in the archives of the Lonergan Research Institute, Toronto, File 508. Most of the lecture was recorded (Lonergan Research Institute Library, TC 693). A transcription of the tape was made by Nicholas Graham (Institute Library, File 693). The tape lacks the first 3½ pages of Lonergan's typescript; those pages are supplied here by relying on his own notes for the lecture. The tape does include a question and answer session at the end of the lecture.

    The editing here is of the autograph typescript, benefiting in places from the fuller expression of the taped lecture and transcription, and including the latter's question and answer session.

    All notes are editorial.

a study of syntax, and also of the extralinguistic contexts in which its use is appropriate, or questions of semantics and pragmatics.

A consequence of this position ... is that the meaning of a word is not explicable by reference or reduction to private mental acts. The usual scholastic doctrine is that words have meaning *because* they express concepts. Meanings are primarily in concepts, private mental acts or states, and then derivatively in language which expresses such a concept. Within this view of language, transcendence does not present too formidable a linguistic problem. A word, such as 'God' can mean a transcendent being, if this is what one intends in using the word. Comforting as such a simple solution might be, it, unfortunately, will not work.[2]

I quote this, not because I propose to speak of God or transcendence, but to have a precise formulation of a difficulty that I feel many of you have with my talk about mental acts.

1   Ordinary Meaning

First, I do not believe that mental acts occur without a sustaining flow of expression. It may not be linguistic. It may not be adequate. It may not be presented to the attention of others. But it occurs. I refer again to Cassirer's treatment of aphasia, agnosia, apraxia.[3]

Secondly, I have no doubt that the ordinary meaningfulness of ordinary language is essentially public and only derivatively private. For language is ordinary if it is in common use. It is in common use, not because some isolated individual happens to have decided what it is to mean, but because all individuals in the relevant group already understand what it means. Similarly, it is by performing expressed mental acts that children and foreigners come to learn a language. But they learn the language by learning how it ordinarily is used, so that private knowledge of ordinary usage is derived from the common usage that essentially is public.

Thirdly, what is true of the ordinary meaningfulness of ordinary language is

---

2 Quoted from Edward MacKinnon, 'Linguistic Analysis and the Transcendence of God,' *Proceedings of the Catholic Theological Society of America* 23 (1968) 30. See Lonergan, *Method in Theology* 254–55. Section 1, Ordinary Meaning, is almost verbatim identical with paragraphs on pp. 255–56 of *Method in Theology.*
3 See the previous lecture, p. 113, n.7.

not true of the original meaningfulness of any language, ordinary, literary, or technical. For all language develops and, at any time, any language consists in the sedimentation of the developments that have occurred and have not become obsolete. Now developments consist in discovering new uses for existing words, in inventing new words, and in diffusing the discoveries and the inventions. All three are a matter of expressed mental acts. The discovery of a new usage is a mental act expressed by the new usage. The invention of a new word is a mental act expressed by the new word. The communication of the developments and inventions can be done technically by introducing definitions, or spontaneously as when *A* utters his verbal constellation, *B* responds, *A* grasps in *B*'s response how successful he was in communicating his meaning and, in the measure he has failed, he seeks and tries out further developments or inventions. Through a process of trial and error, a new usage takes shape, and, if there occurs a sufficiently broad diffusion of the new usage, then a new ordinary usage is established. Unlike ordinary meaningfulness, then, unqualified meaningfulness originates in expressed mental acts, is communicated through them, is perfected in a process of trial and error, and attains ordinariness when the perfected communication is extended to a large enough number of individuals.

2   Systematic Meaning

What is true of ordinary meaning is not only true but also explicit in systematic meaning. Distinguish formal, referential, and empirical system. Let me say that a formal system is one in which primitive terms are fixed by primitive relations, and primitive relations are fixed by primitive terms. Next, a formal system becomes referential when the primitive terms and relations are linked directly or indirectly (through derived terms and relations) to the data of experience. Finally, a referential system becomes empirical when all its implications are verified in the data of experience.

On this showing, meaningfulness develops in three stages. Formal system is meaningful in the sense that the purely hypothetical can be meaningful. Referential system is meaningful in the sense that a hitherto unapplied part of mathematics can be given a physical meaning. Empirical system arises when referential system becomes verified.

Now I feel that many of you will readily grant what I have been saying, as long as it is applied to the field of natural science and, indeed, as long as it is extended to the human sciences, provided they are assumed to have no significant differences from the natural sciences. But I have been asked to explain my strategy, and, very simply, it is a matter of applying the technique of formal, referential, and empirical system, not to the data of external experience, but to the data of internal experience, to the data of consciousness.

2.1 Formal System

The formal system consists of three operators and four sets of operations. The three operators are questions. There are questions for intelligence: What? Why? How? How often? What for? There are questions for reflection: Is that so? Are you certain? Is it only probable? And there are questions for deliberation: Is that worth while? Is it truly good or only apparently good? The four levels of operations are (1) sense experience, (2) insights and formulations, (3) reflective understanding and judgment, and (4) evaluation and decision.

Such are the primitive terms. The primitive relations are implicit in the primitive terms. The first operator, What? Why? How often? What for? promotes consciousness from sense experience to the effort to understand. The effort to understand leads to acts of understanding. Acts of understanding lead to formulations that express both the understanding itself and what is essential to the understanding in the data or schematic image. The second operator, Is that so? promotes consciousness from intelligible formulations to the search for a sufficient reason for affirming the formulations. This leads to acts of reflective understanding in which sufficient reason is grasped. Reflective understanding leads to judgment, to an affirmation or negation because of the sufficient reason that has been grasped. I will leave the third operator and evaluations and decisions to the next lecture.[4]

2.2 Referential System

The transition from formal system to referential system is effected by noting that the foregoing operators, operations, and relations are given in consciousness.

First, then, the operators and operations are expressed by transitive verbs in the active voice; since the verbs are transitive, they are related to objects; moreover, the relation to objects is not merely grammatical but also psychological. By the operator there is intended an object that as yet is not known. By the operation there becomes present an object that otherwise would be unknown. Seeing makes present what is seen; hearing makes present what is

4 Here, chapter 8, 'What Are Judgments of Value?'

heard; touching makes present what is felt; insight makes present the intelligibility of what is understood, and so on. Such is the intentionality of operations and operators.

But there is also a further aspect to them, consciousness. The transitive verbs in the active voice have not only objects but also subjects. By consciousness is meant that the activation of operations or operators makes the subject aware of himself, and of his operators and operations. Note that this awareness does not consist in the presence of an object. The object is what is intended, attended to, sensed, understood, thought, reflected on, affirmed. The subject is aware of himself through his intending, his attending, his inquiring, his coming to understand, his formulation of what he has understood, and so on. The subject is present to himself, not as part of the spectacle, but through his role as spectator.

2.3 Empirical System

The transition from the referential system to the empirical system involves an extension of the ordinary meaning of 'empirical.' Ordinarily, by 'empirical' is meant what is verified by an appeal to sensitive observation or sensible experiment. In the extended sense, we beg leave to use the word 'empirical' to denote what is verified in the data of sense or in the data of consciousness.

Of course, as does happen, by generalizing the meaning of 'empirical' we have also generalized the meaning of 'verification.' Ordinarily, verification is public in the sense that anyone sufficiently in the know and with the proper equipment can repeat for himself the act of verifying, or that several such persons can perform the verification as a team. However, what is verified in the data of consciousness is essentially a private performance. One has to do it by oneself and for oneself. Unless one does so, talk about the data of consciousness will be no more illuminating than a disquisition on color to the blind or a treatise on counterpoint to the deaf.

3   Verification

However, if one wishes to attempt the verifying, the operations to be performed can all be indicated in ordinary, mathematical, or scientific language. So in my book *Insight*,[5] the first chapter is devoted to provoking mathematical insights and begging the reader to advert to them. Chapters 2 to 5 are

5 See above, p. 3, note 2.

concerned with the insights of physicists. Chapters 6 and 7 are devoted to commonsense insights, the insights behind ordinary language. Chapters 9 to 13 are concerned with judgments, their grounds, and their objectivity. Hence, while the actual performance of verifying is private, still the whole process of performing the operations and adverting to them can be under the direction of a publicly meaningful statement.

Moreover, it is rather embarrassing to claim that one has attempted the verification and did not succeed. Either one is going to admit the occurrence of the experience of seeing, hearing, tasting, smelling, touching, or else one will have to claim that one has been living the life of a perpetual sleepwalker. Who is going to tell his pupils that never in his life has he been puzzled, never tried to understand anything, never had the experience of coming to understand and of formulating what he had grasped? Who will preface his books with the declaration that never did he pause to reflect on his opinions, scrutinize them, ask whether there was any evidence for them, indeed ever had any experience of anything that could be named evidence? Who will assure his friends that never has he asked himself whether what he was doing was worth while, never evaluated various courses of action, never made a decision on the grounds that what he decided was the right thing to do?

But if there is a presumption that the operators, the operations, and the relations between them are verifiable in an extended sense of that term, one is not to assume that this type of verifying is as simple as rolling off a log. In the first place, human knowing is not simple. It is a compound of quite different operations, each of which contributes only a part to the whole. The several operations have to coalesce into a single knowing, and the several partial objects of the partial operations have to be compounded into a single object. What is experienced comes to be investigated. What is investigated comes to be understood. What is understood can be formulated intelligently. What is formulated intelligently can be checked. What is checked satisfactorily is found sufficiently grounded to be affirmed.

To simplify the foregoing statement, let us drop some of the operations and say that human knowing consists in experiencing, understanding, and judging. Now experience is either external or internal, either sensitive or conscious. It follows that there are two types of human knowing: one may compound sense experience with understanding and judging; and one may compound experience as conscious with understanding and judging. It is the latter procedure that is needed for our purpose. It will involve consciously experiencing each of the operators, operations, and the relations between them; next it will involve understanding the operators and the operations in each of their several relations; finally it will involve finding the evidence for affirming that the operators and operations exist and have been correctly understood.

To carry out these procedures one has to be operating in a twofold context. There is the lower context of the operations to which one is adverting. There is the upper context of the inquiry in which the adverting takes place. The lower context, for example, may be closing and opening one's eyes, and the upper context will be the scrutiny that adverts not merely to the seen but also to the experience of seeing. Again, the lower context will be any of the endless instances of problem-solving, and the upper context will be an exhaustive scrutiny of all the elements that go into the solution, from the formulation of the problem, the heuristic structure in which the unknown solution is named and all its properties are listed, to the insight that grasps the solution from its properties. At a further stage, the lower context will be supplied successively by each of the different types of judgment, and the upper context will be the investigation that determines just what happens in one's arriving at a judgment. In brief, what I am saying is that introspection is not just an inward look but an investigation that proceeds on two levels: there is the lower level that secures the conscious occurrence of the operations under study, and there is the higher level on which the study takes place.

3.1 Revision

Now it may be felt that such procedures may be interesting or even exciting, but that they cannot arrive at results of philosophic import. Nothing more can be expected at best than an ongoing series of ever better results. That is just psychology. It is not philosophy.

Now I have no doubt that any study of our cognitional operations, no matter how well done, will be open to corrections and improvements due to later studies. But I would note that this process of ongoing revision has its conditions. For one thing, it cannot eliminate the possibility of revision. A revision supposes data that an earlier account overlooked. It supposes fresh insight that accounts satisfactorily both for the earlier data that were known and as well for the new data that were overlooked. It supposes that one will judge that the later, more comprehensive insight will be judged more probable than the insight it would correct. In brief, any revision presupposes a level of experience, where the new data are observed, a level of understanding, where the new insights occur, and a level of judgment, where the new insights are accepted as more valid. In brief, a cognitional theory in terms of experience, understanding, and judgment can be improved by fuller study, but it cannot be changed in its fundamental features without discovering an entirely new meaning to the process named revision. That is a feature that is lacking in other instances of empirical inquiry. Its presence in cognitional theory gives that theory a durability that I should regard of philosophic significance.

Its significance is, of course, the significance of an invariant and, indeed, of an invariant that possesses further implications. By cognitional theory one comes to know just what one is doing when one is knowing. On the basis of a cognitional theory one can come to know just why doing that is knowing; and that is an epistemology. On the twofold basis of cognitional theory and episte- mology one can go on to determining what one knows by cognitional activity, and that is an ontology or metaphysics.[6]

So much for the general strategy, a complement to my first talk.

4   The Real

My next step is whether the world mediated by meaning is real. And there are two main questions: What is meant by reality? What are the criteria for claim- ing to know it?

4.1   Versions of the Real

At a first approximation, there are two candidates for the meaning of the word 'real': the first is the world of immediacy in which one lives in one's infancy; the second is the world one comes to know through successive differentia- tions of consciousness. But the existence of two candidates gives rise at a second approximation to the emergence of a series of other candidates, and I am not meaning them in any historical sense – that is far too complex. I am giving thumbnail sketches.

For the naive realist, the real world is the world mediated by meaning, but it is known, not by experiencing, understanding, and judging, but simply by taking a good look, that is, by employing the criteria relevant to the world of immediacy.

The empiricist takes the naive realist seriously. The criteria for reality *are* the criteria of the world of immediacy. Consequently, one has to empty the world mediated by meaning of all the additions to experience brought about

---

6 Lonergan adds parenthetically, 'And once one has done this investigation, of course, one turns the whole thing over. One takes the primitive terms and starts talking on the basis of that – provided you've done the previous inquiry.'

by inquiry, understanding, formulation, reflection, weighing the evidence, and judging.

The critical idealist takes the empiricist seriously. He is awakened from his dogmatic slumbers. He lays it down that immediate knowledge of objects is only by *Anschauung*, by taking a good look. It follows that the categories of the understanding, of themselves, are empty; they are not immediately referred to objects. They can be applied, however, to the objects presented by *Anschauung* and so, by the mediation of sense, become relevant to objects. Further, it follows that the ideals of reason, of themselves, are empty; they have no immediate reference to objects; they can become related to objects if, and only if, they are employed to guide the use of the categories of understanding when applied to the presentations of sense. Finally, it follows that, while the world mediated by meaning is not the world of things in themselves but only phenomenal, still the use of the categories of the understanding under the guidance of the ideals of reason (properly understood) is the one intelligent and reasonable thing to do.

The absolute idealist wants to restore speculative reason, not indeed in the old Scholastic or rationalist sense in which speculative reason revealed the real world, but in a new sense by new techniques that lead to the mental reconstruction of the universe in all its aspects.

While the absolute idealists enormously enriched the scope of philosophy, their ambition to restore the primacy of speculative reason has not been widely followed. Schopenhauer wrote *Die Welt als Wille und Vorstellung*, the world as will and representation. Kierkegaard took his stand on faith. Newman took his on conscience. Nietzsche turned to the will to power. Dilthey aimed at a *Lebensphilosophie*. Blondel wanted a philosophy of action. Paul Ricoeur has not yet finished his philosophy of will. And in the same direction have proceeded pragmatists, existentialists, and personalists.

While I agree with this tendency and would say that what in the last analysis is decisive is a decision, an option, a commitment, still I do not think that such a decision, option, commitment is either blind or arbitrary. One can commit oneself with one's eyes wide open. But to ask the precise meaning of that metaphor is to raise our second question, What are the criteria that are to be met in claiming to know?

5   Criteria for Knowing the Real

I distinguish a proximate criterion and a remote criterion. The proximate criterion regards single judgments. The remote criterion regards the context of judgments within which any single judgment is inserted, through which it is interpreted, which it corrects or modifies. The remote criterion is that the judgments in the context in which the new judgment is inserted be themselves true, satisfy their proximate criterion. So I begin with the proximate criterion.

5.1 Proximate Criterion

The notion of judgment will be clarified by distinguishing utterance, sentence, proposition, consideration, and assent.

If *A* says, 'The king is dead,' and *B* says, 'The king is dead,' there are two utterances but only one sentence.

If *A* says, 'The king is dead,' and *B* says, 'Der König ist tot,' there are two sentences but only one proposition. Similarly, if *A* writes 2 + 2 = 4 and *B* writes 10 + 10 = 100, there are two sentences but only one proposition.

Now propositions may be merely considered, and then they are no more than objects of thought; but again, propositions may meet with a person's assent, and then they become that person's judgments.

5.1.1 General Form of Judgment

Why does one assent to propositions? I shall indicate a general form, and then apply it to different cases.

The general form is: If *A*, then *B*; but *A*; therefore *B*. In the major, *B* is a conditioned: if *A*, then *B*. In the minor, its conditions are fulfilled: *A*. The fulfilment of the conditions makes a virtually unconditioned; because it is a virtually unconditioned, it is asserted in the conclusion. Because the first two premises together give you a virtually unconditioned, the conditioned is asserted in the conclusion.

However, not all judgments can be conclusions. So one has to proceed from the virtually unconditioned as expressed in propositions to a more primitive virtually unconditioned that arises in the prior activities of experiencing, understanding, and putting the question for reflection, Is that so?

Then the question for reflection, Is that so? will indicate the conditioned. The fulfilment of the conditions will be found in the data of sense or of consciousness. The link between the conditions and the conditioned, the equivalent of 'If *A*, then *B*,' will be found inasmuch as the process from the data to the proposed judgment satisfies the criteria, the exigencies, of intelligence and reasonableness.

5.1.2 Different Cases of Judgment

Let us apply this to different cases of judgment.

First, there are concrete judgments of fact.[7] A worker leaves his neat and tidy home in the morning and returns at evening to find the windows broken, smoke in the air, the walls splashed with water, the furniture soaking wet, and the floor covered with inches of it. He makes a concrete judgment of fact, an extremely restrained one, namely, 'Something happened!'

This judgment can be expressed in syllogistic form: If the data on my home in the evening differ from the data on my home when I left in the morning, then something must have happened. But the two sets of data differ. Therefore something must have happened.

Normally, however, people do not syllogize. In the difference of data on the same object, they grasp the fact of change. Such a grasp is an insight, a direct act of understanding. It's on the second level. Moreover – and this is the important point, where you move on to the level of judgment – it is an invulnerable insight. Insights are vulnerable when there are further relevant questions to be asked. For the further questions may give rise to further insights, and the further insights may complement, qualify, correct the insight already had. But when there are no further relevant questions, when many questions might be raised but would not modify what already has been grasped (Was there a fire? Where is my wife?), the insight in possession is invulnerable. These further questions are not going to change the judgment, 'Something happened.' They presuppose that something happened. And it is that grasp that there is nothing further to be said on this that grounds the concrete judgment of fact.

Next, there are analogies and generalizations. These judgments proceed on the principle that similars are similarly understood. In other words, there has to be a significant difference in the data for one set to be understood one way and another similar set to be understood in another way. Object to an argument from an analogy or to a generalization, and the rejoinder will be, 'What's the difference?'

Third, consider commonsense judgments. Common sense is the development of intelligence, the accumulation of insights, that is expressed in the ordinary language of some people or class at a particular place and time. It is

---

7 Parenthetically, 'We'll take the simplest instance, because these concrete judgments of fact go off in all directions.'

the guide of everyday living, speaking, doing. It is generated by the group, each partly finding things out for himself or herself and partly learning from others. This finding things out is a matter of an insight generating a further relevant question leading to another insight that, in turn, generates a further relevant question, and so on repeatedly until one masters the matter in hand. So, because one has mastered the matter in hand and there are no further relevant questions, one proceeds to judge. Because this goes on in a group, because everyone is finding things out and communicating, we have the sociology of knowledge. It used to be called belief.

Fourth, there are probable judgments. When there are no further relevant questions, a judgment can be certain. When further relevant questions are known or can be expected, there occur judgments that are probable. So, in general, scientific judgments are probable. That something has been discovered may be certain, but that that discovery is definitive, that there will not arise further questions to qualify or modify or correct what now is known, is far from certain.

Fifth, we consider analytic propositions and principles. An analytic proposition is a proposition that follows from the definition of its terms. If A is defined as possessing a relation R to B, there may be derived the analytic proposition, 'Every A has the relation R to a B.'

An analytic principle is an analytic proposition whose terms and relations, in the sense defined, are verified in all relevant instances to which the terms refer.

A provisional analytic principle is one whose terms and relations probably are verified in all relevant instances. Scientific definitions become provisional analytic principles, through the way of using them. Pure water is H_2O.

Serially analytic principles are the principles that generate the ranges of systems, some instances of whose elements can be verified.

5.2 Remote Criterion

Finally, with regard to judgment, one has to note that there are different realms of the world mediated by meaning.

We may say that the moon exists, and that the logarithm of the square root of minus one exists. But this does not mean either that the moon can be derived from suitable postulates or that the logarithm in question can be inspected sailing around the sky.

So we distinguish different realms. The principal realm contains the objects that are verified in the data of sense and consciousness. Subsidiary, qualified realms – the logical, the mathematical, the hypothetical – have various degrees of relevance to the principal realm.

Question:[8] I have a question that alludes back to last week. I would not be unhappy if you tied it in to what you just said. I am trying to understand the difference between your position and that of a positivist or logical empiricist. I'm thinking of something I read a number of years ago, A.J. Ayer's book *Language, Truth and Logic.*[9] He distinguished between words that have cognitive meaning and words that have emotive meaning, and the significance of those with emotive meaning is that they are limited to a series of meaningless questions, in the sense that they didn't lead to answers that could be empirically verified. You seem to be distinguishing – your main category last week was meaning, and I think Ayer's may have been words, or language. You distinguish cognitional, affective [*sic*], and constitutive, if I remember correctly. And I guess I'm drawing an unfair analogy between your cognition and his meaningful words and your affective and his emotional words.
Response: *Effective*, not affective. Affective is emotional. Effective gets things done, like technology.

Question: Oh, you were saying 'effective.' Oh, I'm sorry. Anyway, I remember in one of the earliest essays in your *Collection* you did make a distinction between the position you were stating there and the positivists.[10] You were talking about the response of appetites to motive and the orientation of processes to term, and then you said that a positivist would have no trouble with that statement but would if he moved on to say that appetites respond because of motive, particularly because of the motive of good, and that processes are oriented to terms, particularly to terms ... I don't see the distinction between your position and the positivist one.

---

8 Parts of the questions and comments were not clear, and these are indicated here by ellipses. In general, questioners pursued a line of inquiry for several comments or questions.
9 A.J. Ayer, *Language, Truth and Logic* (London: Gollancz, 1946).
10 [The reference is to Bernard Lonergan, 'Finality, Love, Marriage,' in *Collection,* vol. 4 in Collected Works of Bernard Lonergan, ed. Frederick E. Crowe and Robert M. Doran (Toronto: University of Toronto Press, 1988) 19: 'Any positivist will admit that appetites do respond to motives, that processes are orientated to terms. Quite coherently, any positivist will deny final causality since, beyond such concomitance and correlation, causality requires that appetite respond because of motive, that process be orientated because of term.'

Response: What the positivist position comes to is that human knowledge is natural science; once you get beyond that, you are in trouble. I start my exposition of human knowledge by working from mathematics and science, but I don't stop there.

Question: But your emphasis is on human cognition. That usually is tied to something called epistemology, and normally that is tied to some substitute for a metaphysics of being or a metaphysics of things.
Response: For Aristotle and Aquinas, the fundamental science is the science of being. Next comes the science of things in motion, physics; and then the science of things that are alive, psychology. The fundamental terms in their physics are derived from the metaphysics, and the fundamental terms in biology and psychology are modifications of the terms used in physics. The whole terminology is using that setup. Now the difficulty with that is that you don't get just one metaphysics; you have several schools. And how do you choose between them? Well, up to the start of the Thomist school, doing theology was agreeing with Augustine, with much discussion about whether you agreed with Augustine or not. Afterwards, with the blowup over the Aristotelian-Augustinian controversy at the end of the thirteenth century, doing theology was agreeing with Thomas, the Thomists; and so on – they had these schools. Descartes put the question: Let's start from knowledge. And Kant put it another way. This putting the question starting from knowledge really begins with the beginnings of modern science.

Question: Can't you return the compliment and say that you don't get one epistemology but a proliferation of various kinds of epistemologies that are equally distinguished?
Response: Well, we are working towards one. It is first of all cognitional theory, and any statement in a cognitional theory can be verified in the data of consciousness.

Question: There's a trap there, and I don't know how to get out of it!
Response: That's the point, though.

Question: Would you repeat that?
Response: Any statement in a cognitional theory can be verified in the data of consciousness.

Question: As distinct from metaphysics?

Response: Well, you have no way of solving metaphysical disputes except through a sound cognitional theory and an epistemology. If you can say what you are doing when you are knowing, you can go on to say why doing that is knowing, and that is epistemology.

Question: But there have been many philosophies based in entirely different approaches that have been very respectable, and they may still arise to rule the day before we're through.
Response: Oh yes, one takes one's chances.

Question (same questioner): One of the limitations of trying to apply modern science to solve problems in human society, moral questions, and so on, is that by the very method they use they tend to be limited to what Aristotle might call the efficient cause and not deal with questions that Aristotle or a Thomist would be more equipped to treat with in terms of other forms of causation, like final cause or something like that. And those methods or approaches to the solution of problems allow you to deal with different data, with different contexts, applying your solution to different problems. You talk about vertical finality or absolute finality, factors like that which in modern terminology – I'm not sure about cognitional theory – I suspect cognitional theory doesn't allow you to talk about it.
Response: It's not cognitional theory; it is scientific method, and especially the method of the natural sciences. That's the method that works in that field. But to say that that is the model science and that everything else has to conform to that – that's where the catch comes in.

Question: But I don't understand how your cognitional theory picks up on those other topics.
Response: Well, that is my *Method in Theology.*

Question: I'll read it!
Response: My first book, *Insight,* was largely based on natural science. There was a treatment of common sense, and we did go on to a philosophy, but in the recent book interpretation and history are the main problems.
Comment: I think what my colleague is partially getting at is that in its skeletal form your cognitional theory sounds a great deal like the model of the natural sciences as applied to the context where ... empirical data ... meaning ... verification ... So the distinction of ... the model of method and broadening of the definitions of theology allows the objects of consciousness ... The difficulty

people have learning modern-day mathematics is very similar to many of the aspects of a person learning to make some other thing a part of the world. That area of objects seems singularly unreal ... The time delay before any human mind can accept ... the kind of objects that are being discussed.

Response: Differentiation of consciousness. To add on a new differentiation is a big change and is the main illustration of how knowledge makes a bloody entrance.

Comment: Well, it's very interesting because part of the time you have the ... experience of broadening one's world is almost independent of what one is being taught ... It really consists largely of listening to someone who believes that that world exists long enough for you to come to believe it also, you get immersed.

Question: I was wondering how much your approach leaves for creativity in the formation of new concepts, for trying to give a system of concepts that is different from what one has used before ... and certainly people like Einstein have emphasized that in scientific creativity, it is all so important to let the mind work freely to try to speculate, to try to develop wholly new conceptual systems, and only later worry about trying to tie them back to experience without building them up step by step in a natural sort of way. It seems to me you're discussing a way in which one might build up new concepts in a step-by-step and controlled procedure, but I wonder to what extent – what are the possibilities and what are the limitations in freedom to develop new kinds of concepts in your thinking?

Response: The system is essentially ongoing.

Question: Is there continuity, or can there be radical breaks in the course of the development of concepts?

Response: Take Kuhn's *The Structure of Scientific Revolutions*.[11] There is a period in which you are mopping up. The new ideas have been successful, and to apply them all over the field settles a lot of problems. That is the ordinary situation in the scientific field: you are mopping up the last big achievement. But then there comes another period in which you are turning up problems all over the place. And it is that that brings out something really new, like the

11   Thomas S. Kuhn, *The Structure of Scientific Revolutions* (Chicago: University of Chicago Press, 1962; 2nd, enlarged ed., 1970; 3rd ed., with index, published 1996).

blackbody radiation that Planck was working on. All sorts of things were building up, and you get the breakthrough in quantum theory. My concern, mainly, is precisely with that type of change; I call it higher viewpoints. Higher viewpoints emerge as the previous viewpoint reveals more and more its inadequacy.

Question: Do you think the emergence of such a higher viewpoint is a matter of chance in the individual genius, or is it something that can be controlled or developed systematically?
Response: It's the way that you can say how the thing happens. Take elementary mathematical operations: addition, subtraction, multiplication, division. It is by doing them that you become capable of doing them in a more general form in algebra, and your algebra will go on to further things. Any further advance, insofar as it is a higher viewpoint, is taking the old operations and reshaping the whole thing. The higher viewpoints in physics – just take the main stages in the history of physics. The same with chemistry. Now you can make discoveries statistically more probable, but you can't make them inevitable. You can't set down rules for them, because to discover is taking a new slant, and the mopping up is just keeping on with the old slant.

Question: Could you comment on the span of attention that is implied in this notion of looking at problems as compared with – let me phrase it my way – the history of every concept, which is in some kind of process of revision? Or do concepts die? In other words, if you talk about the processing of immediacy with revision, it presupposes some kind of continuation of life. But is this true for all concepts as one begins to apprehend the nature of reality? Is that a clear question?
Response: It doesn't easily fit into my habitual modes of thought. With regard to concepts, as a theologian I am concerned with their history. It meant this at this time, and it meant this to this person. The meaning of an idea or a term at the present time is *that* history, at least in theology. Is there a generalization as to what happens to concepts? I don't think so. I don't think you can predict.

Question: No, but my question was in a sense by implication from my colleague. You sort of implied that there is a kind of history of science, of concepts, which move through a kind of variety. But is this true of all concepts, and what is the nature of that focus? I would hate to introduce the notion of political theory at this point, but there is something that happens which somehow selects concept from concept in some kind of process.

Response: I think if you want to get what is permanent, you are going to need what I call heuristic concepts, which is the question about the data. For Aristotle, fire was one of the four elements. For people before Lavoisier, it was something to do with phlogiston. For modern chemists, it is a process of oxidation. What's common to them all? Well, there is nothing common to the answers, but they are all answering the same question. What's this here, in flames? What's going on? And that is a heuristic concept.

You can get it in Augustine's notion of the persons in the Trinity: what there are three of in God – a heuristic notion. There aren't three gods, there aren't three Fathers, there aren't three Sons, but there are three. Three what? Well, we'll say 'persons.' But Augustine didn't define 'person.' Regarding the definition of 'person,' there was one by Boethius, another in the twelfth century by Richard of St Victor, another in the thirteenth century by Aquinas. And these were all metaphysical, and so you had a lot of metaphysical theories of personality running through a few centuries. Then Descartes came in with his *Cogito*, and the psychologists developed it, and the interpersonal relations people, the 'I–Thou,' and so on: a succession of different ways of using this word 'person.' What's fundamental is what there are three of, as far as the trinitarian concept goes.

Question: ... your point on durability, and I wanted to ask you, Would what you're proposing here admit of ... What is the element that you think is durable?
Response: The structure: experiencing, understanding, judging, deciding. And the question, the heuristic structure ... the data to which you put the question, and with regard to your formulation you put the question, Is it so? and with regard to your affirmation about reality, Well, what are we going to do about it? What would be the good thing to do, the right thing to do? Those questions, that is what is fundamental. And then what I call the transcendental precepts: Be attentive, Be intelligent, Be reasonable, Be responsible.

Question: I have the suspicion that, as climates of thought change, certainly something of that will carry over, but are there not different ways of slicing up the pie?
Response: I know I'm just one individual in a rather large world. One of my friends at the Florida Congress[12] said, 'We are not your disciples. You taught

12 The reference here is to Ongoing Collaboration: The International
    Lonergan Congress, held at St Leo College, Boca Raton, Florida, 31 March–

us to think for ourselves, and that is what we are doing.' And I welcomed that very much, always did.

Question: Your higher viewpoint reminds me of a philosophy based on dialectic, in which you might have a progression from thesis and antithesis to synthesis, kind of like Plato's divided mind or Hegel's historical evolution towards Spirit. Is there any flavor of that in your higher viewpoint?
Response: Nothing Hegelian. For me, the absolute idealists were a mistaken reaction against Kant's practical reason. They enriched philosophy enormously: philosophy of history, philosophy of right, philosophy of culture, all this sort of thing. As for Hegel's *Phenomenology*, well, as someone said, 'Hegel is fine if you omit the system!'

Question: Can you say what the higher viewpoint would be if it isn't a dialectical progression?
Response: Dialectic for me is the opposition between the intelligent, the reasonable, the responsible, and, on the other hand, the unintelligent, the unreasonable, the irresponsible. Insofar as the second, the dialectic of decline, guides human action, you make the objective situation unintelligible, unmanageable. And from a religious viewpoint, there is need of the category of redemption, undoing evil.

Question: I'm still not quite clear – if you go back to what Thomas Kuhn referred to as paradigms ... new method ... new perspective, I still don't see how that fits with your higher viewpoints.
Response: Well, there's more to the higher viewpoint. As I expressed it, it's very schematic. Kuhn is talking about the concrete process of development. There you have people working on one line, and then another line coming in. It's a higher viewpoint, but in another sense. It's not a mathematical higher viewpoint where rules govern operations, and operations generate terms.

Question: Yes, but what marks the changes in the paradigms is the fact of a new perspective, not from a succession of incremental steps.
Response: These small incremental steps are the process of mopping up, and

---

3 April 1970. Two volumes of the papers given at the Congress, edited by Philip McShane, were subsequently published: *Foundations of Theology* (Dublin and London: Gill and MacMillan, 1971), and *Language Truth and Meaning* (same publisher, 1972).

the new slant – people say, What on earth is he talking about? It's really difficult to come to understand him ...

Lonergan (after a hiatus on the tape): ... classical laws hold, other things being equal. Statistical laws say when other things will be equal – unless you have a scheme of recurrence, such as the planetary system.

Question: You spoke last time of the difference between classical and modern controls, and it might be helpful, in terms of the questions today, if you would speak of the contrast between classical control and logical forms of control, as opposed to this sort of method as a modern type of control.

Response: That puts it well, I think. Classical control believed in universal principles and didn't believe in ongoing system. System for it was something to endure, and that was inbuilt. It's been the main difficulty with the Roman Catholic Church in the present century, and in the last century. It is taken for granted: the pope has this mentality. The modern control is mainly in terms of – no matter what the scientist constructs, what counts are not really his conclusions but his methods. Previous conclusions can all be revised.

Question: How do you move from there to God or theology, or in the world of political science or the humanities, where the methods are not germane and have to be revised, and where you might not be talking about what can be verified because it exists, but about what ought to be because you want to bring it about?

Response: An answer to that question may be found in Gibson Winter's *Elements for a Social Ethic.*[13] He starts off with several types of sociology at the present time: the behaviorist, the intellectualist, the functionalist, the voluntarist (C. Wright Mills), and the intentionalist (the New School of Social Research). He goes on to say that the functionalist and the voluntarist are at one another's throats and their procedures get entirely different sorts of results. The functionalist always favors the status quo, and the voluntarist type is always out for big changes, revolutions, and so on. Is the difference scientific, or is it ideological? Well, you can't answer that on a scientific basis, so he goes on to a social philosophy, and from a social philosophy he goes on to a social ethics, the ethics that is in the *Lebenswelt*, what people praise and blame. And from the ethics he goes on to social policies and planning. The plans are

---

13 Gibson Winter, *Elements for a Social Ethic: The Role of Social Science in Public Policy* (New York: Macmillan, 1966; paperback, 1968; see below, pp. 301–302, note 2).

carried out, and the scientists will give us the feedback for revising these policies. And that seems to be a way in which one can integrate.

Comment: The point is to have a platform on which to stand in order to evaluate the goals or the purposes or the programs that one sets out in such a political or social philosophy. That means having a philosophy in which you not only assert the position on which you stand but defend it against arguments opposed to it.

Response: We will see more about that next week when we talk about values.

8

What Are Judgments of Value?[1]

The world mediated by meaning comes alive with feeling, so we will start with feelings.

1 Feelings

In this I am following Dietrich von Hildebrand, *Christian Ethics,* a book written about 1953,[2] and to some extent also Max Scheler, as presented by Manfred Frings.[3]

Distinguish nonintentional states and trends from intentional responses. The feeling of fatigue is not something that results from apprehending an object; it is a distinct effect. And again, there are nonintentional trends. You can feel hungry, and you have to discover that what is needed is food. You feel tired, and you have to discover that what you need is a rest; you keep on just getting more and more tired. These are nonintentional states and trends. In

---

1 The third of the lectures at the Massachusetts Institute of Technology (see above, p. 107, note 1). There does not seem to be available any original typescript by Lonergan. The lecture was taped, however, and the tape was transcribed by Nicholas Graham. We work here from the tape (at the Lonergan Research Institute, cassette TC 695), with help from the Graham transcription. The tape begins in mid-sentence, and so the first paragraph has been edited. All divisions and footnotes are editorial.
2 Dietrich von Hildebrand, *Christian Ethics* (New York: David McKay, 1953).
3 Manfred S. Frings, *Max Scheler* (Pittsburgh: Duquesne University Press, and Louvain: Nauwelaerts, 1965).

those cases, it is simply the relation of a cause to an effect or a trend to a goal. But there are intentional feelings, intentional responses, and they arise from an object or cause the object to be represented imaginatively. It is these intentional responses that relate the subject to the world mediated by meaning, make it something that is powerful, massive, give it all its momentum.

Feelings are of many different kinds. There are feelings for persons, about our respective situations, about the past, present, and future, about evils to be lamented and remedied, about the good that can and might possibly be accomplished.

Intentional responses fall into two main classes. There are intentional responses to what is agreeable or disagreeable, satisfying or dissatisfying; and there are other intentional responses that respond to values, which may be ontic, and then they are persons, or they may be qualitative, such as beauty, understanding, truth, virtuous acts, noble deeds.

Intentional responses to values move the subject towards self-transcendence and select an object for which or because of which he does transcend himself. Response to the agreeable or disagreeable may be a value or may not; these responses are ambiguous. You can have a response to something disagreeable and nonetheless go ahead and do it without too much lamentation (most of us have a fair amount of that). But value properly so-called is something that calls one to transcend oneself. Such values are vital values: health, strength, grace, vigor; social values: the vital values of the social group; cultural values, which presuppose the vital and the social but rank higher – 'not on bread alone doth man live'; personal values, the incorporation of values in oneself, in one's living, in one's way of life; and finally religious values, which in religious persons are the supreme values, for they determine one's orientation to the universe.

Feelings, like skills, develop, but they do not develop in the same way as skills. Feelings never become something that we can control as we control the movement of our hands or feet, and so on. They are not at the beck and call of our will. While feelings do arise spontaneously, still once they have arisen they can be reinforced or curtailed, and in that way one can change one's spontaneous preferences – by such advertence, approval, or distraction, moving on to something else. The process of education is not merely a matter of advancing in knowledge, it is also a matter of the refinement of one's feelings, creating a climate of discernment in which one can respond to values more fully, more exactly, more precisely.

Feelings as intentional responses are not merely transient; they are not limited to the time of apprehending a value. Some are transient, some can be repressed, but feelings can be in full consciousness so deep and strong, especially when reinforced, that they channel attention, shape horizons, direct one's life; and the great example of this, of course, is being in love.

There are aberrations of feeling. Nietzsche borrowed from the French the word *ressentiment* and gave it a meaning that is his own. Max Scheler modified that meaning, and I am following Scheler,[4] who considered *ressentiment* as a refeeling of a specific value clash with someone else's value qualities, someone else who is one's superior physically or intellectually or morally or spiritually. The response is not any attack on the person but a constant belittling of that value quality, making out that it is not important, or that it is overrated. Without being aggressive it can spread over a whole lifetime, and that anger is neither repudiated nor directly expressed. It can lead to a distortion of a whole scale of values, and can spread not only in an individual but in a whole group, people, social class, and over a whole epoch.

Finally, it is better to take full cognizance of one's feelings, even when they are abominable, to advert to them than to try to repress them or snap them off. It is better to face them fully and do what one can about them.

We spoke of experience, understanding, judging. Feeling is the first fundamental dimension within which knowing emerges, and now we are working on the fourth level, namely, questions for deliberation, evaluations, and decisions. Feelings as well as knowing are presupposed by that fourth level.

2   The Notion of Value

There is a transcendental notion of value. A transcendental notion is what is intended when one asks a question. There are questions for intelligence: What? Why? How? How often? There are questions for reflection: Is that so? And there are questions for deliberation: Is it worth while? Is it truly worth while, or is it merely apparently good? The transcendental notion of value is the capacity to ask that question: Is it worth while? Is this right?

These transcendental notions are the dynamism of our conscious intentionality. They promote the subject from lower to higher levels of consciousness, from experiencing to understanding, from understanding to judging – is it merely a bright idea? – and from knowledge of reality through experience, understanding, and judgment to the question, What are we going to do about it? What is worth doing?

The transcendental notions refer directly to objects. They are the direct intention of the object. You are not knowing any object yet but you are

4 See ibid. chapter 5.

intending it when you are asking, Is it worthwhile? Is it a value? Its answers refer immediately to objects because they are answers to the questions. The transcendental notions not only set up the effort to find the answer but also provide the criteria whether the answer is correct. Your effort to understand may be satisfied by an insight, by some increase in understanding, and insofar as that answer is found fully satisfying you are content, you are happy with it. But insofar as further questions arise, further relevant questions that could modify any understanding you have achieved, you are recognizing the lack of understanding, the incompleteness of your understanding, so that the question provides the criterion that also will decide on the satisfaction, the validity of the attainment.

So one asks questions for understanding, questions for intelligence, and insofar as understanding is fully achieved one is satisfied. If not, further questions arise. Similarly, one asks questions for reflection: Is that so? If one finds the evidence sufficient for saying so, no further questions arise. On the other hand, if there is not sufficient evidence, one keeps doubting. Similarly, the drive for value, the question for deliberation, reveals itself in the good conscience or in the unhappy conscience, the uneasy conscience.

Just as human consciousness is something quite complex, so there are many stages in the process of self-transcendence. The first stage is waking up, or even the dream of the morning in which you are already taking a stance in the world in which you are going to be alive and functioning shortly; and on awaking you become aware of objects all around you. You start asking questions, and you construct a whole hypothetical world in which all these objects find their place and relationships. Then arise questions for reflection. The world ceases to be hypothetical; it is the real world for you. Finally, when the question for deliberation leads to an evaluation, you are becoming a principle of benevolence and beneficence, capable of truly loving, capable of truly collaborating. You are in a world that is not only mediated by meaning but also motivated by value.

The transcendental notions are utterly concrete. They are not concerned with abstractions. They provide the continuous flow of questions, and it is because of this continuous flow of questions that you know that there are many things that you do not know, that there are many questions that you can ask and cannot answer. But the transcendental notions move you towards the totality of satisfactory answers, and consequently the good of value is something concrete, the true is something concrete, the fullness of truth is something concrete, and the intelligible is something concrete.

So much for the transcendental notion of value. Now we turn to judgments of value.

3   Judgments of Value

Judgments of value are simple or comparative. There is the simple judgment of value: *X* is truly good, or, *X* is only apparently good. And there is the comparative judgment: *X* is better than *Y*, or more important, or more urgent.

Judgments of value may be objective or subjective according as they proceed from the self-transcending subject. Is he authentic? As Aristotle put it, the judgment of value is the judgment made by the virtuous man with a good conscience. The criterion there is the same as the criterion in the judgment of truth, namely, self-transcendence. By reaching an unconditioned you reach truth, and by being a virtuous person and making the judgment with a good conscience you are transcending yourself again.

Judgments of value differ in content but not in structure from judgments of fact. They differ in content: something does not have to exist to be right or good, but it has to exist to be affirmed as existing. They do not differ in structure: in both cases there is a criterion and an object. The criterion lies in the self-transcendence, and the object is what you affirm, either in the judgment of fact or in the judgment of value.

Judgments of value go beyond merely cognitional self-transcendence without reaching the fullness of moral self-transcendence.[5] The fullness of self-transcendence is not merely knowing what is right; it is also doing it. It goes beyond merely cognitional self-transcendence: you are not merely knowing what is so, you are also taking a stance with regard to what ought to be. The judgment of value constitutes the subject as proximately capable of full self-transcendence.

Intermediate between judgments of fact and judgments of value lie apprehensions of value. These apprehensions of value occur in feelings that are intentional responses to values: not in nonintentional states and trends, not in intentional responses to what is pleasant or unpleasant, but in the intentional responses to the ontic value of persons and to the qualitative values of beauty, understanding, truth, noble deeds, virtuous acts, great achievements.

In the judgment of value three components unite. There has to be knowledge of reality and especially of human reality. There have to be intentional responses to values. And there has to be the initial thrust to real self-transcendence that is the judgment of value itself. Without knowledge of human life, of human possibilities proximate and remote, of the probable consequences of one's actions, one can have very fine feelings, but the fruit would

---

5 At first, Lonergan said 'real self-transcendence,' but then corrected himself; but see below, two paragraphs later.

be simply moral idealism that has high ideals and probably does much more harm than good. You have to know situations, and what can be done.

Also, as knowledge is not enough, so moral feelings are not enough. Moral feelings have to be criticized and developed. There is honor among thieves, as they say.

Finally, the development of knowledge and the development of moral feelings head one to the existential moment, the existential discovery, where one discovers oneself as a moral being, one discovers the significance of personal value, of personal responsibility. This existential discovery is the discovery where one finds out for oneself that one has to decide for oneself what one is going to make of oneself.

Judgments of value occur in different contexts. There can be the context of growth: one's knowledge of one's operating increases, and one's responses advance up the scale of values; openness to further achievement prevails. At the summit there is the power and vigor of being in love: the love of intimacy, the love of mankind, and the love of God. On the other hand, there can be a context of deviations, neurotic needs, refusal to take risks, distortion of scales of preference, feelings that sour. Bias can set in, rationalization, ideology, even hatred of the good.

Joseph de Finance, a confrère of mine in Rome, in his book *Essai sur l'agir humain*, distinguishes between horizontal and vertical exercises of liberty.[6] In the horizontal exercise, your being in the world is something set, and you keep on operating within that world. The vertical movement of the exercise of liberty selects the stance and the corresponding horizon; you move out of one horizon into another. The foundations of judgments of value are to be found in the exercise of vertical liberty. It is insofar as one has been moving to a fuller and better knowledge and appreciation that one becomes some approximation to the virtuous man whose good conscience provides the criterion for judgments of value.

In this connection, I think something has to be said about beliefs, about what is called now the sociology of knowledge.

4   Beliefs

The appropriation of one's social, cultural, religious heritage is largely a matter of belief. What one finds out for oneself is a small fraction of what one

---

6 Joseph de Finance, *Essai sur l'agir humain* (Rome: Presses de l'Université Grégorienne, 1962). Lonergan's usual reference is to 'pp. 287ff.' A section entitled 'La liberté "verticale"' runs from p. 287 to p. 304.

knows. We live by the experiences and reports of others, by the development of understanding that has been achieved before our day. While we have our own personal judgments, still they live not in some compartment of their own, they live in symbiotic fusion with beliefs one has picked up in various places.

Science often is contrasted with belief, but belief also plays a large role in science. People do make original contributions to knowledge. They can repeat another person's experiments, but there is no mania about repeating other people's experiments. Everyone wants to make his own contribution to the science, and he does that by working in his own area, in his own line. Again, the big verification is not the dropping of a weight from the tower of Pisa or something like that; it is the indirect process of verification that goes on for centuries. Every time a law is tried, applied, either in a laboratory or in an industrial development, you have a further indirect verification of that discovery. And it is this endless cloud of witnesses offering indirect verification that is the surest sign that this thing is correct. But, of course, none of us have the personal knowledge of this endless cloud of witnesses; we are believing that.

There is a division of labor in man's coming to know, and human knowledge is a common fund. One draws on it by believing; one contributes to it by cognitional operations. There develop common sense, common knowledge, common science, common values, a common climate of opinion. There are, of course, oversights, biases, errors, but they are eliminated not by rejecting all belief but by discovering when one has been mistaken in one's knowing and then finding all the things that are to be associated with that mistaken knowing, and also examining a bit the mistaken believer. And it is when you discover a mistaken belief that you have something to be attacked, and all its retinue to be chased around.

There is a process, a logic of believing. The first step is that what is true is not something private; it is independent of the mind that grasps it. You arrive at truth by grasping the unconditioned. I cannot give another my eyes, but I can truly report what I see, what I understand, what I judge.

The second step is a general judgment of value that approves the historical and social division of labor that has enabled mankind to develop down the ages and to allow each generation to stand on the shoulders of its predecessor and move on from there. It will criticize beliefs, and eliminate mistaken beliefs and all their associates, but it does not reject belief itself, which would be simply a return to primitivism. If you reject all belief no one is going to be able to stand on your shoulders. It is just bad.

The third step is a particular judgment of value: this witness is trustworthy, this expert is competent, this teacher, leader, statesman, authority can be relied on. The point at issue fundamentally is, Is the source critical of his sources? How to decide the issue? Usually it is indirect. You can have a concurrence: experts can concur, statements can be coherent. There can be an intrinsic probability for a statement, and when it doesn't seem to have that there can be a limit to my horizon.

The fourth step is a decision to believe. There is the general judgment, 'Believing is a good thing; you cannot get along without it.' There is the particular judgment, 'This can be believed.' You have reason for trusting this person, and the conclusion is, 'This ought to be believed.' If believing is a good thing, and if this can be believed, then it should be believed.

The fifth step is the act of believing. It is the assent of one's judgment that results from the decision. The decision is on the fourth level; the judgment occurs down below. It is another way in which you arrive at knowledge.

Now an analysis may make one suspicious, so let us consider the engineer pulling out his slide rule and using it for calculations. Of course, he knows how a slide rule works and why it works and how to use it. However, the slide rule presupposes enormous trigonometric and logarithmic tables. He has never worked through those tables himself; he believes that they are correct. And he has never calibrated his slide rule to see that they correspond exactly to the table; he is believing that too. If you believe in the division of labor in knowledge, you will say that that is fine. But if you are suspicious of all believing, you are at a loss for a great part of the day.

Finally, let us say something on the structure of the human good. And we will do that by a bit of implicit defining.

5   The Structure of the Human Good[7]

Individual Potentiality	*Actuation*	*Social*	*Ends*
capacity, need	operation	cooperation	particular good
plasticity, perfectibility	development, skill	institution, role, task	good of order
liberty	orientation, conversion	personal relations	terminal value

7 At this point in the lecture, Lonergan writes a schema on the blackboard, similar or identical to that on p. 48 of *Method in Theology*. The latter schema is reproduced here. See below, p. 334.

The first two columns regard the individual, the third the group, and the fourth the ends. Individuals have needs – anything you want in any way, not simply necessities – and the capacities to satisfy needs. By operating they can bring about instances of the particular good – any instance, a meal, an education, and so on. Now usually people are in groups and their operations are cooperations. For the cooperations, there is an already understood and accepted mode of cooperating, and an already understood and accepted way of cooperating is an institution; it can be improved only slowly, it can be ruined in a very short time.

Such institutional frameworks are the family and manners, society and education, the state and the law, economy and technology, the church or sect. People fulfil roles and perform tasks within already understood and accepted ways of cooperating. Individuals have plasticity, perfectibility. The infant who cannot speak becomes the person whose whole life is guided by meaning. Just as operation actuates capacity, so the development of skills actuates one's plasticity, and one does so in order to be able to take on roles and perform tasks within institutions.

Now the institution is one thing and the functioning of that institution is another. The same notions of the family can produce bliss in one case and misery in another. This good of order is the way things actually are working out, and it depends on the efficacy with which people combine within institutions to make the best of everything. To eliminate all that upsets things takes all the knowhow and all the generosity of everyone in the group to make things run well. That is the good of order.

On the third level is liberty, which is not indeterminism but self-determination. It is making the decision on the basis of a judgment of value. By one's liberty one is taking a stance in life, one has an orientation in life, and it can be an orientation to ever greater maturity or, on the other hand, the person may be falling apart.

Taking on the roles and performing the tasks within the institutional framework is shot through with feelings. On these feelings there arise personal relations, and inversely personal relations can give rise to the institutional framework.

Finally, insofar as particular goods are being produced, that is an instance in which there can be or may not be realized a good of order. The good of order materially is not something distinct from the particular goods but is in the whole array of particular goods – education for everyone at MIT, that whole show. The good of order is an ongoing flow; it is an education for so many people a year. Dinner for each one of us is a particular good, but dinner for everyone that earns it is the good of order. Now if particular goods conform to judgments of value, if the good of order conforms to judgments of value, there are being produced terminal values. Insofar as value judgments are ruling the roost, then there are emerging terminal values.

Beyond feelings and values there is the substance of community. People are joined by common experience, by common or complementary insights, by similar judgments of fact and of values, by parallel orientations in life. They are separated, estranged, rendered hostile, when they get out of touch, when they misunderstand one another, when they judge in opposed fashions, when they opt for contrary goals. So personal relations vary from intimacy to ignorance, from love to exploitation, from respect to contempt, from friendliness to enmity. Personal relations bind the community together, or divide it into factions, or tear it apart.

The human good, then, is at once individual and social. It is the work of the group, and the process is not merely the service of man, it is above all the making of man.

That analysis can apply to any community, no matter how primitive. There is the process of progress insofar as people are seeing things that possibly can be done and doing them, and improving on what has been done to get an ongoing process of development. You can have the opposite process: proposals are compromised, mutilated, the situation becomes more and more stupid, unintelligible; finally, the process needs redemption, which is through self-sacrificing love.

Question: I will be glad to start off. In trying to assimilate all this and understand it, of course, you try to put it next to something else you have already heard. Looking at your diagram, as I look at experience, understanding, judgment, and decision, I see shadows in that of Plato's divided line going up proportionately – if I remember correctly – from image to opinion to belief to knowledge, in which knowledge is virtue; in other words, to know the good is to do it. There is no other alternative: once you know the good you do it. As you go up that divided line, I believe you get increasing degrees of reality, the proportion of reality increases as you rise towards knowledge, and also you go from the external pole to the internal pole. These are all dimensions which came out in your discussion last time rather than this time, and I would be curious to know if that is an unfair analogy or what the differences are.
Response: The fundamental difference is that the deliberation, evaluation, decision is not something that is settled by knowledge. This is fundamentally in the line of the critique of practical reason being superior to the critique of

pure reason: Kierkegaard taking his stand on faith; Newman taking his stand on conscience; Blondel's philosophy of action, Dilthey's *Lebensphilosophie* – deciding is really the full control over the whole.

Question: When I'm reading the word 'knowledge' as the word wisdom, I think it is in the same class, but obviously it is different.
Response: Yes, well wisdom is a different thing. The deliberator has to be wise too. But, at least from Aristotle you have too intellectualist a notion of wisdom.

Question: Well I would say that this is different from Aristotle. In Aristotle, you can know the good and do the worst; in Plato you can't.

Question: Could you say something about the origin of feelings – what I mean is, could one say that the feelings one has are previous judgments?
Response: No, I don't think so. Feelings are with you from the start. Karl Stern describes the baby as unlimited receptacle for being loved.

Question: How then would they change?
Response: They differentiate.

Question: If so, how does this come about?
Response: When the baby laughs, the whole baby laughs!

Question: Would this differentiation have anything to do with one's accumulation of knowledge?
Response: Yes, they interpenetrate. Commonsense knowledge is not part of feeling. But when you start getting into systematic knowledge, when you start setting the feelings out, this knowing process is going on but the feelings more or less are there.

Question: You say that the transcendental values are concrete?
Response: The notion is concrete. The good is never an abstraction. Abstractions can be helpful in determining what is good but the good is always concrete. You know the concrete when you know all the answers; when you can answer all the questions with regard to something, you know the thing concretely.

Question: But God can be a good and he may be an abstraction if I don't know all the answers.
Response: But if God exists he isn't an abstraction.

Question: I'm still having trouble with this: something is concrete if you know all the answers ...
Response: You know something concretely if you can answer all the questions regarding it.

Question: My first impulse then is that nothing is concrete.
Response: We don't know anything in its full concreteness, that's true.

Question: I am back to my trouble.
Response: The transcendental notion of value is what you are intending whenever you are asking a question for deliberation. You haven't got the answer yet, but it is the principle of all the questions for deliberation.

Question: By unlimited questioning, I come to know things concretely. But I can't know the answers to an unlimited series of questions.
Response: No, it is the intending.

Question: So the object of my intending would be to get to something concrete, not that it ever is. Then that seems to contradict something that you said earlier, that the notion of a transcendental value is concrete.
Response: It intends towards the concrete.

Question: It intends towards the concrete – like a quest?
Response: Yes.

Question: But operationally ...
Response: It is just the intention.

Question: I don't lay these blocks of concrete around me and then move on to new ones.
Response: No. It is the notion of concrete that is causing the difficulty. I want to distinguish between the concrete and the sensible.

Question: I am tempted to say, are you trying to distinguish between the whole and the part? The concrete could be the whole, and I'm tempted to use the word 'abstract' for the other, though I know it would be the wrong word.
Response: The point is that the word 'abstract' is often abused. You are speaking of a man, let us say. That is not an abstraction because what you are intending is concrete reality. Which concrete reality are you picking out?

Well, you have just a general term, but you're specifying something concrete through a general term. What you mean, though, when you talk about a man is something concrete. And where does that intention of the concrete reside? It resides in your power to ask questions. The transcendental notions correspond to transcendental concepts, but they are not the same. When you objectify your questions for intelligence you talk about the intelligible; when you objectify your questions for reflection you talk about the true, the real; when you objectify your transcendental notion of value you talk about the good, what's worthwhile, what's right.

Question: The problem is in the word 'transcendental.'
Response: Oh yes. It has two different meanings and both of them imply this usage. The Scholastics distinguish between the transcendental and the predicamental. The predicamentals were Aristotle's ten categories: substance, quantity, quality, relation, place, time, action, passion, posture, and habit (like having horns, habit in that sense); and the transcendentals were terms that applied to any one of these ten, like being, intelligible, one, true, real, and so on. The Kantian notion of the transcendental investigation was into the conditions of the possibility of, say, a priori knowledge. And these transcendental notions are transcendental in both senses. They are the conditions of possibility because it is through them that you promote consciousness from the experiential to understanding, from understanding to judging, from judging to deciding. They are the conditions of possibility of the process.

Question: This is the first session I've attended so I don't know if this is worth pursuing at all, but did you speak of relating decision, based on the matrix of processes, to action, to doing?
Response: No. That will be a further ...

Question: ... another three talks, perhaps! I was just wondering about the obligations of the man seeking to live the life of the good.
Response: The process towards the concrete is not just talking about the good but setting up some sort of scheme in which several very different things can proceed to come together. You never arrive fully at the concrete, but to simply repeat after Aristotle that the good is what everyone seeks doesn't take you very far.

Question: A moment ago you distinguished between the sensible and the concrete. That suggests to me something about approximations. Are there conditions of things being sensible or of practices and actions being sensible? Have I gone through enough reflective processes or measurements of experience, understanding, and judgment? Is there an epistemology or cosmology of what is sensible that corresponds to this sort of procedure relating to knowledge?[8]

Response: I'd have to repeat half of the last talk to answer that question! My terms come out of experiencing cognitional operations, and the central one is understanding. You can tie all the others around understanding, one way or another. The sensible is half of what you presuppose whenever you are understanding. There is the internal experience and external experience; external experience is of the sensible.

Question: I'll read the transcripts later and see if I can catch up to you.

Question: Where is the material on the discussion of the human good written up in your work?
Response: *Method in Theology.*

Question: Could you say something more about your friend Joseph de Finance's vertical and horizontal liberty?
Response: He's talking about the exercise of liberty. It is in terms of horizon analysis. You can be in a given orientation towards life, towards activity, and so on, and keep developing within that orientation. That is more or less a horizontal exercise of liberty. Or you can change in some serious way: drop things that before you considered important; promote things that you considered unimportant. And if that is for the good, it is a vertical exercise of liberty.

Question: Raising yourself to a higher horizon?
Response: Yes. A fuller horizon, a richer horizon.

Question: Regarding the similarity between evaluation and cognitive judgment, there are also some differences. In the case of cognitive judgment of existence you are coming into the presence of objects existing independently of us; in the case of values, is it the same?
Response: If your judgment is true ...

8 It seems that the questioner is using the word 'sensible' not in the sense that Lonergan gives it here, but as something like 'intelligent and reasonable and responsible,' as in the expressions, 'He's a sensible person,' or 'That was a sensible thing to do.'

Question: So it is not a creation, it is coming into the presence of something that exists independently of oneself?
Response: Well, in other words, there is this process of self-transcendence. If your judgment of value is true, you are becoming through that judgment of value, in some respect, a principle of benevolence, beneficence, doing what is good, what is right. It is a creative process but it also is true; it is objective, there is a sense in which it is objective.

Question: Presumably the table or the chair has some existence whether we know it or not. But now, in becoming benevolent, does benevolence exist prior to the achievement of it?
Response: No.

Question: So there is that distinction. Would that be true of all values, that they don't exist prior?
Response: Well, they are not known prior to judgments of value.

Question: That could be said of quasars. It is really the question of whether values have a realistic status on all fours with physical entities.
Response: They are in a different order. Judgments of value are part of the dynamism of bringing about values. The self-transcending subject is the originating value, and the values he brings about are terminal values.

Question: He brings them about, that is, he creates them.
Response: He does what is right.

Question: How fixed or stiff is the notion 'terminal values'? Are there not various terminal values of various epochs in history?
Response: Well, that is a different sense of the word 'terminal.' Terminal is what is effected in this process. The self-transcending subject is originating value in his deliberation, evaluation, decision. What he decides to do is the terminal value, the other pole.

Question: As you outline it, it sounds as though these are processes and activities in the mind of an individual coming to apprehend truths, to make a decision, as opposed to collective notions of values as held by large groups or societies. I have trouble with the notions of truth over time, truth in history, since by all reports these notions have changed.
Response: Yes, there are questions of that type. It is a classicism that expects

one and the same thing to hold over time. That is classical culture, a normative notion of culture, with immortal works of art, perennial philosophies ...

Question: Are there many defenders of that type of classicism around?
Response: No, I don't think so ... perhaps some of the older members of the Roman Catholic hierarchy: *semper idem* (always the same) is the motto.

Question: Father Lonergan, in that connection how does your scheme escape the charge of relativism? In other words, you describe a process, a method, by which you recognize whether you are doing the right thing or the wrong thing, but with no criteria about the end product. Is it not open to this charge?
Response: There are a lot of relations involved in it, and that is not what is meant by relativism. Relativism means that there is no true proposition except this one, that there is no true proposition. And I am not saying that.

Question: Well, I mean in the simpleminded way that in each ethic there is a different standard of judgment and nothing in common between ethics. Therefore what happens to be preferred by most good people today is what's good, and the next generation will see a different thing emerge.
Response: You can't do much about what different people think at different times, but you can have a systematic critique, for example, chapter 7 of *Insight* on bias: individual, group, and general bias. This type of critique is the sort of thing that can be done.

Question: It is still, though, a method.
Response: Yes. What is fundamental is method.

Question: Have you taken, for example, that critique in *Insight* and applied it to a people and a culture of a particular time?
Response: I have never worked on that large scale. But I have a book on *Method in Theology* that has just come out.

Question: And that puts all these things together?
Response: It really is dealing with the problem that Roman Catholic theology has been working on. At the beginning of the nineteenth century the German historical school, reacting against Hegel's a priori interpretation of history, developed quite a new technique for dealing with history: 'Critical History,' I have a chapter on that in *Method*, as well as a chapter on 'History and Historians.' But Catholic theology before that had been deductivist. A professor of

theology was supposed to be able to settle things by appealing to the Old Testament and the New, the Apostolic Fathers, the Greek and Latin Fathers, the Scholastics, the Reformation and the Counter Reformation theologians, and so on. That sort of person just became an anachronism. When this new method of doing history was introduced, it was realized you can't be an expert in all these areas. How can you do theology in this new context? That is the problem I am thinking of. You have different kinds of specialties, separate divisions of specializations, yet you want to bring people together even though they are working on different things in different ways. A method is not a set of rules to be followed meticulously by a dolt but a framework for creative collaboration.

PHILOSOPHY OF GOD, AND THEOLOGY

Introduction[1]

The title of my three lectures is rather long, but the meaning it wishes to

1 [This section contains three lectures given by Lonergan at St Michael's Institute, Gonzaga University, Spokane, Washington, on successive evenings, 8, 9, and 10 December 1972. These were the inaugural lectures in an annual series to be known as the 'St Michael's Lecture Series.' The general title given the lectures was 'The Relationship of the Philosophy of God and the Functional Specialty, Systematic Theology.'

   In the following year, the lectures were published under the title *Philosophy of God, and Theology: The Relationship between Philosophy of God and the Functional Speciality, Systematics* (London: Darton, Longman & Todd, and Philadelphia: Westminster, 1973), with a foreword by Patrick B. O'Leary, s.j., Rector of St Michael's Institute, explaining the rationale of the series and introducing the speaker and topic of these particular lectures. Although no editor is indicated in the book, William F.J. Ryan, s.j., has confirmed (e-mail of 7 March 1997) that he in fact was the editor, with Lonergan's approval.

   An Italian translation of the lectures by Giovanni B. Sala was published in 1977, *Ragione e fede di fronte a Dio: Il rapporto tra la filosofia di Dio e la specializzazione funzionale 'sistematica,'* numero 102, *Giornale di teologia* (Brescia: Editrice Queriniana). This translation does not include the questions and responses following each lecture but it has an *editoriale* by Sala, as well as an Italian translation of three related articles of Lonergan as appendices.

   Tape recordings of the lectures are extant (Lonergan Research Institute Library, Toronto, TC 725, 726, 727). In addition, the Institute Archives has two sets of typescript notes by Lonergan (Batch x, File 31), relevant to these lectures. One set has some relation to the first lecture of this series, 'Philosophy of God'; the other, larger set corresponds more extensively to part of the second lecture, 'The Functional Specialty, Systematics.'

   The previously published text, the tape recordings, and the archival notes were all consulted for this edition. Wherever changes were made from the

convey is not self-evident.[2] I shall begin by giving some indication of the meaning of the terms I have employed, and then I shall outline the topics to be treated in the several lectures.

By 'philosophy of God' is meant thought and affirmations or negations concerning God that are not logically derived from revealed religion. In this statement the operative word is 'logically,' for in my opinion the notion of a philosophy of God pertains to a context in which classicism and conceptualism are taken for granted as self-evident. By a classicist I mean a person for whom the rhetorician or orator, Isocrates or Cicero, represents the fine flower of human culture.[3] By a conceptualist I mean a person that is a keen logician, that is extremely precise in his use of terms, and that never imagined that the meaning of terms varied with the acts of understanding that they expressed, that there are as many meanings for terms as there are different developments of intelligence that is expressing itself.

By the functional specialty 'systematics' is meant the effort of human understanding to gain some insight into revealed truths. How can one person be both God and man? How can there be three persons in God? That is the type of question, very generally and very crudely, that systematic theology is concerned with. It differs radically from philosophy of God. It presupposes revealed truths; philosophy of God does not presuppose revealed truths. The two, then, are quite distinct. But there is a further difference. Philosophy of God aims at proving the existence of God and his several attributes. But the functional specialty 'systematics' does not attempt to prove anything. That revealed truths are revealed and are true is established in other functional specialties. Systematics takes over the truths from the other specialties, and its aim is, not to find further proofs, but to understand as best it can what has already been established to be so.

There remains a third term. Our principal topic is, not philosophy of God, not the functional specialty 'systematics,' but the relationship between the two. That relationship, we shall contend, is distinction but not separation.

---

previously published text it is because of material that is found on the tapes of the lectures. Most of these changes have been made silently, and in some cases where differences appear, the editors' decision was to prefer the previously published text to the tapes. Bracketed footnotes are editorial.]

2 [See the previous note. Lonergan gave the title here as 'The Relationship between Philosophy of God and the Functional Specialty "Systematics,"' but the wording of the title given in the previous note is the wording used in official brochures on the lectures.]

3 [Lonergan added in an aside, 'and classicism was still in full flower when I went to school some fifty-five years ago or more.']

The two are quite distinct. In an age dominated by classicism and conceptualism, the two should be separated on those premises. But conditions that obtained in the past no longer prevail. Consequently, there no longer is any reason to separate the two, to have philosophy of God taught by philosophers in a department of philosophy while the functional specialty 'systematics' is taught by theologians in a department of theology or of religious studies.

So much for the meaning of the title of these lectures. By philosophy of God is meant knowledge of God that is not logically derived from revealed religion, from the truths of faith. By the functional specialty 'systematics' is meant the specialty that receives revealed truths from other specialties and seeks some imperfect understanding of them. Finally, the relationship between the two at all times is that they are quite distinct. They have contradictory premises: not from revealed truths, from revealed truths. Under the peculiar circumstances of recent centuries the relationship has been thought to be that the two should be kept quite separate. At the present time it has been my contention in my recent book *Method in Theology* that the two, while distinct, should not be separated.[4] I may add that I believe Karl Rahner to be of the same opinion though not, of course, for the same reasons exactly.

With the terms in the title explained, it is fairly obvious that the topic of the first of these three lectures should be the philosophy of God, that the topic of the second lecture should be the functional specialty 'systematics,' and that the topic of the third lecture should be the relationship between the two.

First of all, then, we are to attempt to grasp what is meant by philosophy of God. As might be expected, there are as many meanings to the phrase as there are philosophic contexts in which it is uttered. Our basic concern, accordingly, will be an attempt to grasp certain fundamental contours relevant to an understanding of variations in philosophic context. It is those variations that account for the fact that the two for a number of centuries were not only distinct but also separated, and the change in the context makes it advisable to bring them together again.

---

4 [For the data on *Method in Theology* see above, p. 12, note 2. In the archival notes (Batch x, file 31, item 1), Lonergan refers to pp. 337–40 in *Method* for the point being made here.]

9

Lecture 1: Philosophy of God

In this title there are two words whose meaning is somewhat obscure. The first of these is 'philosophy,' and the second is 'God.'

The obscurity in question is not, of course, that people have no notion of what is meant by these terms. It is that people have different notions at different times and places. Here the underlying fact is what I have named differentiations of consciousness. The human mind is ever the same, but the techniques it employs develop over time.

A first differentiation of consciousness arises when the infant learns to speak. He or she had been living in a world of immediacy, a world that contained only what could be seen, heard, touched, tasted, smelt, felt. But learning to speak involves an enormous extension of the world of immediacy. It includes not only the present and factual but also the absent, the past, the future, the merely possible or ideal or normative or fantastic. In entering the world mediated by meaning one moves out of one's immediate surroundings towards a world revealed through the memories of other men, through the common sense of community, through the pages of literature, through the labors of scholars, through the investigations of scientists, through the experience of saints, through the meditations of philosophers and theologians.[1]

A second differentiation is observable in the transition from a primitive language to that of an ancient high civilization, and again from the language of practical achievement to the language that has developed a high literature.

A primitive language has little difficulty in expressing all that can be

---

1 Lonergan, *Method in Theology* 28.

pointed out or directly perceived or directly represented. But the generic cannot be directly pointed out or perceived or represented. So in Homer there were words for such specific activities as glancing, peering, staring, but no generic word for seeing. Again, in various American languages of the aborigines one cannot simply say that a man is sick; one also has to retail whether he is near or far, whether he can or cannot be seen; and often the form of the sentence will also reveal his place, position, and posture.

Again, the temporal cannot be pointed out or directly perceived or represented. Time involves a synthesis of all events in a single continuum of earlier and later. So an early language may have an abundance of tenses but they are found to mean, not a synthesis of temporal relationships, but different kinds of action.

Thirdly, the subject and his inner experience lie not on the side of the perceived but on the side of the perceiving. One can point to the whole man or to some part of him, but one cannot point out the pointer. So possessive pronouns develop before personal pronouns, for what one possesses can be pointed out but one oneself as a subject is another story. Again, inner processes of thinking or deliberating are represented in Homer, not as inner processes, but as personalized interchanges. The Homeric heroes do not think or deliberate; they converse with a god or goddess, with their horse or with a river, with some part of themselves such as their heart or their temper.

Finally, the divine is the objective of our questioning our questioning. It cannot be perceived or imagined. But it can be associated with the object or event, the ritual or the recitation, that occasions religious experience, and so there arise the hierophanies.[2]

Early language, then, is abundant on the spatial, the specific, the external, the human, but it is weak on the temporal, the generic, the internal, and the divine. The long transition from primitive fruit gatherers, hunters, and fishers to the large-scale agriculture of the temple states and later the ancient high civilizations brought with it a vast enrichment of language. For men do not do things without first talking about them and planning them, and so there had to be a linguistic development equal to the great works of irrigation, the vast structures of stone or brick, the armies and navies, the complicated processes of bookkeeping, and the beginnings of arithmetic, geometry, and astronomy.[3]

But the discovery and the objectification of the human spirit were achieved

2   Ibid. 87–88.
3   Ibid. 89.

most notably by the Greeks. On a first level there was the literary revelation of
man to himself. Homeric simile drew on the characteristics of inanimate
nature and of plants and animals to illuminate and objectify and distinguish
the varied springs of action in the epic heroes.[4] The lyric poets went on to an
exploration of personal feelings. Intense personal feelings had always been
felt, but they were first expressed through the lyric poets; the language was
found to talk about them. The dramatists exhibited human decisions, their
conflicts and interplay, and their consequences. Within this literary tradition
there occurred reflection on human knowledge. The epic writers explained
their knowledge by referring to the muses. For Homer the muses see everything, and so the bard can describe the past as though he were an eyewitness.
For Hesiod they do not inspire but teach, and they teach not only truth but
also plausible falsehood. As Hesiod proposed to tell the truth about the
struggle in which man ekes out his livelihood, Xenophanes criticized anthropomorphic conceptions and representations of the gods, and Hecataeus
maintained that the stories of the Greeks were many and foolish, that man's
knowledge was not the gift of the gods, that stories of the past were to be
judged by everyday experience, and that knowledge is acquired by planned
and deliberate investigation. This empirical interest lived on in Herodotus,
in the physicians, and in the physicists. But Heraclitus insisted that mere
amassing of information did not make man grow in intelligence. There is an
intelligence, a logos, that steers through all things. It is found in God and man
and beast, the same in all, though in different degrees in each. To know it is
wisdom.[5]

We have been distinguishing a first and a second differentiation of consciousness. The first occurs when one learns to talk; the second occurs when
one learns a language rich and varied and supple enough to portray men in
all their complexity. It is this second differentiation that leads to the third.

Socrates made it his purpose to study, not the universe, but mankind. In
Plato's early dialogues he is seeking universal definitions of temperance or
courage, of knowledge or justice. He explains over and over just what a
universal definition is: it applies to every case, and to nothing that is not a case
of this thing. He admits that he does not know the answers to his own
questions. He can show just where any proposed definition fails. But not many
decades later Aristotle in the *Nicomachean Ethics* was able to define all the

4 [Lonergan added in an aside, 'A lion never retreats. Hector is a lion. And
   you know something about Hector by calling him a lion.']
5 Lonergan, *Method in Theology* 90–91.

virtues and to contrast with each virtue vices that sinned by excess and by defect. What, one may ask, enabled Aristotle to succeed where Socrates and his contemporaries had failed?

To this the answer is a third differentiation of consciousness. Aristotle was able to define because he moved beyond the ordinary language of common sense and the refinements brought to it by literary development, into systematic thinking. He scrutinized words, listed their several meanings, selected the meanings that meshed together to constitute a basic perspective, and made this interlocking group of meanings the primitive terms and relations that provided the basis for derived definitions.

Let me illustrate this shift from ordinary and literary language with a more recent illustration. Sir Arthur Eddington spoke of his two tables. One was brown, rectangular, solid, heavy, plainly visible. The other was mostly empty space with only here and there some mysterious entity that at one moment had to be imagined as a wave and at another as a particle. In fact, of course, there were not two tables, but there were two quite distinct apprehensions of the same reality.[6] The first of these apprehensions was the commonsense apprehension; the second was the systematic apprehension. On the basis of commonsense apprehension, satisfactory universal definitions cannot be produced. This was clear from the Socratic experiment, for every Athenian knew perfectly well the difference between temperance and gluttony, between courage and cowardice, between knowledge and ignorance, between justice and injustice. But it is one thing to know the meaning of words; it is quite another to be able to define that meaning. As our contemporary linguistic analysts keep repeating, one knows the meaning of a word when one is able to use it appropriately. Knowing the meaning of words is knowing how to use them; definition is something later, and it comes when one moves to the differentiation of consciousness that sets up systematic thinking. Any word in any language can be used in several different meanings; definition becomes possible only when a precise set of univocal and interlocking meanings has been selected, clarified, determined.

A further point must be made. While one may make one's entry into the world of systematic meaning by using the already familiar commonsense meanings of words, nonetheless one thereby is entering into a completely new world. We all have the experiences of weight and momentum, but neither of these experiences is precisely what is meant by mass: weight is mg, momentum is mv, but mass is just m; we don't experience just m. We all have

6 [See above, p. 79, note 14.]

experience of heat and cold, but that experience does not coincide with what is meant by temperature. A wooden and a metal object in the same room will be of the same temperature, but one will feel warmer than the other. Feeling warmer and cooler is not what is meant by temperature; temperature is a systematic conception. We all have experience of the endless conveniences provided by electricity, but that experience fails to yield a clue to Maxwell's equations for the electromagnetic field. To move into the systematic differentiation of consciousness does not merely involve the employment of a new set of technical meanings. It involves a new method of inquiry, a new style of understanding, a different mode of conception, a more rigorous manner of verification, and an unprecedented type of social group that can speak to one another in a new way.

In general, a logical system has three characteristics. Its root is a set of basic terms and basic relations, where the relations fix the terms and the terms fix the relations. By means of the basic terms and the basic relations, other derived terms and derived relations may be defined. Through the derived terms and relations the whole system may be related to the data of experience.

Such general characteristics, however, may be found in quite different contexts. Three such contexts merit our attention: there is the Aristotelian type, based on a metaphysics; there is the modern type, based on empirical science; there is the transcendental type, based on intentionality analysis.

Aristotle conceived system as a permanent achievement. It was to be an expression of truth, and what once is true always is true. Further, he conceived that basic terms and basic relations were metaphysical, concerned with being, with reality, with what is, and accordingly that the terms proper to physics, psychology, and similar sciences were to be simply further determinations of the basic terms and basic relations set forth in metaphysics. Finally, in his *Posterior Analytics* he conceived science as a deduction from first principles that expressed objective necessity. It is to be noted, however, that neither Aristotle himself nor his disciple, Thomas Aquinas, went out of their way to provide their work with necessary first principles; they were content to do what they could. In contrast, fourteenth-century theologians paid enormous attention to necessary truth. They were forever distinguishing between what God could do absolutely and what he may be expected to do in this ordered universe. Finally, since God absolutely could do anything that did not involve a strict contradiction, there rapidly followed first skepticism, and then decadence. It would be a contradiction to say, 'I intuit the microphone as existing and present' and 'I do not intuit the microphone as existing and present'; but there is no contradiction in saying, 'I intuit the microphone as existing and present' and 'There is no microphone existing and present.' The contradiction is not there; and you can go on to say, 'Well, if that is what God can do absolutely, how do you know that you are not living in that sort of universe? There is no contradiction.'

A second type of system is found in modern science. Up to the present century it felt itself in possession of necessary truth: there were not only the necessary laws of nature but also the iron laws of economics. A first breach in this wall was effected by the nineteenth-century discovery of non-Euclidean geometry. This was further enlarged by Gödel's theorem that a deductive system, if not trivial, will either be incoherent or incomplete: incoherent, if the same proposition can be both proved and disproved; incomplete, if questions arise in the system but cannot be solved within it. The modesty engendered in mathematicians was extended to physics by the introduction and acceptance of quantum theory. Laplace's determinist world, in which in theory any world situation could be deduced from any other, was replaced by a fundamental indeterminism covered over by statistical regularities.

The systems, then, of modern science differ from the Aristotelian type in three manners. First of all, they fought to liberate science from domination by metaphysics. Instead of borrowing their basic terms and relations from metaphysics, they worked out their own basic terms and relations, such as mass, temperature, the electromagnetic field, the equations of quantum theory, the periodic table, the evolutionary tree. Secondly, they discovered that the intelligibility they attained was the intelligibility, not of what must be so, but of what can be so and happens in fact to be verified. A science in which discoveries have to be verified is a science that discovers not necessities but possibilities. Where Aristotelian system aims to present truth, modern empirical systems aim at an ever fuller understanding and so at an asymptotic approach towards truth. Finally, modern science is more fully aware of the exigences of system. It does not believe that to reach systematic thinking it is enough to add to a word in ordinary language the appendage 'as such,' *qua tale, kath' hauto.* Aristotle was not sufficiently aware of this pitfall, and much less were his fourteenth-century followers.

We have been contrasting two manners in which systematic thinking has been carried out, and we have now to advert to a third. Its basic terms denote the conscious and intentional operations that occur in human knowing. Its basic relations denote the conscious dynamism that leads from some operations to others. Its derived terms and relations are the procedures of common sense, of mathematicians, of empirical scientists, of interpreters and historians, of philosophers and theologians. It begins from cognitional theory: What are you doing when you are knowing? It moves on to epistemology: Why is doing that knowing? It concludes with a metaphysics: What do you know when you do it?

It differs from Aristotelian system inasmuch as its basic terms and relations are not metaphysical but cognitional. It resembles modern science inasmuch as its basic terms and relations are not given to sense, but it differs from modern science inasmuch as its basic terms and relations are given to consciousness. I said that mass, temperature, and so on, are not sensible data; but the basic terms and relations in this case *are* given, but to consciousness and not to sense. Unlike Aristotle and like modern science, its basic truths are not necessities but verified possibilities. Like modern science, its positions can be revised in the sense that they can be refined and filled out indefinitely; but unlike modern science, its basic structures are not open to radical revision, for they contain the conditions of any possible revision, and unless those conditions are fulfilled revision cannot occur.[7]

I have spent so much time on the various systematic differentiations of consciousness because they are highly relevant not only to the conception of philosophy of God but also to the functional specialty entitled systematics. But to these points I shall return.

I have now to note the existence of what I have called the post-systematic differentiation of consciousness. The development of philosophic and scientific systems profoundly affects a culture. But if it modifies the outlook of most of the members in the culture, still it does not do so by transforming them into systematic thinkers.[8] Systematic thinkers are relatively rare. But their achievement is diffused by the commentators, the teachers, the popularizers that illuminate, complete, transpose, simplify. Some of the fruits of systematic thinking are enjoyed, but no real transition is effected from the everyday world mediated by commonsense meaning to the heady atmosphere of the world mediated by systematic meaning.

While other differentiations of consciousness might be described, it will meet present needs if we say something about the religious differentiation of consciousness. I have placed this differentiation in God's gift of his grace. That gift St Paul described when he wrote that '... God's love has flooded our inmost heart through the Holy Spirit he has given us' (Romans 5.5). The power of that gift he described when he wrote, 'For I am convinced that there

---

7 Further properties of this type of system are outlined in the first chapter of *Method in Theology*.

8 [In an aside: 'You don't have to be a physicist to read science fiction.']

is nothing in death or life, in the realm of spirits or superhuman powers, in the world as it is or in the world as it shall be, in the forces of the universe, in heights or depths – nothing in all creation that can separate us from the love of God in Christ Jesus our Lord' (Romans 8.38–39). To the exercise of that gift we are commanded in both the Old Testament and the New: 'Hear, O Israel, the Lord your God is the only Lord; love the Lord your God with all your heart, with all your soul, with all your mind, and with all your strength' (Mark 12.29–30; Deuteronomy 6.4–5).

The exercise of the gift consists in acts of love, but the gift itself is a dynamic state that fulfils the basic thrust of the human spirit to self-transcendence. That fulfilment brings a deep-set joy that can remain despite humiliation, failure, privation, pain, betrayal, desertion. It is a fulfilment that brings a radical peace, the peace that the world cannot give. That joy and peace radiate in a love of one's neighbor equal to one's love of oneself; it abounds in acts of kindness, goodness, fidelity, gentleness, and self-control (Galatians 5.22–23).

In itself and in its fruits, the gift of God's love is conscious. But when I say that it is conscious, I do not mean that it is known. Human knowing is a compound of many different operations. It begins from internal or external experience. It goes on to inquiring, understanding, formulating; then to reflecting, weighing and marshaling the evidence, and finally to affirming or denying. Our conscious acts and states are just the raw materials of human knowing, and to effect the transition from the mere raw materials to the finished product is a long and difficult process.[9]

Not only is the dynamic state of being in love conscious but also it is consciously unrestricted. What scripture commands, God's grace achieves, namely, a love that is with all one's heart and all one's soul and all one's mind

---

9 [In an aside: 'As understood, for example, by client-orientated therapy (Carl Rogers), the function of the therapist is to provide an atmosphere in which a person can discover in himself the conscious feelings he has but can't identify, give a name to, and pick out and recognize their occurrence. And a similar process is the process of intentionality analysis, noting the acts, the operations, that one performs in the process of knowing and naming them, finding them in oneself, for oneself. Or again, Abraham Maslow: there's a posthumous book of his on values, religion, and peak experiences. When he first started studying peak experiences, he thought they were very rare. At the end of his investigations he thought they were very common, but most people didn't know they had them. In other words, they're conscious but they're not known; they haven't been picked out and named and reflected on, and so on.' The Maslow book to which Lonergan refers is *Religions, Values, and Peak-Experiences* (New York: Viking Press, 1970).]

and all one's strength. Moreover, in the unrestricted character of the loving, we discover that it is a love of God, for it would be idolatry to love a creature in so absolute a fashion.

Note, too, that this being in love does not presuppose or depend on any apprehension of God. It is God's free gift. He gives it, not because we have sought and found him, but to lead us on to seeking and finding him. As Blaise Pascal put it, one would not be seeking God unless one had already found him.[10]

It may be objected that we cannot love what we do not know, and I should grant that that generally is the case. Activities on the fourth level of human consciousness presuppose activities on the previous three levels. But God's gift is not something that we produce; it is something that we receive; it is a completion and fulfilment of our being from on high. It is, to repeat what I have already quoted from St Paul, God's love flooding our inmost heart through the Holy Spirit he has given us.

Further, according to the thirteenth chapter of the First Epistle to the Corinthians, charity is necessary for salvation. Again, by common consent, charity is sufficient for salvation. But, as theologians argue from the First Epistle to Timothy (2.4), God wills all men to be saved. Accordingly, he wills to give them all the necessary and sufficient condition for salvation. It follows that he gives all men the gift of his love, and so it further follows that there can be an element in all the religions of mankind that is at once profound and holy.

If I have concluded that there is a common element to all the religions of mankind, I must now add that there is a specific element proper to Christianity. Christianity involves not only the inward gift of being in love with God but also the outward expression of God's love in Christ Jesus dying and rising again. In the paschal mystery the love that is given inwardly is focused and inflamed, and that focusing unites Christians not only with Christ but also with one another.

We have been preparing the ground by discussing differentiations of consciousness. We have noted the differentiations occasioned by the infant's learning to talk, by the technology of the ancient high civilizations, by the objectification of man in the unfolding of Greek literature, by the threefold introduction of system, first in its Aristotelian form, then in the form of empirical science, and thirdly on the basis of intentionality analysis; and,

10 [See Blaise Pascal, *Pensées*, trans. with introduction A.J. Krailsheimer (Harmondsworth, Middlesex: Penguin Books Ltd, 1966) 314.]

finally, we have adverted to the religious differentiation of consciousness, the differentiation that is of basic importance to the present inquiry.

For if it should happen that anyone accepted my views on the religious differentiation of consciousness, he would be led to conclude that Pascal's distinction between the god of the philosophers and the God of Abraham, Isaac, and Jacob need not be taken too seriously. For if both the philosopher and the theologian had experienced the religious differentiation of consciousness, then both would be seeking to know the same God even though they employed means that were quite distinct. Further, since it is highly desirable that there be no ambiguity about the god or God that the philosophy of God sought to know, there exists a preliminary reason for transferring the philosophy of God from the philosophy department into the theology department. For in the theology department there may exist functional specialties named dialectic and foundations that are calculated to reveal whether or not the religious differentiation of consciousness has occurred in any given individual.

A further consideration seems relevant to me. In chapter 19 of my book *Insight*,[11] there is outlined a philosophy of God. Now in Easter week in 1970 at St Leo's near Tampa, Florida, a congress was held – I must add that one of its prime movers was Fr Bernard Tyrrell of this university – and among the topics discussed was that very chapter 19. The discussion was largely unfavorable. It was felt, I think, that that chapter did not at all fit into the direction in which earlier parts of the work had been moving. It seemed to be a mere survival, if not a piece of wreckage, from an earlier age.

At the time my response was brief and noncommittal. I recalled that I had been studying methods generally as a preparation for a work on the method of theology. I had been informed that I was to be shipped to Rome the following year to teach theology at the Gregorian. I foresaw that my ultimate project would have to be postponed. I decided to round off what I had done and publish the result under the title *Insight*. Chapter 19 in that work was part of the process of rounding things off.

Now, of course, I can see that the main incongruity was that, while my cognitional theory was based on a long and methodical appeal to experience, in contrast my account of God's existence and attributes made no appeal to religious experience.

Further, *Insight* insists a great deal on the authenticity of the subject, on his need to reverse his counterpositions and develop his positions, on the impor-

11 [See above, p. 3, note 2.]

tance, in brief, of intellectual conversion. But if *Method in Theology* may be taken as the direction in which *Insight* was moving, then that direction implies not only intellectual but also moral and religious conversion. One might claim that *Insight* leaves room for moral and religious conversion, but one is less likely to assert that the room is very well furnished.

More specifically, proof in any serious meaning of the term presupposes the erection of a system in which all terms and relations have an exact meaning, and all procedures from some propositions to others are rigorous. But the system itself, in turn, has its presuppositions. It presupposes a horizon, a worldview, a differentiation of consciousness, that has unfolded under the conditions and circumstances of a particular culture and a particular historical development.

Now this presupposition of horizon is not a logical presupposition from which conclusions are drawn. On the contrary, it is part of the subject's equipment if he is to understand the meaning of the terms, to grasp the validity of the arguments, to value the goal of the investigation. In the past, and particularly in the Catholic past, the existence of subjective differences was well known, but they were considered to be of merely subjective significance. Moreover, this view was sustained in two ways. On the one hand, there was the Aristotelian belief that there existed first principles that were necessary truths. On the other hand, there was a normative notion of culture. There were not acknowledged as many different cultures as there were differing sets of meanings and values informing different ways of life. That meaning of the word 'culture' had not yet gained currency. To be cultured was to meet certain standards. One met them in the measure one had the right sort of education and so could follow right reason and be a man of good will.

The trouble with chapter 19 in *Insight* was that it did not depart from the traditional line. It treated God's existence and attributes in a purely objective fashion. It made no effort to deal with the subject's religious horizon. It failed to acknowledge that the traditional viewpoint made sense only if one accepted first principles on the ground that they were intrinsically necessary, and if one added the assumption that there is one right culture so that differences in subjectivity are irrelevant.

There emerges from this outline the distinction between different and opposed meanings of the phrase 'philosophy of God.' There is an older meaning that considers philosophy in general, and philosophy of God in particular, to be so objective that it is independent of the mind that thinks it. There is a newer meaning that conceives objectivity to be the fruit of authentic subjectivity. On the former view, philosophy of God need not be concerned with the philosophic subject. On the latter view, philosophy of God must not attempt to prescind from the subject. This means that an intellectual, moral, and religious conversion have to be taken into account.

Now there is no difficulty about theologians in a theology department reflecting on specifically Christian religious experience, but there would be some difficulty in asking philosophers in a philosophy department to reflect on specifically Christian religious experience. Again, there is no difficulty about theologians in a theology department reflecting on Christian religious conversion and employing those reflections to determine the horizon of their theologizing. Nor is there any difficulty about theologians explaining why the god of the philosophers need not be different from the God of Abraham, Isaac, and Jacob. So there is some reason, even at this preliminary stage, for suggesting that it may be possible, and even reasonable, to transfer philosophy of God into the functional specialty 'systematics.'

Question:[12] In a lecture you have entitled 'Dimensions of Meaning,' you stated, '... once philosophy becomes existential and historical, once it asks about man, not in the abstract, not as he would be in some state of pure nature, but as in fact he is here and now in all the concreteness of his living and dying, the very possibility of the old distinction [I presume you mean separation, in the light of the present lecture] between philosophy and theology vanishes.'[13] In the light of this quotation and certain implications of the present lecture, would you not now also hold that the separation, not the distinction, between a natural ethics and a Christian ethics, and between a natural philosophy of man and a theological anthropology should be abolished? This seems to follow immediately from your thought, and to imply the need for a basic shift in the philosophy and theology departments of Christian universities. Am I understanding you correctly?

Response: Right. My concern is with a state of a culture. A theology mediates between a religion and a culture. Its function is to express in terms of the culture the significance and value of the religion. And it does it differently when you have a different culture. Modern science, modern scholarship, and modern philosophy, all three, are quite different from what they were in the

12   [The tape recording indicates that the first four questions were asked by Fr Bernard J. Tyrrell, s.j.]

13   [In *Collection*, vol. 4 of Collected Works of Bernard Lonergan, ed. Frederick E. Crowe and Robert M. Doran (Toronto: University of Toronto Press, 1988) 245; reprinted by the same press, 1993; first published, New York: Herder and Herder, and London: Darton, Longman & Todd, 1967, p. 266.]

Greek world or in the medieval world or in the Renaissance period. I taught theology for twenty-five years under impossible conditions. The whole setup of the school was predicated upon things that were fine in the sixteenth century, but you could not use modern scholarship properly the way things were lined up. The divisions that were introduced by Christian Wolff are not sacrosanct.[14] What is wanted is not philosophy in general, but first of all transcendental method: what is common to all methods, what is the ground of all methods (that is chapter 1 of *Method in Theology*); and an apprehension of the human good (that is chapter 2) so that we are able to say why religion is good; and an account of meaning and all its varieties and differences as a basis for interpretation and history and communication (that is chapter 3); and what is religion (chapter 4), what is the question about God. And the question about God is much more important than the proof of God, because at the present time people deny that the question exists. So, just as the functional specialty doctrines includes not only the dogmas in the traditional sense of the Greek Councils, and so on, but also moral doctrines, so systematics will include both types of doctrines. An introduction to ethics is in chapter 2 of *Method*, but any detailed account of ethics, both natural ethics and Christian ethics, will be in the chapter on systematics.

Question: If you grant that the separation but not the distinction between natural ethics and a Christian ethics should be abolished, then in what functional specialty should 'natural ethics' be taught?
Response: It comes into systematics the way philosophy of God comes into systematics, [but] it should be introduced not only on that level. You have to set up your methodical foundations first. You have to say something in general about the human good, not just that the good is what everything seeks, and leave it at that.

Question: In teaching philosophy of man, I read your section in *Insight* where you said that to prescind from the existential dimension of man is ridiculous. We use a book that takes up Freud, Chardin, Marx, Buber, Heidegger and

14 [Christian Wolff (1679–1754), a German philosopher, professor at the University of Halle. During his career, Wolff developed a comprehensive system of philosophy, publishing treatises on the several traditional areas of philosophy: logic, ontology, cosmology, psychology, natural theology, ethics, and economics. This system of philosophy was taught in most of the German universities in the latter half of the 18th century. *The Oxford Dictionary of the Christian Church*, 2nd ed., ed. F.L. Cross and E.A. Livingstone (London, New York, and Toronto: Oxford University Press, 1974) 1495–96.]

others, trying to view man in a total context. Now is that transposing the philosophy of man into systematics?

Response: I think questions of detail are going to be solved by committees dealing with concrete problems. When I say that the formal object is settled by the method, then you don't ask questions such as, 'Shouldn't it be this subject or that subject?' You are presupposing the old doctrine of formal objects.

Question: You would say, in other words, that the old distinctions between natural morality and Christian morality, between philosophy of man and Christian anthropology are artificial and wrong, and there has to be a reintegration, and it should be done within theology?

Response: They are artificial. And if you're going to have an integration, it can't be outside theology.

Question:[15] It seems that you say that religious conversion is nonconceptual (no insight) and nonjudgmental. If this is so, how can religious conversion serve as the starting point for a philosophy of God and systematics, since these are based upon insights and judgments, as you so strongly aver in *Method in Theology?*

Response: It is a basis insofar as it gives you a new horizon. It gives you the horizon in which questions about God are significant. There are people to whom you can talk about God, and they listen eagerly. There are others who just react, 'What on earth is he talking about? How on earth can he be interested in that?' Conversion is in Ezekiel: God plucking out the heart of stone – the heart of stone doesn't want to get rid of its stoniness – and inserting the heart of flesh. And that is the fundamental thing in religious conversion. I don't say there is nothing else happening, but I am saying that is what the key point is. This key point you can have in all sorts of different contexts. It can be in the context of a hierophany: a god of the moment. In Shintoism there are, I believe, 800,000 gods. In other words, there have been 800,000 hierophanies, occasions of religious experience. A god can be the god of a person: the God of Jacob, or the God of Laban. A god can be the god of a group: the God of the Hebrews. Religious experiences are terrifically varied. So the question arises, 'Is there something that is common to all of them?' I came across this question in the following manner. Wilfred Cantwell Smith, about 1968, read a paper at the University of Toronto,[16] saying that the

15 [The tape recording identifies the questioner as Fr William F.J. Ryan, S.J.]
16 [See Lonergan's reference above, at the beginning of 'Faith and Beliefs.']

historians of religion have done a terrific job of collecting and reporting all observable data connected with religion, but there remains a question: Why is it? What on earth is religious commitment? What is it that makes religion change, transform, people's lives? And he thinks that is a question students of religion have to get after. There you have an example of a student of religion concerned with what is this thing fundamental to religious commitment.

Just as transcendental method is intentionality analysis at its root – you're starting from the subject and his operations – so you can get a theological method if you have something further in the subject that will make that transcendental method into a theological method. And that is again religious experience, religious experience at its finest, God's gift of his love.

Question:[17] The last sentence of your lecture leaves me in some doubt about whether you regard philosophy of God apart from revelation as a real possibility or only a hypothetical one. Insofar as you regard it as a real possibility, you must presuppose that there is genuine religious consciousness apart from Christian revelation. In your lecture, when you discuss religious consciousness, which you define roughly as grace or the result of grace, you do that chiefly with reference to the Bible, but it seems to me that, despite the implications of your exegesis of the passages that you cite, the Bible would deny that there is a genuine religious consciousness apart from the revelation which it itself constitutes. Thus it seems to me that the Bible would deny the possibility of the philosophy of God on your definition.
Response: Well, what about the First Epistle to Timothy, chapter two, verse four: 'God wills all men to be saved?'

Question: The exegesis you give is the traditional Roman Catholic fundamental-theological exegesis, but I think you'd be hard put to find that to be the genuine significance of that verse in any kind of literal sense. Paul is not really thinking that there must be grace bestowed on all men.
Response: I'm just stating what is said there.

Question: God wills the salvation of all men, and thus he has sent his Son to save the world. But Paul says in other places that unless the gospel of Christ is preached and unless the gospel is believed, all men will not be saved. So God is not providing the salvation of all men in any other way than to send his Son to whom the salvation of the world is owed.

17 [The remaining questions are from the floor.]

Response: Well, that's another view, isn't it? But Paul has to say about charity that there isn't salvation without it; and there is lots of evidence of people leading extremely good lives without being Christians.

Question: But your contention that charity is enough for salvation is one that I think Paul would find hard to swallow. Paul never says charity is enough for salvation; for Paul, it is faith in Jesus that is necessary for salvation. Charity is the most important virtue, the most important response, but charity is not enough for salvation, according to Paul.
Response: Well, perhaps according to Paul. In other words, it's an exegetical question. I was suggesting a line of thought.

Question: So you would not at the moment defend in detail –
Response: I am not doing detailed exegesis.

Question: ... that the Bible would allow for genuine religious consciousness outside of revelation.
Response: Well, people have denied that it does.

Question: But you would not want to take up that question except to assert that your exegesis is different from the one that I'm proposing.
Response: Right.

Question: With regard to the motives why you want to move natural theology over to systematic theology: is it that there are commitment implications to a belief in God? In other words, is there is a notional belief in God as opposed to a real belief in God involving action upon coming to the realization that God exists?
Response: My fundamental reason for effecting the change is that when you have natural theology separate, most students coming to theology will say, 'This is just more philosophy; it isn't religious; we don't want it.' That is a fundamental block in teaching theology. On the other hand, natural theology has a lot to gain from being in the context of a religious theology. And the abstraction that would separate the two is foreign to contemporary modes of thinking. We are not chopping up the world with a set of concepts and keeping it all in separate compartments. The whole purpose is the development of the person, and the more one can put together, the more integrated the person will be.

Question: Returning to the element common to all religion, but taking a different approach: I assume this is the love of God; is that correct?
Response: Yes.

Question: Then does this involve the self-revelation of God to all?
Response: No, except insofar as grace is operative in them.

Question: So you would call this in the old terminology 'supernatural revelation,' rather than simply 'natural revelation.'
Response: Right. It is not complete revelation. It is not Christian revelation, which is something that goes beyond it and brings in a specific difference. There is an intersubjective element to love that is present in Christianity, where God is expressing his love in Christ as well as giving you the grace in your heart; and this element is missing when you haven't got a Christian revelation.

Question: Daniélou has said that the Jewish-Christian revelation presents us with 'God in search of man,' whereas the other world religions speak of 'man in search of God.' Do you accept that?
Response: No. I would say with Pascal, 'You would not be seeking me unless you had already found me.'[18]

Question: God is always searching for man. Can you conceive of man in search of God?
Response: Well, insofar as he is, it is because he has been given God's grace.

Question: He has always been given God's grace?
Response: Yes.

18 [See above, note 10.]

10

Lecture 2: The Functional Specialty 'Systematics'[1]

The title of these lectures is 'The Relationship between the Philosophy of God and the Functional Specialty "Systematics."' We have spoken about the philosophy of God. Our topic here will be the functional specialty 'systematics.' Following that, our concern will be the relationship between the two.

1   Functional Specialization

For the orientation of any that have not read chapter 5 of my book *Method in Theology*,[2] I feel I should say something about functional specialization. Very briefly, then, specialization is of three kinds. There is field specialization that divides the field of data into different parts so that each specialist concentrates on his part of the total field. There is subject specialization that divides the results of investigations into different subjects so that different professors give different courses on different subjects. Finally, there is functional specialization. It divides the process from data to results into different stages. Each stage pursues its own proper end in its own proper manner. The task of a method in theology is to distinguish between these proper ends and determine each of the proper manners of pursuing the proper ends.

The notion of functional specialization may be illustrated by the difference

---

1 [The second of three lectures given by Lonergan at St Michael's Institute, Gonzaga University, Spokane, on 9 December 1972. Divisions, subtitles, and bracketed footnotes are editorial.]
2 [See above, p. 12, note 2.]

between experimental and theoretical physics. Only the experimental physicist can handle the cyclotron. But only the theoretical physicist can decide what experiments seem worth trying, and again, only the theoretical physicist can tell how significant the results of the experiment are.[3] Similarly, the textual critic, the exegete, and the historian work on the same data but they perform quite different tasks. The textual critic studies the various readings found in the many manuscripts and citations in an effort to determine what the original text was. The exegete takes over to determine what the text originally meant. The historian takes over from several exegetes in the hope of arriving at an account of the course of events recounted in the manuscripts.

Now the notion of functional specialization is not entirely new in theology. In the past, people were familiar with the distinction between dogmatic theology, concerned mainly with the doctrines defined by the church, and systematic or Scholastic theology, concerned mainly with the meaning, significance, relevance of church doctrines. To these in more recent centuries were added positive or historical theology to meet the exigences of modern historical mindedness.

From these remarks you will correctly infer that theology is not the same thing as religion. Theology is reflection on religion. It mediates between a religion and a culture. Its function is to bring to light the significance and value of a religion in a given culture. It follows that, even though the religion remains unchanged, still a theology will vary with cultural variations.

So in *Method in Theology* eight functional specialties are distinguished. There is *research* to make available the relevant data. There is *interpretation* to ascertain their proper meaning. There is *history* to determine what was going forward in the past. There is *dialectic* to compare and evaluate the conflicting views of historians, the diverse interpretations of exegetes, the varying emphases of researchers. There is *foundations* that sets forth the horizon, the standpoint, that allows religious affirmations to have meaning and reveal values. There is *doctrines* that on the basis of foundations makes a selection from the alternatives presented by dialectic. There is *systematics* to clarify the meaning of doctrines. Finally, there is *communications*, concerned with the task of preaching and teaching the doctrines to all men in every culture and in every class of each culture.

Of the eight functional specialties our concern here is only with the seventh, systematics. A first question that arises is how the Christian religion

3 [In an aside: 'So the same process with regard to the same data is divided up between two quite different types of specialists.']

ever allowed itself to be involved in systematic thinking; after all, such thinking is not mentioned in the Sermon on the Mount. The answer is, of course, that it did so gradually. Let me briefly recall successive stages in the process.

2   Stages

2.1   The New Testament

In New Testament writings, different layers may be distinguished. According to Reginald Fuller,[4] a first layer corresponds to the gospel as it was preached to Jews that read the Old Testament in their native language. A second layer represents the gospel as it was preached to Jews that read the Old Testament in a Greek translation. A third layer accords with the gospel as it would be preached to Gentiles that did not read the Old Testament at all. What differences resulted, Professor Fuller sets forth in successive chapters. But the point we would make is that the New Testament bears witness to the fact that preaching the gospel to all nations necessitates preaching it differently to different nations. Cultural differences can be overlooked only at the cost of creating misunderstanding and misinterpretation.

Moreover, in the New Testament we also have a first adumbration of the distinction between philosophy of God and the functional specialty 'systematics.' The functional specialty presupposes revelation, as did the Jews that read the Old Testament. Philosophy of God does not use revelation as a logical premise for its conclusions, [and this was the case also with][5] the Gentiles that did not read the Old Testament.

2.2   The Apologists

A further step was taken by the Apologists of the second and third centuries. They had to take into account the pagans that accepted neither the Old Testament nor the New, that misinterpreted Christianity, and persecuted Christians. The Apologists' task was to make clear what Christians really believed and taught. To make it clear to pagans they had to enter into the

4 Reginald H. Fuller, *The Foundations of New Testament Christology* (New York: Charles Scribner's Sons, 1965). [The stage of the New Testament writings is treated in Lonergan's archival typescript, Batch x, File 31, Item 2, pp. 2–3.]
5 [Lonergan's wording is 'as did the Gentiles ...' This is not clear and is subject to misunderstanding. The words substituted and placed in brackets are an editorial addition.]

mind of the pagans, to discern what they would accept as legitimate assumptions, and to proceed from that basis to a clarification of Christian doctrine. If you ask why the Apologists were not content to preach the Sermon on the Mount, the answer is that the gospel can be preached by Christians only if Christians are allowed to exist. Justin Martyr was a second-century Apologist. If one finds it strange that Justin wrote two apologies, at least one can infer from his martyrdom that he had some reason for his writing.[6]

2.3 The Interpretation of Scripture

A third step arose in the interpretation of scripture. The fanciful interpretations proposed by many Gnostics had to be resisted, and the only successful way to resist them was to lay down the principles of a hermeneutics and to apply them. Early in his *Miscellanies*, Clement of Alexandria argued that the liberal arts of the Greeks along with philosophy came from God, and by philosophy he meant not the Stoic or Platonic or Epicurean or Aristotelian school but a selection from them of what was correctly said and of what taught justice along with piety.[7] In the last book of the same work he presented a selection from the liberal arts when he explained how one is to determine the meaning of a text. He began from the gospel precept, 'Ask and you will receive; seek and you will find; knock and the door will be opened' (Matthew 7.7; Luke 11.9). His application was to asking and answering questions relevant to the matter in hand in an orderly fashion without contentiousness or vaingloriousness.[8] He then went on to urge a methodical ordering of the questions asked, the definition of each of the words used, where the definitions were clearer than what they defined and where they were admitted by all. Once the words were defined, one was to determine whether or not any reality corresponded to the words. With that correspondence established, one was to inquire into the object's nature and its qualities. Further notes were added on proofs, signs, analysis, suppositions, genera, differences, species, categories, causes.[9] One has only to read a few

---

6 [See the entry 'Justin Martyr' in *The Oxford Dictionary of the Christian Church*, ed. F.L. Cross and E.A. Livingstone (2nd ed., London: Oxford University Press, 1974) 770.]

7 Clement of Alexandria, *Stromata* I, c. 7, 37, 1.6, in *PG* 8, 731 B and D, and in Stählin's edition (see above, p. 100, note 40) II, 24–25.

8 *Stromata*, VIII, 1 ff.; *PG* 9, 558 ff.; Stählin III, 80–81.

9 *PG* 9, 562 ff.; Stählin III, 81–82.

samples of Gnostic exegesis to see that Clement had found the tool that would cut short many an endless disputation.[10]

2.4 The Apprehension of God

A fourth step regarded one's apprehension of God. The pre-Socratic thinker Xenophanes had criticized the anthropomorphic gods of the Greeks and had remarked that, were they able to carve or paint, lions, horses, and oxen would represent their gods in their own image. The point was not lost on Clement of Alexandria, who urged Christians to interpret not literally but allegorically the anthropomorphisms of the Bible.[11] 'Let no one think, even though it is written in scripture, that the Father of all stands up and sits down, gets angry and repents, has a right hand and a left,' and so on. But if Christians were not to take the Bible literally, then they had to have recourse to some other source for their notion of God. For them this was no easy matter. Unless people are initiated philosophically, and not always then, they are unaware of the differences between the infant's world of immediacy and the adult's world mediated by meaning. Spontaneously they adopt the position of the naive realist with its materialistic implications. Readily they ask with Tertullian, Who will say that God is not a body? He wouldn't be real if he was not a body.[12] Or with Irenaeus they conceive the omnipotent as the one that contains all the rest.[13] Or with Clement of Alexandria's *Excerpta ex Theodoto* (*Excerpts from Theodotus*), they will argue that God the Father has a shape because the angels of little children contemplate his face and because the pure of heart will see him.[14] Again, because he who sees me sees the Father, they conclude that the Son is the face of the Father.[15] Further, since the devils suffer they must have bodies;

10 See for example Irenaeus, *Adversus Haereses*, I, 3, 1.2; I, 3, 6; I, 8, 4; William W. Harvey, *S. Irenaei ... libri V adversus haereses*, I, 24–26; 30–31; 73–75.
11 Clement of Alexandria, *Stromata* v, c. 11, 68, 3; v, c. 11, 71, 4; *PG* 9, 103 B and 110 A; Stählin II, 371, lines 18–22 and 374, lines 15–17. On Clement's interpretation of Xenophanes, see Bruno Snell, *The Discovery of the Mind: The Greek Origins of European Thought* (see above, p. 102, note 46) 142.
12 *Tertullian's Treatise against Praxeas*, 7, ed. Ernest Evans (London: Society for Promoting Christian Knowledge, 1948) 96, and see the note on pp. 234–36. Also Michel Spanneut, *Le Stoïcisme des pères de l'église, De Clément de Rome à Clément d'Alexandrie* (Paris: Editions du Seuil, 1957).
13 Irenaeus, *Adversus Haereses*, II, 1, 5; Harvey, I, 253–54.
14 Clement of Alexandria, *Excerpta ex Theodoto*, 11. Editions by Robert P. Casey (London: Christophers, 1934) 48–50, and by François Sagnard, *Sources chrétiennes* 23 (Paris: Editions du Cerf, 1948) 80–83.
15 Ibid. 12 [Casey 50, Sagnard 83–85].

angels are said to be without bodies only inasmuch as their bodies are less crass than ours; even the human soul is a body, otherwise Lazarus would be unable to dip his finger into water and place a drop on the tongue of the rich man in hell.[16]

In brief, ancient Christian writers had philosophic problems, and gradually they discovered their existence. Irenaeus could conceive God in the Old Testament narrative style as the creator of heaven and earth, the producer of the garden of Eden, the author of the deluge, the God of Abraham, Isaac, and Jacob, and eventually the Father of Jesus Christ, the Lord of the universe.[17] But he was aware in implicit fashion that, besides faith, there are also the preambles of faith. So he praised Justin Martyr because, in his book against Marcion, he had stated that he would not believe Christ if Christ had announced some god other than the creator and lord of all things.[18] So it was that Clement of Alexandria set about explaining how one should conceive God by abstracting from everything corporeal.[19] So Origen allied himself with the Middle Platonism to insist on the strict spirituality of the divine hypostases, of the angels, and of human souls.[20] It was a revision of the biblical notion of God that entailed a revision of the biblical notion of Christ, and brought on the controversies with Arians, Nestorians, and Monophysites, the emergence of a distinctive Christian apprehension of reality that had not been anticipated by Platonists or Aristotelians, Stoics or Gnostics.[21]

2.5   The Middle Ages

Though much profound thinking was expressed by the writers of the patristic

---

16 Ibid. 14 [Casey 52A, Sagnard 86–87].

17 Irenaeus, *Adversus Haereses*, II, 30, 9; Harvey, I, 368.

18 Irenaeus, *Adversus Haereses*, IV, 6, 2; Harvey, II, 158–59. [In an aside: 'Marcion considered the God of the OT wicked, the source of the evils in the world; the good God was the God of Jesus Christ.']

19 Clement of Alexandria, *Stromata* V, c. 11, 71, 2.3.5; V, c. 12, 81, 5 ff.; in *PG* 9, 102B ff.; 115B ff.; Stählin, II, 370–74 and 377–83.

20 Origen, *De principiis*, Book 1, chapter 1; Koetschau [see above, p. 103, note 49] 16–27; *In Ioannem commentarii*, IV, 21 ff.; E. Preuschen, 244 ff. But note the qualifications in *De principiis*, Book 2, chapter 2; Koetschau 81–82.

21 Bernard Lonergan, 'The Origins of Christian Realism,' *Theology Digest* 20 (1972) 292–305; reprinted in *A Second Collection* (see above, p. 22, note 12) 239–61. [There is also an earlier paper with the same name that makes a similar point, now published as 'The Origins of Christian Realism (1961),' in *Philosophical and Theological Papers 1958–1964* (see above, p. 111, note 5) 80–93.]

era, it remains that theology did not seriously aspire to be systematic until the Middle Ages. Nor was that aspiration arbitrary. It arose out of the inner exigences of the situation. Theologians read; they were puzzled; they asked questions. Their reading was facilitated by anthologies, by books of Sentences, by commentaries. Their questioning became an organized and ongoing procedure. Peter Abelard in his *Sic et non* had argued from scripture, from patristic writings, and from reason that each of one hundred and fifty-eight theological propositions should be both affirmed and denied. Gilbert of Porrée advanced that there existed a question in theology when one proved from authority or from reason that the same proposition should be both affirmed and denied. This released a grand program of reconciliation. First, the existence of the question was to be proved by listing first the arguments against a proposition (*Videtur quod non ...*) and then the arguments in its favor (*Sed contra est ...*). Secondly, general principles of solution were to be presented (*Respondeo dicendum quod ...*). Finally, the general principles were to be applied to each of the arguments alleged in proving the existence of the question (*Ad 1m, Ad 2m ...*).

The question, accordingly, was a technique for reconciling differing authorities in matters of faith and apparent oppositions between faith and reason. It could be applied to random issues, as in the Quodlibetal Disputations, when the master undertook to resolve any question that was raised. It could be applied to an orderly series of questions on a single topic, for example, to all the questions concerned with truth or power or evil (*De veritate, De potentia, De malo*). It could be applied to all the questions that arose in reading a classified set of quotations from scriptural or patristic writings, such as were Peter Lombard's *Libri quattuor sententiarum*, four books of sentences, four books of the opinions of the Fathers. Finally, it could be applied to all the questions that arose in an account of the whole of Christian doctrine, as in Thomas Aquinas's *Summa theologiae*.

However, the larger the scale of the operations, the graver became a fresh problem. How was one to make sure that the many principles of solution that were proposed were themselves free from contradiction?[22] The one obvious solution was to derive one's principles of solution from some system. If the system was coherent, the solutions too would be coherent. If the system lacked coherence, this lack would be magnified in the solutions, and this magnification would lead to a correction of the system.

---

22 [In an aside: 'There'd be hardly any use eliminating the contradictions in the sources if the work of eliminating introduced new contradictions.']

Now the simplest manner of moving from a commonsense to a systematic differentiation of consciousness is to adopt and perhaps also adapt a system that already exists. So it was that medieval theologians found in Arabic and Greek thinkers models for imitation and adaptation. Of these the most influential turned out to be Aristotle.

Still, one cannot move from commonsense to systematic thinking without creating a crisis. One is introducing a new technical language, a new mode of formulating one's convictions and beliefs, a new mode of intellectual development, a new mode of verification. Automatically there is formed a new social group that understands the new technical language, that is expert in transposing from prior to later modes of expression, that is raising new questions and solving them in a new way. Automatically there also is formed a far larger social group that greets the new movement with incomprehension.

It happened that the spokesmen for the new group were largely Dominicans while those for the old ways were Franciscans. And towards the end of the thirteenth century, there was a knockdown controversy. John Peckham, who became Archbishop of Canterbury in 1272, wrote to Rome that the doctrines of the two Orders were opposed to each other on every debatable point, that one of these Orders set aside and to some extent belittled the teachings of the saints, that it relied almost entirely on philosophic dogmas.[23] This, of course, was a plausible view from a commonsense viewpoint.[24] But what was going on, as subsequent judgment would have it, was quite different. Aquinas did not set Augustine aside or belittle him; he revered him, and his later works are more fully and accurately Augustinian than his earlier ones. Again, Aquinas did not derive his religious doctrine from Aristotle; he derived his religious doctrine from the Christian tradition, but he used Aristotle, partly as a master and partly as a quarry, to construct a systematic presentation of Christian doctrine.

It is probable enough that thirteenth-century theologians could not have done better than turn to Aristotle for help. It remains that Aristotle had his limitations. He conceived science as a deduction of conclusions from necessary first principles. He believed such principles could be reached empirically after the fashion in which a rout ends in a rally; when one man makes a

---

23 Franz Ehrle, 'John Peckham über den Kampf des Augustinismus und Aristotelismus in der zweiten Hälfte des 13. Jahrhunderts,' *Zeitschrift für katholische Theologie* 13 (1889) 181. The relevant passage from Peckham has been quoted in my *De Deo trino* (Rome: Gregorian University Press, 1964) in the *Pars systematica*, at p. 49.
24 [In an aside: 'that didn't know what was going on.']

stand, others join him, and still more come to his side.[25] But if this is a good illustration of the way in which insights accumulate and cluster to generate a discovery, still what is discovered is not a necessary truth but a postulate or a hypothesis. Moreover, Aristotle wanted the basic terms and relations of the sciences to be further determinations of the basic terms and relations of metaphysics. He was not sufficiently on his guard against a tendency to attempt to transform a commonsense meaning into a systematic meaning by adding the qualifier 'as such,' *qua tale, kath' hauto.* Finally, he was quite unacquainted with relatively recent scholarship in hermeneutics and in history.

Let us now attempt a thumbnail sketch of subsequent developments. Ecclesiastical decrees in Paris and Canterbury banned the constructive genius of Thomas Aquinas, who had operated within the methodical mold of *lectio* and *quaestio* (of reading and question), a genuinely scientific method that arose and was developed spontaneously in the High Middle Ages. Aquinas took *lectio* seriously. He wrote commentaries on numerous books in the Old and New Testaments, on many of Aristotle's works, on the pseudo-Dionysius, on Al Farabi, in whose writing he recognized a re-presentation of the *Elementatio theologica* of Proclus, a neo-Platonist. His familiarity with the whole of Aristotle protected him from any illusions that might be generated by the *Posterior Analytics.* In his *Contra Gentiles* he distinguished between matters in which both faith and reason could have a say and others in which faith alone was the issue. The former were treated in the first three books, and they included man's naturally desired end, the beatific vision, and the external and internal means to that end, the law and the gift of grace. Things on which only faith could say something were treated in the fourth book; they were the Trinity, the Incarnation, original sin, and the sacraments. In the first three books not only demonstrative but also probable arguments were to be employed. In the fourth book the objections of adversaries were to be resolved, and probable arguments were to be adduced to confirm the faithful in their beliefs.[26]

When one turns from this cool implementation of faith's search for understanding, an understanding that may be certain or merely probable, to the writings of John Duns Scotus or William of Ockham, one finds oneself in a quite different world. They were by-products of the Augustinian-Aristotelian conflict. They accepted Aristotle's logical works. His other writings they disregarded as merely pagan. In consequence they took the *Posterior Analytics*

---

25 Aristotle, *Posterior Analytics*, I, 2, 71b 8–12; II, 19, 100a 11–13.
26 Thomas Aquinas, *Summa contra Gentiles*, 1, c. 13, § 3.

at face value. Their basic concern was whether or not this or that issue could be settled demonstratively. When that approach combined with questions on what could be done by God's absolute power, the one way to certitude was through the principle of noncontradiction. Absolutely, God could do anything that did not involve a contradiction. There is no contradiction between the occurrence of a hallucination and the absence of the hallucinated object.[27]

But the Augustinian-Aristotelian conflict left its mark on all schools. Fr Congar has expressed surprise that Scotist vocabulary became the vocabulary of subsequent Scholasticism.[28] But clarity and rigor, though they may convey little understanding, at least are great advantages in a debate, and it was the debate that aroused interest and passion. Today with our concern for sources we may be amazed that Capreolus wrote his commentary, not on the Lombard's *Sentences* (which was a collection, a source book on scripture and the Fathers), but on Aquinas's commentary on the Lombard's *Sentences*. Still stranger was Cajetan's commentary on the purely systematic work, the *Summa theologiae* of Aquinas. Theology seemed to be painting itself into a corner, to be getting away from its sources and just discussing systems.

2.6 The Reformation

A new orientation arose from the Reformation and from humanism. Out of the Reformation came the Counter-Reformation, the Council of Trent, and Bellarmine's *De controversiis*. Humanism gave us Melchior Cano's *De locis theologicis*. He insisted on a return to sources. Theology was to consist in a set of medieval doctrines to be proved by an appeal to scriptural and patristic writings, to the councils and the consensus of theologians, and from *ratio theologica* (theological reason), which sought to transform the ancient *fides quaerens intellectum* (faith seeking understanding) into an argument that somehow did not prove. Perhaps more than a century passed before Cano's *De locis* became dominant, but his influence has extended right into the twentieth century.

27 Frederick Copleston, *A History of Philosophy*, vol. 3, part 1 (Garden City, NY: Doubleday, 1963) 77. See DS 1033, 1948. [In an aside: 'and how do you know that you are not living in that sort of world?']
28 Yves Congar, *A History of Theology*, ed. and trans. Hunter Guthrie (Garden City, NY: Doubleday, 1968) 130–31.

2.7 The Modern Period

Melchior Cano died in 1560, and his *De locis* was published posthumously. But in the last four hundred years the notions of science, of philosophy, and of scholarship have radically changed. Where Aristotle conceived science as a permanent acquisition of truth, our contemporaries conceive it as an ever fuller understanding of the data, and so an ever closer approximation to truth. Where Aristotle conceived philosophy as basically a metaphysics whence all other disciplines derived their basic terms and basic relations, philosophy today, at least in my opinion, is basically a cognitional theory whence all other disciplines are able to derive an explicit account of their methods. Where Aristotle had only a perfunctory notion of hermeneutics and no serious concern for history, our contemporaries are eminent in the practice both of hermeneutics and of history.

It is the development of modern hermeneutics and history that has forced Catholic theology out of the manualist tradition, the tradition that goes back to Melchior Cano. The old-style dogmatic theologian was expected to establish a series of propositions or theses, from the Old Testament and the New, from patristic writings and the consensus of theologians, and from *ratio theologica*. But modern scholarship set up an endless array of specialists between the dogmatic theologian and his sources. With the specialists the dogmatic theologian just could not compete. Without an appeal to his sources, the dogmatic theologian had nothing to say. Such has been a basic and, as well, a most palpable element in the crisis of contemporary Roman Catholic theology. Along with the changes in the notion of science and the notion of philosophy, this change has been my motive in devoting years to working out a method in theology.

3   Philosophy of God in Theology

It is only on the basis of a full understanding and a complete acceptance of the developments in the contemporary notions of science, philosophy, and scholarship that my account of the functional specialty 'systematics' can be understood. Similarly, it is only on the basis of a full acceptance of the developments in contemporary notions of science, philosophy, and scholarship that there can be understood, let alone accepted, my proposal that philosophy of God be taught by theologians in a department of theology.

My aim, of course, is not to disqualify philosophers from teaching or speaking about God. My aim is to qualify theologians for a task that once was theirs, that subsequently ceased to be theirs, and once more I believe should become theirs.[29]

The reason for this belief is that changes in the notion of science, philosophy, scholarship, and theology require adjustments. Former views were Aristotelian. They took for granted that the basic discipline was metaphysics and that other disciplines had to derive their basic terms and relations by adding further determinations to the basic terms and relations of metaphysics. The result is a cosmology that no longer exists and a faculty psychology that is pretty well discredited. They took for granted that each discipline had its field defined by a material object and its approach defined by a formal object. They conceived theology as a science about God and about all other things in their relation to God. They were taken by surprise by modern methods in exegesis and in history and put up a protracted resistance to them.

That resistance has ended. But there are other, no less important changes. The basic discipline, I believe, is not metaphysics but cognitional theory. By cognitional theory is meant, not a faculty psychology that presupposes a metaphysics, but an intentionality analysis that presupposes the data of consciousness. From the cognitional theory there can be derived an epistemology, and from both the cognitional theory and the epistemology there can be derived a metaphysics. These three are related to all other disciplines, not by supplying them with elements for their basic terms and relations, but by providing the nucleus for the formulation of their methods. Instead of speaking of material objects one speaks of data or fields, and instead of speaking of formal objects one simply applies to the data the operations prescribed by the method. While theology used to be defined as the science about God, today I believe it is to be defined as reflection on the significance and value of a religion in a culture. From this view of theology it follows that theology is not some one system valid for all times and places, as the Aristotelian and Thomist notion of system assumes, but as manifold as are the many cultures within which a religion has significance and value.

The proposal, then, that philosophy of God be treated along with the functional specialty 'systematics' does not stand alone. It is not a proposal that presupposes the notion of philosophy presented to me as a student forty-five years ago or the notion of theology presented to me as a student thirty-eight

29 [In an aside: 'Not only in Aquinas but in Scotus and Ockham, you have no separation; you have a distinction between philosophy and theology, but no separation.']

years ago. On the contrary, its suppositions are a radical revision of those notions. There is supposed a notion of science based, not on the extra-scientific notions of science assumed by modern scientists, but on the analysis of scientific practice presented, for example, in my work *Insight*. There is supposed a notion of philosophy that is in accord with the achievements of modern science, that can ground the methods of modern science, that does not attempt to dominate science by telling it what its basic terms and relations must be. There is supposed a notion of theology that integrates a religion with the culture in which it functions, that conceives the formal object of a theology by stating its method, that integrates within theology and its method what formerly were conceived as merely auxiliary disciplines.

Textual criticism and the edition and indexing of texts used to be considered as merely auxiliary disciplines, but in *Method in Theology* they are regarded as the functional specialty 'research.' Exegesis once was considered to be an auxiliary discipline, but in *Method in Theology* it is regarded as the functional specialty 'interpretation.' History once was considered an auxiliary discipline, but in *Method in Theology* it is regarded as the functional specialty 'history.' Doctrines regarding the divine legate, the church, the inspiration of scripture once were considered to be fundamental theology, but in *Method in Theology* these doctrines along with all others are included in the functional specialty 'doctrines,' while their foundational function has been handed over to the evaluations and decisions of the functional specialties 'dialectic' and 'foundations.' Philosophy used to be regarded as the *ancilla theologiae*, the handmaid of theology; it happens, however, that the handmaid for some centuries has gone in for women's liberation, and so in *Method in Theology* the philosophy that the theologian needs is included in the first four chapters, on Method, The Human Good, Meaning, and Religion. Finally, what in Aquinas were considered probable arguments for the truths of faith, or reasons for confirming Christians in their faith, in a later age became proofs from theological reason. In *Method in Theology* they are placed in the functional specialty 'systematics,' and its function is not to prove but to endeavor to find some understanding of the propositions established as true in the preceding functional specialty 'doctrines.'

I have mentioned these differences to obviate objections. My proposal to unify philosophy of God and the functional specialty 'systematics' is not compatible with what everyone used to hold about textual criticism, exegesis, history, fundamental theology, philosophy, and theological reason. My proposal is compatible with quite different views. And it is only the latter compatibility that I can defend.

Question:[30] Cannot man by his own volition and free will separate himself from the love of God?

Response: Yes, he can. Connected with it is one of the fundamental problems on grace. His separating himself of his own free will from the love of God is simple fact. But it is not explicable, for sin is an irrational; there is no explanation of why he does it. It is just revolt; but it can happen.

Question (continued): Can the denial of existence render existence invalid? That is, can the absolute refusal on the part of such a man to accept the existence of God in fact render the power of God's love impotent?

Response: A person can be confused. If his negation of God's existence is that he can't prove it, or that the notion of God presented to him is not a satisfactory notion and he is rebelling against that unsatisfactory notion, he can be what Rahner would call an 'anonymous Christian,' a person who is in the state of grace but doesn't express himself the way people in the state of grace usually do. In other words, God's gift of his love is just that. It leads to a transformation in life, but more on the order of practice than on the order of intellectual knowledge. There are interpretations, for example, of Buddhism that consider that their atheism really isn't atheism at all, that they are mystics and they have no way of expressing their mystical experience except by denying the existence of God. This question can be extremely complex. We must not expect people's lives – concrete living – to be coherent. It's a tendency towards coherence.

Question (continued): Can a man's refusal bring the power of God's love to a screeching halt?

Response: Insofar as it is sinful. He is refusing God's love and its advantages.

Question (continued): So where he exists there is sort of a blank?

Response: Well, no. It is just that he is not acknowledging God's existence. He no longer has the gift of God's love. It is the opposition: being in the state of grace and being in the state of mortal sin.

---

30 [For the first twenty minutes or so of the question period, written questions that had been submitted were read by Fr Tim Fallon, s.j., and Fr Bill Ryan, s.j. The person who submitted the question had an option to pursue it further. These questions were not on the lecture topic, but were the result of discussions on the first lecture.]

Question (continued): That is not rendering God's love impotent?
Response: No, that is not the proper way to put it. If you don't want to love in return, that at least for the moment ends that initiative on God's part. There is this mysterious thing sin, as well as this mysterious thing God's grace, and they are opposites.

Question: Is not the plucking out of the heart of stone in religious conversion a two-sided affair? The man must want it or it can't happen?
Response: If it happens, the man will want it, simply because his heart is a heart of flesh. The man that didn't want it is the man who had a heart of stone. And that is the doctrine of the priority of God's grace.

Question (continued): Can it remain a heart of stone if God plucks it?
Response: Not then and there, no, if it has occurred. But God can do it and the man can refuse it. Then you have the surd of sin coming in.

Question: You say in your lecture[31] that 'being in love does not presuppose or depend on any apprehension of God.' In *Method in Theology* you cite Karl Rahner's statement to the effect that 'consolation without a cause' means 'consolation with a content but without an object' (p. 106, n. 4). Could you explain more precisely what this content without an object is?
Response: The content is a dynamic state of being in love, and being in love without restriction. It is conscious but it is not known. What it refers to is something that can be inferred insofar as you make it advance from being merely conscious to being known. And then because it is unrestricted, you can infer that it refers to an absolute being. But the gift of itself does not include these ulterior steps. They are further steps. And consequently this content without a known object is an occurrence, a fundamental occurrence, the ultimate stage in a person's self-transcendence. It is God's free gift. It involves a transvaluation of values in your living, but it is not something produced by knowing. It is going beyond your present horizon; it is taking you beyond your present horizon.

Question (continued): There would be no insight, no concept, no judgment?
Response: Not of itself, no. You can say it is on the fifth level. It is self-transcendence reaching its summit, and that summit can be developed and enriched, and so on. But of itself it is permanent.

31 [The reference is to the first lecture. See above, p. 170.]

Question: Can mystical works such as St John of the Cross's *Spiritual Canticle* and *Living Flame of Love* be said to be the result of insight, since they are not the content of mystical experience but the content of reason seeking to articulate what transcends pure speculative understanding? In other words, do insights occur on the notional, speculative level when the intellect tries to express what the soul has experienced mystically? In terms of chapter 19 of *Insight* ('General Transcendent Knowledge') how could insights be said *not* to occur when reason attempts to formulate in language the content of mystical experience of the transcendent?

Response: There is mystical experience of the transcendent. There is the effort to say what is happening, to find out what is happening: 'Am I going nuts?' People with that experience are profoundly disturbed, and they can be very apprehensive.

Question (continued): But in that case you're objectifying. You said previously you had a content without an object. Aren't you making an object out of content now?

Response: Yes, you are discovering it. There isn't an already apprehended object. But you can find the object by reflecting, and that reflection involves insight, and so on. Writing the *Living Flame of Love* or the *Spiritual Canticle* is like any other writing – a matter of experience and understanding and judgment and verbal creativity. But that doesn't mean that the mystical experience itself is that. It is one thing to have the experience. It is another thing to describe it and express it and talk about it and evaluate it.

Question: You identify three questions that one might ask. Cognitional theory: What are you doing when you are knowing? Epistemology: why is doing that knowing? Metaphysics: What do you know when you do it? How does question 2 differ from question 1? It would seem to add nothing. Is it not the same to ask: What are you doing when you are knowing? and to ask: Why is doing that knowing?

Response: After you have answered the first question, knowing has taken on a different meaning. It means performing this set of operations. Why is performing this set of operations something relevant to knowing an independent reality? Why are the immanent criteria in your operations – the requirement to attend, to be intelligent, to be reasonable – what on earth have they to do with my ability to know something that is totally different from myself? That is the epistemological problem. We talk about knowing, but what precisely happens when one is doing mathematics, when one is doing empirical science, when one is using one's common sense? Those are the questions in cognitional theory. The epistemological question is why these operations possess any relevance to knowing. And here you get another question about knowledge: the validity of knowledge. The first is concerned with what occurs, the occurrence, an accurate account of what occurs when you are coming to know. You next reflect on that series of occurrences and ask, 'Is that really knowledge? Is it valid?' – the question that was raised by Descartes and Kant, and so on. The third question goes beyond the other two: What is the basic heuristic structure of everything that you are going to know?

Question: In doing natural theology, a great deal of time was spent on the proofs of the existence of God. Since you stress that it is conversion and not proof which is most crucial for the Christian, and since you are putting natural theology within the specialty 'systematics,' whose aim is not to prove anything, does the idea of actually trying to prove the existence of God really make any sense in our contemporary culture?
Response: The objection is very logical. The whole idea of method is that we take all the means to attain an end. When I propose that philosophy of God be included, be taken along with systematics, I don't mean that it has ceased to be philosophy of God. I mean that the two cooperate, reinforce one another, have a common origin and a common goal. It is a performative unity; it is not a logical unity. It is not systematics dictating to philosophy of God or philosophy of God dictating to systematics. But it is mutual support, mutual clarification, each doing its own thing but at the same time helping the other.

Question (continued): Won't the proofs that you work out through reason in natural theology seem pale compared to the conviction you already have through conversion?
Response: The thing is that proof is never the fundamental thing. Proof always presupposes premises, and it presupposes premises accurately formulated within a horizon. You can never prove a horizon. You arrive at it from a different horizon, by going beyond the previous one, because you have found something that makes the previous horizon illegitimate. But growth in knowledge is precisely that. There are proofs for the existence of God. I formulated them as best I could in chapter 19 in *Insight*, and I'm not repudiating that at all. But I say it is not a matter of comparing the two; it is using the resources of both. It is not letting the student of theology brush aside all systematic theology because 'that's just more philosophy and we have wasted enough time on that already.' Similarly, there would be the

theologian brushing aside philosophy because 'that doesn't presuppose the scriptures.'

Question (continued): Or a convinced Christian brushing aside both?
Response: Yes.

Question:[32] You said you were going to speak about some of the problems of the philosophy of God. What is God?
Response: It is something that most people know about. St Thomas has five arguments for the existence of God. One is from the first Mover: he proves there is a first Mover, and he says that is what everyone means by God. He is presupposing a notion of God. And he does it for the second argument and for the third; he has something different for the fourth and the fifth. He identifies the conclusion with what everyone considers to be God. That, to my mind, is the fundamental notion of God, and it is resulting from God's gift of his love.

Now you can go on and ask further questions on the basis of that knowledge, and you can proceed to answering those questions, either along the lines of philosophy of God, natural theology, or along the lines of systematic theology. And the two are complementary. Take Thomas's theological *Summa.* There he treats God as one (questions 2 to 26); in questions 30 to 43 he treats God as three persons. But in questions 27 to 29, he is preparing the fundamental elements of his trinitarian doctrine about God. He asks, 'Are there processions in God? Are there relations in God? Are these relations persons?' He is effecting the transition out of a natural theology into a systematic theology.

The two just marvelously fit together, and to want to pull them apart just creates repetitions. You can do philosophy of God in a philosophy department for people who aren't going to do theology later on. But if people are going to do theology, too, I would say, why break that up? That is my point.

Question: You have spoken of 'primitive language.' You are approaching it from a very philosophical standpoint. Most anthropologists would say that what you say is objectively wrong.
Response: My source is *Philosophy of Symbolic Forms* by Cassirer.

Question (continued): He is not an anthropologist. If you approach this particular problem which you're dealing with in these lectures in a purely

32 [At this point the questions were thrown open to the floor.]

philosophical way and ignore the social sciences, aren't you at the very same time undermining the theory of conceptualization?

Response: The fundamental issue is to form notions about language so that you will have the tools, the models, when you come to do the empirical side of the study. There is an intelligibility that can be reached that way. It eliminates an awful lot of occult entities that obfuscate thinking. You will find that point elaborated in the last section of my third chapter, on Meaning, in *Method in Theology*. It is not at all a matter of brushing these people aside; it is to set up a heuristic structure within which specialists in different fields can construct models that will help people enter into mentalities quite different from their own. Simple description does not suffice. There are fundamental tools that underlie language and that account for differences in languages and in the development of languages. The empirical study can be helped by this, or you can start from the empirical and move up to it. But if you move up to it, you will move not into speculative philosophy, but cognitional theory.

Question: How would you define sin?

Response: Mortal sin at the present time among moral theologians is, I believe, conceived in terms of fundamental options. There are fundamental options that are a turning against yourself, and against God, and against your neighbor. And that is what is meant by sin.

Question (continued): What is the criterion for knowing what to do?

Response: The criterion for a value judgment is that it occurs in a virtuous person who pronounces a judgment with a good conscience. If you are vicious, you may have a good conscience when making a bad judgment. But if you are virtuous, you will have a bad conscience if you make a bad judgment. Such briefly is the criterion. I treat judgments of value in the second chapter, on the Human Good, in *Method in Theology*.

Question: What about the criterion of a good conscience?

Response: The good conscience means that, when you listen to an explanation, either you are satisfied or you put further questions. The satisfaction that comes with the act of understanding (or the dissatisfaction when you find the understanding inadequate) is something that is immediate. Similarly, you ought to make a judgment. Metaphorically you marshal and weigh the evidence. There is a more technical expression of that in the tenth chapter of *Insight*, but you know when your evidence is sufficient. A man comes home. He had left his beautiful home in the morning, everything in perfect order, and he finds windows broken, water on the floor, smoke in the air. If he says, 'Something happened,' he knows he is absolutely right. If he says, 'There was a fire,' well, all of this could have been faked. And if he sees that, he won't say, 'There must have been a fire' – that is only a highly probable judgment. And similarly, the judgment of value in a good person reveals its truth insofar as it occurs with a good conscience and reveals its weakness by an uneasy conscience. Objectivity is the fruit of authentic subjectivity, all along the line. Insofar as you are attentive, intelligent, reasonable, responsible, you will also be objective. They are the criteria. If you want to have something else, you will box yourself up in some corner.

11

Lecture 3: The Relationship between Philosophy of God and the Functional Specialty 'Systematics'[1]

There are two issues. First, there is the basic issue of the viewpoint to be assumed in this discussion. Secondly, once the basic issue is settled, there is the detailed issue of working towards an account of the relationship between philosophy of God and the functional specialty 'systematics.'

1   Static and Dynamic Viewpoints

The basic issue is between a static and a dynamic viewpoint. If the viewpoint is static, then from the very start everything really is settled. Nothing new can be added at any point after one has started. On the other hand, if the viewpoint is dynamic, then there can be added any number of reflections and discoveries that at the start were not included in one's assumptions.

The static viewpoint is the ideal of deductivist logic. One determines one's basic terms and relations. One determines how further terms and relations may be derived from the basic terms and relations. One sets forth one's postulates. One determines rules for valid inference. From this starting point, as a fixed basis, one proceeds.[2] But all that one can discover is what one has

---

1 [This is the third and last lecture of a series given by Lonergan at St Michael's Institute, Gonzaga University, Spokane. The lecture was delivered on 10 December 1972. Divisions, subtitles, and bracketed footnotes are editorial.]

2 [In an aside, 'If you want to change the basis, you're setting up another system. You're dropping one and setting up another one. Everything you're going to get in this system is already implicitly present in the system. And

already settled implicitly, for any conclusion one reaches must already be implicit in one's premises or else the result of faulty reasoning.

The dynamic viewpoint, on the contrary, is a moving viewpoint. One starts from what one already knows or thinks one knows. One advances by learning what others have discovered, and perhaps occasionally one may discover something for oneself. No limits are placed on what others or one oneself may discover. One's goal is not settled in advance. One may guess or make predictions, but it is not impossible that the guesses or predictions may prove mistaken.

Now this distinction between a static and a dynamic viewpoint is cardinal in our inquiry. If a static viewpoint is assumed to be the relevant viewpoint, then one has to conclude that philosophy of God and the functional specialty 'systematics' are bound to be not only distinct but also separate. For if the static viewpoint is adopted, then both philosophy of God and the functional specialty 'systematics' must be constructed in accord with the ideal of deductivist logic. But philosophy of God and the functional specialty 'systematics' cannot form one and the same deductivist system. For one and the same deductivist system either does or does not have premises derived from revealed religion. If it does, then philosophy of God is eliminated; and if it does not, then the functional specialty 'systematics' is eliminated. It would seem, therefore, that if you mean to unite philosophy of God and the functional specialty 'systematics' into a single deductivist system, then you are attempting the impossible.

But what is not possible from a static viewpoint may very well be possible from a dynamic viewpoint. The philosophy of God and the functional specialty 'systematics' may have something in common in their origin and in their goal; each may go its separate way and yet, at the same time, each may borrow from the other and reinforce the other. While their procedures differ, this does not imply that they must be kept in different departments, treated by different professors, expounded in different books. While they cannot have the unity of a single deductivist process, they may very well have the unity of a single collaborative process.

Some, no doubt, may feel that to be content with a dynamic viewpoint and unity is to desert the notion of science properly so-called. But while I would grant that it does desert a narrow reading of Aristotle's *Posterior Analytics*, I think many would hesitate to agree that that narrow reading possesses any

----

that's the reason why it's static.' Lonergan's understanding of the logical deductivist ideal is presented in some detail in part 1 of *Phenomenology and Logic* (CWL 18).]

positive significance in the context of modern science, modern scholarship, or modern philosophy. Indeed, it would seem that only the older generation of contemporary theologians have any acquaintance with Aristotle's *Posterior Analytics* either in a narrow reading or in the more intelligent reading that takes into account Aristotle's practice and even theory in his other works.

Indeed, if one accepts the theorem propounded by Kurt Gödel,[3] one will conclude with him that realizations of the deductivist ideal are either trivial or incomplete or incoherent. They are trivial when their content is largely tautologous. They are incomplete when they lead to contradictory alternatives which they cannot resolve. They are incoherent when they demonstrate both the affirmation and the negation of the same proposition.

In brief, like the mortician, the logician achieves a steady state only temporarily. The mortician prevents not the ultimate but only the immediate decomposition of the corpse. In similar fashion, the logician brings about not the clarity, the coherence, and the rigor that will last forever but only the clarity, the coherence, and the rigor that will bring to light the inadequacy of current views and thereby give rise to the discovery of a more adequate position.

The shift from the static to the dynamic viewpoint relativizes logic and emphasizes method. It relativizes logic. It recognizes to the fullest extent the value of the clarity, coherence, and rigor that logic brings about. But it does not consider logic's achievement to be permanent. On the contrary, it considers it to be recurrent. Human knowledge can be constantly advancing, and the function of logic is to hasten that advance by revealing clearly, coherently, and rigorously the deficiencies of current achievement.

I have said that the shift from the static to the dynamic viewpoint not only relativizes logic but also emphasizes method. For it is method that shows the way from the logically clear, coherent, and rigorous position of today to the quite different but logically clear, coherent, and rigorous position of tomorrow.

Method, however, can be conceived in quite different manners. Method can be thought of as a set of recipes that can be observed by a blockhead yet lead infallibly to astounding discoveries. Such a notion of method I consider sheer illusion. The function of method is to spell out for each discipline the implications of the transcendental precepts: Be attentive, Be intelligent, Be reasonable, Be responsible. Nor does the explicitness of method make the occurrence of discoveries infallible. The most it can achieve is to make discoveries more probable. The greater the number of investigators following

3 [See Lonergan's presentation of Gödel's theorem and of Gödelian limitations, ibid. 49–62.]

a sound method, the greater the likelihood that someone will attend to the data that are significant. The greater the likelihood of attention focusing on the data that are significant in the solution of current problems, the greater the likelihood that the intelligent hypothesis will be proposed. The greater the likelihood of the intelligent hypothesis being proposed, the greater the likelihood of there being worked out the proper series of experiments to check and verify the hypothesis.

I have been contrasting a static and a dynamic viewpoint, and I have been bringing the two together in a higher unity by urging that logic brings to each successive discovery the clarity, coherence, and rigor that will reveal the inadequacy of the discovery, while method shows the way from one discovery to the next. But while logic and method do enter into a higher functional unity, nonetheless a position that rests solely on the logical deductivist ideal without any awareness of the compensating values of method results in an extremely one-sided position.

This one-sidedness appears in the merely logical view of objectivity, of the basic discipline in human knowledge, of the relation of the basic discipline to other disciplines, of the notion of system, and of the conception of theology.

For the man that knows his logic and does not think of method, objectivity is apt to be conceived as the fruit of immediate experience, of self-evident and necessary truths, and of rigorous inferences. When method is added to the picture, one may succeed in discovering that objectivity is the fruit of authentic subjectivity, of being attentive, intelligent, reasonable, and responsible.[4]

For the man who knows his logic and does not think of method, the basic discipline will regard objects generally. It will be a metaphysic. But when method is added to the picture, the basic discipline will regard not objects but subjects: it will be not a metaphysic but a cognitional theory; and the cognitional theory will provide the critical basis both for an epistemology and for a metaphysic.

For the man who knows his logic and does not think of method, the relation of the basic discipline to other disciplines will be logical. The basic discipline will provide the basic terms and relations. The other disciplines will add the further specifications to the terms and relations provided by the basic discipline. But when method is added to the picture, the relationship between the basic discipline and other disciplines lies in the field not of logic but of method. The basic discipline sets up a transcendental method, a manner of

---

4 [In an aside, 'And (one may discover that) it isn't necessary that we be attentive, intelligent, reasonable, and responsible.']

proceeding in any and every cognitional enterprise. The other disciplines add to transcendental method the categorial determinations appropriate to their specific enterprise.

For the man who knows his logic and does not think of method, the term 'system' will have only one meaning. Systems are either true or false. True system is the realization of the deductivist ideal that happens to be true, and in each department of human knowledge there is only one true system. But when method is added to the picture, three notions of system are distinguished. There is the mistaken notion of system that supposes that it comprehends the eternal verities. There is the empirical notion of system that regards systems as successive expressions of an ever fuller understanding of the relevant data and that considers the currently accepted system not as eternal truth but as the best available scientific opinion. Finally, there is system in the third sense that results from the appropriation of one's own conscious and intentional operations.[5]

From these differences there arise different conceptions of theology. When the logical view prevails, theology is conceived as the science of God and of all things in their relation to God. As the methodical view develops, theology is conceived as reflection on the significance and value of a religion within a culture, and culture itself is conceived, not normatively as though in principle there was but one human culture, but empirically and so with a full recognition of the many different manners in which sets of meanings and of values have informed human ways of life.

So much, then, for the preliminaries. I advocate the unity of the functional specialty 'systematics' and of the philosophy of God not on any and every set of assumptions but only on one precise meaning of unity, and only on certain assumptions concerning the meaning of objectivity, the content of the basic disciplines, the relationship between the basic and other disciplines, the nature of system, and the concept of theology. It is on these assumptions that I shall proceed to argue that the philosophy of God and the functional specialty 'systematics' have a common origin, that each complements and reinforces the other, and that they have a common goal even though they proceed in different manners.

2   A Common Origin

First, then, the two have a common origin in religious experience. Such

5 [In an aside, 'transcendental method.']

experience varies with every difference of culture, class, or individual. But I have suggested on theological grounds that at the root of such experience is God's gift of his love. There is a gift of God's love that floods our inmost hearts through the Holy Spirit that God gives us (Romans 5.5). The acceptance of that gift of love is necessary for salvation (1 Corinthians 13). And God wills all men to be saved and to come to knowledge of the truth (1 Timothy 2.4).

Further, I have argued that it is this gift that leads men to seek knowledge of God. God's gift of his love is God's free and gratuitous gift. It does not suppose that we know God. It does not proceed from our knowledge of God. On the contrary, I have suggested that the gift occurs with indeed a determinate content but without an intellectually apprehended object. Religious experience at its root is experience of an unconditioned and unrestricted being in love. But what we are in love with remains something that we have to find out. When we find it out in the context of a philosophy, there results a philosophy of God. When we find it out in the context of a functionally differentiated theology, there results a functional specialty, systematics. So it turns out that one and the same God has unknowingly been found and is differently being sought by both philosopher and theologian.

Now it could be objected that the priority of a supernatural gift introduces a non-philosophic element, with the result that philosophy of God ceases to be itself. Such a conclusion, I readily admit, would follow on the assumption of the static viewpoint. For on that viewpoint objectivity is simply a matter of self-evident principles, immediate experience, and rigorous conclusions. To admit any other influence would be to rob pure reason of its purity. But what holds on the static viewpoint turns out to be ridiculous on the dynamic viewpoint. For there objectivity is conceived as the fruit of authentic subjectivity, and to be genuinely in love with God is the very height of authentic subjectivity.

Again, it may be objected that our position does not square with the decree of the First Vatican Council to the effect that from the existence of creatures by the natural light of reason man can know with certainty the existence of God.[6] Now I grant that this conclusion would follow if the decree meant that fallen man without grace can know with certainty the existence of God. But most certainly that is not the meaning of the decree, for an earlier stage of the decree said precisely that, while the final version omitted the words 'fallen' and 'demonstrated.'[7]

6 [DS 3004, 3026.]
7 The third schema of the Constitution *Dei Filius* in the corresponding canon read: 'per ea quae facta sunt, naturali ratione ab homine lapso certo

Finally, may I point out once more the great advantage that accrues to philosophy of God when it is acknowledged to be seeking the same God as do the theologians – and, indeed, as do all men, for '... he is not far from each one of us, for in him we live and move, in him we exist' (Acts 17. 27–28). It was Blaise Pascal that contrasted the god of philosophers with the God of Abraham, Isaac, and Jacob.[8] That contrast has since been so extended that the god of the philosophers has become another god, a usurper, an idol. In such a climate of opinion it is of extreme importance to ascertain that it is one and the same God that unknowingly has been found, though differently sought, by both philosophers and theologians.

3   The Question of God

Our first point, then, has been that philosophy of God and the functional specialty 'systematics' have the same source and origin in God's gift of his love. In both disciplines man is seeking to know whom he is in love with. Our second point will be that the philosophy of God needs to stand in the context of the functional specialty 'systematics.' Here our basic argument will be that the question of God arises on a series of successive levels, that it may begin as a purely metaphysical question but it becomes a moral and eventually a religious question, and that to deal with all of these levels requires putting an end to the isolation of philosophy of God.

I suggested in *Method in Theology* that the basic form of the question of God arises when one questions one's questioning.[9] Now our questioning is of different kinds. There are our questions for intelligence, and by them we ask, What? and Why? and How? and What for? Next, there are our questions for reflection, and by them we ask, Is that so or is it not so? Is it certain or is it only probable?[10] Thirdly, there are our questions for deliberation, and by them we ask whether what we are doing is really worth while, whether it is

---

cognosci et demonstrari posse ...' [through what has been made, it can certainly be known and demonstrated by natural reason on the part of fallen man] J.D. Mansi, *Sacrorum conciliorum nova et amplissima collectio* [see above, p. 89, note 28], vol. 53, col. 168. See also the article 'Natural Knowledge of God' (see above, p. 83, note 23).

8 [Pascal, *Pensées* (see above, p. 19, note 9) 449.]

9 Lonergan, *Method in Theology* 101–103.

10 [In an aside, 'The second type of question can be answered by a yes or a no, but the first cannot.']

truly good or only apparently good. Finally, there is the religious question: we are suffering from an unconditioned, unrestricted love; with whom, then, are we in love?

A first form of the question of God may be derived from our questions for intelligence. Answers to such questions are reached when the desire to understand expressed in the question is met by the satisfaction of actually understanding: I've got it! Eureka! Still, the desire to understand is not simply a desire for a subjective satisfaction. It wants more. It wants to understand the persons and things that make up one's milieu and environment. How is it, then, that the subjective satisfaction of an act of understanding can be the revelation of the nature of the persons and things in one's milieu and environment? Obviously, if intelligence can reveal them, they must be intelligible. But how can they be intelligible? Does not the intelligibility of the object presuppose an intelligent ground? Does not an intelligent ground for everything in the universe presuppose the existence of God? Such is a first form in which arises the question of God.[11]

A second form of the question of God arises when we reflect on our questions for reflection. In *Insight*, I concluded that answering questions for reflection supposes that we reach a virtually unconditioned.[12] The meaning of this phrase 'virtually unconditioned' has its simplest expression in the hypothetical syllogism 'If A, then B. But A. Therefore B.' In the major premise, 'If A, then B,' the consequent, B, is conditioned by A: that is, B if A. In the minor premise, 'But A,' the condition is fulfilled. In the conclusion, 'Therefore B,' there is posited the virtually unconditioned, namely, B was a conditioned, but its condition has been fulfilled, and so virtually it is an unconditioned.

Now all the objects in our sensible universe are known only as virtually unconditioned. Their existence is not necessary but conditioned, something that you verify, not something that you deduce from 'pure reason.' They are contingent beings, and so they can be known to exist only when their existence has been verified. But can everything be contingent? Must there not exist some necessary being, whose existence is unconditioned, to account for the existence of the beings whose existence is conditioned? In this fashion there once more arises the question of God.

A third form of the question of God is had when one deliberates about

---

11 [In an aside, 'Note that I'm not proving that God exists. I'm proving that the question about God arises out of the mere fact that we question our questioning.']

12 [Lonergan, *Insight* 305–306.]

one's deliberating. To deliberate is to ask whether this or that course of action is worth while. To deliberate about one's deliberating is to ask whether it is worth while ever to stop and ask whether one's course of action is worth while. Is deliberating worth while? No doubt, we are moral beings. No doubt, we are forever praising *X* and blaming *Y*. But the fundamental question is whether or not morality begins with the human race. If it does, then basically the universe is amoral; and if basically the universe is amoral, then are not man's aspirations to be moral doomed to failure? But if man is not the first instance of moral aspiration, if basically the universe is moral, then once more there arises the question of God. One asks whether the necessarily existing and intelligent ground of the universe also is a moral being, and that is another form of the question.

A fourth form of the question of God arises when one reflects on religious experience. No doubt, such experience takes many forms. No doubt, it suffers many aberrations. But it keeps recurring. Its many forms can be explained by the many varieties of human culture. Its many aberrations can be accounted for by the precariousness of the human achievement of authenticity. Underneath the many forms and prior to the many aberrations some have found that there exists an unrestricted being in love, a mystery of love and awe, a being grasped by ultimate concern, a happiness that has a determinate content but no intellectually apprehended object. Such people will ask, 'With whom are we in love?' So in the fourth and final manner there arises the question of God.

Now if the question of God arises on four different levels, it does not follow that there are four distinct and separate questions. The questions are distinct but they also are cumulative. The question of God is epistemological when we ask how the universe can be intelligible. It is philosophic when we ask why we should bow to the principle of sufficient reason when there is no sufficient reason for the existence of contingent things. It is moral when we ask whether the universe has a moral ground and so a moral goal. It finally is religious when we ask whether there is anyone for us to love with all our heart and all our soul and all our mind and all our strength.

It can quite plausibly be argued that the fourth question would not occur if man existed in what has been called the state of pure nature. In that case the philosophy of God would not only be distinct from the functional specialty 'systematics' but that functional specialty would not exist. But man at present does not exist in the hypothetical state of affairs named pure nature. The question of God can be raised in all four ways. The four ways are cumulative; they belong together. So we should put an end to the practice of isolating from each other the philosophy of God and the functional specialty 'systematics.'[13]

But further, one must not think that the question of God fundamentally is philosophic, that in the state of pure nature it would not extend into theological terrain, that accidentally in the present state of affairs it merely happens to move out of its proper sphere and touch on matters that are theological. The vast majority of mankind have been religious. One cannot claim that their religion has been based on some philosophy of God. One can easily argue that their religious concern arose out of their religious experience. In that case the basic question of God is the fourth question, which arises out of religious experience. It is only in the climate of a philosophically differentiated culture that there occurs reflection on our questions for intelligence, our questions for reflection, and our questions for deliberation.

4   A Common Objective

Finally, it is only in the climate of religious experience that philosophy of God flourishes. I do not think it difficult to establish God's existence. I do think it a lifelong labor to analyze and refute all the objections that philosophers have thought up against the existence of God. But I see no pressing need for every student of religion to penetrate into that labyrinth and then work his way out. Much more necessary and also much more fruitful is the self-appropriation that grounds cognitional theory, epistemology, and metaphysics, that provides the criteria for distinguishing positions from counterpositions, that leads into an account of the human good, that extends into a general theory of meaning, that brings to light man's capacity for self-transcendence and the relation between that capacity and religion. Now such are the topics treated in the first four chapters of *Method in Theology*. They underpin the practice of theology. But they also underpin rational arguments that establish God's existence and attributes. It is in this climate of reflection on religion that philosophy of God acquires its proper significance and attains its proper effectiveness.[14]

But if philosophy of God has much to gain by being joined by the functional specialty 'systematics,' it is no less true that the functional specialty has much

13 [In an aside, 'Notice the dynamic viewpoint: you move from one level to another; there is continuity.']
14 [In an aside, 'So the importance of the climate of religious experience is that it obviates, on sound grounds, the endless difficulties that can be constructed on the basis of mistaken philosophies, and that have been constructed.']

to gain by the same union. For the categories employed by the theologian are both general and special. The special categories are employed only by theologians. The general categories are employed in other disciplines as well: in philosophy, in the sciences, in hermeneutics and history. For theology, insofar as it acquires a method, becomes a reflection on the significance and value of a religion within a culture; because it treats of a religion, it has its own special terms; because it is concerned with the significance and value of the religion within a given culture, it has to have recourse to the general terms that refer to significance, value, and culture in their many aspects.

In brief, the world of the theologian is not some isolated sphere cut off from the affairs of men. The static viewpoint, of course, inevitably leads to such isolation. By rejecting the static viewpoint, by conceiving theology as an ongoing process guided by a method, one puts an end to isolationism. The concern of the theologian is not just a set of propositions but a concrete religion as it has been lived, as it is being lived, and as it is to be lived. So conceived, theology has to draw on the resources not only of scientists and historians but also of philosophers.

It is true, of course, that dropping the static and accepting the dynamic viewpoint imply that one is setting aside the old-time notions of philosophy and theology. Logic ceases to rule the roost. The dominant issue is method. The possibility of method is a multiple differentiation of consciousness: the religious, the linguistic, the literary, the systematic, the scientific, the scholarly, and the self-appropriation of intentionality analysis. When all of these differentiations of consciousness have been achieved, the consequent notions of philosophy and theology are quite different from what they were when only the first four differentiations had occurred. For example, the Thomist and especially the neo-Thomist conceptions of philosophy and theology rest on the religious, the linguistic, the literary, and the systematic differentiations of consciousness. Commonly they are unfamiliar with the differentiations resulting from modern science, modern scholarship, and contemporary intentionality analysis.

The importance of the closest relationship between philosophy and theology in the present situation is revealed by the contemporary breakdown of Scholasticism. People generally no longer accept or even consider a Scholastic metaphysics. The consequence has been that they water down or reject the truths of faith. This they excuse on the ground that the early church at Jerusalem, Antioch, Corinth, Rome had no interest in metaphysics. This they further excuse on the ground that they have no idea how there could be any development of revealed truth. But a lack of understanding proves nothing but one's own incompetence.[15] Before one can judge whether or not a development of revealed truth is possible and legitimate, one had best understand how it could be conceived to be possible and legitimate. To communicate such an understanding cannot be attempted in the present paper. But at least a clue can be thrown out. The possibility of a development in doctrine arises whenever there occurs a new differentiation of consciousness, for with every differentiation of consciousness the same object becomes apprehended in a different and a more adequate fashion.

I have claimed that philosophy of God and the functional specialty 'systematics' have a common origin and a common objective: their origin is religious experience, and their objective is to discover its significance and estimate its value. I have argued that philosophic questions concerning God lead into strictly religious questions, and that the philosophic inquiry needs the support of the properly religious context for the full and effective attainment of its goal. I also have argued that the functional specialty 'systematics' is concerned not only with the strictly supernatural but also with the effect of God's gift of his love on man's life and history in this world; hence the functional specialty not only has its own special and strictly religious categories but also the categories it shares with other fields, and notably the ones it shares with philosophy. I have pointed out the havoc wrought on people's faith when their philosophy is jettisoned without being replaced. I have now to add a final consideration. It has to do with the contemporary notion of person.

5   The Contemporary Notion of Person

The traditional view was the product of trinitarian and christological problems as these were conceived within the systematic differentiation of consciousness as originated by Aristotle and transposed to Christian soil by Thomas Aquinas. The contemporary view comes out of genetic biology and psychology. From the 'we' of the parents comes the symbiosis of mother and child. From the 'we' of the parents and the symbiosis of mother and child comes the 'we' of the family. Within the 'we' of the family emerges the 'I' of the child. In other

---

15 [In an aside, 'As Chesterton said, Someone comes along and sees a gate in the wall, and says, "Why is there a gate there? I don't see any reason for having it there." And Chesterton said, "Well, if you did see some reason, you might have some reason for taking it down. But if you don't know why it went up in the first place, you don't know enough to decide whether to take it down or not."']

words the person is not the primordial fact. What is primordial is the community. It is within community, and through the intersubjective relations that are the life of community, that there arises the differentiation of the individual person.

It follows that 'person' is never a general term. It always denotes this or that person with all of his or her individual characteristics resulting from the communities in which he or she has lived and through which he or she has been formed and has formed himself or herself. The person is the resultant of the relationships he or she has had with others and of the capacities that have developed in him or her to relate to others.[16]

Now extremely relevant to the notion of the development of the person conceived in this fashion has been our conception of religious experience and our view of the philosophy of God and of the functional specialty 'systematics' as arising from religious experience and as aiming at its clarification. For the strongest and the best of the relationships between persons is love. Religious experience at its first root is the love of God with one's whole heart and whole soul, with all one's mind and all one's strength, and from it flows the love of one's neighbor as oneself. If persons are the products of community, if the strongest and the best of communities is based on love, then religious experience and the emergence of personality go hand in hand.

It follows that, as philosophy of God and the functional specialty 'systematics' have a common origin in religious experience, so also they have a common goal in the development of persons. But each person is one, a whole, and not just a set of parts. It follows that the study of what makes persons persons is not to be carried on under different principles and in different departments. Philosophy of God and the functional specialty 'systematics' may and should unite. They have a common origin; they complement and reinforce each other; they are concerned with a common goal: the promotion into clear consciousness of the major factor in the integration and development of persons.

Question:[17] How can you justify starting methodology with cognitional theory? Does not the basic judgment of existence underpin every act of perception,

---

16 Maurice Nédoncelle, *La réciprocité des consciences. Essai sur la nature de la personne* (Paris: Aubier, 1942).
17 [For the first twenty minutes or so of the session, written questions submitted in advance were presented by Fr Vincent Beuzer, s.j., Chair of the Theology

questioning, and affirming? Don't I implicitly affirm, 'Something exists,' from the beginning of any act of awareness? If so, isn't metaphysics implicitly prior to cognitional theory?

Response: Metaphysics is prior if you consider that what you are studying is fully known objects. In other words, it is dealing with objects. When you start out that way, you have no way of critically justifying your metaphysics. You can critically justify it if you derive it from a cognitional theory and an epistemology. And you can critically justify the cognitional theory by finding it in yourself: the terms of the theory are found in your own operations, of which you are conscious and which you are able to identify in your own experience, and the relations connecting the terms are to be found in the dynamism relating one operation to the other.

Question (continued): Is that question presuming that there is a real disagreement between metaphysicians, one using the object, and the other seeing and using subjectivity as a proper means?

Response: There is a fundamental difference there. This question presupposes a position like Gilson's in his *Réalisme thomiste et critique de la connaisance*, written about 1939.[18] I discussed it in 'Metaphysics as Horizon,' the chapter in *Collection*, comparing Coreth, Gilson, and Kant.[19]

Question (continued): This, then, becomes a problematic between people like Maritain, Gilson, and yourself (and Rahner perhaps)?

Response: Yes. Rahner's philosophic position is expressed by Coreth in his *Metaphysik*,[20] and what he begins with are the questions. He says there is a question about the starting point, so let us take the question *as* the starting point. Your knowledge of existence: *An sit?* Is it so? is the first question you ever raise, and if you do you will say, 'Something exists,' and it fits the affirmation that something exists from the beginning of my acts of awareness.

That is implicit if you need it; but you don't need it. Judgments result

Department at Gonzaga University and Fr Thomas Royce, s.j., Chair of the Philosophy Department, with the option of the person who submitted the question to pursue it further.]
18 [Etienne Gilson, *Réalisme thomiste et critique de la connaissance* (Paris: J. Vrin, 1939); in English, *Thomistic Realism and the Critique of Knowledge*, trans. Mark A. Wauck (San Francisco: Ignatius Press, 1986).]
19 [Lonergan, *Collection* (see above, p. 131, note 10) 188–204.]
20 [Emerich Coreth, *Metaphysik. Eine methodisch-systematische Grundlegung* (Innsbruck, Vienna, Munich: Tyrolia-Verlag, 1961).]

from sufficient evidence, and sufficient evidence for something precise that has been conceived. So your questions for intelligence precede your questions for reflection, your judgments, and your experience has to precede your acts of understanding; otherwise, you will have nothing to be understood. But you may want to conceive human knowing as taking a look – What is it to know? it is to take a good look; and what does your intellect do? it takes an intellectual look at an abstraction. Gilson escapes from that by introducing this 'implicit judgment.' Well, an implicit judgment is a judgment that hasn't occurred yet.

Question (continued): It seems you are leading to, are liable to the charge of subjectivism. Could you explain 'authentic subjectivity,' a phrase you have been using in these lectures?

Response: Subjectivity is authentic in the measure that it is attentive, intelligent, reasonable, responsible. Those are the conditions of being an authentic person. The thing is that our knowing is discursive. It is not a matter of taking a look, it is not intuitive; it is discursive. Until you have clear concepts, you cannot observe. Suppose there is a bug on a table. All I can say about it is that it is a bug. But an entomologist can tell you 100 or 150 or 200 things about it, and he can do so because he has the words and the concepts, and he has studied the thing carefully under all its aspects. I once was at a discussion of scientists and philosophers at Loyola in Los Angeles, and the question arose whether science kept on developing indefinitely. The chairman of the department of chemistry (this was almost ten years ago) said that in the last five years theoretical discoveries in chemistry have enormously enlarged the data we can see. Until you have got understanding and clear concepts, you may feel a little ill at ease, but you don't really attend to the objects.

People talk about Maréchal. Maréchal was the one that effectively introduced in Catholic circles the notion that human knowledge is discursive and that you know when you affirm. An affirmation is a detail of the process, the third level. I was taught philosophy on an intuitive basis, naive realism, and I took refuge in Newman's *Grammar of Assent.* Later I read a book by J.A. Stewart, *Plato's Doctrine of Ideas;*[21] it was a book that influenced me unconsciously a great deal. I started reading it recently to prepare a talk and I discovered that, according to Stewart, Plato's ideas are what the scientist is trying to discover, and what Plato is doing in the Dialogues is setting up a methodology.

---

21 [J.A. Stewart, *Plato's Doctrine of Ideas* (Oxford: Clarendon Press, 1909).]

Question: It seems, then, that the authentic Christian mystic is best suited to explore the meaning of God.

Response: The trouble with mystics is that they are not interested in any of these questions. They consider all these books rather silly and superfluous. They don't even want to read books on mysticism. While they have certain advantages – they're beautiful persons – you can't interest them in joining any investigation.

Question (continued): What good are they to theology?

Response: They are good to the church. Luigi Sturzo has said that there are two components in the ongoing history of the church, the organizational and the mystical.[22] The mystical brings things to life again, and the organizational keeps them going even though you have no more mystics. When the need for more mystics becomes evident, then divine providence, we hope, will step in.

Question: In your writing you have stated that the present crisis of modern man is not one of faith but of culture. I have taken this to mean that the shift in world views via the rise of modern science, and especially today in the social sciences, has made it difficult for modern man to understand his place in the universe, and thus properly to order himself and his society. Yet the contemporary moves attacking human life, the family, and authority appear to me as perhaps not a cultural change but a godless, at best humanistic, movement which may best be met by Christian faith. Could you please clarify what you mean by this cultural shift we are witnessing?

Response: What I am talking about is a crisis in the church, the crisis in the church that involves radical change in theology brought on by the inadequacy of the philosophy and the scholarship and the notions of science that we had in the past. That is the fundamental problem in the church at the present time. Fr Greeley, in his interview with a Bishops' committee after his sociological report, said that the fundamental need at the present time is theory. The fundamental problem is not celibacy or faith but theory, and that is what I am saying. I am not talking about the world problems.

The origins of this atheism and lack of faith are the eighteenth-century Enlightenment, which through universal education has been communicated to the masses. In the general situation, the emphasis made by the question is

22 [Luigi Sturzo, *Church and State*, trans. Barbara Barclay Carter (London: Geoffrey Bles, 1939). See Lonergan's reference to the translator's preface, in *A Third Collection*, ed. Frederick E. Crowe (Mahwah, NJ: Paulist Press, 1985) 11–12.]

correct, namely, in the general field of human society. In general, the eighteenth century wanted to get rid of positive religion, revealed religion; and to get rid of it they said, 'Let's get rid of tradition.' And when you get rid of tradition, you move back to the state of pre-Cro-Magnon man. There is a crisis in our tradition today. It is a cultural crisis because it is affecting our tradition.

Question: If the possibility exists that man can separate himself from the love of God by his own free will, are men who possess a love for God equally exposed to the elements that make up this potential separation?
Response: St Paul says, 'Make out your salvation in fear and trembling,' and 'Pray for perseverance.' It is the thing to be prayed for, and therefore, because it has to be prayed for, it is not something you already possess securely. Human authenticity is always precarious, but if you have the love of God in your heart you are that much better off. Aristotle said that virtues make you do the right thing promptly, easily, and with pleasure; and Aquinas said, 'Well, at least not with too much pain.'

Question: What do you think of the concept of God derived from process philosophy? Is a god who changes in perfection compatible with the Christian notion of God discussed in systematics, or the philosophical notion of God in *Insight?*
Response: Everyone admits that there are contingent predications of God: things that are true about God and not necessarily true. God created the world, and he need not have created the world. This is a contingent predication about God. Does that imply that there is a real change in God? If you are a process philosopher you will say yes, and if you are not one you will say no. The question is, Is the metaphysics of God the same as the metaphysics about man? If you make a new decision, there is a real change in you. If God decides to create a world, is there a real change in him? Is the metaphysics of an infinite being the same as the metaphysics of a finite being? That is the fundamental form of the question.

Now the concept of God in *Insight* is a concept of an unrestricted act of understanding, an absolute intelligibility. In Whitehead's *Process and Reality* God is the first accident.[23] There is a radical opposition there because an accident is something that is not intelligible; it just happens.

The questions concerned with the basis of the contingent predication

---

23 [See Alfred North Whitehead, *Process and Reality. An Essay in Cosmology* (New York: The Free Press, 1969) 403–13.]

about God started out in Aristotle. With him, the action is in what is moved, not in the mover. The mover does not change; it is what moves that changes, per se. If no one is learning, you are not doing any teaching because teaching and learning are the same thing. It is the thing in the person that learns, but it is from the person that teaches. Sound and hearing are the same thing. The bell can put longitudinal waves in the air, but that is not sound. Sound is what is in potency in the ear when there is nothing ringing, and what actually is in the ear when something is ringing. But it is sounding insofar as it is from the bell, and it is hearing insofar as it is in you. You have there a first instance in which predications imply not a reality in the agent but a reality in the effect.

That is the basis of the Thomist doctrine that creation is a notional relation in God and a real relation in us. There are shifts in terminology when you move from one to the other. That is just a rough outline. I can go on to the question of understanding and willing, and so forth, whether those predications are the same. God is an infinite being: what do you add to him?

With regard to God as undergoing change in the course of time, it is an anthropomorphic conception of God, God being more like us. It conceives God not as a God of the universe but as part of the universe, an accident within the universe.[24]

Question (continued): Have process philosophy and process theology any sure role to play in our own development of thought?
Response: We have to get over the notion that metaphysics is static; what is static is logic. There are conceptions of substance that are ludicrous, and often current. There is a purification of metaphysical concepts that is needed and that process philosophy attempts. I don't think that process philosophers have succeeded in effecting the purification that they want.

Question:[25] Suppose I were a philosopher with a well worked-out philosophy of God and a theologian with a highly developed systematics. What further developments would be open to me?
Response: Well, you can go on to communications, expressing what you have acquired to people in every class and in every culture, or at least getting to know one class of some culture very well and saying it to them. And communications is not simply a matter of one person doing something. What

24 [Lonergan made a side reference to Langdon Gilkey as supporting his view, but it is not clear what work of Gilkey's he had in mind.]
25 [The remaining questions are directed from the floor.]

is the church? The church is an ongoing process of communication of the message of the gospel, of the message that is what the Christian knows, of the content that informs his life, and of the precepts that guide his actions. That communication is the fruit, the final stage of theology; it is the eighth of the functional specialties.

Question: In light of your ideas of 'I' and 'We' and the artificial means of birth being developed with test-tube babies, do you think this technology would be dehumanizing?
Response: Without the love of the parents the infant is retarded. I think the psychologists will agree with that. You don't get mother's love in an incubator. There is not developed the attachment the mother has to her own child if she has not carried that child. There is a psychological dimension to it.

Question: If authentic subjectivity is a prerequisite to inquiry, then to what extent does that subjectivity not also become content, or a product, of the inquiry, and then how, if it is content or product, can my inquiry be communicable to you subjectively?
Response: 'Subjective' does not mean anything distinct from objective; it is the source of objectivity. How one person understands another person is an extremely complex process. Learning new words, catching on to new uses of words: you make the gesture, someone else interprets it; you see the corrections you should make in your gesture to get him to understand what you really mean. The gestures can be made manually or vocally or any other way. That is the communication side.

   The inquiry does not presuppose authentic subjectivity. The roots of authentic subjectivity are already there in your attentiveness, intelligence, reasonableness, and responsibleness. That is the source of your questions on these different levels. Subjectivity, insofar as it accepts mistaken notions, beliefs, is distorted, and it has to work itself out of a blunder, and correcting errors is not easy. But there is a process: by muddling through you can get there. Your position is a rather static one, wanting logical explanations for everything.

Question: This question arises out of my religious experience. With whom am I in love? Do I go back to another level when I ask another question that arises out of my religious experience?[26]
Response: You are going back to a speculative level, aren't you? That was

   26 [Part of this question could not be deciphered from the tape.]

Anselm's question. The religious experience of the Christian is specifically distinct from religious experience in general. It is intersubjective. It is not only this gift of God's love, but it has an objective manifestation of God's love in Christ Jesus. That intersubjective component creates a difference, and because it creates a difference, insofar as you advert to that intersubjective element in your love with Christ, you are proceeding from experience. Your question is coming out of your experience. It is insofar as you are related to Christ as God.

Question: Does what you have said have any bearing on the relationship between the functional specialty of doctrines, for example, the Christian teaching about God, and the systematic understanding of God? What is the distinction between those two?

Response: Doctrines is the previous functional specialty. All eight interact, but conception of them is sequential. Doctrines come out of a dialectic that lines up the differences between historians, interpreters, researchers, and reduces those differences to their roots. You have opposed positions and counterpositions coming out of dialectics. Foundations give you the horizon within which religious statements have a meaning. By applying foundations to dialectics you get doctrines. In systematics you can say, 'What on earth does this mean?'

Question (continued): In doctrines do you get a statement about God in which you have no understanding of the meaning of it?

Response: You have some understanding; you have a catechetical under-standing of it. Or you can have a historical understanding, insofar as you have been studying the history.

THE LARKIN-STUART LECTURES AT

TRINITY COLLEGE, UNIVERSITY OF TORONTO

12

A New Pastoral Theology[1]

General Introduction to the Larkin-Stuart Lectures

I felt greatly honored, two years ago, when the former Provost of Trinity College, Professor Derwyn Owen, invited me to give the Larkin-Stuart Lectures in 1973. My happy feelings were confirmed when his successor as Provost, Dr George Ignatieff, reiterated the invitation. To both of them, to their Selection Committee, and to Trinity College, faculty and students, I must begin by expressing my sincere appreciation and warm gratitude.

1 [The first of the Larkin-Stuart Lectures, which Lonergan delivered at Trinity College in the University of Toronto, November 1973. The date of this lecture is 12 November. Under the general title 'Revolution in Catholic Theology?' the series consisted of four lectures on successive evenings, the others being 'Variations in Fundamental Theology' (13 November); 'Sacralization and Secularization' (14 November); and 'The Scope of Renewal' (15 November).

The following February, under the auspices of More House at Yale University, Lonergan repeated the first three of these lectures as the St Thomas More Lectures on 11, 12, and 13 February respectively, under the general title 'Change in Roman Catholic Theology.' Given different audiences, it is understandable that the introductions and conclusions would vary, but the main text of the lectures was substantially the same. For this first lecture, it seemed best to include in the text the respective introductions and conclusions, while leaving to footnotes indication of other variations in the text. Accordingly, the sequence will be: general introduction to the Larkin-Stuart Lectures, general introduction to the Thomas More Lectures, main text of the first lecture of both series with the conclusion of the Larkin-Stuart lecture, followed by the conclusion of the Thomas More lecture.

As a general title for the four lectures I chose 'Revolution in Roman Catholic Theology?' To the title was appended a question mark, to have it denote, not a statement of fact, but an inquiry. In selecting this title, I was thinking, not of revolution in Chile or Cuba or China or even Russia, but of a rather celebrated little book by a historian of science. Its title was *The Structure of Scientific Revolutions* and its author was Thomas Kuhn.[2]

For Dr Kuhn science meant, not the content of textbooks, but the ongoing occupation of a scientific community. Normally that occupation is an ongoing series of minor achievements. It is a matter of working out, of clarifying, of applying in a great variety of manners, the implications of the last great breakthrough. It is something like the work of mopping up carried out by an army after a decisive victory. Only intermittently do there occur in the field of science the major achievements that change the whole face of things and initiate a new period of normal science in which the new viewpoint is assimilated, its implications worked out, and their significance applied to problems that had long existed but now could be seen in a far clearer and more revealing light. It was such major achievements, the uphill battle of gaining them recognition, their eventual acceptance by a new majority constituted by a later generation, that for Thomas Kuhn were to be named scientific revolutions.

The library of the Lonergan Research Institute has tapes (TC 771, 773, 777) of the Larkin-Stuart Lectures (except the third), as well as the autograph texts prepared for delivery (Library, Files 771, 773, 775, 777). No tapes of the Thomas More Lectures are extant, but the Institute library has the typescript of these lectures, incorporating Lonergan's changes (Files 789, 791, 793) . File 719 of Batch XIII in the Archives has a photocopy of the Thomas More typescripts. All these materials were drawn upon in editing the lectures. File 719 in the Archives is particularly significant in that Lonergan typed on the file 'LECTURES 1974 Trinity Yale SMU BC Final Reworking.' 'SMU' refers to the fact that 'Sacralization and Secularization' was delivered at the Perkins School of Theology at Southern Methodist University on 21 March 1974. It would appear, however, that the version that was delivered there was not the one found in File 719 but the earlier 1973 autograph. 'BC' probably refers to the fact that Lonergan delivered both 'A New Pastoral Theology' and 'Sacralization and Secularization' at the first Lonergan Workshop, on 18 June and 20 June 1974, respectively.

With the typescript of the Thomas More Lectures is an announcement regarding the lectures. The following description is given of 'A New Pastoral Theology': 'When Vatican II promulgated "A Pastoral Constitution on the Church in the Modern World," pastoral theology had to enlarge its concern from the parish to the world.']

2 [Thomas S. Kuhn, *The Structure of Scientific Revolutions* (see above, p. 134, note 11).]

Such, then, is the analogy I had in mind when I proposed to speak on revolution in the Roman Catholic theological community. Up to the Second Vatican Council, it had enjoyed not a mere few decades but whole centuries of normal science in which achievements were very minor indeed. The Second Vatican Council startled the press, if not the world, with its unexpected vitality. During the Council, it is known, theologians had been busy behind the scenes. Since then, there was for a time a spate of books and articles by Catholics on theological issues, but recently popular support seems to have died down, and a number of Catholic publishers have closed their doors.

I cannot offer an adequate survey of the last eight years of Catholic theology. My first three lectures will be concerned to present indications of change, first, in the notion of a pastoral theology, secondly, in the field of fundamental theology, thirdly, through the theme of sacralization and secularization that relates the church to the world. My fourth and final lecture, on the scope of renewal, will inquire how deep is the change and whether it modifies theology deeply without breaking faith with the past.

General Introduction to the Thomas More Lectures

My topic for this series of three lectures is 'Change in Roman Catholic Theology,' and a few preliminary words of explanation may not be out of place. The notion of change, of course, calls for no comment: it merely means that things are no longer what they were, whether for better or for worse. The locus of change is circumscribed: it is change, not in religion in general, not in Christianity, but in Roman Catholicism and, indeed, in Roman Catholicism since the Second Vatican Council. The issue, finally, is change in theology: our concern in these lectures centers directly, not on Roman Catholic beliefs, not on Roman Catholic Church doctrines, but on that reflection on doctrines and beliefs that for some centuries has gone by the name of theology.

The matter might be handled in various ways. One might attempt a general survey of the books and articles published by Catholic theologians in the last nine years to conclude with a catalogue of the items that were new or in some manner different. If that approach were rejected as too minute and multitudinous in detail and, at the same time, too summary and unsubstantial in content, one might veer to the opposite extreme and select some one massive phenomenon, such as the disappearance of Scholasticism, that can be held to account both for an outpouring of novelties and a lack of any unifying structure and coherence.

But this second alternative would be found, I think, to reach too far and cut too deeply. It is true enough that a disappearance of Scholasticism has been conspicuous in Catholic theology since Vatican II. It remains that Vatican II merely released the manifestation of a change that had begun long before and sooner or later was bound to emerge. The German Historical School of the first half of the nineteenth century introduced into theology the critical history and the interpretative techniques that in the first half of the twentieth century had discredited in the eyes of Catholic theologians many basic procedures of Scholastic research. Modern philosophies – critical, idealist, positivist, pragmatist, voluntarist, personalist, phenomenological, existential, linguistic – piled up in the wake of modern natural and human science to necessitate a stance and style for which the Aristotelian corpus and the Thomist *Summa* were no adequate preparation.

So it is that I have sought a middle way. I have selected three specific areas of change. They illustrate positively the too general and too negative theme of the disappearance of Scholasticism. Because they are specific they can make some claim to be not just items in a far larger, secular change, but consequences of Vatican II. No doubt, more learned or more discriminating speakers might well prefer a different selection, a shift in perspective, a better documented presentation. But perhaps I can hope to have chosen topics that, in your indulgence, you will consider to have some bearing on the issue and to possess some interest of their own.

My topic this evening, 'A New Pastoral Theology,' easily comes out of the Second Vatican Council as a pastoral council. The second lecture is on 'Variations in Fundamental Theology.' It answers the Council's desire for an overhauling of theological teaching, and the answer is a *volte-face*. The third is entitled 'Sacralization and Secularization.' It is a new venture in Catholic theology and, however tentative, involves a thorough remodeling of ways of thought.

1   A Pastoral Council

There is no lack of evidence that Pope John XXIII intended the Second Vatican Council to be a pastoral council. At the solemn inauguration on October 11, 1962, he addressed the assembled bishops, and in the course of his remarks he pointed out both what was and what was not his purpose in summoning them to the Council. There was no point, he said, in their gathering together merely to repeat what anyone could find in familiar theological handbooks. Equally, there was no point in going over ancient decrees and clearing up this or that obscurity to satisfy the interest of antiquarians. What was desired was advertence to the distinction between the unchanging deposit of faith and the changing modes of its presentation to meet the needs of different times. What was required today was a fresh presentation, one that met current needs, one that fitted in with the function of the teaching office of the church, a teaching office that in the main was pastoral.[3]

During the first session of the Council there came to light divergent views on the precise meaning of the word 'pastoral.' Pope John had no intention of entering into these debates. His interventions were incidental, rare, pragmatic, strategic, and readily understood by the majority of the bishops. Still, a few weeks after the first session had come to an end, in responding to the Christmas greetings of the curial cardinals and prelates, Pope John harked back to his inaugural address. The inspiration he had had in calling the Council was hope for a widespread and more fervent renewal in the life of the church. It was for a new and more vigorous spread of the gospel in the whole world. He wanted our contemporaries to be made aware of the church's striving for the spiritual and, no less, the material betterment of the whole of mankind. He begged leave to repeat the point he had endeavored to make in his inaugural address on October 11. Undoubtedly a first duty of the Council was fidelity to the basic truths of the deposit of faith and of the church's teaching. But this duty was not to be fulfilled by any wrapping of one's talent in a napkin and burying it in the ground. It called for a prompt and fearless will to draw upon ancient doctrine and to apply it under the conditions of our day. The business of the Council, he then had insisted, was not the discussion of this or that topic in the fundamental doctrines of the church. It was not any elaboration of the teachings of the Fathers or of ancient or modern theologians. That sort of thing can be done very well without holding a council. What was expected was a leap forward (*un balzo innanzi*) that would set forth the faith in the mental forms and literary style of modern thought while satisfying the requirements of the teaching office, an office, he repeated, that predominantly was pastoral.[4]

John XXIII died before the second session met. But in the first session Giovanni Cardinal Montini had shown that he understood the meaning of a pastoral council, and when he became Paul VI, he had the Council continue its work for three more years. It can be maintained, I feel sure, that the further sessions revealed how well the vast majority of the assembled bishops

3 *Acta Apostolicae Sedis* 54 (1962) 791–92.
4 *Acta Apostolicae Sedis* 55 (1963) 43–45.

understood the spirit and the scope of the Council. But for present purposes it will suffice to recall the longest of the documents, 'Gaudium et spes,' which was entitled 'A Pastoral Constitution on the Church in the Modern World.' It began with an expression of worldwide solidarity. The joy and hope, the sorrow and anguish of men today are also the joy and hope, the sorrow and anguish of the disciples of Christ. So the statements of the decree were addressed not only to those that invoke the name of Christ but to the whole of mankind. Its aim was to present its conception of the role of the church in the world of today. That role included no earthly ambition. It was to be led by the Paraclete, and it was to continue the work of Christ, who came into the world not to judge but to save, not to be served but to serve.[5]

2   The Notion of a Pastoral Council

In ecumenical councils from Nicea on, a distinction was customary between a doctrinal section that expounded the truths of faith and a disciplinary section that sought remedies for current defects and abuses. But Pope John's pastoral council seemed to evade these categories. It expounded truths but hurled no anathemas. It was concerned with concrete living but its thrust was positive rather than remedial.

The Council itself did not resolve this issue directly. But the issue, nonetheless, was a live one in the conciliar debates. Indeed, there was a single touchstone commonly employed to settle whether or not a topic for discussion or a proposal for an amendment was relevant. That touchstone was the question, Is it pastoral? Moreover, in the wings of the Council were a flock of theologians with their own notions of what was and what was not pastoral.

Let us take one answer to this question, which I happen to find particularly clear and penetrating. It is from the pen of Marie-Dominique Chenu, O.P., and it was written in January 1963, that is, just a few weeks after the first session of the council closed. In April of that year it appeared in the review *Parole et mission,* and a year later it was included in a two-volume collection of Fr Chenu's writings.[6]

---

5 'Gaudium et spes, Pastoral Constitution on the Church in the Modern World,' in *Vatican Council II: The Conciliar and Post Conciliar Documents,* ed. Austin Flannery, O.P. (Northport, NY: Costello Publishing Co., 1992) §§ 1–3, pp. 903–905.

6 Marie-Dominique Chenu, 'Un Concile "Pastoral,"' in *Parole et mission* 21 (15 avril 1963) 182–202, reprinted in *La Parole de Dieu, II. L'Evangile dans le temps* (Paris: Editions du Cerf, 1964) 655–72.

After noting that in the council the term 'pastoral' had functioned as the criterion of the truths to be formulated and promulgated, he set forth the views of Cardinal Siri, Archbishop of Turin, on the topic. For the cardinal, 'pastoral' did not mean mere smiles and condescension. First and foremost, it meant presenting the truths revealed by our Lord. Further, since every council had conceived its aim to be the presentation of revealed truths, the term 'pastoral' could not be the distinguishing mark of any council.

Fr Chenu felt that some such opinion underlay the work of the pre-conciliar committees. Theirs had been the task of putting together the suggestions, the requests, the plaints of the bishops, and of presenting initial drafts, named schemata, for the council to approve, modify, or reject. In fact, however, the Council had rejected more than one of these schemata, pronouncing them to be abstract and Scholastic, and neither biblical nor pastoral nor ecumenical.

What, then, does 'pastoral' mean? For Fr Chenu, difficulty arises when one puts the cart before the horse. If first one clarifies the meaning of doctrine and then sets about explaining the meaning of 'pastoral,' one tends to reduce 'pastoral' to the application of doctrine, and to reduce the application of doctrine to the devices and dodges, the simplifications and elaborations, of classical oratory. But what comes first in fact is the word of God. The task of the church is the kerygma, announcing the good news, preaching the gospel. That preaching is pastoral. It is the concrete reality. From it one may abstract doctrines, and theologians may work the doctrines into conceptual systems. But the doctrines and systems, however valuable and true, are but the skeleton of the original message. A word is the word of a person, but doctrine objectifies and depersonalizes. The word of God comes to us through the God-man. The church has to mediate to the world not just a doctrine but the living Christ.

God spoke in the prophets, he spoke in his Son, he still speaks today in scripture and tradition, in the biblical movement, the liturgical movement, the catechetical movement, the ecumenical movement. First and foremost he speaks to the poor, to the poor in the underdeveloped nations, to the poor in the slums of industrialized nations. And if the word of God is not preached to the poor, then the church has failed. So it was in the theme of the word of God preached to the poor – a theme so lucidly and powerfully set forth by, among others, Cardinal Lercaro[7] – that the bishops, assembled in council, together

---

7　[Cardinal Giacomo Lercaro, Archbishop of Bologna, President of the Concilium for the Implementation of the Constitution on the Sacred Liturgy.]

discovered and collectively responded to the momentous meaning of the phrase 'a pastoral council.'

Alive, personal, communal, the word of God also is historic. As the old covenant, so also the new names a dispensation, an economy, an ongoing disposition of divine providence both emergent in human history and carrying it forward to an ultimate, an eschatological goal. With its origins in the distant past and its term in an unknown future, its scope extends to the ends of the earth and its mission to all men. Once more there comes to light the complete inadequacy of attempting to begin from doctrines and then attempting to flesh them out into living speech, when it is living speech that, from the start, alone can be at once concrete and alive, interpersonal and communal, historic and ecumenical.

Let me add just one more point from Fr Chenu's account. An ideology can be expressed in the propositions of a doctrine, in the premises and multitudinous conclusions of a system. But the words of a pastor, of a shepherd of souls, are far more than any ideology. They are words spoken in faith, and awakening faith. They are words of salvation, a salvation that is God's gift of himself, of his peace and joy, of his eternal hope.

3   Pastoral Theology

On December 7, 1965, there was promulgated the 'Pastoral Constitution on the Church in the Modern World.' One may well regard it as, by and large, a vindication of Fr Chenu's conception of a pastoral council. But there is a further aspect to the matter, and to this we must now attend. When one thinks or speaks of a pastoral constitution on the church, one is employing the word 'pastoral' in a far broader, a far more comprehensive sense, than the sense commonly envisaged by pastoral theology.

There is a material difference between the pastoral operations of the whole church in the world and, on the other hand, the operations of a vicar in his parish. There is as well the formal difference between the view propounded by Fr Chenu and the view attributed to Cardinal Siri. But, however much one may prefer Fr Chenu's word of God as already alive to Cardinal Siri's efforts to bring to life doctrinal abstractions, it remains that the Cardinal's position corresponds to traditional views on pastoral theology. For the traditional position, at least in the Catholic Church, very much was a matter of learning one's fundamental, doctrinal, systematic, and moral theology, and then perhaps devoting some thought to the arts of human communication.

In fact, this view at times seems to have been pushed to incredible extremes.

In 1953 I began teaching in Rome, and, for the first time, was directing a doctoral dissertation. The candidate was a young priest from France, and for some time I was puzzled by his complaints about the irrelevance of theology to preaching. Eventually, I grasped the point to his remarks and said, 'No one in a sermon presents a thesis taken out of a theological textbook.' He answered, briefly and appositely, 'In France, one does – one has to!' At the time I missed the more recent implications of his reply. Preaching can become, not just the application of doctrine, but doctrine pure and simple. It is preaching as an arid event, an event that necessitates a pastoral council. This larger issue was bound to come to the fore when the adjective 'pastoral' was shifted from the priest in his parish to the church in the world. Such a shift had had its forerunners long before the Council. In 1841 Anton Graf (1811–1867) at Tübingen had published an account of what he preferred to term 'practical theology.' It was concerned with the activity of the church as a whole and in its several parts; and it sought to overcome the myopia that concentrated on the pastor, presented the unrelated multiplicity of his tasks, and overlooked the originating, coordinating, and supporting activities of other members in the body of the church. Unfortunately, Graf's ideas were taken over by a Joseph Amberger (1816–1889), who divided practical theology into two parts: one part was pastoral theology in the traditional sense, treating the tasks of the priest in his parish; the other part was handed over to canon law where, naturally enough, it remained canon law.[8]

In our own century, two works by Franz Xaver Arnold, in 1949 and 1956 respectively, restored the approach to pastoral theology through practical theology, and in 1960, when word of the Council was in the air, Karl Rahner had printed as a manuscript a paper entitled 'Plan and Sketch of a Handbook of Pastoral Theology.'[9] The plan was grandiose, and its execution was both rapid and massive. A group of five editors sorted out the tasks, solicited the collaboration, and assembled the contributions, of a host of specialists in theology, in the human sciences, and in relevant interdisciplinary fields. A first, thick volume appeared in 1964, a second and double volume in 1966, a third volume in 1968, and a fourth in 1970. Also in 1970 there came out a

---

8 See Franz Xaver Arnold, Karl Rahner, Viktor Schurr, Leonhard M. Weber, Ferdinand Klostermann, *Handbuch der Pastoraltheologie*, vol. 1, 2nd ed. (Freiburg, Basel, Wien: Herder, 1970) 56–62.
9 See Heinz Schuster, 'The Nature and Function of Pastoral Theology,' in *The Pastoral Mission of the Church, Concilium*, vol. 3, ed. Karl Rahner (1965) 5, note 1.

second edition of the first volume, and an index of the whole work was promised.[10]

A mere inventory of the many excellent points made in these volumes would occupy most of these lectures. Even then an independent evaluation could not be attempted without first setting up its own criteria. Accordingly, it seems best at this juncture to describe a distinct but similar venture that is at once more broadly based, more massive, and, because ongoing, more fluid and more adaptable to the multitudinous and multiform eventualities of our age. I refer to the post-conciliar periodical *Concilium.*

The center of the stage in the Second Vatican Council was held by some twenty-three hundred bishops who, in the course of four years, revised and rewrote and by large majorities approved some sixteen documents. But behind the scenes there also labored some hundreds of theologians. They came from many countries. All made their contribution great or small. And when finally the council came to a close, it was natural enough for them to feel that the episode in their lives occasioned by the Council, the give-and-take of four years of discussions, the sharpening and refashioning of mind that came about in so intimate and intense a milieu, should not suddenly and irrevocably come to an end.

So, one surmises, was founded *Concilium.* It was to be in many ways a continuation of the type of work done by theologians during the Council. It was addressed to those carrying out pastoral tasks within the church. It took its stand on the lessons learnt or reinforced during the Council, namely, that theology has much to learn from pastoral practice, that no less current pastoral practice cannot be content with the theology learnt by pastors years ago. More basically, it stood for the view that a new theology was coming into being, that its distinguishing marks admitted no brief description or summary sketch, that it was to be the as yet unformulated resultant of taking one's stand on scripture and on the history of salvation, while humbly yet courageously confronting the problems of our time.

Such was the general orientation set forth over the names of Karl Rahner and Edward Schillebeeckx in the preface to the first volume of the new series,

---

10 [The autograph text of the Larkin-Stuart lecture adds here, 'I have not seen that index but it should prove indispensable in tracking down specific issues in over two thousand, six hundred, and fifty pages.' The sentence does not appear in the Thomas More lecture. The promise was fulfilled with vol. v, *Lexikon der Pastoraltheologie,* ed. Ferdinand Klostermann, Karl Rahner, Hansjörg Schild (Freiburg, Basel, Wien: Herder, 1972).]

Concilium.[11] In the eight years since the series began publication, well over eighty volumes have appeared. Under the guidance of a general editorial board, each volume had its own editorial committee, and these committees were drawn from an initial three hundred thinkers and writers in twenty-six countries. Each volume has been confined to some one of nine areas in theology. Each has been published in English, German, French, Dutch, Italian, Spanish, Portuguese, with at times partial publication in Polish and Japanese. Finally, each volume might fairly be described as somewhat left of center.

Together they operate on the assumption that the redemptive work of Christ is carried on not exclusively by individual pastors of souls but by all members of Christ's mystical body. It follows that this work is to be performed by all, at times as individuals, at times as members of this or that larger or smaller group, at times as members or as officials of the whole body. Further, this work is to be performed not in a vacuum but in the concrete situations that condition the lives of individuals, of groups, of the whole of humanity. And since there is no divine revelation of what each of these successive situations are, what is possible in them, what would be the probable outcome of this or that initiative, there is required an ongoing practical or pastoral theology concerned with apprehending and understanding situations, settling policies, working out plans, seeing to their implementation, and examining the feedback that may lead to an adjustment of policies or a revision of plans.

4   Existential Theology

In the third volume of *Concilium*, Heinz Schuster referred to such a practical or pastoral theology as an existential ecclesiology.[12] The word 'ecclesiology,' despite its Greek roots, occasions no difficulty; it simply denotes a doctrine concerned with the church. But the adjective 'existential' may be found highly ambiguous. Is it the implicit existentialism of Kierkegaard, the existentialism disavowed by Heidegger, the existentialism proclaimed by Sartre, or some other variety?

A positive or, rather, a definite answer to any of those questions would, I fear, risk being misleading. For one might arrive at some doctrine or other in the sense that we found Fr Chenu urging that doctrine was not enough. One

---

11 Karl Rahner and Edward Schillebeeckx, 'General Introduction,' in *The Church and Mankind, Concilium*, vol. 1 (Glen Rock, NJ: Paulist Press, 1964) 1–4.
12 Schuster, 'The Nature and Function of Pastoral Theology' (see above, note 9) 8.

arrives at the existential, first of all, when one arrives at oneself – at oneself not asleep but awake, not heavy-eyed but attentive, not obtuse but trying to understand and in some measure succeeding, not irrational but both yielding to what evidence there is and not going a millimeter beyond it, not amoral but responsibly evaluating and freely deciding. Such one is when authentically human, when one's existing is the existing proper to a human being.

As one can exist as a human being, so too a human being can exist as a Christian. That is the existing of one whose heart is flooded by God's love through the Holy Spirit given him or her (Romans 5.5). It is a being-in-love manifested, to the discerning, in joy and peace, patience and kindness, goodness and fidelity, gentleness and self-control (Galatians 5.22). It is a being-in-love that is eschatological, looking towards a last end in hope, that responds with faith to the preaching of the gospel, that joins with all the faithful in desiring and praying for and contributing to the human destiny we name salvation, a salvation that consists in God's gift of himself to us in this life and, more fully and overtly, in the next.

At the risk of being tedious, let me insist: existing does not reside in the words I have used; it does not reside in grasping the meaning of such words; it does not reside in any object intended as object. It resides in the subject that may or may not use the words, that may or may not understand what the words mean, but that lives the reality that is meant. Such living is the luminous experience out of which accounts of authentic human and authentic Christian experience may come. Such living is the source from which there springs a genuine response to such accounts.

Now it happens that this is a topic to which we have already adverted. We did so prior to the present context and, to some extent, in different language. But many of you no doubt have found that my present point has been echoing Fr Chenu's paper on a pastoral council and, in particular, his contrast of the doctrinal with the pastoral. For it is authentic Christian experience that is alive. It is that experience as shared by two or more that is intersubjective; that, as shared by many, is community; that, as transmitted down the ages, is historic; that, as intended for all Christians, is ecumenical and, as intended for all men, is universalist; it is the same experience, as headed for an ultimate goal, that is eschatological. So a single human reality, in its many aspects, and through its many realizations, at once is alive and intersubjective, communal and historic, ecumenical and universalist and eschatological.

Still, this gives rise to a grave question. Few would dispute that a pastoral council should spring from roots that were alive, intersubjective, communal and historic, ecumenical, universalist, and eschatological. Fewer, perhaps, would deny that what is granted to a pastoral council also should be granted to a pastoral theology, whether pastoral theology was understood as guiding the operations of a vicar in his parish or the whole church in the whole earth. But the real issue, surely, is both larger and more momentous. Might not what is true of a pastoral council also be true of a doctrinal council? Might not what is true of a pastoral theology also be true of a doctrinal theology? Might not one go further and claim that what is true of pastoral and doctrinal theology also is true of systematic theology, of fundamental theology, of historical theology?

Such questions, I believe, naturally arise from the occurrence of a pastoral council, from the enlarged notion of pastoral theology that was disseminated by the Council, from the announcement of a new theology by Karl Rahner and Edward Schillebeeckx in their preface to the first volume of the series, *Concilium.*

As I believe these questions arise, so I feel that they demand an affirmative answer. If the epithet 'pastoral' means no more than the logical application of universal norms to particular cases, there is no need for a pastoral council or even for a serious pastoral theology. But if the epithet 'pastoral' means something more, then that something has to be found in what escapes the universal, in the individual and the personal in the concrete community and the ongoing process of history.[13] Finally, if the individual, personal, communitarian, historical is really significant, then its consideration cannot be confined to a pastoral theology. For the whole of theology is a reflection on religion; the individual, the personal, the communitarian, the historical are essential to the Christian religion; and so, it would seem, the individual, the personal, the communitarian, the historical are relevant not just to a part of theology but to the whole of it.

Thomas Aquinas, in the first question of his *Summa theologiae,* defended the view that theology was a science. Meeting the objection that science dealt with the universal but theology with particulars, he answered: 'Particulars are treated in sacred doctrine, but not as though they were the principal topic; they are introduced as models of life in the moral sciences or as presentations of the authority of those through whom divine revelation came to us ...'[14] The

---

13 [The wording from 'in the individual' is the way Lonergan rewrote this part of the sentence for the Thomas More lecture. In the autograph of the Larkin-Stuart lecture, he wrote, 'in the individual, the personal, the concrete community, the ongoing process of history.']

14 *Summa theologiae,* 1, q. 1, a. 2, ad 2m. [The translation here seems to be Lonergan's own.]

Thomist position was inevitable as long as theology was conceived as a science and science was deemed to deal with the universal. But commitment to the universal is not the norm of modern science, which would explain all phenomena; it is not the norm of modern scholarship, which would understand the thought of individuals and narrate the histories of peoples; it is not the norm of a modern philosophy which can take its stand on the inner experience of the individual and from that basis proceed to an understanding of human process, human community, human history. Today, theology not only can be concerned with the individual, the personal, the communitarian, the historical – it just cannot avoid embracing that concern and adopting that viewpoint.

5   The Shift to the Human Subject[15]

Now the shift to the existential human subject includes much more than the transition from universal essences to the personal experience of individuals. It drops the Aristotelian primacy of metaphysics to draw its basic concepts from the data of consciousness. It replaces a faculty psychology by an intentionality analysis. It subsumes the value of truth under the more comprehensive value of the good, to sublate what was called speculative intellect under the free and responsible deliberations, evaluations, decisions of a subject that is existential before being practical. It acknowledges the ongoing character of human investigation, and so conceives logic as a tool within the larger domain ruled by method.

This shift to the subject had its antecedents in the writings of Augustine, Pascal, Kierkegaard, Newman. It developed its techniques in the interplay of modern thinkers, the meditations of Descartes, the critiques of Kant, the comprehensive systems of the absolute idealists, the subsequent scattering of philosophic, scientific, and scholarly opinion that agreed only in rejecting the ambitions of the idealists.

Roman Catholic thinkers were slow to join their contemporaries and become personalists or phenomenologists or pragmatists or existentialists. Their tardiness is easily understood. There stood in their way papal patronage of the works of Thomas Aquinas, a patronage that emanated from the Roman curia to bishops throughout the world, and from bishops to the rectors that presided over seminaries.

Still, this patronage came with its own remedy. The more Aquinas was

15   [Lonergan added, in the Larkin-Stuart lecture, 'die anthropologische Wende.']

extolled, the greater the value and the importance of grasping exactly what he thought. There was begun a critical edition of his works. Medieval Institutes fostered and spread the application to his writings of the best contemporary techniques in hermeneutics and history. It was not long before students of Aquinas banished from the classroom the old-style interpretation that quoted and then argued. What alone could be valid, what alone was acceptable, was the prolonged and tedious study and comparison of texts that rarely arrived at results that were both significant and certain. Devotion to the thought of Aquinas had been intended to provide a Maginot Line that ensured doctrinal uniformity and immobility. But modern scholarship tended to change it into a vast forest, and only a lifelong expertise enabled one to say which trees had been chopped down, which still stood, and what new ones had recently sprung up.

For an even longer period the same process had been going forward in patristics, so that there grew up, even in Roman Catholic circles, a large body of theological opinion familiar with the procedures and techniques initiated by the German Historical School in the early nineteenth century. This opinion was quite aware that the methods already applied in the fields of patristic and medieval studies inevitably were to be extended to the study of scripture. That extension, long vetoed by Roman curial opinion, finally was acknowledged, approved, and praised by Pius XII in his celebrated encyclical *Divino afflante Spiritu*, issued on the feast of St Jerome, September 30, 1943.

Now one cannot but be happy over these developments. It was a good thing for Catholic researchers to become familiar with their sources, biblical, patristic, medieval, and modern, by employing the best available procedures and techniques. It was no less a good thing for them to be freed from the limitations of Greek and medieval systems of thought. Still, these good and, indeed, excellent things also presented a supreme challenge. Where traditional theology had felt it could proceed deductively from scripture to the councils, modern scholarship revealed more than a sea change. Where traditional theology felt itself in possession of necessary and self-evident truths,[16] modern reflection scrutinized a field of contingent developments, developments that were contingent both in the proximate objects investigated and in the merely probable conclusions reached by investigators.[17]

---

16 [In the Thomas More lecture this is rewritten to read, 'Where traditional theology retained an ideal of necessary and self-evident truths ...']

17 [It is at this point that the Larkin-Stuart lecture and the Thomas More lecture begin to vary considerably. The following paragraph is the last

It is this challenge that explains, I believe, the sudden disarray of Catholic theologians. Ever since Vatican II, the world has been astounded by the manifold of novel opinions put forward in Catholic theology. But even more notable is the impotence of those who would sustain traditional positions. For what is traditional has for centuries been Scholastic, and what is Scholastic is open to the criticism uttered during the Council, namely, that pre-conciliar draft decrees were not only Scholastic but also abstract, and neither biblical nor pastoral nor ecumenical.

6   A Choice of Revolutions [Conclusion to the Larkin-Stuart Lecture]

The word 'revolution' has many meanings. For present purposes it will suffice to distinguish two of them. There is the revolution of the political type that involves a repudiation of the past. There is the revolution of the scientific type that goes beyond the past yet preserves it in a new synthesis. What I have called the political type of revolution may be illustrated by the French, the Russian, or the Chinese revolution. What I have called the scientific type may be illustrated by Einstein's special theory of relativity that included Newtonian mechanics as a particular case in a broader and different scheme of things.

The theological relevance of this distinction may be illustrated by the age-old question, What think you of Christ? In the issue for May and June of this year, the *International Catholic Review* contains an article with the title, 'In What Way Is Jesus Christ Unique?' The first paragraph of the article sets forth with admirable clarity just what the title means. It recounts that 'Until a few years ago, every Christian, at least every Catholic Christian, would unhesitatingly have answered the question why he professed faith in Jesus by saying that Jesus is more than a human being, the God-man, the eternal Son of God incarnate. Today this answer has become questionable, and other answers are offered: We believe in Jesus as the true, exemplary, new human being. This change in the understanding of Christ and the profession of faith in Christ is particularly clear in theological thought.'[18]

---

paragraph in this section of the Larkin-Stuart lecture, and the section that follows it is the concluding section of the same lecture. The Thomas More lecture does not contain the following paragraph, but rather adds one sentence to the present paragraph. See the material at note 20 below.]

18 Klaus Reinhardt, 'In What Way Is Jesus Christ Unique?' in *International Catholic Review* 2 (1973) 131; in German, *Internationale katholische Zeitschrift* 2 (1973) 206. [Lonergan's note adds, 'This review is published simultaneously in several languages; my references are to the English and German editions.']

Such is the contention of Klaus Reinhardt and of a number of the theologians to whom he refers. In its substance the contention is startling.[19] Traditional Christians who accept the councils of Nicea, Ephesus, and Chalcedon will say that Mary is the Mother of God. Those who feel that, after all, these councils went astray will be content to say that Mary is the mother not of God but of the true, exemplary, new human being. This view is revolutionary, and, since it repudiates a notable element in the Christian past, the revolution resembles the political type.

But besides the political type of revolution, there also is the scientific type. So far from repudiating the past, it retains it, to incorporate it with its original sense and meaning unchanged within a new perspective. It will grant that the systematic theology of the past that accepted the Aristotelian priority of metaphysics has had its day. It will point out that there has long been maturing what the Germans name *die anthropologische Wende*, the shift to the human subject. It will derive its basic concepts not from a metaphysics but from immediate human experience as brought to light by intentionality analysis. It will be able, I am convinced, to express in the formulations of elementary experience what Chalcedon sought to convey when it mentioned one person and two natures.

There we must leave the matter. Already I have spoken too long, and, while the matter can and must be carried further, it will remain for younger theologians of today – if any happen to agree with me – to effect the needed clarifications and developments that will make the alternative of a scientific revolution not just a possibility but an actuality.

***

In an extremely quiet fashion there had come about a profound change in the structure and the procedures of theology.[20]

Conclusion to the Thomas More Lecture

If I have acknowledged a profound change in the structure and the procedure of Catholic theology, I must add that the change envisaged has long been awaited, that it is carefully motivated, that it is substantially limited.

19 [In the autograph text, Lonergan had typed 'not new' but then changed this to 'startling.']
20 [This sentence appears at the end of the section 'The Shift to the Human Subject,' in the Thomas More lecture. See above, at note 17. This sentence is followed by the conclusion written for the Thomas More lecture.]

The change has been long awaited. It dates not from 1965, when the Second Vatican Council closed, but rather from 1845, when Newman completed his *Essay on the Development of Christian Doctrine*.

The change is carefully motivated. It is not the too frequent blind and total rejection of medieval achievement. It is a recognition of precise shortcomings that have been brought to light by modern science, modern scholarship, modern philosophy. It is not any undiscriminating acceptance of the modern. It is an acceptance that, at least for me, was prepared by years of teaching theology and by two detailed studies of Aquinas, one on *Grace and Freedom*, the other on *Word and Idea*.[21] It is an acceptance worked out step by step in two books, *Insight* and *Method in Theology*,[22] with the composition of the first beginning in 1949 and the completion of the second occurring in 1972.

The change is limited. Its aim is filling out the old by the new, *vetera novis augere et perficere*. If it gives cognitional theory a priority over metaphysics, it does so not to downgrade metaphysics but to ground it critically. And it wants a critically grounded metaphysics because any statement with an objective reference contains implicitly a metaphysics and there occur occasions, even in theology, when it is well to make the implicit explicit.

It places orthopraxis above orthodoxy, but it has no doubt that 'doing the truth' involves 'saying the truth,' that 'saying the truth' heads into the broader context of 'writing the truth,' that symbolic and anthropomorphic speaking and writing have eventually to give an account of themselves with a literalness and coherence that meet the requirements of logic. So the unfolding of Christian teaching mounts a succession of terraces. To discern the many routes followed at each stage of the ascent, to understand each and to measure its validity, calls for work that resembles closely Aloys Grillmeier's *Christ in Christian Tradition*[23] and differs vastly from Piet Schoonenberg's *The Christ*.[24]

---

21 *Grace and Freedom: Operative Grace in the Thought of St Thomas Aquinas*, vol. 1 of Collected Works of Bernard Lonergan, ed. Frederick E. Crowe and Robert M. Doran (Toronto: University of Toronto Press, 2000); *Verbum: Word and Idea in Aquinas*, vol. 2 of Collected Works of Bernard Lonergan, ed. Frederick E. Crowe and Robert M. Doran (Toronto: University of Toronto Press, 1997).
22 [See above, p. 3, note 1, and p. 12, note 2.]
23 Aloys Grillmeier, *Christ in Christian Tradition: From the Apostolic Age to Chalcedon (451)*, trans. J.S. Bowden (London: Mowbray & Co. Ltd., 1965). [This is the volume to which Lonergan referred; subsequent volumes have appeared since.]
24 Originally in Dutch, this book has been translated into German, English, and French. Piet Schoonenberg, *Hij een God van Mensen* ('s Hertogenbosch:

A many-terraced unfolding of Christian doctrine by itself gives rise at each stage to a new and narrower elite and thereby threatens an increasing alienation of ever greater numbers.[25] So the very development of doctrine calls for a doctrinal pluralism,[26] for as many manners of teaching the same basic message as there are distinct classes dividing each of the many cultures of mankind. It is this pluralism that must be had both to preach the gospel to all nations and to reconcile the fact of doctrinal and theological development with the pastoral concern of Pope John XXIII and his Second Vatican Council.

Malmberg, 1969); *Ein Gott der Menschen* (Einsiedeln: Benziger, 1969); *The Christ: A Study of the God–man Relationship in the Whole of Creation and in Jesus Christ*, trans. Della Cowling (New York: Herder and Herder, 1971); *Il est le Dieu des hommes* (Paris, Editions du Cerf, 1973).

    Comments from *Acta Apostolicae Sedis* 64 (1972) 238, § 3. Mark Schoof, 'Dutch Catholic Theology: A New Approach to Christology,' *Cross Currents* 22 (Winter, 1973) 415–27. Bernard Sesboué, 'Bulletin de théologie dogmatique: Christologie,' *Recherches de science religieuse* 61 (1973) 423–65; on Schoonenberg, 447–54. Bernard Lonergan, 'The Origins of Christian Realism' (see above, p. 184, note 21).

25 Alienation is provoked rather than allayed by an article that begins as follows: 'A far-reaching change is taking place in the way in which Christ is thought of at the present time. Until a few years ago, every Christian, at least every Catholic Christian, would unhesitatingly have answered the question why he professed faith in Jesus by saying that Jesus is more than a human being, the God-man, the eternal Son of God incarnate. Today this answer has become questionable, and other answers are offered: We believe in Jesus as the true, exemplary, new human being. This change in the understanding of Christ and in the profession of faith in Christ is particularly clear in theological thought.' So Klaus Reinhardt, 'In What Way Is Jesus Christ Unique?' [see above, note 18].

26 Internationale Theologenkommission, *Die Einheit des Glaubens und der theologische Pluralismus* (Einsiedeln: Johannes Verlag, 1973). French, Italian, and Spanish translations have been announced. See also Bernard Lonergan, *Doctrinal Pluralism* (Milwaukee: Marquette University Press, 1971 [see above, pp. 70–104]).

13

Variations in Fundamental Theology[1]

I have already had occasion to mention *Concilium*. It is a series of volumes on current theological issues in which the theological consultants at the Second Vatican Council continued the type of work they did during the council. So far over eighty volumes have appeared. Up to 1970 they averaged about one hundred and eighty pages each. Since then the average has dropped to about one hundred and fifty.

---

1 [The second of the Larkin-Stuart Lectures, Trinity College on 13 November 1973, and the second of the St Thomas More Lectures, delivered at Yale University 12 February 1974; see above, p. 221, note 1. A version of this lecture, edited by Frederick E. Crowe, was published in *Method: Journal of Lonergan Studies* 16:1 (1998) 5–24.

   The sources used here are the autograph text of the 1973 lecture, the tape recording of the same lecture, the typescript for the 1974 lecture, and the version published in *Method*. (For information on the first three of these sources, see above, p. 221, note 1.) Lonergan's own section headings, added for the 1974 lecture, have been retained. The two public lectures had distinct concluding summaries. The slightly longer version of the Yale lecture is given first, since it is the version that was preserved by Lonergan in his private papers (Archives item A2589). The shorter version of the Trinity College lecture follows. Three other differences between the 1973 autograph and the 1974 typescript will be indicated at the proper places.

   The announcement of the Thomas More lectures describes this lecture as follows: 'A style in fundamental theology, dating from the early seventeenth century, and commonly followed in Catholic schools up to Vatican II, now has practically vanished. Proposals for a successor are numerous and, despite some measure of convergence, they remain for conservatives quite novel.']

My topic this evening comes from volume 46, published in 1969. Its title is *The Development of Fundamental Theology*, and its contributors come from around the world. They are Claude Geffré at Paris, René Latourelle at Rome, Raymond Panikkar in India and various places in the United States, Heinrich Fries at Munich, Juan Segundo at Montevideo, Jan Walgrave at Louvain, Joseph Cahill then at Notre Dame and now at Edmonton, Karl Rahner then at Münster, Langdon Gilkey in Chicago, and John Macquarrie then in New York and now at Oxford.

1   The Traditional Conception

Interest in my topic lies, not in fundamental theology itself, but in the fact that the traditional conception of it was rejected by many representatives both of the thinking that went into the Second Vatican Council and of the spirit that the council fostered or at least released. This rejection marks a notable reversal of opinion. Prior to the council and during it, it was customary in most Catholic theological schools to devote to fundamental theology the whole first year of the four-year basic course. Vatican II called for an overhauling of the teaching of theology. Four years after the council closed, René Latourelle, a brilliant French Canadian, Dean of the faculty of theology at the Gregorian University in Rome, reported: 'Key experiments, in Europe or America, demonstrate that fundamental theology at the present time is confronted with the alternatives either of dismemberment and disappearance or of beginning a new and different life.'[2]

These alternatives are startling. What had been the staple of the first year of theological studies now is offered the grim choice. On the one hand, it may be dismembered and disappear.[3] On the other hand, it may be transformed into something else.

So abrupt a change may be accounted for in two ways. First, there is the general cause that accounts for so many of the seeming novelties that emerged during or after Vatican II: change was long overdue. What might have been an extended series of almost imperceptible modifications running over centu-

2 [This quotation has no reference in Lonergan's typescripts, but agrees in sense if not verbatim with reflections found in Latourelle's paper, 'Dismemberment or Renewal of Fundamental Theology?' in *Concilium* 46: *The Development of Fundamental Theology*, ed. Johannes B. Metz (New York: Paulist Press, 1969) 29–30.]
3 [In the Trinity College lecture, Lonergan added, 'a little bit here and a little bit there.']

ries turned into an enormous cumulation of differences that eventually emerged as a single massive sweep.

In the second place, fundamental theology was a highly technical conception. It was concerned with presenting the reasonableness of faith. But that reasonableness may be presented in at least three different manners, and fundamental theology denoted, not all three manners, but only one. That one was the most technical of the three, and the one most involved in the peculiarities of the thought and temper of an age that had passed away.

The reasonableness of faith, then, may be shown on the basis of the faith itself. Such showing, of course, is not a logical proof. To a logician it is merely arguing in a circle, concluding to the faith by presupposing the faith. Still, logic never took anyone beyond what he already knew implicitly, for there is nothing in any strictly logical conclusion that is not already contained in the premises. What advances matters is developing understanding, coming to understand what previously one did not understand. Such is the secret of all teaching. Such, too, is the most effective way of coming to understand the faith. To appeal to such faith as people already have is the most rapid and convincing way to make them begin to feel at home in what hitherto they have not grasped.

Besides those that already believe, there are those still outside the faith. To them too the reasonableness of the faith may be shown. But now the argument will presuppose, not the tenets of faith, but the convictions of reasonable men and women. Its purpose will be, not to demonstrate, but to persuade. It will start from people as they happen to be. It will take into account their strengths and their weaknesses. It will proceed in some approximation to the artistry developed in Greece by an Isocrates and codified by an Aristotle, then developed in a new key in Rome by a Cicero and codified by a Quintilian. Its success will vary with the time and place, with the skill of the advocate and the good will of his hearers or readers.

Besides these two ways there is a third, and it is the way of a fundamental theology. It is not content with the first way, even for believers, for they can feel that the beliefs they happen to entertain are the fruit of some accident. They are believers because their parents were, or because their more inspiring and persuasive teachers were, or because their country, like Kierkegaard's Denmark, is a Christian country. But what alone has an intrinsic claim upon them is the fact they are and/or wish to be reasonable men or women. Why should one, they ask, simply because he or she wishes to be reasonable, accept the tenets of the Christian religion as presented in this or that communion?

The third way, then, at once resembles and differs from both the first and the second. It resembles the first inasmuch as it speaks to believers. It resembles the second and differs from the first inasmuch as it speaks to nonbelievers. And it differs from the second inasmuch as it proposes to proceed, not by rhetoric, but by logic. It is by this concern to proceed rigorously and, in that sense, to be scientific that the way of fundamental theology differs from the other two.

It is this third way, it would seem, that Karl Rahner refers to as traditional fundamental theology. It is the way that by many today is repudiated, despite the oblique reaffirmation of its essential validity by Pius XII in his encyclical *Humani generis* (DS 3876). Its origins lie in the controversies of the Reformation period, in the triumph of rationalism in the Enlightenment, and in the cultural phenomenon of atheism. It has a threefold structure that goes back to *Les trois vérités* of Pierre Charron (1593) and to the *De veritate religionis christianae* (1627) of Hugo Grotius. This threefold structure involved demonstrations, first, of the existence of God and of religion, secondly, of the Christian religion, thirdly, of the true church. A natural theology established the existence of God. A natural ethics established the obligation of worshipping God. The prophecies of the Old Testament and the miracles of the New established the divine origin of the Christian religion, and the Christian message settled the identity of the true church.

Now there is an obvious difficulty to this procedure. It starts from data of common experience. It advances by human reason and historical testimony. It concludes to a religion and a church that not only may acknowledge the mysteries of the Trinity and the Incarnation but also may claim that these mysteries are not within the reach of human reason. Somewhere it would seem there must be a fallacy, for a valid argument has nothing in its conclusions that is not contained in its premises. But here the premises are presented as within the reach of human reason, while the conclusion contains what may lie beyond the reach of human reason.

To this objection there are answers, and some I think are invalid while others are valid. One may distinguish between the fact and the content of revelation, hold that the argument proves the fact, deny that it concludes or at least should conclude to the truth of the mysteries. Against such a view I would be inclined to accept Claude Geffré's contention that the distinction is unsatisfactory.[4] The fact of revelation becomes an abstraction. It sets aside a very notable element in the content of revelation, namely, the revelation that

4 [Claude Geffré, 'Recent Developments in Fundamental Theology: An Interpretation,' in *Concilium* 46, *The Development of Fundamental Theology* 11.]

a revelation has occurred. Again, the distinction between the fact and content of revelation leads to a further distinction. It is one thing to establish by natural reason the possibility of believing an indeterminate revelation; it is another to establish the possibility of believing mysteries that transcend human reason. The former does not include the latter, for by strict logic human reason cannot transcend itself.[5] And so the objection stands.

However, it is possible to give substantially the same argument a quite different interpretation. It concludes not to the truth of the Christian message but to its divine origin. It concludes that man is to hearken to the message, that the message creates a situation, that the situation is one of encounter, that man is to bow and adore, and in his adoration, which is unrestricted submission, he is to believe. On this interpretation, I think, the objection fails. But it fails precisely because it introduces a hiatus between the alleged objective science and the act of the believer. It is the existence of this hiatus that Jan Walgrave reported when he acknowledged a broad consensus that '... it is in no sense the function of fundamental theology to "prove" the truth of the Christian message. All that is expected of it is that it should deal with the reasons which can justify the acceptance of the faith as a moral option for a serious conscience.'[6]

But there remains a more radical objection. Professor Joseph Cahill, now at Edmonton, traced current fundamental theology back to the works of John Perrone written between 1835 and 1842. He claimed that its failure sprang from its attempt to do too much. He pointed to the 'naive and uncritical treatment of Scripture' in the textbooks. He noted, beyond an overtly polemic tone and intent, the further weakness of parochialism quite out of place in contemporary ecumenism, a pluralistic world, and a crisis of faith. As a final seal of its obsolescence he observed that traditional fundamental theology does not provide any room for the universes of discourse set up by such sciences as history, archeology, psychology, biology, psychiatry, sociology, and philosophy.[7]

A similar point is made with no less vigor and greater amplitude by Karl Rahner in a paper entitled 'Reflections on the Contemporary Intellectual

5 [The 1973 autograph reads, '... for human reason cannot strictly transcend itself.' The text here follows the 1974 typescript.]
6 Jan Walgrave, 'The Essence of Modern Fundamental Theology,' in *Concilium* 46, *The Development of Fundamental Theology* 82. [In the 1973 lecture, at the end of this quotation Lonergan added the remark, 'It proves that the question arises.']
7 Joseph Cahill, 'A Fundamental Theology of Our Time,' ibid. at p. 94.

Formation of Future Priests.'[8] Traditional fundamental theology, he would say, presupposes a view of scientific knowledge that belongs only to an earlier age. Then it was possible for a single mind on the basis of personal investigation to arrive at assured mastery in this or that field and so to be capable of a personal judgment on the issues that arose in that field. But the modern sciences are not individual but community enterprises. They are not fixed achievements but ongoing developments. They are not isolated from one another but interdependent, usually in highly complex manners. The range of data to which they appeal and on which they rest is mastered, not by the individual but by the group, and not by the group of this or that moment but by the ongoing group that critically receives and independently tests each new contribution. Finally, while the natural sciences admit secure generalizations and seriations, the fields of human studies confront the student with such vast diversity that each situation calls for a special investigation even though the results of the investigation may turn out to be matched by other instances.

It is within such a perspective that Rahner asks how a young student of theology – or for that matter an elderly professor of dogmatics such as himself – can form a personal judgment on relevant elements in the New Testament without being an expert in the Jewish theology of the time of Jesus, a Qumran specialist, a form critic, a historian of ancient religions, and many other things besides. He goes on to add that the student, if he becomes at least honestly conversant with the contemporary problems in these matters, cannot but feel that, so far from being capable of forming a personal judgment on which to base his own life and his future ministry, he is on the contrary bound to remain in all such matters a pitiful amateur.[9]

Rahner has further pregnant remarks on the plight of candidates for the priesthood, but they are far less relevant to our present concern. We have been considering a traditional fundamental theology that characterized itself as scientific and so distinguished itself from the rhetoric of apologetics. But we have come upon serious objections to such a claim. There was a time when the procedures of traditional fundamental theology might pass for science, but the science of Newton and the scholarship of von Ranke have radically transformed what is, and what is thought to be, scientific. Traditional funda-

8 [Karl Rahner, 'Reflections on the Contemporary Intellectual Formation of Future Priests,' *Theological Investigations*, vol. 6, trans. Karl-H. and Boniface Kruger (Baltimore: Helicon Press and London: Darton, Longman & Todd, 1969) 113–38.]
9 Ibid. 117.

mental theology differs from apologetics, not by being scientific, but by being a more jejune and abstruse piece of rhetoric. Further, even if traditional fundamental theology were scientific, it would not reach its goal. At most it can set forth prolegomena. But the prolegomena are only remotely relevant to an encounter, an act of adoration, and, in the adoration, an act of faith.

2   The New Outlook

However, my own purpose in these reflections on fundamental theology is to intimate to you some comprehension of the post-conciliar breakdown and disappearance of neo-Scholasticism, and some brief introduction to its successor, *die anthropologische Wende*, the turn to the human subject. This turn is conceived differently by different Catholic theologians, and an account of these differences would call for a bulky volume. I can do no more than present my own view of the matter, in the hope that it may be found helpful by those among you that wish to investigate the issues more fully.

First, then, the turn to the human subject is an acceptance of a cognitional fact unknown to Aristotle, namely, modern science.[10] This means that the ideal of science is to be conceived not in terms of deductive logic but in terms of method. The foundations on which science relies are not some set of self-evident premises or of necessary and eternal truths. What the scientist relies on ultimately is his method; and when his present method fails, then his reliance shifts to the improved method that that very failure, understood as failure, will bring forth. Similarly, the conclusions which science reaches are not the necessary consequents of necessary truths. As hypotheses, they are verifiable possibilities; as verified, they become the best available scientific opinion. Hence, science is no longer conceived as a permanent achievement but as an ongoing process; and it no longer is constituted by an acquired habit in the mind of an individual; rather it consists in the current stage in the cumulative development of a scientific community.

Already in these contrasts there may be envisaged the turn to the human subject. It is a turn from idealized objects, objects of infallible intuitions, of self-evident truths, of necessary conclusions. It is a turn to the actual reality of human subjects, to a community of men and women in a common attentiveness, in a common development of human understanding, in a common

10 [The 1973 autograph reads, '... the turn to the subject is an acceptance of modern science as cognitional fact.' The text here follows the 1974 typescript.]

reflection on the validity of current achievement, in a common deliberation on the potentialities brought to light by that achievement.

I cannot insist too much that this turn to the subject is totally misconceived when it is thought to be a turn from the truly objective to the merely subjective. Human subjects, their attention, their developing understanding, their reflective scrutiny, their responsible deliberations are the objective realities. Infallible intuitions, self-evident premises, necessary conclusions are the merely subjective constructions that may have served their purpose in their day but have been definitively swept aside by the science and scholarship of recent centuries.

I have been indicating the turn to the human subject – as I happen to conceive it – in its first and basic moment. But that first moment is only the thin edge of the wedge. For the shift from an ideal in terms of logic to an ideal in terms of method involves a shift not only in the ideal of scientific endeavor but also in the ideal of philosophic inquiry. As long as one's ideal is in terms of logic, then one's first philosophy will be, like Aristotle's, a metaphysic. For logic operates on propositions, and it is metaphysical propositions that are presupposed by all other propositions. But method orders cognitional operations,[11] and there are cognitional operations that are prepropositional, preverbal, prejudgmental, preconceptual; to these prior operations all propositions, including metaphysical propositions, reduce; and so from the viewpoint of method, as opposed to the viewpoint of logic, priority passes from metaphysics to cognitional theory.

It turns out, however, that the priority of cognitional theory is only relative, and the priority of cognitional operations qualified. The cognitional yields to the moral, and the moral to the interpersonal. To make a sound moral judgment one has to know the relevant facts, possibilities, probabilities; but with those conditions fulfilled, the moral judgment proceeds on its own criteria and towards its own ends. Again, moral judgments and commitments underpin personal relations; but with the underpinning presupposed or even merely hoped for, interpersonal commitment takes its own initiative and runs its own course.

I am touching here upon a key point. I have already mentioned a hiatus between the arguments of a fundamental theology and, on the other hand, the act of faith. That hiatus frequently is referred to as a leap of faith. That affirmation of a leap I would not deny or diminish. But while acknowledging

11 [In an aside, in the Trinity College lecture, 'It tells what to do: first, second, third.']

its unique aspects, I would urge that it is not unparalleled. For a distinction may be drawn between sublating and sublated operations, where the sublating operations go beyond the sublated, add a quite new principle, give the sublated a higher organization, enormously extend their range and bestow upon them a new and higher relevance. So inquiry and understanding stand to the data of sense; so reflection, checking, verifying stand to the formulations[12] of understanding; so deliberating on what is truly good, really worth while, stands to experience, understanding, and factual judgment; so, finally, interpersonal commitments stand to cognitional and moral operations.

The successive sublations of which I speak are, not at all the mysterious surmounting of contradictions in a Hegelian dialectic, but the inner dynamic structure of our conscious living. In its natural mode, as perhaps Edmund Husserl would say, such living is just lived. It is not adverted to explicitly; its elements are not distinguished, identified, named; the patterns of their interconnections have not been studied, scrutinized, delineated. But if we hold back from the world of objects, if our whole attention is not absorbed by them, then along with the spectacle we can advert to the spectator, along with the sounds we can find ourselves aware of our hearing. So too, problems let us find ourselves inquiring; solutions let us find the insights of the solver; judgments bring us to the subject critically surveying the evidence and rationally yielding to it; decisions point not only outwardly to our practical concerns but also inwardly to the existential subject aware of good and evil and concerned whether his own decisions are making him a good or evil man. But beyond all these, beyond the subject as experiencing, as intelligent, as reasonable in his judgments, as free and responsible in his decisions, there is the subject in love. On that ultimate level we can learn to say with Augustine, *amor meus pondus meum*, my being in love is the gravitational field in which I am carried along.

Our loves are many and many-sided and manifold. They are the ever fascinating theme of novelists, the pulse of poetry, the throb of music, the strength, the grace, the passion, the tumult of dance. They are the fever of youth, the steadfastness of maturity, the serenity of age. But on an endless topic, let us be brief and indicate three dimensions in which we may be in love. There is domestic love, the love that makes a home, in which parents and children, each in his or her own ever-nuanced and adaptive way, sustains and is sustained by each of the others. There is the love that is loyalty to one's fellows: it reaches out through kinsmen, friends, acquaintances, through all the bonds – cultural, social, civil, economic, technological – of human coop-

12 [In the Trinity College lecture, Lonergan added, 'the hypotheses.']

eration, to unite ever more members of the human race in the acceptance of a common lot, in sharing a burden to be borne by all, in building a common future for themselves and future generations. But above all, at once most secret and most comprehensive, there is the love of God. It is twofold. On the one hand, it is God's love for us: 'God loved the world so much that he gave his only Son, that everyone who has faith in him may not die but have eternal life' (John 3.16). On the other hand, it is the love that God bestows upon us: '... God's love has flooded our inmost heart through the Holy Spirit he has given us' (Romans 5.5).

I have been indicating two distinct components in the task of apologetics or, if you will, of fundamental theology. The precise character of these components varies with the historical unfolding of the Christian religion and with the personal development of individual inquirers. In the early church the two came together in the reply '... repent and be baptized, everyone of you, in the name of Jesus the Messiah; and you will receive the gift of the Holy Spirit' (Acts 2.38). For inasmuch as one was baptized in the name of Jesus the Messiah, one entered into the objective history of salvation; and inasmuch as one's repentance became efficacious through the gift of the Spirit, one entered upon a new life. But as the centuries slipped by, both the early simplicity remained for many, and a more complex account was needed, whether for the more erudite or for the more perverse. So in the First Vatican Council the two components appear: the first as the signs of divine revelation and, particularly, as the prophecies and miracles that show forth the omniscience and the omnipotence of God; the second as the help of the Holy Spirit given us within (DS 3009).

Today, the signs of divine revelation, the prophecies of the Old Testament and the miracles of the New, have been engulfed in the mountainous extent and intricate subtlety of biblical studies and critical history. God's gift of his grace is as frequent, as powerful, but also as silent and secret as ever, while we are perturbed by the probing of depth psychology and bewildered by the claims of linguistic analysts, by the obscurities of phenomenology, by the oddities of existentialism, by the programs of economic, social, and ecological reformers, by the beckoning of ecumenists and universalists.

3   New Positions

If I have attempted an overview of the issues, I must now report, even if with more brevity than justice, on positions that have been adopted and solutions that have been proposed. Certain basic attitudes are common to Henri

Bouillard, Heinrich Fries, Claude Geffré, and Jan Walgrave, and from them I shall begin. In contrast, the views of Karl Rahner and Raymond Panikkar introduce new and distinct issues that call for separate treatment.

In general, all agree that traditional fundamental theology has had its day. Juan Segundo of Montevideo succeeds in being quite amusing on the topic of a year of lectures establishing the fact of revelation without getting around to studying what was revealed.[13] Heinrich Fries depicts the controversialists that dilated on the apostasy of opponents but failed to grasp what they prized and defended, and he contrasts such an approach with the contemporary effort not to rebut error but to open doors, to listen and ask questions, to seek seriously an answer to questions.[14] Jan Walgrave speaks of a reversal of former positions: the old demonstrations from miracles and prophecy are often relegated to some intellectual limbo or are allowed to appear as incidental matter on the fringe of the real issues.[15] For Henri Bouillard, the real issues have their root in human experience of human life. He considers the word 'unbelief' a negative name for a positive reality. The positive reality he finds stated by Paul VI in his encyclical *Ecclesiam suam*, where it is asserted that there exist authentic human and spiritual values at the heart of non-Christian religions and at the basis of the arguments used by atheists to explain the nature of man.[16]

This appeal to common human experience evokes the memory of Maurice Blondel, once the victim of old-guard attacks but now mentioned explicitly by Geffré[17] and Walgrave.[18] However, the language employed seems to fit most easily into an adaptation of Heidegger. For Heidegger, *Verstehen*, understanding, was the condition of the possibility of the project and so of *Dasein*, of being a man.[19] For these writers, faith is the condition of the possibility at once of being fully a man and of being a Christian. Bouillard develops the point at

---

13 Juan Segundo, 'Fundamental Theology and Dialogue,' in *Concilium* 46, *The Development of Fundamental Theology* 69–79.
14 Heinrich Fries, 'From Apologetics to Fundamental Theology,' ibid. at p. 58.
15 Walgrave, 'The Essence of Modern Fundamental Theology' 82.
16 Henri Bouillard, 'Human Experience as the Starting Point of Fundamental Theology,' *Concilium* 6: *The Church and the World* (New York: Paulist Press, 1965) 82.
17 Geffré, 'Recent Developments in Fundamental Theology: An Interpretation' 13.
18 Walgrave, 'The Essence of Modern Fundamental Theology' 82–83.
19 [The 1973 autograph reads, 'For Heidegger *verstehen*, understanding, was the condition of the possibility of *Dasein*, of being a man.' The text here follows the 1974 typescript.]

some length but the gist of his thought would seem contained in the sentences: '... God's revelation would have no meaning for us if it were not at the same time the revelation of the meaning of our own existence. For the signs of revelation to be understood for what they are, the subject must grasp that there is an intrinsic relationship between the mystery which they are said to manifest and our own existence. The subject must at least glimpse what the Christian faith contributes to the fulfilment of his destiny. No apologetic will touch him if it does not in some way achieve this.'[20]

Heinrich Fries writes: '... faith is one of man's basic possibilities and actions – insofar as it essentially means "I believe in *you*," and not "I believe *that*."'[21] What is said of faith in general as a basic human possibility is applied to Christian faith: 'The tenets of faith must strike man in such a way that he is real in them and finds himself in an authentic encounter. In this encounter, man should really come to understand himself; he should find his "self" and the answers to his questions. Otherwise, faith is simply ideology.'[22]

Jan Walgrave, who like Heinrich Fries is a student of John Henry Newman, feels that other approaches run into difficulties because they do not go to the heart of the matter. So we are to confront the Christian message 'with the deepened self-understanding of man and the philosophy which analyzes the motives that live in that self-understanding.' This, of course, repeats in more general terms the point made by Bouillard and Fries, to which Walgrave adds that what is to be reached in that self-understanding is existential, prereflective, already a reality before it is clarified, *vécu* before it can be *thématique*.[23]

Claude Geffré presents not so much a view of his own as a critical survey of the current situation. He finds the ultimate refinements of traditional fundamental theology in the writings of Ambrose Gardeil and Reginald Garrigou-Lagrange.[24] He observes that contemporary thought has been reacting not merely against an obsolete fundamental theology but more basically against the once pervasive intellectualist and objectivist assumptions of neo-Thomism. Accordingly, the background of more recent efforts lies in post-Kantian developments of man's understanding.[25] To the whole of theology he as-

20 Bouillard, 'Human Experience as the Starting Point of Fundamental Theology' 87.
21 Fries, 'From Apologetics to Fundamental Theology' 62.
22 Ibid. 61–62.
23 Walgrave, 'The Essence of Modern Fundamental Theology' 84.
24 Geffré, 'Recent Developments in Fundamental Theology: An Interpretation' 9.
25 Ibid. 14–15.

cribes an anthropocentric dimension, to which fundamental theology pays special attention. For him the human subject is no longer a passive receptacle into which supernatural truths are to be deposited; on the contrary, the meaningful activity of God's people is accounted a constitutive element in revelation itself. So modern theology draws out the implications of Bultmann's intuition on the preunderstanding requisite for reading the Christian message. The gift of God's revelation is also a revelation of man to himself, so that, as Ricoeur has it, revelation as such is an opening up of existence, a possibility of existing,[26] or as Schillebeeckx put it, understanding the faith and self-interpretation cannot be separated.[27]

With Rahner, Geffré feels that the distinction between fundamental and dogmatic theology will tend to vanish, the more that dogmatic theology tends to be hermeneutical, that is, to find its basic terms in immediate human experience. He feels, as Rahner suggests, that there should be a far greater interpenetration of fundamental and dogmatic theology than at present exists, and thinks this will come about the more dogmatic theology becomes hermeneutical,[28] that is, derives its basic terms from immediate human experience.[29] With others, however, he finds, if not dangers, yet an excessive abstractness in Rahner's emphasis on an anthropocentric theology,[30] and devotes considerable space to the views of Johannes Metz and Jürgen Moltmann on eschatology as the key to the integration of theology in human historical process.[31]

4   Rahner and Panikkar

While Rahner's anthropocentrism[32] (which goes back to the 1940s)[33] comes up for criticism in volume 46 of *Concilium*, Rahner himself is off on quite a

26 Ibid. 16 and note 18.
27 Ibid. 19 and note 25.
28 Ibid. 19.
29 [Both of the preceding two sentences are found both in the 1973 autograph and in the 1974 typescript. In the Trinity College lecture, Lonergan did not read the words from 'that is' to the end of the sentence. Despite the seeming repetition, both sentences have been left in the text here.]
30 Ibid. 21 [with explicit reference to Hans Urs von Balthasar].
31 Ibid. 23–25.
32 [On the tape recording, Lonergan adds, 'Really, it is an identification of theocentrism and anthropocentrism.']
33 [In the Trinity College lecture, Lonergan adds a reference to Rahner's book *Hörer des Wortes*.]

different tack. His topic is theological pluralism. For two theologies to be contradictory, they have to share to some extent a common universe of discourse; otherwise, the putative contradiction would be merely a misunderstanding. For propositions to be contradictory, they must employ the same terms and attribute to them the same meaning. But it is just these identities that tend to be lacking in the modern world. As Rahner puts it: 'We are encountering basic positions, held by alien theologians, which do not spring from a shared horizon of fundamental understanding and which do not directly contradict our own theology. The disparity is not clear-cut, so that we cannot tackle it directly. In such cases we cannot adopt a clear yes or no toward the other side.'[34]

He does not hesitate to illustrate his point from his own Germanic world. He asks:

> Who among us can say for sure whether the basic conception of Barth's doctrine of justification is Catholic or not? If someone feels that he can, I would like to shake his hand. But where do we go, if we cannot even do that?
>
>   Who can say for sure that the ultimate root positions of Rudolf Bultmann are really un-Catholic? Who can say that the ultimate conclusions to be drawn from the postulates of the Bultmann school actually undercut his real intention and are unacceptable to Catholics, whether the Bultmann school realizes it or not? What do we do if we are not in a position to form some clear and responsible stance toward the other positions which confront us?[35]

Rahner gives further examples from within Catholic thought, but what he is up to is plain enough. Any science, any academic enterprise is the work of a group, of a scientific or academic community. For the work to prosper, the conditions for its possibility must be fulfilled. What Rahner is observing is that their medieval heritage had given Roman Catholic theologians a common and to some extent unambiguous language. There did exist different schools of thought, but the schools were of ancient lineage, and each had a fair notion of the ambiguities endemic in other positions. But Scholasticism and neo-

34 Karl Rahner, 'Pluralism in Theology and the Oneness of the Church's Profession of Faith,' in *Concilium* 46, *The Development of Fundamental Theology* 109.
35 Ibid.

Scholasticism had long been inadequate to modern needs, and their influence simply evaporated with Vatican II. Thereby, the Roman Catholic theologian and, no less, the teaching office of the church, the magisterium, are
confronted with basic, foundational problems that hitherto they were able to
neglect. A solution will have to be ongoing, dynamic and not static, for human
knowledge is a process of development. It will have to be securely anchored in
history; otherwise, it will be irrelevant to a historical religion. It will have to
have criteria for distinguishing between genuine development and mere
aberration.

Raymond Panikkar is, if anything, more radical than Rahner. He argues
that if '... fundamental theology is to have any relevance at all in our time of
world communication, it has to make sense to those outside the cultural area
of the Western world and, incidentally, also to those within it who no longer
think, imagine and act according to the paradigms of traditional fundamental
theology.'[36] Again, he urges: 'The real challenge to Christian faith today
comes from within – i.e., from its own exigence of universality ... The Christian
faith will either accept this challenge or declare its particular allegiance to a
single culture and thus renounce its claim of being the carrier of a universally
acceptable message, which does not destroy any particular value.'[37] He finds
that acceptance of the Christian message is blocked, not by its religious or
theological content, but by its philosophic or cultural accretions. 'The Bud-
dhist would like to believe in the whole message of Christ, and he sincerely
thinks that he could accept it and even understand it better if it could be
purified from what he considers its theistic superstructure. The Hindu will
wonder why he has to join a physical and cultural community simply because
of his belief in the divinity of Christ and in his resurrection. The "death of
God" theologian, or whatever name we choose for him, will say that it is
precisely because Christ is the Savior that he can dispense with any conception of a transcendent God or a physical miracle.'[38]

The solution envisaged by Panikkar is notably clear though not notably
precise. It is not any set of epistemological or ontological presuppositions that
once more would tie theology to some philosophic kite. Fundamental theology is to be fundamentally theology.[39] Its immense difficulty is that it is to be
an Exodus theology, a theological justification of a theological as well as a

36 Raymond Panikkar, 'Metatheology or Diacritical Theology as Fundamental
    Theology,' in *Concilium* 46, *The Development of Fundamental Theology* 46.
37 Ibid.
38 Ibid. 49.
39 Ibid. 47–48.

religious pluralism.[40] It would show '... that the Christian message may be-come meaningful in any authentic human attitude and genuine philosophi-cal position, ... that the Christian kerygma is not in principle tied down to any particular philosophical system or cultural scheme, or even to any particular religious tradition. Its role is to explain, for instance, not simply that the acceptance of the existence of God is a necessary prerequisite to understand and accept the Christian faith, but also that under the hypothesis of there being no God, if this is existentially given, the Christian proclamation could look for a justification and a meaning.'[41]

The source of the solution is a pluritheological dialogue. It is not to be assumed that there must be a kind of objectifiable common ground or certain universally formulable common statements. The plea is for a really open dialogue, one in which its meeting ground may first have to be created, one in which the very intermingling of religious currents, ideas, and beliefs may release a more powerful stream of light, service, understanding.[42] There are to be no rules of the game laid out in advance. Fundamental theology be-comes lived religion. It becomes mystical faith because it is previous to and beyond any formulation. It is the religious quest for a ground of understand-ing, for a common concern, which has to be lived, delimited, verbalized.[43]

5   Summary

By way of a concluding summary one may place generically and specifically the fundamental theology that once was traditional and now is widely rejected. Generically it was a logically ordered set of propositions. Specifically it was worked out in the context of a distinction and a separation: the distinction was the medieval distinction between nature and grace; the separation was the Cartesian reinforcement of the medieval distinction between philosophy and theology.

The logical operations were in a cumulative series. A first topic was the existence and attributes of God: it was considered philosophic and named a natural theology. A second topic was ethical: it established man's duty of worshiping God. A third topic was the true religion, and there it was argued that Jesus Christ was God's plenipotentiary in this matter. A fourth topic was

40 Ibid. 51.
41 Ibid. 52–53.
42 Ibid. 52.
43 Ibid. 54.

the true church: it examined the divisions within Christianity and determined which was the true church and what were its legitimate claims. With this concluded, the rest of theology had its foundation: for the true church demanded acceptance of all it believed and taught; and it was equipped to settle any further issues of moment that might arise.

In its day, this procedure was well adapted to the tactic of entering through another's door and coming out one's own. One entered the rationalist door of abstract right reason, and one came out in the all but palpable embrace of authoritarian religion. But in the course of time it came to pass that the rationalist door led nowhere. Authoritarian religion lived on, but it did so not as a logical conclusion but as a concrete community with a long and complicated history. There still was process but now it was, not from premises to conclusions, but from the original mustard seed to the large and conspicuously different tree. There still were cognitional operations, but now they terminated in the responsibility and freedom of total commitment.

Such has been the shift to the human subject, *die anthropologische Wende*, explored by Bouillard, Fries, Geffré, Walgrave. Such also is the historical process that breaks the bounds of some single universe of discourse, and scatters in Rahner's manifold of disparate yet not totally dissimilar modes of speech and thought. Such, to an undisclosed extent, may be the working of the one Spirit of God in diverse cultures and traditions to ground Panikkar's metatheology.

If I have been stressing differences between the Catholic present and past, I must stress equally that the past in question is a relatively recent past. There was a late Scholasticism that took over and expanded the mistakes in Aristotle's *Posterior Analytics*. Its tendencies, which were widely influential, were extended by the controversies of the sixteenth century and by the rationalism of the Enlightenment. Such, I should say, were the antecedents of traditional fundamental theology. But there also was an earlier and more celebrated Scholasticism. Its aim was not to demonstrate but to understand. It brought together and classified the data of scripture and tradition. It sought to reconcile discrepancies. It partly adopted and partly adapted a terminology, a single, coherent *Begrifflichkeit*, from the Aristotelian corpus. In this technical terminology it aimed to express a motivated clarification and orderly synthesis of the often seemingly opposed doctrines contained in its sources.

This procedure was a commonly understood and accepted if not explicitly formulated method. Its cumulative and progressive character can be seen in the succession of commentaries on Peter Lombard's four books of *Sentences*. If, for example, one compares the questions and articles of Aquinas with the corresponding passages in the Lombard, one can understand the manifest differences of thought and expression only through the theological development that occurred in the intervening century.

But though it was methodical, this work had a basic defect. It was not informed by historical consciousness, and so it projected, as it were, on a flat surface without the perspectives of time and change what can properly be apprehended only as the successive strata of an ongoing process.

Contemporary Catholic theology, then, is rightly new inasmuch as it makes its own all that is to be learned from modern conceptions and techniques of science, of interpretation, of history. But I believe that all this can be achieved without any repudiation of what is valid in the Catholic past. Indeed, as my own various writings will show, it can be done in a style and with a content that has a basic isomorphism[44] with the thought of Aquinas. So in this year, in which the seventh centenary of his death is celebrated, you will, I trust, permit me to end tonight's paper with this brief tribute to his name.

Concluding Summary of Larkin-Stuart Lecture[45]

By way of a concluding summary, one may locate the traditional fundamental theology, so widely rejected at the present time, as logically ordered operations on propositions, within the context of a medieval distinction between nature and grace and a Cartesian separation of philosophy and theology.

Within this context, a first task was to establish the existence and attributes of God, and, as this lay within the realm of human nature, it was termed a natural theology. The second task was ethical; it established man's duty of worshiping God, and the relevant arguments were assembled in a treatise on religion. A third task envisaged the multiplicity of religions, raised the question of the true religion, and undertook to show that Jesus the Christ was God's plenipotentiary in this matter. A fourth task confronted the divisions within the multitude of Christians and set about determining which was the true church and what were its claims. Finally, since the true church claimed complete submission and obedience, a foundation in principle had been found for the solution of every other theological question.

The hollowness of such a scheme became painfully obvious in an age when logic was no more than a subordinate tool within the larger framework of

44 Bernard Lonergan, 'Isomorphism of Thomist and Scientific Thought,' in *Collection* (see above, p. 76, note 7) 133–41.
45 [See above, note 1.]

method, and when the biblical movement, personalism, phenomenology, and existential concern moved attention on the European continent from words to their real antecedents in operations and attitudes.

The scattering of views I have illustrated may, perhaps, be given some unity by referring to my *Method in Theology*.[46] The preverbal and, indeed, pre-conceptual foundation of theology proposed by Panikkar intends to be a common starting point for all religions. Insofar as one starts from it and moves towards Christ, the Word of God, it corresponds to the foundational reality set forth in chapter 11 of *Method*, a reality conceived by Christians in terms of St Paul's statement: 'God's love has flooded our inmost hearts through the Holy Spirit he has given us' (Romans 5.5).

For Rahner's puzzlement over the swarm of disparate theologies that resist precise classification and so escape theological judgment, we may offer a set of larger containers, namely, the ordered multiplicity of differentiations of consciousness and their diversification by the presence or absence of religious, moral, or intellectual conversion. Such broad genetic differences can serve to mark off frontiers that contain conceptually disparate views.

Finally, the views of Bouillard, Fries, Geffré, and Walgrave form a separate class. They do not single out some preverbal and preconceptual foundation with Panikkar, and they do not stress with Rahner the disparateness of the views they discuss. Nonetheless, their existential concern both relates them implicitly to Panikkar's emphasis and, at the same time, enables their argument to be relevant to the disparate positions to which Rahner draws attention.

46 [See above, p. 12, note 2.]

14

Sacralization and Secularization[1]

It may well be thought strange that an account of post-conciliar change in Roman Catholic theology should venture to mention a topic on which the principal theorist has been Friedrich Gogarten and the renowned names are Karl Barth and more particularly Dietrich Bonhoeffer.

1 [The third of the Larkin-Stuart Lectures, delivered at Trinity College, University of Toronto, on 14 November 1973, and the third and final of the St Thomas More Lectures, delivered at Yale University on 13 February 1974; see above, p. 219, note 1.

The sources used in this editing of the lecture are the autograph text prepared for the Larkin-Stuart lecture; a dittoed reproduction of the same for a Faculty Seminar at Regis College on 17 November 1973; and a typescript of the St Thomas More lecture. All three of these documents can be found in the library of the Lonergan Research Institute, Toronto. The Thomas More typescript includes revisions to the Larkin-Stuart autograph, and these have been preserved in the text produced here. Variations will be indicated in notes, and the longer conclusion of the 1973 autograph will be added at the end.

No tape recording of this lecture is available.

It seems that the original autograph text was used again by Lonergan as the Willis M. Tate-Willson Lecture, Southern Methodist University, on 21 March 1974. See File 799 in the library of the Lonergan Research Institute.

The announcement of the Thomas More Lectures describes 'Sacralization and Secularization' as follows: 'The topic is introduced by reports on (1) Paul Ricoeur on the Freudian critique of religion and (2) M.-D. Chenu and Jean Daniélou on the "Constantinian era." There follow accounts of infra-structure and suprastructure in religion, and the fragments are collected in a dialectic on the ambiguities of "sacred" and "profane," "sacral" and "secular."']

But one of the features of post-conciliar Catholic thought is precisely the fact that Protestant initiatives are all the more readily transferred to the Catholic milieu and there undergo the sea change of a fresh significance and a new treatment. So last December in the London periodical, *The Month*, Nicholas Lash had an article of purely Catholic concern on 'Faith and the Secular,'[2] while the international periodical *Concilium* has devoted at least three volumes to similar matters. Volume 16 was entitled *Is God Dead?* Volume 19 was on *Spirituality in the Secular City*. And volume 47 was devoted, as is the present lecture, to *Sacralization and Secularization*.[3]

I shall introduce my subject by outlining an article of Paul Ricoeur's on the atheism of Freudian psychoanalysis, and by sketching Claude Geffré's contrast of Marie-Dominique Chenu's and Jean Cardinal Daniélou's radically opposed views on the end of the Constantinian era. I shall work towards an understanding of the issues by a discussion of the social construction of reality, not without a bow to Peter Berger and Thomas Luckmann. I shall close with an attempt at clarifying terms and presenting a genealogy of differences.[4]

---

2 [Nicholas Lash, 'Faith and the Secular,' *The Month* (December 1973) 403–408.]

3 [*Concilium* 16, *Is God Dead?* (New York: Paulist Press, 1966); *Concilium* 19, *Spirituality in the Secular City* (New York: Paulist Press, 1966); *Concilium* 47, *Sacralization and Secularization*, ed. Roger Aubert (New York: Paulist Press, 1969). No editor is named for vols. 16 and 19.]

4 [The 1973 autograph has a different set of introductory paragraphs. They read as follows.

'The theologians that, as advisers, *periti*, took part in the Second Vatican Council wished to perpetuate the service they had rendered during the council. So they banded together and under the title *Concilium* have published over eighty volumes bearing on religious issues of the day. The forty-seventh volume in this series was entitled *Sacralization and Secularization*. From that volume I have borrowed the title for this evening's lecture. A notable part of my material, however, will be drawn not only from that volume but also from volumes 16 and 19 entitled, respectively, *Is God Dead?* and *Spirituality in the Secular City*.

'In the earliest of these three volumes there is a paper by Paul Ricoeur entitled "The Atheism of Freudian Psychoanalysis." I shall begin by offering some account of its contents, for I know no quicker or better way to point out the relevance and indeed the high seriousness of our topic. Professor Ricoeur's contention is at once simple and heartening. He grants that Freud has reinforced the faith of unbelievers; but he would show us how to make use of Freud to reinforce the faith of believers (*C* 16:71).']

1   Paul Ricoeur: 'The Atheism of Freudian Psychoanalysis'[5]

Writing on the general topic, *Is God Dead?* Professor Ricoeur began by recognizing Sigmund Freud as one of the outstanding atheists of our culture. Freud's atheism he found evident in such writings as *The Future of an Illusion, Civilization and Its Discontents, Moses and Monotheism.* But what makes this atheism outstanding lies in Freud's originality and in his profound influence on modern man's understanding of himself.

Freud's originality is that his atheism is not just another instance of philosophic empiricism or scientific positivism. For his work differs from that of natural science both in its data and in its technique. Its data are not the outer data of sense but the inner data of consciousness, even the data of dreams. Its technique is not the correlation of measurements but the interpretation of personal experiences. So it is that the work of the psychoanalyst bears little resemblance to that of a physicist and a great resemblance to that of a textual critic or an exegete.

Differing from natural science both in its data and in its technique, psychoanalysis concerns itself with the mental hygiene not only of individuals but also of cultures and civilizations. In this fashion Freudian thought comes to be classed along with the thought of Feuerbach, Marx, and Nietzsche. As they did, it too criticizes culture and, along with culture, religion as a cultural phenomenon. As they did, it too reduces religion to a hidden movement of consciousness that is the source of an illusion and expresses itself in myth. As they did, it too is not content to destroy religion; it has a positive aim and would restore to man what is proper to him but had been displaced and lost in an alien transcendence.

After conceding the originality of Freudian atheism, Ricoeur proceeds to reveal his own originality. Where other religiously-minded critics tend to dispute in principle the legitimacy of psychoanalytic pronouncements on art, morality, religion, Ricoeur is at pains to grant explicitly that legitimacy insofar as art, morality, religion are cultural phenomena. The tension between human instinct and socially acceptable behavior is not confined to the individual psyche but is a real and significant component in the tensions of society itself. The Freudian 'censor,' 'superego,' 'father image' are psychic functions within the individual but they stand in vital correspondence with social demands. Finally, if these psychic functions are to succeed in meeting social demands,

5 [Paul Ricoeur, 'The Atheism of Freudian Psychoanalysis,' trans. Ruth Dowd, *Concilium* 16 (1966) 59–72.]

if they are to banish even the thought of incest, murder, cannibalism, then they need to be reinforced by some compensating factor at once terrible and consoling: terrible enough to preclude transgression; consoling enough to hide privation.

Now it is religion that can and does fulfil this twofold role. It can threaten punishments painful beyond measure and, to boot, everlasting. It can promise joys that no one has known in this world. But as meeting a psychic need, as a cultural phenomenon that meets the need, religion is no more than an instance of wish fulfilment. Its threats and promises are what men may need, what men may wish but, unfortunately, what men cannot bring about. Wishing effects nothing. We are not in fairyland.

I have spoken of Ricoeur's originality in granting that the Freudian critique of religion was, in principle, legitimate. But there is a further aspect to that originality to which attention must now be drawn. For in granting the legitimacy of the critique in principle, Ricoeur does not grant that the critique is in fact complete. Something more has to be said, and its tenor will be that, as in the past Freud has reinforced the faith of unbelievers, so in the future he may be used to reinforce the faith of believers.

The incompleteness of Freudian thought comes to light in two manners. On the one hand, Freudian analysis moves from a contemporary psychic situation in a patient back to its origins in childhood, in infancy, in prenatal experience. But this backward movement necessarily presupposes in the patient or client a previous forward movement that proceeded from the origins to the present state of affairs. Besides the archeology that discovers traces of the past in the present, there also exists a teleology along which the present emerged from the past. Moreover – and this is the second element in the matter – that process of emergence can be disturbed and distorted, and such disturbances and distortions, in principle, can be corrected or remedied. For if no correction or remedy is possible, then it would be useless to consult a psychoanalyst on one's neurosis or to listen to one when he would liberate civilizations from their illusions.

But what is true of human development in general also would seem to be true of man's religious development. It has its beginnings, its incomplete and rudimentary stages, its tendencies towards a fullness and balance that may be named a maturity. But traces of the rudimentary can survive in developed instances, and there can arise disturbances that, if let run their course, result in distortions. As in other domains, so too in the domain of religion infantile fears can outlast the time of their inevitability. They can color or pervade or dominate in religious feelings of guilt. But it does not at once follow, and it is not at once to be assumed, that such fears represent religious maturity and not religious retardation. One cannot simply ignore the fact that, as religious people advance in the life of the spirit, fear gives place to love, and the terrors of guilt yield to shame for one's lack of responsibility and sorrow for one's lack of love. Again, insofar as religious hope renounces the satisfactions of this life for the sake of the satisfactions of the future life, we have to do not with the maturity of hope but with the law, which for St Paul was just our pedagogue in Christ. True hope may for a time express itself as a hope for recompense, but until it grows into a confidence that relies simply on the goodness of God, then on a day of bitter trial the satisfactions of the present may seem the better bargain.

I have been sketching in bold outline and with simplified emphases the reflections of Paul Ricoeur on the atheism of Freudian psychoanalysis. For a fuller account you must go not only to the article I have mentioned but also to the book *De l'interprétation: Essai sur Freud.*[6] But enough perhaps has been said to introduce you into the climate in which such terms as sacralization and secularization can assume a precise meaning. Their clarification cannot be attempted at once, but it can at once be said that they deal with development and retardation, with mistaking retardation for development and mistaking development for retardation and, most disastrous of all, with triumphantly living out a mistake as though it were the truth, or living out a truth in the agony of fearing it to be a mistake.

2   Claude Geffré, o.p.: 'Desacralization and the Spiritual Life'[7]

In the nineteenth volume of *Concilium*, bearing the title *Spirituality in the Secular City*, Claude Geffré reviews a number of debates turning upon the tension between the inner life of prayer and the secular, desacralized world in which we live. Of these debates our attention will have to be limited to that between Marie-Dominique Chenu, who favors desacralization, and Jean Cardinal Daniélou, whose elevation to the cardinalate was preceded by a book entitled *L'Oraison, problème politique.*[8]

6 [Paul Ricoeur, *De l'interprétation: Essai sur Freud* (Paris: Editions du Seuil, 1965); in English, *Freud and Philosophy: An Essay on Interpretation*, trans. Denis Savage (New Haven: Yale University Press, 1970).]
7 [Claude Geffré, 'Desacralization and the Spiritual Life,' trans. Theodore L. Westow, *Concilium* 19 (1966) 111–31.]
8 [Jean Cardinal Daniélou, *L'Oraison, problème politique* (Paris: Librairie Arthème Fayard, 1965); English trans., J.R. Kirwan, *Prayer as a Political Problem* (New York: Sheed and Ward, 1967).]

For Chenu, the changed situation of Christianity in Western Europe simply marks the end of the era of Constantine. It was Constantine that decreed the end of the persecution of Christians. He it was that initiated the fateful alliance of church and state that for centuries, despite changing circumstances and profoundly altered situations, despite quarrels and enmities and violence, nevertheless did define a basic state of affairs, a dyarchy of *imperium* and *sacerdotium*, of throne and altar.

It has been Chenu's thesis, if not his words, that the end of the era of Constantine means a passage from Christendom to Christianity. From being a power in the world, the church is to become a presence in the world. It is a change that he holds to be all to the good. His protracted study of the ways in which the Word of God is incarnated in time has led him to the conclusion that the more the world is itself, the more men will be themselves and the more the Word of God will be itself. This triple authenticity frees the Word of God to be a pure presence, to be unentangled in worldly affairs, to follow freely the rhythms, embedded in history, of man's advance in humanness. A disciple of Aquinas, of the thinker who broke with the symbolic thought of his medieval predecessors and contemporaries, who acknowledged the reality of human nature and the legitimacy of its proper sphere of activity, Chenu 'gladly supports the progress of natural and profane forces all through history, and he is of the opinion that this support, far from jeopardizing the domain of grace, ensures its transcendence and richness.'[9]

In terms of our topic, sacralization and secularization, one would seek to discern in Chenu's position four aspects: (1) a sacralization to be dropped and (2) a sacralization to be fostered; (3) a secularization to be welcomed and (4) a secularization to be resisted. Of these the first and third are complementary and stand in a clear light. Chenu welcomes the contemporary movement of secularization and laicization insofar as it compels us through the force of circumstance to get out of the mental and institutional complex of Christendom. He contemplates with equanimity the church's abandonment of outdated institutions and past involvements. He expects the Christian of the future to take with a grain of salt certain institutions and heavy-handed procedures that prevailed in the past. He pictures that future Christian as eager to be a missionary of the gospel and loath to be the protector of a civilization he himself has organized.

As the first and third, so also the second of the four elements we mentioned appears quite clearly. Besides a sacralization to be dropped and a secularization

9 Geffré, 'Desacralization and the Spiritual Life' 114.

to be welcomed, there is a new sacralization to be fostered. The Second Vatican Council advocated the Christian's discernment of the signs of the times. Among such signs Chenu would include man's becoming more human, his socialization, peace among nations, the rise of conscience in the peoples of the world. Such signs reveal the autonomous process proper to the world, but Chenu sees them as 'toothing stones,' as a new kind of *praeparatio evangelica* leading to the ultimate destiny of man. The function of the Christian is not to despise such human values but to lift them up; it is not to bring about a sociological Christianization of the masses, or to set up a Christian world alongside the world, but to be in the world without being of it, to respect and promote its genuine values without being confined to them and without identifying Christian values with them.

I have accounted for three of four elements in Chenu's position, but if we look for the fourth element – the resistance to secularization – we find it not in Geffre's account of Chenu's views but rather in the diametrically opposed views of Jean Cardinal Daniélou. For Daniélou, 'The conversion of Constantine made the Gospel accessible to the poor.' 'The faith can really take root in a country only when it has penetrated its civilization, when there exists a Christendom.' 'There can be no Christianity for the masses without a Christendom; there lies the choice.' 'In a world threatened by atheism, we must defend the substance of the sacred wherever it is found.'[10] While those that follow Chenu rejoice in the church's abandonment of secular institutions, Daniélou wants to restore a Christendom. As opposed to those who rejoice in the desacralization of the world (it has even become a slogan), Daniélou insists in an almost provocative way on resacralization of the world before it can be sanctified.

So Geffré paints the opposition between Chenu and Daniélou in bold strokes and in the plainest possible manner. But he does so in a single paragraph and proceeds to add six more not to mitigate the opposition but to locate it precisely. He insists that both Chenu and Daniélou want faith to penetrate social and political life and that both reject an oversimplified separation of the spiritual and the temporal, the sacred and the profane, the Christian and the political element. Again, both are haunted by the evangelization of the world, by a realistic presence of the church in the world. Where they differ is in their view of man in his concrete situation. Chenu would have progress in Christian life promote the natural processes and inherent freedom of this world. Daniélou, while he has abandoned the dream of a Christen-

10 [Ibid. 115–16.]

dom as it existed in the Middle Ages, wants the faith to have other securities than God's word alone. He wants some kind of sociological preparation for the faith, certain zones where sacred and religious elements are preserved so that the faith of the poor is not left without cultural and social foundations.

But to this debate we shall return later when certain further factors in the matter have been clarified.

3   One's World[11]

The word 'world' is used in many senses. It may be used absolutely to denote the sum of all that exists. It may also be used relatively to denote as much as I happen in one way or another to apprehend. It is in the latter sense that I may speak of 'my world,' 'the world for me,' 'the world as I happen to apprehend it.'

Now it is common to associate sacralization with primitive times and secularization with advanced civilizations, and in this connection a further distinction is relevant. It regards 'my world,' and it is between 'a world of immediacy' and 'a world mediated by meaning.' The world of immediacy is the world of the infant, the world of the nursery as given to sense, as accompanied by feelings of comfort and distress, as beginning to stretch out in time through memories and anticipations. In contrast, the world mediated by meaning is the world into which the child plunges with eager glee as it learns to speak and listen. It is a world that includes the absent as well as the present, the far as well as the near, a long, long past behind and an indefinitely long future ahead, a world of probabilities and possibilities as well as facts, a world of rights and duties, a world enriched by stories, by travelers' tales, by discoveries and inventions, by the meditations of saints, the reflections of philosophers, the investigations of historians, the achievements of scientists.

Now two sociologists, Peter Berger and Thomas Luckmann, have written an illuminating book entitled *The Social Construction of Reality.*[12] If we need not

11   [In the 1973 autograph, the heading for this section is, 'Leonardus Laeyendecker, "The Sociological Approach to Secularization,"' and the brief first paragraph reads: 'Professor Laeyendecker follows the view of Peter Berger and Thomas Luckmann that reality is socially constructed. As this view is paradoxical yet contains an important truth, it will be worth while to draw a few distinctions and attempt to locate its meaning.' There are a few other differences in the early part of the section, but they do not affect the meaning.]

12   Peter Berger and Thomas Luckmann, *The Social Construction of Reality: A Treatise in the Sociology of Knowledge* (Garden City, NY: Doubleday, 1966).

bother to ask whether the world of immediacy is socially constructed, there remains a significant distinction to be drawn with regard to the social construction of the world mediated by meaning. If the claim is that our knowledge of that world is not an independent personal achievement, then certainly there has to be acknowledged a social contribution and a consequent dependence of our knowledge on that contribution. But if the claim is that not merely our knowledge but also the things known are socially constructed, then there becomes relevant the ancient distinction between nature and art. The objects studied by natural scientists are known through scientific collaboration; but in the main they are not in the first instance constructed by scientific collaboration. On the other hand, knowledge of human artifacts, of Plato's houses and tables and beds, is knowledge of what in the first instance was constructed by man; and the sociologists' point would be, I believe, that social realities – family and custom, community and education, state and law, economy and technology, and indeed all that results from human counsel and decision – are products of human activity; and as there is very little that individual men achieve all by themselves, there is a vast region of human reality that is not naturally given but socially constructed.

Now the construction of human reality gives rise to a distinction between an infrastructure and a suprastructure. It has long been obvious that animals in hive and pack, flock and herd, anticipate human social structures. The fables of Aesop and La Fontaine drew human morals from plausible fictions in which animals provided the cast of characters; but it was reserved for the ethologists of our own day, recently awarded Nobel prizes, to give detailed accounts of the behavioral codes of insects, birds, and beasts.

By the social infrastructure, then, is meant simple prolongations of prehuman achievement. If I may quote what I wrote some years ago:

> ... primitive community is intersubjective. Its schemes of recurrence are simple prolongations of prehuman attainment, too obvious to be discussed or criticized, too closely linked with more elementary processes to be sharply distinguished from them. The bond of mother and child, man and wife, father and son, reaches into a past of ancestors to give meaning and cohesion to the clan or tribe or nation. A sense of belonging together provides the dynamic premise for common enterprise, for mutual aid and succor, for the sympathy that augments joys and divides sorrows. Even after civilization is attained, intersubjective community survives in the family with its circle of relatives and its accretion of friends, in customs and folkways, in basic

arts and crafts and skills, in language and song and dance, and most concretely of all in the inner psychology and radiating influence of women. Nor is the abiding significance and efficacy of the intersubjective overlooked when motley states name themselves nations, when constitutions are attributed to founding fathers, when image and symbol, anthem and assembly, emotion and sentiment are invoked to impart an elemental vigor and pitch to the vast and cold technological, economic, and political structures of human invention and convention. Finally, as intersubjective community precedes civilization and underpins it, so also it remains when civilization suffers disintegration and decay. The collapse of imperial Rome was the resurgence of family and clan, feudal dynasty and nation.[13]

What once I described as intersubjective community may be identified, I believe, with the infrastructure of some sociologists. It is any set of social arrangements that goes beyond prehuman attainment but does so with a maximum of obviousness, directness, simplicity. It can be the society of primitive fruit gatherers, or hunters, or fishers. It can make its home in the tropics, in polar regions, or with the animals in the plains of America. It can adjust to the hurdle of large-scale agriculture introduced by the discovery of the ox and the invention of the plough to give the ancient high civilizations their peasantry and to encircle their frontiers with parasitical nomads. Through the vicissitudes of European history it can preserve the folk songs and stories that nineteenth-century romantics have uncovered by their research and celebrated by their theories.

As there is a social, so too there is a religious infrastructure. Arnold Toynbee has remarked, not without penetration, that 'The pith of primitive religion is not belief but action, and the test of conformity is not assent to a creed but participation in ritual performances.'[14] In brief, religious experience may be objectified in two manners. It may do so in the world mediated by a meaning that leaps beyond the world of immediacy; then a creed enters into its essence, and assent to a creed becomes the manifest test of conformity. But it also may do so in a manner that clings to the world of immediacy; it will fixate on sacred objects, it will acknowledge sacred places, it will hallow sacred times, it will celebrate sacred rites; it will conform to the dictum that the

13 Lonergan, *Insight* 237–38.
14 Arnold Toynbee, *A Study of History, Abridgement of Volumes VII–X*, by David C. Somervell (London, New York, Toronto: Oxford University Press, 1957) 95.

metaphysics of primitive man are expressed in the sedate and rhythmic movements we associate with the dance. So, for the religious infrastructure, for the primitive in any age even our own, creeds are just words, and insistence on assent to creeds is an alien intrusion or, at best, insistence on a formality.

Religions of the infrastructure can, in principle, be as authentic and genuine as any, for I do not suppose that the grace of God is refused to certain stages in the unfolding of human culture yet granted to other stages. Nonetheless, it is true that the religions of the infrastructure, like all things human, are under the dialectic of progress and decline, righteousness and aberration. More than other religions, the religions of the infrastructure are open to palpable idolatry and superstition, to orgiastic and cruel cults, even to the ritual murder of human sacrifice. So it was with reason that Abraham was called to leave the land of his fathers and to sojourn in a strange land, that Moses was ordered to lead the people of Israel away from the fleshpots of Egypt and into the desert, that the book of Deuteronomy in its most solemn manner commanded: 'Hear, O Israel: The Lord our God is one Lord, and you shall love the Lord your God with all your heart and with all your soul and with all your might' (Deuteronomy 6.4). It was a momentous command, spelt out positively in the many ways in which the Old Testament makes known the transcendence of God and, more practically, negatively by the prohibition of any sharing in the cults of neighboring peoples. It was a difficult command, as witnessed by the repeated backsliding of the people of God; and, if one would understand that difficulty today, I can only suggest that one think of it as an epochal transition in which religious experience of transcendence began to express itself in the style, not of the infrastructure but of the suprastructure. For if Hebrew religion had its sacred objects, its sacred places and times, its sacred recitals and rituals, still its God was hidden, powerful above all, creator of heaven and earth, one sole Lord God brooking no strange gods before him despite all the diversity of creation and despite the contradictions in which man implicated himself.

The Christian doctrine of the Incarnation of the Son of God, the eternal Word, binds together both styles of expression: the style of the infrastructure, for Christ was man, and the style of the suprastructure, for Christ was God. At the same time it affirms the dialectic by which the one must decrease that the other increase. As the sacred temple and the holy city of Jerusalem were destroyed, so too Christ suffered in the flesh and died to rise again, to sit at the right hand of the Father, to rule the living and in a heavenly Jerusalem to rule the dead. If it was sacralization for Christ according to the flesh to be esteemed, revered, listened to, followed, so it was secularization for the secular power to condemn him to suffering and death. But it was a new and far superior sacralization for him to rise again according to the flesh, to sit at the right hand of the Father, to rule in a kingdom that has no end. Finally, as Christ attained his full stature when he entered into the glory of his Father, so too for Christian hope 'coming of age' is not some human perfection attained in this life but being received by Christ in the kingdom of his Father.

4   A Clarification of Terms[15]

I have been illustrating the realities that may be subsumed under such terms as 'sacralization' and 'secularization,' and the illustrations have come from very different fields: from Freudian psychoanalysis, from Constantinian and later establishments of the Christian religion and from the secular revolutions of recent centuries, from religions objectified in the style of the social infrastructure or in the style of the social suprastructure. It is now, you may feel, high time to clarify basic terms and, if possible, to state clear conclusions.

First, then, the words 'secular,' 'secularize,' 'secularization,' 'secularist' are in common use. They are neutral terms that replace the older adjective 'profane,' the verb 'to profane,' the noun 'profanation.' While 'profanation' suggests something like sacrilege, 'secularization' may denote what is good, what is bad, and what is indifferent.

Secondly, what 'secular' does for 'profane' 'sacral' does for 'sacred.' Similarly, 'sacralize' and 'desacralize' denote the actions meant by 'consecrate' and 'desecrate,' while omitting the moral judgments the latter terms express.

Thirdly, while 'secular' is in common use – there has been a good deal of secularizing going on for some time – 'sacral' is not. It is true that dictionaries acknowledge its anatomical meaning, but of the four I consulted only one acknowledges the usage of anthropologists. Finally, the derivatives of 'sacral,' such as 'sacralize,' 'desacralize,' 'resacralize' can be found in technical writing but have not yet made their way into the dictionaries.

Fourthly, the reason for the additional terms is simple enough. One wishes to state matters of fact without making judgments of value. In the Hellenistic empire, meat from animals offered in sacrifice was regarded as sacred by the pagans. Such sacredness was overruled by St Paul as in principle of no account (1 Corinthians 10.25–27). If one wishes to state matters of fact without commit-

---

15 [In the 1973 autograph, the title of this section is 'Collecting the Fragments.']

ting oneself to judgments of value, one may say that meat sacralized by pagans was desacralized by Christians.

Fifthly, to move from verbal to real issues, one may observe that any regularly recurrent human activity tends to generate roles for persons, to appropriate special places and times for the exercise of the roles, and to reserve material objects for use in that exercise. Now let us say that roles, places, times, objects are sacral when the activity involved is regarded as religious by the participants. Again, let us say that the roles, places, times, objects are secular when the activity involved is not regarded as religious by the participants.

Sixthly, by this definition – which is not meant to be authoritative – the terms 'sacral' and 'secular' are relative in meaning. They do not tell what really is sacred and what really is profane. They only tell what the participants regard as sacred and what they regard as profane.

Seventhly, the transition from 'sacral' to 'really sacred' and from 'secular' to 'really profane' involves three criteria: the personal, the communal, and the historical. The personal criterion is the authenticity of the individual, an authenticity that results cumulatively from his attentiveness, his intelligence, his reasonableness, his responsibility. The communal criterion is the authenticity of the individual's tradition, for it is only a partial and qualified authenticity that results from an authentic appropriation of a defective tradition.[16] Finally, the historical criterion arises inasmuch as religion itself develops, for what is authentic at one stage of religious development may no longer be authentic at another; and again, one style of religious development may be defective in comparison with another style.[17]

5   A Genealogy of Differences[18]

It would seem that the earliest stages of religion, as of society and culture, pertain to the infrastructure. Within that matrix the sacral and the secular may

16 [The 1973 autograph has the more familiar 'from an authentic appropriation of an unauthentic tradition.']
17 [The 1973 autograph has, '... for what is authentic religion at one stage of human development need no longer be authentic tradition (*sic*) either when the same process has reached a later and higher stage or when one takes into consideration another and distinct process of human development.']
18 [This section heading was added in the 1974 revision of the lecture. The entire section shows marked differences from the conclusion of the 1973 autograph, which simply ran on here in the same section, without a new division. The text of the last pages of the 1973 autograph will be given below, beginning at p. 276.]

exist and may operate. But they will be implicit rather than explicit, acted out but not named, shown rather than said, *vécu* but not *thématique*. From such indistinction it would follow that religious roles and tasks, religious places, times, and objects can develop without at once claiming the exclusiveness we associate with the sacred. In similar fashion secular business can be penetrated with concerns and precautions that we would be inclined to label religious.

Now if such initial indistinction implies a de facto secularization of the sacral and a de facto sacralizing of the secular, one may also expect its prolongation into subsequent periods. It is true enough that 'sacred' and 'profane' are not recondite notions and that their application to concrete activities is not difficult. But it is another matter to think of them generally, to discern the proper sphere of each, and, above all, to adjudicate the extent to which religious thought and feeling may reach beyond a strict interpretation of its proper sphere and exert a suzerainty over certain aspects of the secular domain. Indeed, before such issues can be formulated, before legitimate and illegitimate sacralizations can be distinguished, before the former can be approved and the latter effectively abolished, there are needed matters of fact.

It has been thought, for instance, that large-scale, long-term cultivation of the soil could only become possible after the institution of property in land, that the original institution of such property was under the auspices of religion, that such was the origin of the temple states that preceded the empires in Mesopotamia and still functioned in Cappadocia and Phyrgia down to Roman times.[19]

Again, when the empires succeeded to the temple states, when even the Roman empire succeeded to the oligarchical city states of Greece and Rome, it could be argued that the one way to secure the respect of a vast and motley population was some association between the imperial power and divinity. In any case, in point of fact, the pharaohs of Egypt were regarded as divine beings, the monarchs of Assyria were the adopted sons of God, this royal ideology found its way into Israelite thought, and the Roman emperors were accounted lords and gods, *kurioi kai theoi*.

Christianity had a basis for a sharp distinction between 'sacred' and 'profane' in the celebrated response: 'Render to Caesar the things that are Caesars's and to God the things that are God's' (Mark 12.17). It lived out this

19 Christopher Dawson, *The Age of the Gods* (New York: Sheed and Ward, 1933) 111–13.

distinction during intermittent persecutions over two and a half centuries. Its long travail ended with the advent of Constantine, but the new era of tolerance first mixed politics with the affairs of religion and later, in the slow decay of empire in the West, witnessed a gradual decline of secular talent and prestige and the consequent transfer to local bishops of an increasing share in the burden of secular offices.

In the dark and medieval periods, the beginnings of Western civilization found traditions and structures that had been cradled in the church and served to reinforce incipient feudal economies and polities. But a sacralization of the secular, justified by the decline of one civilization and again by the weak initial stages of its successor, was bound to be challenged all the more forcibly the more that laymen became capable and eager to handle their own affairs. So a series of secularizations in the body politic, now in this country and now in that, were the ambition or the achievement of feudal overlords, of Renaissance admirers of ancient Greece and Rome, of the Reformers' affirmations of the rights of individual or regional conscience, of Enlightenment propaganda, and of Marxist denunciations of the opium of the people.

I have been attending principally to the sacralization and secularization of social arrangements, of the already understood and commonly accepted modes of cooperation, such as custom and the family, community and education, state and law, economy and technology. But in the history of Europe and America the issues were not only social but also cultural, and on this more basic terrain one has to distinguish not only sacralization and secularization, but also secularism and resacralization. For the sacralization of Western Europe in the medieval period went well beyond social arrangements. It penetrated art and literature. Its canon law was a principal source of the common law. Its theology aimed not only at a reflective statement of religious motives and beliefs but also at a synthesis that made philosophy and science subordinate parts of a world view.

But if the Babylonian cosmology implicit in scripture could easily come to terms with Ptolemaic astronomy, if the Greek elements in the New Testament and the apocrypha could facilitate a fusion of the biblical view of man with Aristotelian anthropology, if the science borrowed from Greeks and Arabs could hold its own against scattered Western developments, still all of these in time only illustrated the disadvantage of building one's house not on a rock but upon sand. For this sacralized construct of man and his universe was impugned, and impugned successfully, by Copernicus, Galileo, and Newton, by Darwin and Freud, and by the swarm of philosophies and counter-philosophies that began at least with Descartes.

But the success was not recognized by all. A persistent age-long rearguard action was maintained in Roman Catholic and in other circles against these pernicious novelties. The result was not merely secularization but secularism – the outraged and outright rejection of all religion as the futile champion of a dead and unlamented past. Nor was this all. The rejection began indeed as an attack on religion but in due course it became, in philosophy and science and in the broader fields of literature and education, an unquestioned and unquestionable assumption. In Nietzsche's phrase, God had died.

To the medieval sacralization of philosophy and science, of society and law, there later was added a defensive sacralization of scholarship. In the seventeenth century Richard Simon (1638–1712) introduced the methods later known as biblical criticism. Three centuries later such methods were implicitly approved and defended by the Second Vatican Council. But Jacques Bénigne Bossuet, a very celebrated preacher and the Bishop of Meaux, had no foreknowledge of this event. He had the Royal Council confiscate thirteen hundred copies of Simon's basic work, *Histoire critique du Vieux Testament* (Paris, 1678), and he had most of Simon's writings placed on the Index of Prohibited Books, where they remained up to the final edition of that publication.[20]

Such was the extension of the mantle of religion over the opinions of ignorant men. Its result was that, in the intervening centuries, Catholic biblical studies, when not condemned, remained in an ever more archaic rut. The whole of Catholic theology was deprived of the problems whose challenge would have brought about a revision of its methods and a reorientation of its concern. It is the abrupt and fragmentary occurrence of such revision and reorientation that has followed the Second Vatican Council that has aroused the misgivings and dismay of many loyal Catholics, that has been encouraging others to an indiscriminate rejection of the past, and now to this and now to that venturesome restructuring not only of Catholic thought but also of Catholic living.

For at this point[21] there becomes relevant a somewhat subtle distinction between secularization and desacralization. For secularization is the liberation of a secular domain from the once but no longer appropriate extension of the sacral. Still, for it to be known as secularization, there also must be

---

20   Enrique Dussel, 'From Secularization to Secularism: Science from the Renaissance to the Enlightenment,' *Concilium* 47 (1969) 93–119.

21   [This and the following three paragraphs are the concluding paragraphs in the Thomas More lecture of 1974. They will be followed by the concluding paragraphs of the Trinity College lecture of 1973.]

known that the extension of religious feeling over the domain is no longer appropriate. When this second item of knowledge is lacking, there is apparent a withdrawal of sacrality, a desacralization, but there is no realization that this withdrawal was overdue, that it simply grants to the secular what belongs to it. For those unaware of the profound developments in historical scholarship that occurred basically in the nineteenth century, the new style in Catholic biblical scholarship is not an overdue secularization but an incomprehensible desacralization. For those unaware that modern science has not merely added new elements to earlier accumulations but more radically has changed the very concept of science, changes in Catholic theology and philosophy are not overdue secularizations but incomprehensible desacralizations.

But if the wind should be tempered to the shorn lamb – and this perhaps is the justice of Cardinal Daniélou's contention – there remain more complex issues represented by Paul Ricoeur's study of Sigmund Freud. There do arise new developments that cast a searching light on human affairs but present their findings in an unsatisfactory manner. They are not to be rejected outright. They are not to be swallowed whole. They are to be met with a distinction: not indeed with a distinction expressed by two Latin adverbs and found in a textbook, but with a distinction that presupposes a basis in long and patient study and that can be formulated only when the mischievous oversight has been pinpointed and the relevant insight has uncovered the appropriate correction. It was only after completing three books of his *Philosophy of the Will*,[22] and adding over five hundred pages in a study of Freud,[23] that Ricoeur was able to write his paper on 'The Atheism of Freudian Psychoanalysis'[24] and to announce that if, in the past, Freud had reinforced the unbelief of many, Freud now could be used to reinforce the belief of many.

Ricoeur, I believe, has made a point in depth psychology. But I am much more firmly convinced that he has set an example. The example illustrates the principle that, when secularization becomes secularism, the secularism can be overcome by a resacralization. The example not only illustrates the principle but also shows how the principle is to be applied. As Ricoeur

---

22 Paul Ricoeur, *Philosophie de la volonté* I. *Le volontaire et l'involontaire*; II. *Finitude et culpabilité*: 1. *L'homme faillible*, 2. *La symbolique du mal* (Paris: Aubier, 1950, 1960). English translations: *Freedom and Nature: The Voluntary and the Involuntary*, trans. Erazim V. Kohak (Evanston: Northwestern University Press, 1966); *Fallible Man*, trans. Charles Kelbley (Chicago: Regnery, 1965); *The Symbolism of Evil*, trans. Emerson Buchanan (New York: Harper & Row, 1967).
23 See above, note 6.
24 See above, note 5.

studied Freud, so other believers can study in detail other leaders in contemporary secularism. As Ricoeur had the detachment and the patience to come to understand what was correct and valuable in Freud, so other believers can labor in detachment and patience to understand other leaders in secularism. As Ricoeur had the penetration and the good luck – all discovery presupposes some luck – to uncover what Freud assumed yet did not explicitly acknowledge, so other believers can come to uncover the shortcomings of other secularists. As Ricoeur was able to use his discovery to turn the tables, so too other believers can work on other fronts to tackle secularism on its own ground and to resacralize what never should have been secularized.

Others no doubt will tell you that the errors of secularism need to be denounced so that the shorn lambs be not exposed to the shock of desacralization. I would have you grant that their contention is true, but I would also have you live and work – with much labor and commonly with little encouragement – in the light of another, complementary truth. It is that modern science makes no claim to truth. It claims to be no more than the best available opinion. Its claim is met, and its theories are abandoned, not because they have not yet reached the full truth but only because another theory is recognized by the majority of the scientific community both to provide a more satisfactory account of the available data and to promise a more fruitful line of investigation.

6   Conclusion of the 1973 Lecture[25]

So much for generalities, for the clarification of terms and the criteria of their objective reference. Let us turn now to specifics, to processes of sacralization and secularization in politics, in science and scholarship, in philosophy and methodology, and in religion itself.

In the field of politics our attention returns to the Constantinian era. It began with a respect that ended persecution and recognized the power of spiritual influence. But the long and slow decay of the empire – one of Arnold Toynbee's moribund universal states – created a vacuum of talent and prestige that gradually transferred to local bishops an increasing share in the burden of secular offices. Again, the beginnings of Western civilization in the

---

25 [See above, p. 271, at note 18. The text picks up from the paragraph that ends '... another and distinct process of human development' (see above, note 18). While many of the same items are included as in the 1974 text just given, the wording is different enough to warrant full reproduction here.]

dark and the medieval periods found in the church traditions and structures that cradled and later reinforced feudal economics and polities. But what is justified by the decline of a civilization or by the weak initial stages of its successor is bound to experience an ever diminishing role as its successor or successors become capable of handling their own affairs. So a series of secularizations in the body politic, now in this country and now in that, have followed upon Renaissance admiration for ancient Greece and Rome, upon the Reformers' affirmations of the rights of local or of individual conscience, upon the ideals of the eighteenth-century Enlightenment and the revolutions that ensued, upon Marxist demythologization of religion and the subsequent Soviet occupation of Eastern Europe.

Secularization in the body politic has been reinforced by secularization in science, in philosophy, in literature, in education. The Babylonian cosmology implicit in scripture easily came to terms with Ptolemaic astronomy. The Greek elements in the apocrypha and the New Testament facilitated a fusion of the biblical view of man with Aristotelian anthropology. But this sacralized construct of man and his universe not merely was impugned successfully by Copernicus, Galileo, Newton, Darwin, Freud, and the series of philosophies beginning at least with Descartes, but a persistent, age-long rearguard action was maintained in Roman Catholic and other circles against their pernicious novelties. The result was not merely secularization but secularism – the outright rejection of religion as the futile champion of a dead and unlamented past. This rejection began indeed as an attack on religion but soon became in the broad fields of literature and education an unquestioned and unquestionable assumption. In Nietzsche's phrase, God had died.

As sacralization in science and philosophy, so sacralization in scholarship was the extension of the mantle of religion over the quite traditional opinions of ignorant men. In the seventeenth century Richard Simon (1638–1712), a priest of the Oratory, introduced the methods later known as biblical criticism. Three centuries later they were approved and defended by the Second Vatican Council. Unfortunately, Jacques Bénigne Bossuet, a celebrated preacher and the Bishop of Meaux, had no foreknowledge of this event. He divined in Simon's work an attempt to undermine religion. He had the royal council confiscate thirteen hundred copies of Simon's basic work, *Histoire critique du Vieux Testament* (Paris, 1678). Most of Simon's writings were placed on the Index of Prohibited Books, and they remained there until the final edition of that publication. In the intervening centuries Catholic biblical studies, when not condemned, remained in an archaic rut, and the whole of Catholic theology was deprived of the problems whose challenge would have brought about a revision of its methods and a reorientation of its concern. It is the abrupt and fragmentary occurrence of such revision and reorientation since Vatican II that has aroused the misgivings and dismay of many loyal Catholics while moving others to work out their own brand of secularization and even secularism.

To the basic pair of terms 'sacralization' and 'secularization,' the more ominous term of 'secularism' has just been added. Let us attempt by way of conclusion a clarification of this triad of terms, 'sacralization,' 'secularization,' 'secularism.'

Our starting point will be Heidegger's existential, being in the world, but it will be that existential in its twofold form: from infancy one is in a world of immediacy; as one learns to speak and to undergo acculturation, one enters into a world mediated by meaning and motivated by values.

There are many cultures and many degrees of cultural development. For present purposes it will suffice to distinguish four degrees. The first includes some measure, great or small, of linguistic, religious, artistic, literary development. The second adds the radical new departure of systematic development: it may be represented by Greek mathematics, Archimedean mechanics, Aristotelian logic and philosophy, and Thomist theology. The third is a further radical departure that partly reinterprets and partly goes beyond and replaces the second degree. It is the development characterized by modern science and modern scholarship: where the second degree aimed at truth and so at a system that would be eternally valid, the third degree aims at an ever fuller intelligibility, with truth postponed to the attainment of the ideal limit where there are no unexplained phenomena. The fourth degree, finally, is a philosophy and theology that works out of modern science and scholarship as the basis of a contemporary cognitional theory and undertakes to overcome the relativism and agnosticism that are the *prima facie* implications of modern science and scholarship.

Now what can be sharply formulated on the second, the third, or the fourth degree of cultural development is not simply unknown on the first degree. It is the object of aspiration, intention, striving. While the tools for its proper formulation are not available, still it does not remain locked up in the aspiring, intending, striving subject, but is objectified symbolically in a transmogrification of nature and in an endowment with fuller meaning of human deeds, human words, human constructs and artifacts. Insofar as such symbolization expresses man's religious experience, there is constituted a sacralization of the world mediated by meaning and motivated by value.

Such symbolization, however, is not destined to be the last word. The emergence of further degrees of development is marked by the introduction of distinctions between symbolic and literal meaning, and philosophers work out techniques, named metaphysics, that map out the realm of what really is so. So Socrates was regarded as an atheist and condemned to death on the ground, among others, of secularizing the clouds and the moon. He was accused of teaching that the clouds were just water and the moon just earth.

A far more comprehensive and much earlier secularization had been the work of the Hebrew prophets. Distinct from heavens and earth and all they contain was their Lord and Maker. To worship any created thing was denounced as idolatry. But even Hebrew achievement was incomplete. It directed worship to the true God and to him alone. But its apprehension of the true God was shot through with anthropomorphism. So it was, centuries later, that when the Gnostics borrowed from Greek thought the means to criticize and ridicule the God of Hebrews and Christians, the Christian Fathers, and still later the Scholastic theologians, borrowed from the Greeks the conceptual and verbal tools for purifying their apprehension of God.

It remains that such patristic and medieval purification of biblical thought forms was not enough. It has been the fruit of both modern science and modern scholarship that a desacralization of the world of the Bible should be completed by a desacralization of the Bible itself. The Bible told how Joshua commanded the sun to stand still, and the sun stood still for about a whole day (Joshua 10.12–13). The first chapter of Genesis described the creation of vegetation on the third day, of fishes and birds on the fifth, of animals and man and woman on the sixth. But a full-fledged secularization of such sacralized views was advocated by Galileo in the first instance, and by Darwin in the second. Their contentions were resisted vigorously and for a long time, to set up a radical opposition between science and religion and to turn many secularizers into secularists.

The difference between the two is simple enough. The secularizer denies literal meaning to the symbol, but he does not deny it all objective significance. But for the secularist, the only meaning of the symbol is purely subjective; it expresses in some inadequate fashion the feelings of religious people but says nothing about what really is so. When Galileo claimed that the Holy Spirit did not intend to teach astronomy in inspiring the Bible, he was claiming no more than St Augustine had claimed before him and the bishops at Vatican II eventually acknowledged. The secularizer may consider that symbols belong to the childhood of the human race, but the secularist considers himself to have come fully of age; for him the hermeneutics and the metaphysics that find a real meaning for the symbol are as childish as the symbols themselves.

Finally, I should perhaps revert to the writers on whom I have drawn without making any comment of my own. I find, then, in Paul Ricoeur's treatment of Freud a model for handling all similar issues. Acknowledge the insight of the critic of religion, and pin it down exactly. Discover the oversight that makes him a critic of religion. Use his insight for the purification of religion, and use his oversight for a renewal of its vitality and power.

With both Fr Chenu and Cardinal Daniélou I agree but with qualifications. I wholeheartedly share Chenu's acceptance of progress in all its forms; but I would refer back to chapter 7 of my little book *Insight* for an account of the many ways in which progress is corrupted by bias and turned into decline; and I would refer to chapter 20 of the same book for an indication of the redemptive role of religion in overcoming bias and restoring progress.

Cardinal Daniélou speaks of the poor. It is a worthy topic, but I feel that the basic step in aiding them in a notable manner is a matter of spending one's nights and days in a deep and prolonged study of economic analysis. It remains that there is a real religious issue that regards not only the poor but also the rich and the middle class. It is that while all sane men need symbols, only a small minority ever seriously get beyond the limitations of symbolic thinking. Hence, in a developed culture, religion has to be pluralist: it needs some measure of symbolization for all; it needs only a limited measure for the few that get beyond symbolic thinking; and it needs a bounteous dose for the many that do not.

With regard to symbolization, however, we may be anything but glib. In the industrially advanced nations, urbanization has separated man from his roots in the rhythms and processes of nature; the ever shifting opportunities of commerce, of industry, of finance scatter the once stable circle of relatives, friends, and acquaintances, and keep scattering new group formations; technological processes, finally, by their complexity and abstruseness are understood only by relevant teams of experts while for the many they are just a black box; men know that if you put in x out will come y, but it is all they know, however much they may need to know more. It would be difficult to conceive a soil less open to the genesis and cultivation of intersubjective community, and while some lines of solution have been thought out in terms of intersubjectivity, they seem to offer no more than a sacralization of an infrastructure. Far more promising is the dedication of highly competent people to a common task. Recently I had a hurried note from a nun. She is working in a hospital in the British West Indies where all the doctors and nurses are volunteers. She refers to them as 'a tremendous group of people with whom to share the work of caring for the sick,' and she adds, 'there is always an atmosphere of joy and peace.' Such an atmosphere, I would suggest, is the human community's coming of age in any era, and a foretaste of the ultimate coming of age that, we hope, will join us to Christ in the kingdom of his Father.

15

The Scope of Renewal[1]

I must begin by asking you to distinguish between two renewals, a great renewal and a small renewal. The great renewal was the one intended in the Second Vatican Council, the renewal of the whole church. The small renewal is the renewal of theology. Our topic in these lectures has been Roman Catholic theology since Vatican II, and so the topic of the present lecture is how far-reaching and, in particular, how radical has been or is to be the renewal in contemporary Roman Catholic theology.

1   The Passing of Thomism

A first symptom and, indeed, a first measure of this change is the passing of Thomism. In 1879 Pope Leo XIII in a bull, *Aeterni Patris*,[2] enjoined the study of St Thomas of Aquin on all theological students. In 1918 the then new Code of Canon Law imposed the study of Aquinas on all students of philosophy and

---

1 [The fourth and final of the Larkin-Stuart Lectures delivered at Trinity College on 15 November 1973. No corresponding lecture was given in the St Thomas More Lectures at Yale University (see above, p. 219, note 1).

The following sources were used in editing this lecture: the autograph text prepared for the lecture (file 777 in the library of the Lonergan Research Institute, Toronto), the tape recording of the lecture, and an edited version that appeared in *Method: Journal of Lonergan Studies* 16:2 (1998) 83–101, ed. Robert C. Croken. Headings for sections and subsections have been added to the text.]

2 [DS 3135–40.]

theology. But in the Second Vatican Council we find that the adjective 'Scholastic' had become a term of reproach. What was Scholastic certainly was not pastoral; what was not pastoral had no place in a pastoral council; and so when a bishop wished to disparage effectively a certain type of proposal or amendment, he would tend to refer to it as 'Scholastic.'

This change of attitude was no passing whim. For decades, three factors had been at work to bring it about, and the Council provided the occasion to articulate publicly throughout the church what already was widely felt.

1.1   First Factor: Historical Scholarship

The first of the three factors, I would say, was historical scholarship. When the study of Aquinas was enjoined on all students of philosophy and theology, what was envisaged was the assimilation of the basic tenets of Thomist thought. But the first concern of historical scholarship is not to set forth and convince readers or hearers of the profundity of an author's thought, the breadth of his vision, the universal relevance of his conclusions. That sort of thing may be allowed to pad a preface or to fill out a conclusion. But the heart of the matter is elsewhere. It is a long journey through variant readings, shifts in vocabulary, enriching perspectives – all duly documented – that establish as definitively as can be expected what the great man thought on some minor topic within the horizon of this time and place, and with no great relevance to other times or places. Only from a long series of such dissertations can the full picture be constructed – a picture as accurate as it is intricate, broad indeed but with endless detail, rich in implications for other times if only one has the time to sort them out, discern the precise import of each, and infer exactly what does and does not follow. In brief, the Aquinas of historical scholarship called for the full time of a specialist. That Aquinas was not to be tucked into a corner of courses for all students of philosophy and theology. And the students had heard enough about historical scholarship to be quite incredulous when a professor would propound this or that interpretation of Aquinas as the genuine thought of the great medieval theologian.

The inner exigences of historical scholarship went much further. To be a specialist, to rank as an expert, entitled one to no more than the best available opinion of one's day. Like the results of natural science, the results of scholarship stood within a cumulative, ongoing process. The process would extend beyond one's span of years and into that remote future when there would remain no unexplained phenomena. And this slippery underfooting confronted one not only in medieval studies but in study of the councils, the

Fathers, the scriptures. Catholic theology, whether in the medieval style of the *quaestio* or in the post-Renaissance style of the thesis, found both its basic supposition and its method called in question. For the supposition had been that texts had the same meaning both for their authors and for the readers that chanced upon them centuries later. And the method had been either a dialectic that sought a middle way between contrary views or else a deduction that inferred conclusions from principles. But now, under the new scholarly dispensation, whether views had really been contrary, and what precisely had been the content of the alleged principles, were in the first place unknowns that had to be determined by interpreters working within the original historical contexts. Not only did those prior tasks extend indefinitely into the future, but also what could be anticipated were not permanent views to be reconciled or fixed principles for inferences but rather the starting points of developments that transposed from lesser to more complex modes of human apprehension.

1.2 Second Factor: Modern Science

There was a profounder shock in store. Aristotle's theory of the syllogism and the theory of science he had constructed on that basis in his *Posterior Analytics* had fostered the view that a science consisted in a system of permanent truths. Its principles were to be necessary and self-evident. Its conclusions were to follow necessarily from the principles. Even though such an ideal might not yet be realized at any given time and place, yet in the eternal order of things it was something that eventually was to be had. Such a view was not confined to Aristotelians. All through the nineteenth century the propagandists of science kept referring to the necessary laws of nature, and even the economists backed up their affirmations with a reference to the iron laws obtaining in their field. But the necessary laws of nature were shaken by Einstein's special relativity in 1905, and they were forgotten with the advent of quantum theory in 1926, while the iron laws of economics relaxed remarkably only a little later in the heat of the great depression and the remedies proposed by Lord Keynes.

This illusion of necessity might have vanished earlier. For empirical science is verified science. Any claim to probability or truth that it has results not from the intrinsic merit of its principles but simply from the fact that its proposals happen to be verified. No doubt, what the scientist discovers is intelligible. But the intelligibility that is discovered is the intelligibility not of a necessity but of a possibility. Were it the intelligibility of a necessity, then verification would be superfluous. Because it is only the intelligibility of what might or might not be, only by verification can one settle that in fact it exists.

I have spoken of the slippery footing supplied by scholarship, for there may ever be a better informed or profounder scholar to come. But the same is to be said of scientific systems generally. They are not Thucydidean attainments for all time. They are just systems on the move: smaller systems that move into and are transformed by larger systems; larger systems that give way to more comprehensive views.

1.3   Third Factor: Modern Philosophy

But if science and scholarship are ever no more than the best available opinions of their day, can our third factor, philosophy, escape such relativity if not relativism? Here, I think, a very massive phenomenon has to be noted. Some two hundred years ago, Immanuel Kant had proclaimed the subordination of pure reason to practical reason: pure reason knew neither the noumenal world nor the human soul nor God; but practical reason could come to terms with these issues. Kant was challenged by the absolute idealists – Fichte, Schelling, Hegel – who put practical reason back in its minor role and assigned supremacy to speculative reason. But the absolute idealists did not have the last word. In many and differing ways, in a variety of contexts, with widely differing implications, a succession of thinkers tended to reverse the view that had been held not only by absolute idealists but by rationalists, and before them by Aristotelians. In this new style Schopenhauer wrote on *Die Welt als Wille und Vorstellung.* Kierkegaard took his stand on faith. Newman toasted conscience first and only then the pope. Nietzsche extolled the will to power. Dilthey set up a *Lebensphilosophie,* a philosophy of concrete living. Blondel aspired to a philosophy of action. Utilitarians sought the greatest good of the greatest number, pragmatists stressed decision, personalists dwelt on intersubjectivity. While Edmund Husserl aimed at making philosophy a rigorous science, his phenomenology was taken over by others as a descriptive technique and employed in any of a variety of manners. Logical positivists, finally, discovered what they named a verification principle, and while it has not been verified, personally I should say that it is true if cast in the form of an empirical principle. It was in this sense that in my book *Insight* I distinguished between analytic propositions and analytic principles.[3] Analytic propositions are just tautologies derived from the definitions of their terms: one cannot

3 [Lonergan, *Insight* 329–34.]

accept the definitions without accepting the analytic proposition they entail. But analytic principles are analytic propositions with a difference: each of their terms has been verified in precisely the sense that was defined; to accept the terms in their defined sense, and also to accept the verification of that sense, is to accept the verification of the proposition.

1.4 Summary

I have been speaking of the passing of Thomism in Roman Catholic theological circles. Its occasion was the rejection of views named Scholastic in the Second Vatican Council. But its roots were old and deep. The development of historical scholarship, particularly in the nineteenth century, undermined both the medieval method of the *quaestio* and the later method of the thesis. It made the interpretation not only of St Thomas but also of scripture and the Fathers the work not of youthful seminarians but of aging specialists. Further, the notion of a science to be derived from Aristotle's *Posterior Analytics* and implicit in the commentaries and the *obiter dicta* of Aquinas was the notion of a permanent achievement, of universal and necessary truths valid for all times. But both modern scholarship and modern science held a radically different view. Their endless research aimed not at discovering what was self-evident and necessary, but what ingenuity might discover and patient skill verify; and what was so discovered and verified was not truth but only the best available opinion of the day. Finally, what scholars and scientists had learnt by experience, the philosophers, for all their disagreement, seemed to be concluding from whatever methods they happened to follow. Kant's rejection of the rationalists was followed, indeed, by the absolute idealists' rejection of Kant; but a large and imposing number of nineteenth- and twentieth-century thinkers rejected the absolute idealists' rejection and, though they might differ from Kant, did accept the empirical principle. Metaphysics based on some a priori type of knowledge was rejected, and in general this meant that no metaphysics whatever was accepted.

Did it follow that there had to be rejected Thomist metaphysics with its basis in *principia per se nota*? I do not think that this question has been found exciting. It could be left to medievalists specializing in Thomist philosophy. It could be left to professional philosophers. It could be left to speculative theologians. But it certainly was not to be an urgent issue for the masses, for the mass of the faithful, for the pastorally-minded products of the Second Vatican Council intent on forgetting old mistakes and pressing forward in winning all men to Christ.

If this pastoral optimism or euphoria is general, there do exist dissenting voices. They are not advocating a return to Thomist metaphysics, but they are adverting to a twofold contemporary need. This twofold need corresponds to the twofold goal Aquinas set himself in writing his *Contra Gentiles*.[4] As he put it, there are two kinds of truths for the theologian to defend, and two contrary types of error for him to refute. One of these lies within the province of the human mind; the other exceeds its capacity. With regard to the former, demonstrative arguments can be had both to establish what is true and to refute what is false. But with regard to the latter, the refutation of errors is possible, since faith does not run counter to reason, but no more than suasive or probable arguments can be had for the truth, since faith exceeds the province of reason.

So Aquinas. On both these counts one finds in contemporary Catholic theology that the passing of Thomism is a reality. One finds it in the realm in which Aquinas would expect demonstrative arguments for establishing truth and for rejecting error. One finds it in the other realm in which Aquinas would grant only suasive arguments for the truth to exist, while contending there were certain arguments for the refutation of error. Let me dwell on both the former point and on the latter.

2   Contemporary Views

In 1968 Patmos-Verlag in Düsseldorf, and in 1969 Newman Press in New York, published a series of interviews with six outstanding Catholic theologians.[5] Two were French: Yves Congar and Jean Daniélou. Two were Dutch: Edward Schillebeeckx and Piet Schoonenberg. Two were German: Karl Rahner and Johannes Metz. The Frenchmen and the Dutchmen were interviewed singly, but the Germans, Rahner and Metz, formed a team, each speaking in turn, each agreeing in the main with what the other had just said, but each going on to add not a little more that changed the other's perspective.

2.1   Yves Congar

For Congar, the great task facing the theologian today was to appropriate an adequate anthropology. This need he found particularly relevant in combat-

4   Thomas Aquinas, *Summa contra Gentiles*, 1, c. 9.
5   [*The Crucial Questions on Problems Facing the Church Today*, ed. Frank Fehmers (New York: Newman Press, 1969). References here are to the Newman Press

ing atheism, since most forms of atheism begin by affirming man and only as a consequence go on to the denial of God. So far from admitting that theology was concerned not with man but with God, he urged that in scripture the affirmation of God and of man go hand in hand.[6]

Again, Congar was concerned that the third world should make its contribution to Catholic theology. Even at the council it was obvious that the church is Western, though a considerable proportion of the bishops there were non-European. He added that countries that do not belong to Western civilization have, until now, contributed nothing to the theological thinking of the church, and he desired that the human vitality of the third world should begin to have its counterpart in the area of religion.[7]

2.2   Jean Daniélou

Cardinal Daniélou found that in contemporary circles, even religious circles, doubts were widespread about the capacity of the human mind for coming to a knowledge of God, whether through the exercise of reason or by appealing to the truths of revelation. The question was the radical question of the possibility of man attaining knowledge of the divine. The combat between the church and the world today takes place, he contended, not on the level of revelation but on a preceding level where man's apprehension of himself and of human values is formed. The issue is not the obscurity of mysteries hidden in God but the obscurity of the philosophies devised by men.[8]

As Congar, so also Daniélou adverted to the related issue of Christianity and culture. While people today were urging the separation of Christianity from its setting in Western culture, he felt that Christianity is not truly implanted in a country when it is present merely in a number of individuals, or when it exists institutionally simply because the church has been set up there. It must also acquire a cultural expression within the country, and it is implanted there only when it has sufficiently penetrated the country's social and cultural patrimony. Accordingly, he found an ironic contrast between the will in the West to separate Christianity from its Western expression and, on

---

edition. They were provided also by Lonergan in the margin of the autograph. The German title is *Die Antwort der Theologen* (Düsseldorf: Patmos-Verlag, 1968).]

6   Ibid. 9.
7   Ibid. 10.
8   Ibid. 26.

the other hand, the recognition that the main problem in evangelizing other world cultures – in China, in India, in the Arab world – was the need to incarnate Christianity in these cultures.[9]

2.3 Edward Schillebeeckx

Schillebeeckx noted the widespread secularization of the modern world. In the past man's whole personal and social life was imbued with religion. It was not that, in some first instance, religion was something apart and then, in a later instance, it penetrated into secular life. On the contrary, secular life itself was seen and experienced as religious. But now with the massive advance of secularization, everything has been placed within the horizon of rational understanding and, by that fact, withdrawn from religion and the world of religion. In this fashion secularization has come to coincide with desacralization. So there has arisen the question, What place is left for faith? Gradually there has come the answer that faith is concerned with a superstructure, that it in no way impinges on the flow of earthly events, that it is superfluous and humanly irrelevant.[10]

Accordingly, Schillebeeckx would argue for a new form of natural theology, not something in the line of the old *theologia naturalis*, but a discipline that would show that it is possible to speak about God, not only on the basis of revelation but on the basis of secular life itself. If this should not be possible, he feared that there is to be a permanent split between the secularized world and religion, and that religion is to be swept away as no longer relevant. Pointing his moral, he concluded that the ultimate consequence of fideism, of relying on faith and neglecting reason, is atheism in all its varieties, not excluding Christian atheism.[11]

2.4 Piet Schoonenberg

In his contribution, Piet Schoonenberg contrasted orthodoxy and orthopraxis, right thinking and right doing, and he felt that we needed to get used to the idea that orthodoxy was not simply absolute but had a certain relativity with respect to orthopraxis.[12]

9 Ibid. 38.
10 Ibid. 53–54.
11 Ibid. 54.
12 Ibid. 106–107.

2.5   Karl Rahner and Johannes Metz

On the same issue, Karl Rahner affirmed: '... the question whether we really live Christianity, even in contradiction to the world, or only speak cleverly about it, seems to me to be really almost the ultimate question, and it can naturally be solved neither by institutional measures nor by a modern, more sublime theology.'[13]

Again, the Rahner-Metz team shared, with Congar, Daniélou, and Schillebeeckx, an awareness of the secularism of the modern world. Rahner remarked that the crucial postconciliar questions were not the questions treated in the council, and that the first of these crucial issues was that the very question of God had become lost.[14] Metz complemented this by saying that our environment is a post-atheistic humanism, that it does not offer a world design, an existence design, *against* God but rather a world-and-existence-design *without* God. No longer can we take for granted the former common basis for a confrontation between Christianity and atheism. Indeed, one of the greatest embarrassments of the believer and the church today is how and in what manner should faith and the church give an answer to the 'world,' when this 'world' no longer has any questions about the church and about the faith the church offers for consideration.[15]

Rahner followed this up by pointing to the paradox of his own position. For over twenty years he had been considered a progressive theologian by those about him. He had not shared their view, but then suddenly he found that, without any change in his own position, he had become a very traditional defender of the church's central positions. In brief, he felt that the church all of a sudden had been confronted with a radical opposition within itself, that the church had to defend the question of the living God and the question of Jesus Christ against a fashionable secularism, against a fashionable desacralization, in its own midst. To express himself forthrightly, he said that in the coming decades we shall have to be clear about one thing: we shall have to deal with a situation in which genuinely unchristian heresies spring up in the church, whose adherents would not want to leave the church. Against them, the church in his opinion must have the courage to pronounce in a completely old-fashioned way an unambiguous 'No,' a real condemnation. He considered it obvious that such a thing should occur only after trial, with

13 Ibid. 162.
14 Ibid. 144, 145.
15 Ibid. 147–48.

caution, in love, after real, genuine dialogue, with a real understanding of the grounds which lead to such heresies within the church. But he added that we must realistically and soberly reckon with such heresies within the church, heresies which, even while they want to set up house within the church, attack the very substance of Christianity in the name of the progress of the church and in the name of the modern period and its tasks.[16]

Disclaiming any wish to underestimate or minimize the danger Rahner had been sketching, Metz wished to shift the accent. The church, he felt, has still to learn a genuine pluralism, a pluralism that no longer admits a theoretical formulation. The church has to learn to become a real field of tension, taking up within itself and carrying out initiatives of the most varied theological and social origins. It is, he felt, precisely in the ability to take up and assimilate such tensions that the positive integrating power of the institution 'church' becomes evident. He argued for a transformation of the apologia to those without the faith to an apologia for those within, for a deeper appreciation of the difficulties of faith that come up within the church itself, a deeper appreciation of the fact that the person for whom faith must be justified is not so much the person living outside the church but rather the individual believer living within the church.[17]

With all of this Rahner expressed his agreement with his customary vehement explicitness: for the need of a genuine theological pluralism, for the greater importance of the apologia to those within, for the need of a critical openness in the church, for an openness to which the faithful and the theologians, the bishops and perhaps the popes, are not accustomed, for an openness, finally, that is the one means that will make the church's contribution to the modern world credible. Nonetheless, he returned to his previous point. Is the situation, he asked, in which the church under certain circumstances can and must say an unambiguous 'No' still a remote one, still a theoretical possibility which one can concede in principle but which still has no real meaning for the immediate future? Such remoteness, he urged, was doubtful, since he had recently met a Catholic theologian, still teaching in the church, who explained that one could still preserve the substance of Christianity under the supposition that Jesus never existed at all. The theologian in question did not, it is true, deny the purely historical existence of Jesus, but he did hold it to be a more or less irrelevant question as far as faith

16 Ibid. 148–49.
17 Ibid. 149–50.

is concerned. If such things already occur today, Rahner continued, if there is talk in such an undifferentiated way about demythologizing and desacralization, as one can already hear everywhere, one must consider such a 'No' on the part of the church, not as an abstract possibility, but as a realistic decision forced upon the church by the circumstances.[18]

2.6 Summary

Perhaps enough has been said to indicate what seems to have been lost by the passing of Thomism. The theologians I have been quoting stand in the front rank. Congar urged that the great need facing the theologian today was an adequate anthropology. Daniélou contended that the issue was not the obscurity of the mysteries but doubt about the capacity of the human mind to know anything more than the visible universe. Schillebeeckx pointed out that, unless a new natural theology, quite different from the old one, were worked out, there would result a permanent split between the secularized world and religion, and it would follow that religion would be swept away as irrelevant. Rahner and Metz fully acknowledged the fact of secularism but went on to tackle problems of faith within the church. Nor was the source of these problems obscure to them.

Rahner granted that the proximate possibility of the church having to condemn views held by Catholics was due basically to the fact that theology had not achieved sufficiently what it should achieve today. He said that theology should be able to come to terms with such problems through its own inner strength and not through official ecclesiastical measures. While he granted that purely ecclesiastical measures as such do not solve the problem, he also urged that the church is not to be confronted with the alternatives either of remaining silent or of promoting the development of a theology that would make such measures superfluous.[19]

Before concluding this section I should state that I have not been offering you the substance of a book of over one hundred and seventy pages. Each of the six theologians raised several distinct issues. I have been quoting them only to add to my own point of the passing of Thomism the further point that currently something like Thomism is very much to be desired.

18 Ibid. 151–53.
19 Ibid. 153.

3   What Is Desired

If, however, I am asked what this something else is to be, I must insist that half a century would be a short time for ideas already in gestation to mature and reach wide acceptance. Until then, each one can do no more than express the view on which he has labored and leave it for contemporaries to criticize and for pupils to improve. It is only on this understanding and in this spirit that I venture to present what I have been thinking.

What is desired will be, I should say, first, an assimilation of what is new, secondly, in continuity with the old, and thirdly, dialectical. More concretely, an assimilation of what is new will have to involve, first, an understanding of modern science, secondly, an understanding of modern scholarship, and thirdly, a philosophy that is at home in modern science and modern scholarship. Next, continuity with what is old will be a matter of analogy and, indeed, of analogy of proportion; so a theology will be continuous with Thomism, to take one example, if it stands to modern science, modern scholarship, and an associated philosophy as Thomism stood to Aristotelianism. Finally, the theology will be dialectical if it distinguishes systematically between the authentic and the unauthentic, between positions and counterpositions, and if it can settle issues by appealing to this distinction.

3.1 Assimilation of the New

This is all very general but, if I am asked to be more specific, unfortunately I cannot do better than refer to what I have already written. By an understanding of modern science I mean, not agreeing with what scientists hold and repeating their scientific and extra-scientific opinions, but attending to their performance, figuring out what is involved in any process from inquiry through discovery to experimentation and verification, and assembling the elements of the larger movement from one discovery to another. In brief, it is doing the sort of thing I attempted in the early chapters of my book *Insight*. In similar fashion, understanding modern scholarship is not just practicing it but understanding the practice: what is going on in learning another language, what are the ups and downs in interpreting an ancient text, how does history differ from chronicle, and critical history from the previous stage of uncritical history. Once more, if you wish a concrete example, it is doing the sort of thing I attempted in certain chapters of *Method in Theology*.

A somewhat fuller answer must be given the next question, What is meant by a philosophy that is at home in modern science and modern scholarship? Here, I should say, there arises a basic disjunction. Either the philosophy follows what above I referred to as the empirical principle or else it does not. If it follows the empirical principle, all its statements will be in some sense verifiable. If it does not, then it will be constructed by deducing conclusions from analytic principles, from what Aquinas or Aristotle would call *principia per se nota*.

Now in *Insight* I accepted the first member of the disjunction. All philosophic statements, if valid, are in some sense verifiable; and they are in some sense verifiable if the empirical principle is always applied, though of course it is not always applied in the same manner. Let me list such different manners. There is the simple and direct application of the empirical principle in the empirical method of the natural sciences, where verification is in the data of sense as given. There is a simple but less direct application of the empirical principle in the empirical method of interpreters and historians, where verification is in the data of sense, not simply as given, but as given and as carriers of meaning. From simple and direct one turns to simple and indirect applications when one uses ordinary,[20] mathematical, scientific, or scholarly language to direct attention to the data of consciousness. Such is the generalized empirical method employed in *Insight*, a method that operates on the data of consciousness as the method of natural science operates on the data of sense.

Now generalized empirical method not merely enables the subject to assimilate modern science and modern scholarship but also enables him to appropriate his own conscious reality as an existential subject. As a conscious subject he can attend, inquire intelligently, judge reasonably, decide freely and responsibly, love totally. As a conscious existential subject he confronts and accepts the fact that ultimately it is up to him to decide whether he will really love, whether his free decisions will be responsible, whether his judgments will be reasonable, whether his investigations will be intelligent or biased, whether he will advert to the data both of sense and of consciousness or induce the blind spots that eliminate what for him are the more unpleasant facts of life.

In brief, generalized empirical method goes beyond the empirical to the normative. It reveals the human subject to himself, reveals norms immanent

20 [Some editorial work was involved here. The autograph reads, 'From simple and direct to simple and indirect applications one turns to the use of ordinary ...']

in his own operations, confronts him with the alternatives of being an authentic human being or, in some measure, unauthentic, and leaves him with the responsibility of making himself whatever he makes himself.

3.2 Dialectical Analysis

This transition from the empirical to the normative provides the foundation for a dialectical analysis. For dialectic has to do with the concrete, the dynamic, and the contradictory. But the existential subject is concrete; he is dynamic, for his living is operating; he is confronted with the contradictory alternatives of being an authentic or an unauthentic human being.

Further, while the psychological reality of authenticity and its opposite are accessible only within the consciousness of the individual subject, it remains that these inward events and transactions have their outer manifestation in silence and speech, in words and deeds, in motives that move some and not others, in goals that some pursue and others oppose. So it is that from the inner opposition of authenticity and unauthenticity there proceeds the generally accessible opposition of positions and counterpositions; and it is only a fuller manifestation of the radicalness of this opposition when it is covered over with the confusion that ensues when the authentic name positions what the unauthentic name counterpositions and, vice versa, when the authentic name counterpositions what the unauthentic name positions.

3.3 Continuity with the Old

Something has been said on two of the three points to be presented. There was to be an assimilation of what is new, and this was obtained through a generalized empirical method reaching an understanding of modern science and modern scholarship. There was to be attained a dialectic, and this was reached in a transition from the empirical through the norms of authenticity to the opposition between authentic and unauthentic and to its manifestations in an opposition and a confusion of positions and counterpositions. It remains, however, that this new style has to be continuous with the old style if it is to make use of what was valid in previous achievement.

Now this third and last requirement calls for a longer disquisition than can be attempted tonight, and so I propose to be content with indicating an analogy and a difference between the old *theologia naturalis* of the Thomist tradition and the new natural theology desired by Schillebeeckx if we are to meet the challenge of secularism.

Let me begin by recalling a point made by another eminent member of the Order of Preachers. I have already quoted Congar to the effect that contemporary atheism denies the existence of God because it affirms, or because it insists on making room for, the full reality of man. For this reason he urged that the main task facing the theologian today is to appropriate an adequate anthropology.

Now for me the basic step in such an appropriation is the appropriation of one's own reality as existential subject and, in consequence, freely and responsibly though not necessarily, the decision to become and remain an authentic human being. In brief, to appropriate one's own reality as existential subject raises the question for deliberation, Will I be an authentic human person? It can be met by the judgment of value: it is supremely worth while for me to become and to remain an authentic human person. And this judgment of value may and should be followed by a decision that underpins all the honorable decisions of a lifetime.

The secularist, who denies God that he may affirm man, who rejects institutional religion because he finds it blocking human development, can hardly reject the existential subject's discovery of himself, acceptance of himself, realization of his own potentialities. He cannot but share the effort to apprehend the workings of human understanding in mathematics, in science, in common sense, in scholarship. He cannot but distinguish between the merely bright ideas of understanding and the affirmations of sound judgment, and so prefer astronomy to astrology, chemistry to alchemy, science to magic, history to legend, philosophy to myth. From such objective realms he will turn in upon the subject, upon his capacities for attention, for intelligent inquiry, for reasonable judgment. From the cognitional theory of grasping what happens when one knows, he will derive an epistemology that explains why such happenings are knowing. From both cognitional theory and epistemology he will derive an account of what one knows when such happenings occur; and it is such an account that is what the hardheaded mean by metaphysics. Further, the secularist is neither premoral as the child nor amoral as the psychopath. He is aware of his feelings, of the values they can reveal, of the moment of moral truth in which he finds himself when he asks himself whether this or that course of action is truly good, really worth while. Because he would affirm all that is good in man, he will face the existential challenge and make the existential decision to be guided not by satisfaction but by value, to seek not just the maximum of satisfaction for the greatest number but, far more, the greatest value realized by the greatest number.

But the appropriation of one's own reality as existential subject can lead one further still. One can observe that the whole development of science and scholarship rests on two pillars. The first is the rejection of obscurantism, of the failure to face the relevant questions that arise. The second is the empirical principle, that answers to questions be verified in the data of experience. From the two principles the secularist concludes that science can know only objects in this world, that it can never attain knowledge of anything beyond this world. But one may ask whether science is the only knowledge man can attain. The question is relevant, for scientific knowledge is of its nature bound to be incomplete. It can reduce every x to some y; but every reduction ultimately is a mere matter of fact; it happens to be verified, and it would not be true if it did not happen to be verified. Every scientific affirmation gives rise to the further question, Does it really just happen? Is there not a massive obscurantism involved in brushing aside the question that obviously arises whenever any scientific proposition happens to be verified?

I need not carry the argument further, for my purpose has been no more than to indicate the lines along which the new natural theology desired by Schillebeeckx might be worked out. It starts from the self-appropriation of the existential subject, and it advances beyond the realms of science and scholarship and existential subjectivity by pushing further the questions by which subjectivity comes to appropriate itself and to constitute itself. It differs from the old *theologia naturalis* both in its starting point and in its procedure. Where the old *theologia naturalis* begins from the material universe, the new begins from the self-appropriation of the existential subject. Where the old proceeds from the material universe to God by invoking the principles of a metaphysics, the new advances from the existential subject to God by the claims of a full rejection of obscurantism. The old and the new are analogous, for they proceed from knowledge of the finite to a conclusion about the infinite. The old and the new differ, for the old thinks of objects and objective principles while the new adverts to the subject and the exigences of his intelligence and reasonableness.

It remains that the new has a triple excellence relevant to the needs of our times. It concludes to God as did the old. But it does so in a manner that begins from what the secularist can discover in his own reality to overcome his own secularism. At the same time it is a tool that churchmen can bring to bear only if they repudiate the very obscurantism that in the past led men beyond secularization to secularism. At a single stroke it would recall those that have gone astray and, as well, remove the scandal that led them to go astray.

4   Conclusion

My question in these lectures was 'Revolution in Roman Catholic Theology?'
I have offered instances of profound change in the notion of pastoral theology, in the conception of fundamental theology, in a critique of both sacralization and secularization. I have endeavored to make it clear, both in the
previous lectures and in the present one, that in an extremely serious manner
the whole mindset of Roman Catholic theology is being overhauled.

As yet, issues are unsettled. There is the danger that new notions in
science, scholarship, philosophy can be exploited in the manner Karl Rahner
would name substantial heresy. There is the opposite danger that the whole
effort of renewal give rise to a panic that now, as on earlier occasions, would
close doors, and shut eyes, and stop ears. But there exists the third possibility
that the new can be analogous to the old, that it can preserve all that is valid in
the old, that it can achieve the higher synthesis mentioned by Leo XIII in his
bull *Aeterni Patris: vetera novis augere et perficere*, augmenting and perfecting the
old by what is new. To that end we must labor and for it we must pray.

1974–1979

16

Moral Theology and the Human Sciences[1]

1   A Distinction of Cases

Not all human sciences are equally developed in all their parts, and so we begin with a distinction of cases.

Case 1. Both morally good and morally evil courses of action are possible in areas in which neither the science itself nor its possible applications are in doubt. Such, for example, is often the case in medical ethics.

Case 2. The science is not sufficiently determinate to yield fully concrete applications. None of its proposals is morally objectionable. Which proposal would yield the best results cannot be determined a priori. There is advised a course of social experimentation in which social scientists, social philosophers, and moralists (1) collaborate, (2) are guided by feedback from the implementation of their proposals, (3) gradually discover ever better policies, plans, procedures.[2]

---

1 This essay was submitted by Bernard Lonergan in 1974 to the International Theological Commission in response to a request from its president at the time, Francis Cardinal Seper. It was previously edited by Frederick E. Crowe and published in *METHOD: Journal of Lonergan Studies* 15:1 (1997) 1–20. A photocopy of the essay was found posthumously in File 105-31 of Lonergan's papers (A1015), along with a covering letter dated 28 February 1974 addressed to Cardinal Seper. The letter identifies the essay as an interim report concerning the topic of the title of the essay. The report, Lonergan says, 'envisages methodological matters of relevance to moral theologians and human scientists.'
2 See Gibson Winter, *Elements for a Social Ethic: Scientific Perspectives on Social*

Case 3. The human science is itself open to suspicion. Its representatives are divided ideologically. They advocate contrary courses of action, all of which have their respective good points, but none is without very serious defects. The notorious instance at the present time is economics.

In Case 1 neither the science nor its applications are in doubt. In Case 2 the applications are in doubt. In Case 3 the science itself is under suspicion.

If the three cases are distinct, the list by no means pretends to be exhaustive. Its purpose is simply to indicate something of the diversity of the issues involved, and thereby to reconcile the reader to that larger consideration that goes beyond simple conflict between natural law and technical possibility, and moves toward the enlargement of the attainable human good and toward the critique of certain human sciences.

With this goal in mind it seemed appropriate to begin with a clarification of the notion of human science. First, we shall speak of human science as science, and so treat its empirical principle. Secondly, the topic will be human science as human, and so there is considered its dialectical principle. Thirdly, there is the concrete realization of both the empirical and the dialectical principle in the ongoing scientific community. So it is only in the fourth place that we come to Catholic Action, or, under favorable circumstances, Christian Action, which operates beneficently both on the human community to which human sciences are applied and on the scientific community that develops and revises the human sciences.

2   The Empirical Principle

Human science as science is subject to an empirical principle. This principle is positive in its content but negative in its enunciation. It is that there are no true factual judgments without a foundation in relevant data.

Relevant data include the data of consciousness as well as the data of sense. Hence the empirical principle does not imply the behaviorist principle, which would confine human psychology to the methods available in animal

---

Process (New York: Macmillan; London: Collier-Macmillan, 1966; paperback, 1968 [Lonergan gave the subtitle as *The Role of Social Science in Public Policy*; this was indeed the subtitle used on the cover of the 1968 paperback edition, but the title page had the one given here.]). Also Bernard Lonergan, 'The Example of Gibson Winter,' *Social Compass: International Review of Socio-Religious Studies* 17 (1970) 280–82 [reprinted, Bernard Lonergan, *A Second Collection* (see above, p. 22, note 12) 189–92].

psychology. It does not imply the positivist principle, which overlooks the a priori contained in man's questions for intelligence, for reflection, for deliberation. It is not to be confused with the verification or falsification principle, which confines human knowledge to the world of experience. Finally, statements about factual judgments are not to be extended to moral judgments, to judgments of value, and the like, which are not factual but normative.

While the ultimate significance of data is their bearing on judgment, their proximate significance regards human understanding which operates and develops with respect to data. This Aristotelian and Thomist principle becomes a dynamic principle in empirical science. There, observations yield descriptions, contrasting descriptions yield problems, problems sooner or later lead to discoveries, discoveries are formulated in hypotheses, hypotheses are expanded in processes of experimentation, experiments yield new observations which either confirm the hypothesis or lead to new discovery, hypothesis, experiment, and so on indefinitely.

Hence, the modern notion of science differs profoundly from the ideal notion projected by Aristotle in his *Posterior Analytics*. Modern science is not *certa rerum per causas cognitio*.[3] It is not knowledge but hypothesis, theory, system. It is not in terms of final, efficient, material, formal causes, but of whatever intelligibility is brought to light by scientific method. While it may be certain in rejecting earlier views, its own positive contribution claims no more than probability. Hence a modern science offers, not demonstration, but the best available contemporary opinion; and so to object that it has not demonstrated is just *ignoratio elenchi*.

Finally, one may note that modern science implies a continuity of theory and practice: as developing human understanding mounts to its presuppositions, it becomes theory; as it descends to its applications, it becomes practice; and so theory and practice are distinct parts of a single reality.

3   The Dialectical Principle

Human science as human is subject to a dialectical principle. For the data on man are ambiguous: man's actions may be good or evil; his statements may be true or false; his development may be authentic or unauthentic.

This ambiguity is radical. It affects the very data on which an empirical

3 [certain knowledge of things through their causes. See Aristotle, *Posterior Analytics*, I, 2, 71b 10–12.]

science rises and rests. To cope with this radical ambiguity is the office of the dialectical principle. Its precise nature must be our immediate concern.

In general, mathematics and the sciences have to presuppose in their data (or quasi data) an intelligibility to be discovered. In both fields there is the recurrence of the phenomenon that anticipated intelligibility does not exist, so that anticipations have to be revised and fundamental categories modified. So surds are not fractions. Imaginary numbers cannot be approximated on a linear continuum. Uniform rectilinear motion continues indefinitely as long as no cause intervenes. Time is not a parameter but a fourth dimension. Etc., etc.

The peculiarity of the human sciences is that error, evil, unauthenticity may be not merely an absence of intelligibility but an unintelligible absence. The point was acknowledged by Aquinas: he granted that God indirectly willed the evil of natural defect and the evil of penalty because of a good with which that evil was connected; but he denied that God in any manner willed the evil of sin.[4] He urged that God neither willed evils to occur nor willed evils not to occur, but willed to permit evils to occur.[5] He granted that, as the creature would slip into nothingness unless sustained by God, so it would fall into the non-good unless sustained by God; but he denied that it would tumble into sin unless sustained by divine grace.[6] He denied the existence in things of an ontological falsity, when things are referred to the divine intellect; but nonetheless made an exception for the evil of sin, which in scripture is accounted a falsity and a lie.[7] Finally, for the relevance of the nonintelligibility of sin in a reconciliation of sin with divine providence, I refer to my *Grace and Freedom in Aquinas*.[8]

Now if the term 'dialectic' is employed to refer to a concrete process involved in contradictions, it has a twofold application in human science.

4 Thomas Aquinas, *Summa theologiae*, 1, q. 19, a. 9 c.
5 Ibid., ad 3m.
6 Thomas Aquinas, *De malo*, q. 16, a. 4, ad 22m.
7 *Summa theologiae*, 1, q. 17, a. 1 c.
8 [Lonergan referred to pp. 109–15 in *Grace and Freedom: Operative Grace in the Thought of St. Thomas Aquinas*, ed. J. Patout Burns (London: Darton, Longman & Todd, and New York: Herder and Herder, 1971). This corresponds to pp. 111–16 in the Collected Works edition, the section 'The Possibility of Sin.' See above, p. 238, note 21. Probably respecting the international character of the Commission, Lonergan gave the references also to the Italian translation (*Grazia e Libertà: La grazia operante nel pensiero di S. Tommaso*, trans. Natalino Spaccapelo [Rome: Gregorian University Press, 1970] 154–60), and to the original publication in *Theological Studies* 3 (1942) 547–52.]

There is a first application to the object, which falls short of intelligibility. There is a second application to the subject of human science, who may or may not anticipate complete intelligibility in his object.

First, then, with regard to the object, a human group, reflecting on its situation, may reach a new insight; the insight leads to a new project; the new project to a new course of action; the new course of action to a change in the situation. Insofar as the insight was relevant, the new situation will be an improvement on the old; but insofar as the insight was inadequate, the improvement will itself be incomplete; such incompleteness may lead to a new, further insight that complements the old; and its implementation may produce a further improvement that itself is incomplete. This process of gradual but ever incomplete improvements corresponds in the social order to the gradual but ever incomplete advances that characterize empirical science. It is a process that in some sense may be named progress, and it may be illustrated abundantly from Arnold Toynbee's account in his *Study of History* of the factor he names 'Challenge and Response.'[9]

It remains that progress is not the sole possibility, for man is subject to bias. There is the latent bias of unconscious motivation. There is the conspicuous bias of individual egoism that endeavors to circumvent public purpose for private gain. There are the shared delusions of group bias which considers its self-interest a contribution to the well-being of mankind. There is the general bias of all men of common sense, for common sense includes the common nonsense of its omnicompetence, and so it insists on palpable short-term benefits at the cost of long-term evils.

Bias begins by conferring an elemental vigor to every process of change, provided, of course, that the change is in the right direction. The result is that changes are not only incomplete but also distorted improvements. The further result is that every attempt to complete the incomplete and to rectify the distorted meets with resistance and succeeds only when mangled in the mill of compromise. The cumulative irrationality of decisions and actions brings about an ever more distorted, unintelligible, irrational social situation, and, as the situation mounts in unintelligibility, its capacity to suggest intelligible courses of action keeps decreasing until in the limit stagnation sets in. Such is the minor dialectic of sin. It changes progress into decline and decline into disaster.

9 [See Arnold Toynbee, *A Study of History*, vol. 3: *The Growths of Civilizations* (London: Oxford University Press, 1934); index, Challenge-and-Response. See the indices also of vol. 6, *The Disintegrations of Civilizations, Part Two* (1939) and of vol. 10, *The Inspiration of Historians* (1954).]

But there is also a major dialectic. For the unintelligibility of the situation is an objective fact that both mirrors and reinforces a subjective spirit of darkness. Men are not content to decide and to act out of bias. They want their bias justified. They provide a market for an ideology that would justify their ways in the eyes of faltering followers and envious opponents. Nor is this enough. The ideology has to meet a far deeper need. Intelligence, reasonableness, responsibility can yield cumulative development in virgin territory. But the situation produced by sustained decline is not virgin territory. Mere ideas no longer work. The creative minority becomes a dominant minority. It needs the power to compel, the power of technology, of economic pressures, of political discrimination, of passionate ideology. But the ideology of the oppressors evokes a contrary ideology of the oppressed. Ideologies themselves splinter, divide, conflict. In the resultant confusion men speculate on utopia, put their confidence in leaders, or sink into apathy and despair.

4   The Conjunction of the Principles

On the Aristotelian notion of science, science could be a habit in the mind of a man, and its principles could be logical premises. On the modern notion, science is the cumulative product of a scientific community. Its members have to submit to an initiatory program in a university and a graduate school. They achieve standing by the significance of their contributions to the common endeavor. They themselves by their authenticity – by their attentiveness, their intelligence, their reasonableness, their responsibility – are the principles whence the ongoing science proceeds and in whom, accordingly, the norms of empirical and dialectical procedure have to be incarnated.

In an appendix added to the second printing of his *The Structure of Scientific Revolutions*, Thomas S. Kuhn remarked that, were he to rewrite his work, it would 'open with a discussion of the community structure of science, a topic that has recently become a significant subject of sociological research and that historians of science are also beginning to take seriously.'[10] In fact, his work as written does center on the notion of the scientific community. It is the scientific community that shares the paradigms that came into existence or survived the last breakthrough. It is the scientific community that normally is engaged in 'mopping up,' that is, in resolving the host of puzzles that will extend the dominion of the last breakthrough over the whole field. It is this

10   Thomas S. Kuhn, *The Structure of Scientific Revolutions* (see above, p. 134, note 11) 176.

backward-looking concern that makes most scientists resist each new break-through and so gives each new breakthrough the attributes of a revolution. Finally, it is the revolutionary character of the new that makes its acceptance a pragmatic affair, a matter of a gradual shift of the members of the scientific community from resistance to acceptance of the new view.

Now it is of major importance to our present inquiry that science is, not just an accidental form radicated in a possible intellect but the ongoing occupation of a group and indeed a community of persons. For this implies that the moral theologian has to consider, not a single but a double set of moral issues. On the one hand, there are the moral issues that arise in the object studied in the human science. On the other hand, there are the moral issues that arise in the subjects that do the studying of the object of the human science.

Moreover, just as sin and the justification of sin by ideology are to be found on the side of the object, so too they may infect the scientific subject. In particular, ideology is contagious. The sinner gains little from his justifying ideology, if the human scientist points out to all and sundry that the justification is merely ideology. Again, the warfare of conflicting ideologies is stultifying. It makes it difficult, if not impossible, for the scientist to have recourse to the philosopher or the theologian for a clarification of underlying issues. It makes it persuasive and even mandatory for scientists to eschew all theological and all philosophical issues and to pursue their proper tasks with complete autonomy and even contemptuous independence.

5   Functions of Moral Theology

Our concern is with issues in which the moral theologian is to operate, not in isolation but in conjunction with others. But the measure of this collaboration varies in different cases. In what we named Case 1, the human scientist presents an account of available techniques and of their relevant presuppositions and consequences; on the basis of this material the moral theologian passes a moral judgment. In Case 2, however, the issue is not so much a matter of avoiding evil as of achieving the good; positive precepts rather than prohibitions are relevant; and the precepts regard the collaboration of all those involved in the experimental process – the collaboration not only of moralists and scientists but also of all participants in the execution and the amelioration of the program. But it is in Case 3 that the full challenge comes to light; what is at stake is the renovation of society; and it may be that the renovation can succeed only by going beyond the local scene to the regional, beyond the regional to the national, beyond the national to the international.

Further, complicating all cases, but the later more than the earlier, there is a real measure of indeterminacy. There is the general measure consequent on human freedom: courses of action cannot be demonstrated.[11] There is the specific measure consequent on the nature of empirical and especially human science: modern sciences do not demonstrate; they can offer the best available opinion; but even that opinion can be distorted by ideology; and still more can the acceptance of that opinion be opposed and impeded.

To some it may seem that we have moved beyond the scope of moral theology and are engaged in the practical theology – or the pastoral theology as practical theology – that has been set forth by Arnold, Rahner, Schurr, Weber, and Klostermann in *Handbuch der Pastoraltheologie*.[12] But if the latter already exists as an idea in many volumes, I am not aware that it is as yet an ongoing process conducted by a scientific community. Indeed, I suspect that in most countries and for some time to come we shall have to count on the already highly practical men engaged in moral theology. In any case my present terms of reference are to moral theology, and it is to them or, alternatively, through them to others that I must address my more general and my more specific remarks.

My general remarks are addressed to Catholics and indeed, where ecumenical collaboration is operative, to Christians. In the first instance they are in terms of conversion: religious, moral, intellectual. Religious conversion is the basic precept of the Old Covenant and the New: 'Love the Lord your God with all your heart, with all your soul, with all your mind, and with all your strength' and 'Love your neighbor as yourself' (Mark 12.30–31; see Deuteronomy 6.5). Its fulfilment occurs basically when 'God's love has flooded our inmost heart through the Holy Spirit he has given us' (Romans 5.5). Its fruit is described in 1 Corinthians 13, and its harvest in Galatians 5.22–23. From religious conversion there follows moral conversion, when the criteria of our practical judgments shift from satisfactions to values. From religious and moral conversion there emerges in the course of time an intellectual conversion: it adverts to the fact that the world apprehended by faith is a world mediated by meaning; it reflects that the world of every adult also is a world mediated by meaning; it concludes that the naive realism of childhood has to

11 Aquinas, *Summa theologiae*, 1, q. 83, a. 1 c.
12 *Handbuch der Pastoraltheologie*, ed. Franz Xaver Arnold, Ferdinand Klostermann, Karl Rahner, Viktor Schurr, and Leonhard M. Weber, 5 vols. (Freiburg, Basel, Wien: Herder, 1964 [2nd revised ed., 1970], 1966, 1968, 1969, 1972 [Index volume]).

be replaced by a critical realism, a realism that knows the real because it knows what is true. On these topics a fuller account may be had in my *Method in Theology*, chapter 11 on Foundations, chapter 4 on Religion, chapter 2 on The Human Good, and chapter 1 on Method.

But if one is to 'use good to defeat evil' (Romans 12.21), conversion to God, to the good, to the true, has to be complemented with knowledge of evil and with the will to overcome it. To knowledge of evil I have already alluded in the section on the dialectical principle. I have treated the same matter from a particular viewpoint in *Insight* on dramatic bias; on tension, dialectic, and bias in community; on liberation from moral impotence; on the role of faith, hope, and charity in overcoming social evil.[13] On the similar role of Christian suffering, see thesis 17 in my *De Verbo incarnato*.[14] The relevance of the last chapter of *Insight* to an ecclesiology has been developed by Bishop B.C. Butler in a chapter 'Lonergan and Ecclesiology' in *Foundations of Theology*.[15] Aquinas on moral impotence was set forth in *Grace and Freedom*.[16]

Very briefly, the perpetuation of social evils by the strict justice (*ad aequalitatem*) of 'an eye for an eye' is broken by Christian charity. The determinisms of the technology, the economy, the polity, the sociocultural heritage can be withstood by Christian hope. The ineffectualness of truth in the midst of passionately competing ideologies is remedied by the power of faith.

The general procedure, finally, is a matter of developing positions and reversing counterpositions, where positions express religious, moral, and intellectual conversion, while counterpositions are opposed to any one or two or all three of these. Positions are developed by finding ever more situations in which faith, hope, charity advance the cause of the good. Counterpositions are reversed inasmuch as Christian acceptance of suffering robs evil of its power to blind, to threaten, to endure.

Specific procedures may be divided by their greater relevance to Case 1, Case 2, or Case 3.

---

13 *Insight* 214–31 on dramatic bias; 239–67 on tension, dialectic, and bias in community; 643–56 on liberation from moral impotence; 718–25 on the role of faith, hope, and charity in overcoming social evil. [Lonergan gave the pagination of the 1957 and 1958 editions.]
14 *De Verbo incarnato*, 3rd ed. (Rome: Gregorian University Press, 1964) 552–93.
15 B.C. Butler, 'Lonergan and Ecclesiology,' in *Foundations of Theology*, ed. Philip McShane (Dublin: Gill, and Notre Dame: University of Notre Dame Press, 1971) 1–21.
16 See above, p. 238, note 21.

Case 1 has long been familiar in moral theology, and I at least can say no more than *consulantur probati auctores.*[17]

Case 2 regards collaboration of moral theologians and scientists in an experimental process that brings about a development of social policy. Here everything depends on the competence of the persons involved, and no more than a few general suggestions occur to me.

The first I draw from Gibson Winter in the work already referred to. He adverted to the fact that sociologists were divided into approximately four schools, with a right wing of phenomenologists, a left wing of behaviorists, and a center of conflicting functionalists (Talcott Parsons) and voluntarists (C. Wright Mills). Confronted with such diversity, a person with no real apprehension of modern science might attempt to reduce conclusions to their logical principles and then adjudicate between the principles. In contrast, a modern scientist is aware that the truth of principles is revealed mainly in their consequences, and so Gibson Winter asked himself which type of sociological theory would be most likely to prove helpful in dealing with various types of problems. He found behaviorists most likely to be helpful in dealing with traffic problems, voluntarists in analyzing revolutionary situations, functionalists in understanding ongoing processes, and phenomenologists in entering into the mentalities and aspirations that motivate and direct social continuity and change. In brief, as it is by their fruits that one knows men, so too it is by their fruits that one evaluates human sciences. While I do not consider this the whole story, anyone who wishes may find the complement I would add in my little book *Insight.*

A second but allied suggestion is a distinction between external and internal criticism. The external critic draws, not on the science he is criticizing but on some distinct source. So the obligation to pay a family wage may be concluded from evident moral principles. But the de facto operative economic theory may be that of a market economy, so that any employer that does pay a family wage sooner or later goes bankrupt because his wicked competitors do not pay a family wage. The de facto result is that a family wage is not paid and, indeed, cannot be paid until a modification of the market economy is brought about either by recurrent legislation on minimum wages or by a more radical criticism of the market economy itself.

In contrast, the internal critic operates along the very lines of scientific development. His criticism consists either in adverting to data that have been overlooked, or in bringing to bear fresh insights, clarifications, distinctions, or

17 [let the approved authors be consulted].

both of these. So the notion of religion in the History of Religions has undergone a series of developments in virtue of internal criticism, and in each case the developments have been effected by investigators in the field. Talcott Parsons has sketched the process from the speculations of anthropologists such as Tylor, who conceived religion as pseudoscience, through the shifts brought about by Pareto, Malinowski, Weber, and Durkheim,[18] to the position of topmost control in the cybernetic analysis of social continuity.[19] While the progress is only from contempt of religion to respect for it, it nonetheless is progress and involves an openness to further developments.

For radical internal criticism of a human science one has to turn from the practitioners of 'normal' science to the independent minds that belong to a larger scientific community and so possess an independent base for criticism. Such was Paul Ricoeur who, after completing the first two volumes of his *Philosophie de la volonté*, did a five-hundred-page study of Freud,[20] and later was able to boast that hitherto Freud had confirmed the unbelief of many, but henceforth he could confirm the belief of many.[21] His technique in this achievement was the application to dialectic of the program of developing positions and reversing counterpositions in the particularized form of a twofold hermeneutic, a hermeneutic of suspicion and a hermeneutic of recovery.

In the opinion of the present writer, the human science 'economics' is in need of similar radical criticism. Its three principal variants, all operative to some extent, are the traditional market economy, the Marxist-inspired socialist economy, and the new transactional economy constituted by the giant corporations which are not socialist and are not controlled by the market. In all three the influence of ideology is discernible, and what, I believe, is needed in the first place is a pure economic analysis of the exchange process untainted by any ideology. Until it is achieved, of course, it will be confidently pronounced to be no more than a pipe dream. For recent appraisals of the situation in the United States see John Kenneth Galbraith, *Economics*

18 Talcott Parsons, 'The Theoretical Development of the Sociology of Religion,' in *Essays in Sociological Theory Pure and Applied* (New York: The Free Press, 1949) 52–66 (revised ed. 1954, 197–211).
19 Talcott Parsons, 'Introduction' (to Part IV: 'Culture and the Social System'), *Theories of Society*, ed. Talcott Parsons et al. (Glencoe, IL: The Free Press, 1961) 963–93; see also Robert N. Bellah, *Beyond Belief* (New York: Harper and Row, 1970), chapters 1 and 2.
20 Paul Ricoeur, *De l'interprétation: Essai sur Freud* (see above, p. 263, note 6)
21 Paul Ricoeur, 'The Atheism of Freudian Psychoanalysis' (see above, p. 261, note 5).

and the Public Purpose,[22] and Richard N. Goodwin, 'Reflections: The American Condition.'[23]

6   Conclusion

The conclusion to the present paper is simple enough. What can be done principally on the basis of moral theology, as in Case 1, already seems to be being done. What calls for collaboration between moral theologians and those engaged in other fields, which in general are not theological, would seem to be extremely important. It is not, however, the type of work in which the Theological Commission up to the present has been engaged. It has seemed to me that it would be acting *ultra vires* for the organizer of the fourth section of a subcommittee to take the initiative in the matter without higher authorization.

Whether or not there exist cases distinct in a significant fashion from the three that have been considered is an issue on which the views of others might profitably be sought. I am of the opinion that such further cases do exist, but that they are to be subsumed under some such rubric as Pastoral Theology or Practical as Pastoral Theology rather than under Moral Theology in its established sense and function.

22 John Kenneth Galbraith, *Economics and the Public Purpose* (Boston: Houghton Mifflin, 1973).
23 Richard N. Goodwin, 'Reflections: The American Condition,' *The New Yorker*, 21 and 28 January and 4 February 1974; I, 35–60; II, 36–68; III, 48–91.

17

Self-transcendence: Intellectual, Moral, Religious[1]

It was suggested that I speak to you of self-transcendence: intellectual, moral, and religious. That provides me with five topics: first, the self; second, self-transcendence; third, intellectual self-transcendence; fourth, moral self-transcendence; and fifth, religious self-transcendence.

1   The Self

To speak of the self or of being oneself is to speak in public about what is private, intimate, more intimate perhaps than one has explicitly conceived.

---

1 [A lecture delivered on 10 October 1974 at Hobart and William Smith Colleges in Geneva, New York. The lecture was followed by a short question period. On the afternoon of that day Lonergan had held a seminar, principally on *Insight*. The same lecture was delivered on 3 December 1975 at Boston University.

Three tapes of the 1974 lecture are in the library of the Lonergan Research Institute, and the original tape has been graciously lent to the Institute by Mary Gerhart. Marcela Dayao transcribed the tape recording to computer, and Gregory Carruthers subsequently made some corrections on the transcription. Both the tape recording and the transcription have been used in this editing, as well as a photocopy of Lonergan's autograph of the lecture (Archives, File 722, item A2603). Greg Lauzon, audio archivist at the Lonergan Research Institute, has subsequently made a compact disc from the original tape. It is clear from the autograph that Lonergan took portions of the lecture from other sources, adapting those sources slightly in his preparation and delivery: '*Existenz* and *Aggiornamento*' in *Collection* (CWL 4), 'The Response of the Jesuit as Priest and Apostle in the Modern World,' in

Such existential speaking cannot be tidily tucked away into a single category: at once it is psychological, sociological, historical, philosophic, theological, religious, ascetic, perhaps for some even mystical; but it is all of them because the person is all and involved in all.

At the same time, it is not personal in a merely individual sense: it is not exhibitionism on the part of the speaker; it is not exhortation for those that listen. It is what the Germans call a *Besinnung*, a becoming aware, a growth in self-consciousness, a heightening of one's self-appropriation, that is possible because our separate, unrevealed, hidden cores have a common circle of reference, the human community, and for believers an ultimate point of reference, which is God, who is all in all.

Now with regard to the self, the first distinction is between substance and subject. When one is sound asleep, one is actually a substance and only potentially a subject. To be a subject, one at least must dream. But the dreamer is only the minimal subject: one is more a subject when one is awake, still more when one is actively intelligent, still more when one actively is reasonable, still more in one's deliberations and decisions when one actively is responsible and free.

Of the human substance it is true that human nature is always the same; a man is a man whether he is awake or asleep, young or old, sane or crazy, sober or drunk, a genius or a moron, a saint or a sinner. From the viewpoint of substance, these differences are merely accidental. But they are not accidental to the subject, for the subject is not an abstraction; he or she is a concrete reality, a being in the luminousness of being.

Substance prescinds from the difference between the opaque being that is merely substance and the luminous being that is conscious. Subject denotes the luminous being.

The being of the subject is becoming. One becomes oneself. When I was a child, I was a subject; but I had not yet reached the use of reason; I was not expected to be able to draw reasonably the elementary distinctions between right and wrong, true and false. When I was a boy, I was a subject; but I was a minor; I had not reached the degree of freedom and responsibility that would make me accountable before the law. The self I am today is not numerically different from the self I was as a child or boy; but it is qualitatively different.

A *Second Collection* (latest printing, Toronto: University of Toronto Press, 1996), 'Dimensions of Meaning' (again in *Collection*), and 'Religious Commitment' (see above, p. 30, note 1). The bracketed notes (all but what here is note 8) are editorial.]

Were it not, you would not be listening to me. Were you yourselves not, I would not be talking to you in this way.

The subject has more and more to do with his own becoming. When an adult underestimates a child's development and tries to do for the child what the child can do for himself, the child will resent the interference and exclaim, 'Let me do it.' Development is a matter of increasing the number of things that one does for oneself, that one decides for oneself, that one finds out for oneself. Parents and teachers and professors and superiors let people do more and more for themselves, decide more and more for themselves, find out more and more for themselves.

There is a critical point in the increasing autonomy of the subject. It is reached when the subject finds out for himself that it is up to himself to decide what he is to make of himself. At first sight, doing for oneself, deciding for oneself, finding out for oneself are busy with objects. But on reflection it appears that deeds, decisions, discoveries affect the subject more deeply than they affect the objects with which they are concerned. They accumulate as dispositions and habits of the subject; they determine him or her; they make him or her what they are and what they are to be.

The self in the first period makes itself; but in a second period this making oneself is open-eyed, deliberate. Autonomy decides what autonomy is to be.

The opposite to this open-eyed, deliberate self-control is drifting. The drifter has not yet found himself; he has not yet discovered his own deed, and so is content to do what everyone else is doing; he has not yet discovered his own will, and so he is content to choose what everyone else is choosing; he has not yet discovered a mind of his own, and so he is content to think and say what everyone else is thinking and saying; and the others too are apt to be drifters, each of them doing and choosing and thinking and saying what others happen to be doing and choosing and thinking and saying.

I have spoken of the opposite to drifting, of autonomy disposing of itself, of open-eyed, deliberate self-control. But I must not misrepresent. We do not know ourselves very well; we cannot chart the future; we cannot control our environment completely or the influences that work on us; we cannot explore our unconscious and preconscious mechanisms. Our course is in the night; our control is only rough and approximate; we have to believe and trust, to risk and dare.

In this life the critical point is never transcended. It is one thing to decide what one is to make of oneself. It is another to execute the decision. Today's resolutions do not predetermine the free choice of tomorrow, of next week or next year, or ten years from now. What has been achieved is always precarious:

it can slip, fall, shatter. What is to be achieved can be ever expanding, deepening. To meet one challenge is to effect a development that reveals a further and graver challenge.[2]

2   Self-transcendence

A distinction has been drawn between the autonomous human subject and the mere drifter. Now it is in the autonomous human subject that self-transcendence occurs. Our account of it will consist in a description of six stages: first, dreamless sleep; second, dreaming; third, waking; fourth, inquiring; fifth, reflecting; and sixth, deliberating. To these six there will be added later a seventh, being in love. But the six suffice to introduce intellectual and moral self-transcendence, and it will be time enough to speak of being in love when we come to religious self-transcendence.

In dreamless sleep we are substance without being subject. Still, we are alive. We are operating in accord with the laws of physics, chemistry, and biology. It may be said that we are ourselves but not that we are reaching beyond ourselves and much less that we are rising above ourselves. But when we begin to dream, consciousness emerges. However helpless, however lacking in initiative, the dreamer is an intending subject. What is intended, commonly is obscure, fragmentary, symbolic. In so-called dreams of the night the source of the dream is one's somatic state, say, the state of one's digestion. But in dreams of the morning the dreamer is anticipating his waking state; he is recollecting his world; he is beginning to adopt a stance within that world. In the dream of the morning, then, the dreamer has got beyond himself; he is concerned with what is distinct from himself; he is anticipating his self-transcendence.

An enormously richer self-transcendence emerges when one awakes. There is the endless variety of things to be seen, sounds to be heard, odors to be sniffed, tastes to be palated, shapes and textures to be touched. We feel pleasure and pain, desire and fear, joy and sorrow, and in such feelings there seem to reside the mass and momentum of our lives. We move about in various manners, assume now this and now that posture and position, and by the fleeting movements of our facial muscles communicate to others the quiet pulse or sudden surge of our feelings.

2 [On the page of 'Notes,' Lonergan entered a note at this point indicating that the paragraphs in this section had been taken from '*Existenz* and *Aggiornamento*.' The relevant pages in the Collected Works edition are 222–24.]

Still, sensations, feelings, movements are confined to the narrow strip of space-time occupied by immediate experience. But beyond that there is a vastly larger world. Nor is anyone content with immediate experience. Imagination wants to fill out and round off the picture. Language makes questions possible. Intelligence makes them fascinating. So we ask why and what and what for and how. Our answers construct, serialize, extrapolate, generalize. Memory and tradition and belief put at our disposal the tales of travelers, the stories of clans or nations, the exploits of heroes, the treasures of literature, the discoveries of science, the reflections of philosophers, and the meditations of holy men. Each of us has his own little world of immediacy, but all such worlds are just minute strips within a far larger world, a world constructed by imagination and intelligence, mediated by words and meaning, and based largely on belief. We haven't been there.[3]

If the larger world is one and the same, still there are as many different constructions of it as there are stages in human development and differences in human cultures. But such diversity only serves to bring to light a still further dimension of self-transcendence. Beyond questions for intelligence – such as what and why and how and what for – there are the questions for reflection that ask, Is that so or is it not so? Is that certain or is it only probable? Unlike questions for intelligence, these can be answered by a simple yes or no. How we can give such answers is beside my present purpose; but what such answers mean is very much to it. For when we say that this or that really and truly is so, we do not mean that this is what appears, or what we imagine, or what we would like, or what we think, or what seems to be so, or what we would be inclined to say. No doubt we frequently have to be content with such lesser statements. But the point I would make is that the greater statement is not reducible to the lesser. When we seriously affirm that something really and truly is so, we are making the claim that we have got beyond ourselves in some absolute fashion, somehow have got hold of something that is independent of ourselves, somehow have reached beyond, transcended ourselves.

I have been endeavoring to clarify the notion of self-transcendence by contrasting, first, dreamless sleep with the beginnings of consciousness in the dream; secondly, the dreaming with the waking subject; thirdly, the world of immediate experience and the enormously vaster real world in which we live our lives; fourthly, that larger world as constructed by intelligence with the same larger world as known to have been constructed as it really is.

---

3 [This sentence was added in the lecture at Hobart and William Smith Colleges. It does not appear in the autograph.]

There remains a still further dimension of self-transcendence. Our illustrations so far have mainly regarded knowledge. There remains action. Beyond questions for intelligence – what? why? how? what for? – there are questions for reflection – is that so? But beyond both there are questions for deliberation. Beyond the pleasures we enjoy and the pains we dread, there are the values to which we may respond with the whole of our being. On the topmost level of human consciousness, the subject deliberates, evaluates, decides, controls, acts. At once he is practical and existential: practical inasmuch as he is concerned with concrete courses of action; existential inasmuch as control includes self-control, and the possibility of self-control involves responsibility for the effects of one's actions on others and more basically on oneself. The topmost level of human consciousness is conscience.

However, man's self-control can proceed from quite different grounds. It can tend to be mere selfishness. Then the process of deliberation, evaluation, decision is limited to determining what is most to one's advantage, what best serves one's interests, what on the whole yields a maximum of pleasure and a minimum of pain. At the opposite pole it can tend to be concerned solely with values: with the vital values of health and strength; with the social values enshrined in family and custom, society and education, the state and the law, the economy and technology, the church or sect; with the cultural values of religion and art, language and literature, science, philosophy, history, theology; with the achieved personal value of one dedicated to realizing values in himself and promoting their realization in others.

In the measure that one's living, one's aims, one's achievements are a response to values, in that measure self-transcendence is effected in the field of action. One has got beyond mere selfishness. One has become a principle of benevolence and beneficence. One has become capable of genuine collaboration and of true love. In the measure that self-transcendence in the field of action characterizes the members of a society, in that measure their world not only is constructed by imagination and intelligence, mediated by words and meaning, based by and large on belief; it also is a world motivated and regulated not by self-seeking but by values, not by what is only apparently good but by what is truly good.

Now if we compare the last four of our modes of self-transcendence, we find that they form an interlocking unity. Experiencing is presupposed and complemented by inquiry and understanding. Experiencing and understanding are presupposed and complemented by reflecting and judging. Experiencing, understanding, and judging are presupposed and complemented by deliberating and deciding. The four modes are interdependent, and each later level sublates those that precede in the sense that it goes beyond them, introduces something entirely new, makes that new element a new basis of operation; but so far from crowding or interfering with its predecessors, it preserves them, perfects them, and extends their relevance and significance. Inquiry sharpens our powers of observation, understanding enormously extends the field of data one can master, reflection and judgment force inquiry to attain to ever further data and force understanding to revise its previous achievements, deliberation turns attention from what is to what can be, to what probably would be, and above all to what really is worth while.

To conclude, human authenticity is a matter of following the built-in law of the human spirit. Because we can experience, we should attend. Because we can understand, we should inquire. Because we can reach the truth, we should reflect and check. Because we can realize values in ourselves and promote them in others, we should deliberate. In the measure that we follow these precepts, in the measure we fulfil these conditions of being human persons, we also achieve self-transcendence, both in the field of knowledge and in the field of action.[4]

3   Intellectual Self-transcendence

The problem of intellectual self-transcendence seems connected with language. More precisely, it is connected with the transition from the stage at which one does not yet speak, to the later stage in which one does. But let me explain.

As long as one is an infant, etymologically a non-talker, one is busy learning to develop, differentiate, combine, group in ever broader syntheses one's capacities for operation in the movements of head and mouth, neck and arms, eyes and hands, in mastering the intricacies of standing on one's feet, then of tottering from one spot to another: all that Piaget describes in his account of the first twenty-four months of the lives of his three children;[5] you learn a lot in those two years. When first hearing and speech develop, they are directed to present objects, and so meaning initially is confined to a world of immediacy, to a world no bigger than the nursery, and seemingly no better known because it is not merely experienced but also meant, talked about, pointed out.

4 [The page of 'Notes' indicates that this section was taken from 'The Response of the Jesuit ...' 166–70.]
5 [See Jean Piaget, *The Origins of Intelligence in Children*, trans. Margaret Cook (New York: International Universities Press, 1952).]

But as the command and use of language develops, there comes a reversal of roles. For words denote not only what is present but also what is absent, not only what is near but also what is far, not only the past but also the future, not only the factual but also the possible, the ideal, the ought-to-be for which we keep on striving though we never attain. So we come to live, not as the infant in a world of immediate experience, but in a far vaster world that is brought to us through the memories of other men, through the common sense of the community, through the pages of literature, through the labors of scholars, through the investigations of scientists, through the experience of saints, through the meditations of philosophers and theologians.

This larger world mediated through meaning does not lie within anyone's immediate experience. It is not even the sum, the integral, of the totality of all worlds of immediate experience. For meaning is an act that does not merely repeat but goes beyond experiencing. What is meant is not only experienced but also somehow understood and, commonly, also affirmed. It is this addition of understanding and judgment that makes possible the larger world mediated by meaning, that gives it its structure and its unity, that arranges it in an orderly whole of almost endless differences partly known and familiar, partly in a surrounding penumbra of things we know about but have never examined or explored, partly in an unmeasured region of what we do not know at all. It is this larger world mediated by meaning that we refer to when we speak of the real world, and in it we live out our lives. It is this larger world mediated by meaning that we know to be insecure, because meaning is insecure, since besides truth there is error, besides fact there is fiction, besides honesty there is deceit, besides science there is myth.[6]

I have been contrasting a world of immediacy and a world mediated by meaning. But it is very much to our purpose to make quite clear where differences lie and where identity obtains.

It is the one and the same person that once was an infant and now is an adult. Such is a first identity.

Again, in becoming an adult one does not migrate from one world to another quite different world; one doesn't go from earth to Mars. When one grows up, one is still in the same world one was in when an infant. And that is a second identity.

---

6 [The page of 'Notes' refers to 'Dimensions of Meaning.' The relevant pages in the Collected Works edition are 232–33. At this point Lonergan turns from previously published materials to material written expressly for this lecture. He will return to some earlier material later.]

On the other hand, there is a difference between the world as apprehended by the infant and the world as apprehended by the adult. For the latter apprehension includes an endless multitude of things which the infant did not know.

Further, the apprehension of the adult differs from the apprehension of the infant. For the infant's world of immediacy need include no more than what is given to sense. But the adult's world includes sense but adds to sense both what is grasped by intelligence and what is affirmed or denied by judgment. It adds the unifications and relations, the constructions and extrapolations, the serializations and generalizations of intelligence. It also adds the distinctions of judgment between science and myth, honesty and deceit, fact and fiction, truth and error.

Finally, as the relevant cognitional operations differ, so too the criteria of objectivity differ. For the world of immediacy there suffice the criteria of experience, the visible givenness of what is seen, the audible givenness of what is heard, the sensible givenness of what is felt. But for the world mediated by meaning, while all the criteria of experience are required, still alone they do not suffice. There also are needed the criteria for the appropriate use of human intelligence and, no less, the further criteria on the necessary and sufficient evidence for a true judgment.

Now while there is a certain complexity to the ambiguities I have been pointing out, there would seem to be no real difficulty. It remains that what I have said is extremely general and abstract, while the difficulties arise in the concrete, in saying just what happens and why when mathematicians do mathematics, scientists do science, men and women of common sense make their commonsense pronouncements, historians do history, even philosophers do philosophy. Only too easily people can drift from infancy through childhood and a long educational process only to practice adult cognitional procedures with no clear notion of what they are doing. They have a firm grasp of impressions on their senses and feelings. They have a sure appreciation of the intelligence or dullness, the reasonableness or silliness that emerge in the spoken or written word. But what goes on between the input from sense and the output in language, that is obscure, vague, unconvincing. To them the human mind is just a black box. The input is clear enough. The output is clear enough. But the inner working is a mystery.

Intellectual self-transcendence is taking possession of one's own mind. It is a matter of attending to each of its many operations, of identifying them, of comparing them, of distinguishing them, naming them, relating them to one another, grasping the dynamic structure of their emergence and development, and so coming to clarify the workings of the mind in mathematics, in science, in common sense, in history, in philosophy.

If a comparison would be helpful, it is a labor not unlike Carl Rogers' client-centered therapy.[7] People have feelings that are distorting their lives, feelings they experience, feelings however they have yet to identify, compare, distinguish, name, relate to their occasions, to their causes, to their consequences.

What is true of the neurotic and his feelings also can be true of the normal man or woman and their insights. Insights are not rare and marvelous events. They are a dime a dozen. They occur easily and frequently in the intelligent, more rarely and with greater difficulty in the retarded. But for the most part not even the intelligent have any clear notion of what an insight is, under what conditions it occurs, how frequent are merely bright ideas that remain only half-baked, what a long succession and cumulation of insights is required for a genuine discovery.

In brief, for intellectual self-transcendence a price must be paid. My little book *Insight* provides a set of exercises for those who wish to find out what goes on in their own black boxes. But it is only a set of exercises. What counts is doing them.

Should one attempt to do them? As long as one is content to be guided by one's common sense, to disregard the pundits of every class whether scientific or cultural or religious, one need not learn what goes on in one's own black box. But when one moves beyond the limits of commonsense competence, when one wishes to have an opinion of one's own on larger issues, then one had best know just what one is doing. Otherwise, one too easily will be duped and too readily be exploited. Then explicit intellectual self-transcendence can become a real need.

4   Moral Self-transcendence

A recent work with the intriguing title *Towards Deep Subjectivity*[8] begins with two photographs. The first is of two benches set at right angles in a park in the Czech city of Prague. On one of the benches are seated three Russian soldiers, and they are looking straight ahead. One surmises that they are avoid-

---

7 [Carl Rogers, *On Becoming a Person* (Boston: Houghton Mifflin, 1961).]
8 Roger Poole, *Towards Deep Subjectivity* (London: Allen Lane / Penguin Press, 1972 and New York: Harper Torchbooks, 1976).

ing the eyes of the two Czech civilians, a young man and a young woman, seated on the bench at right angles to theirs, and looking right at them.

As the book explains, the picture has a moral. Rather, to adopt the author's expression, it illustrates ethical space. It sets forth in the objective world the subjective reality of two moral judgments: the moral judgment of the Czechs whose gaze amounts to the question, What right have you to be here? and the moral acquiescence of the Russians who do not care to look the Czechs in the eye.

There are many morals to the picture.

The first is, perhaps, that there is nothing recondite about morality. We are all forever praising this and blaming that, praising what we consider right and good, blaming what we consider wrong and evil.

The second is that good and evil bear witness to each other. The open gaze of the Czechs bears witness to the fact that they were wronged. The Russians' avoidance of the Czechs' eyes transmits the blame from their helpless selves to their powerful and exacting masters.

The third is that people commonly are unwilling to accept blame. They pass it along to those higher up or those lower down or those to the right or those to the left. They retort it, and so it is always safer to leave throwing the first stone to the man that is without sin.

The fourth is pretense. One's cause is not blameless, but one points to a greater good, to the long run, to the extenuating circumstances, to the example of one's betters, to the hypocrisy of one's rivals or opponents, to the dangers that menace one. After all, one has to confess – who does not? – that one is not a saint. Or again, one explains that one has to live. In the kingdom of crooks one has to be a crook to survive.

A fifth is ideology. Now it happens that ideology has two basic meanings. In the language mostly of people that do not attempt to think seriously, it is no more than an otiose synonym for systematic thought. But properly it denotes systematic rationalization, that is, a system of thought worked out to defend, justify, legitimate an iniquitous style of living, of economic arrangements, of political government, of any of the organized forms of human activity. So for Marx capitalist economics was the ideology of the bourgeoisie. For the advocates of free enterprise, communism is the ideology of the Soviet commissars. So in its proper meaning the term 'ideology' includes a moral judgment of reprobation both of the system of thought that one opposes and of the system of action that that system of thought would legitimate.

A sixth feature is impotence. When one grows up, one can easily see through the nonsense of children each blaming the other for some mishap.

But it is a far more difficult task to obtain accurate information, to understand lengthy and minute analyses, to follow protracted chains of reasoning, to come to appreciate or see through the claims of clusters of nations armed with thermonuclear bombs.

But impotence on the grand scale is coupled in each of us with impotence on the small, the private scale. For virtuous action has two conditions: sound judgment and good will. Unfortunately we are not born equipped either with sound judgment or with good will. They have to be acquired. But acquiring them is a long and difficult task. More than any other it calls for sound judgment so that we know what we have to do, and for good will so that we actually do it. But if sound judgment is a prerequisite for acquiring sound judgment, how are we ever to acquire it? If good will is a prerequisite for acquiring good will, how are we ever to acquire good will?

Is then moral development just a trap? Is it caught in a vicious circle in which, to acquire what one does not have, one must already have it? Call it a trap or a vicious circle if you please. But at least note that another interpretation of the human situation is available. One becomes a moral being by transcending oneself.

There are questions for intelligence that promote our being from a world of sense impressions, images, feelings into a world of intelligence, discovery, endless vistas. There are questions for reflection that promote our being from a world of sense and intelligence to the rationality of a world in which one discerns clearly and efficiently between fact and fiction, astronomy and astrology, chemistry and alchemy, history and legend, philosophy and myth, science and ideology. There are questions for deliberation, and they are of two kinds. There are the self-regarding questions that merely ask what is in it for me or for this or that group of which I am a part. There are the moral questions that ask what is worth while, what is truly and not merely apparently good.

Both sets of questions are practical. On them hinges what courses of action will be adopted and followed. Both sets of questions are interpersonal, for on both the lives of other persons are affected for good or ill. Both sets of questions are existential, for on both there is being settled what I am to make of myself, what I am to be.

But along with these common features there also are grave differences. If basically one's questions are of the self-regarding type, then one has not attempted moral self-transcendence. One has merely added oneself to the world's already teeming population of moral drifters. One has merely added another humble contributor to the economic and political determinism resulting from competing egoisms. But when one's basic questions for deliberation regard not satisfactions but values – the vital values of health and skill, the social values that secure the vital values of the group, the cultural values that make worth while social goals and the satisfaction of vital needs – then moral self-transcendence has begun. One has ceased to need the carrot of desire and the stick of fear; one has become a self-starter, a principle of benevolence and beneficence, a genuine person whose words and deeds inspire and invite those that know him or her to aspire themselves to moral self-transcendence, to become themselves genuine persons.

5   Religious Self-transcendence

Man's questions for intelligence, for reflection, for deliberation reveal man's capacity for self-transcendence. But capacity, hankering, intermittent trying are one thing; stable achievement is another. Such stable achievement seems to occur when one falls in love. Then one's being becomes being-in-love. Such being-in-love has its antecedents, its causes, its conditions, its occasions. But once it has blossomed forth and as long as it lasts, it takes over. It becomes the first principle. From it flow one's desires and fears, one's joys and sorrows, one's discernment of values, one's decisions and deeds.

Being-in-love is of different kinds. There is the love of intimacy, of husband and wife, of parents and children. There is the love of one's fellow men with its fruit in the achievement of human welfare. There is the love of God with one's whole heart and whole soul, with all one's mind and all one's strength (Deuteronomy 6.4–5; Mark 12.29–30). It is God's love flooding our hearts through the Holy Spirit given to us (Romans 5.5). It grounds the conviction of St Paul that there is nothing in death or life, in the realm of spirits or superhuman powers, in the world as it is or the world as it shall be, in the forces of the universe, in heights or depths – nothing in all creation that can separate us from the love of God in Christ Jesus our Lord (Romans 8.38–39).[9]

I have been speaking in terms of the Judeo-Christian experience. It has its parallels, as Professor Heiler has explained at some length, in Islam, Zoroastrian Mazdaism, Hinduism, Buddhism, Taoism.[10] But in this already crowded lecture I had best stay on native soil, Christianity, and note that

---

9 [The page of 'Notes' refers to 'Religious Commitment,' as published in *The Pilgrim People: A Vision with Hope*, ed. Joseph Papin (Villanova, PA: Villanova University Press, 1970) 56 for this paragraph and part of the previous one.]

10 [Friedrich Heiler, 'The History of Religions as a Preparation for the Cooperation of Religions' (see above, p. 40, note 25).]

religious love is the basic fulfilment of our conscious intentionality, of our questions for intelligence, for reflection, for deliberation. It is a fulfilment that brings a deep-set joy that can remain despite humiliation, failure, privation, pain, betrayal, desertion. That fulfilment brings a radical peace, the peace that the world cannot give. That fulfilment bears fruit in a love of one's neighbor that strives mightily to bring about the kingdom of God on this earth. On the other hand, the absence of that fulfilment opens the way to the trivialization of human life stemming from the ruthless exercise of power, to despair about human welfare springing from the conviction that the universe is absurd.[11]

One of the oldest convictions of spiritual writers and directors is that religious experiences are highly ambiguous. What really reveals the man or woman is not inner experience but outward deed. As scripture put it, 'By their fruits you shall know them' (Matthew 7.16).

Hence, if anyone wishes to ascertain whether he loves God, he is not to attempt psychological introspection, but he is to consider his own palpable behavior. A person can be profoundly in love with God yet fail to find it in his inner experience. As Professor Maslow put it, most people do have peak experiences, but most of them are not aware of the fact.[12] Psychological introspection is a highly difficult art.

Now being in love with God, if not a peak experience, at least is a peak state, indeed a peak dynamic state. Further, it will be marked by its unrestricted character. It is with one's whole heart and whole soul, and all one's mind and all one's strength. Hence, while all love is self-surrender, being in love with God is being in love without limits or qualifications or conditions or reservations. Just as unrestricted questioning is our capacity for self-transcendence, so being in love in an unrestricted fashion is the proper fulfilment of that capacity.

Such fulfilment is not the product of our knowledge and choice. It is God's free gift. So far from resulting from our knowing and choosing, it dismantles and abolishes the horizon in which our knowing and choosing went on, and it constructs a new horizon in which the love of God transvalues our values and the eyes of that love transform our knowing.

Though not the product of our knowing and choosing, it is a conscious,

---

11 [The 'Notes' indicate that part of this paragraph is taken from 'Religious Commitment' 56 as in note 9 above.]

12 [Abraham H. Maslow, *Religions, Values, and Peak-Experiences* (see above, p. 169, note 9) 22, 86, 88–90.]

dynamic state of love, joy, peace that manifests itself in acts of kindness, goodness, fidelity, gentleness, and self-control (Galatians 5.22).

To say that this dynamic state is conscious is not to say that it is known. For consciousness is just experience, while full human knowing is a compound of experiencing, understanding, judging.

Because the dynamic state is conscious without being known, it is an experience of mystery. Because it is being in love, the mystery is not merely attractive, it is fascinating; to it one belongs; by it one is possessed. Because it is an unmeasured love, the mystery is otherworldly; it evokes awe; in certain psychic contexts it can evoke terror. Of itself, then, inasmuch as it is conscious without being known, the gift of God's love recalls Rudolph Otto's idea of the holy, his *mysterium fascinans et tremendum*.[13] Again, it seems to correspond to what Paul Tillich named a being grasped by ultimate concern.[14] Thirdly, it is like St Ignatius Loyola's consolation without a cause, as expounded by Karl Rahner, namely, a consolation that has a content but is without an apprehended object.[15]

I have been concentrating on religious experience but I must not overlook the religious word. By the word is meant any expression of religious meaning or value. Its carrier may be intersubjectivity, or art, or symbol, or language, or the portrayed lives or deeds or achievements of individuals or groups. Normally all modes of expression are employed but, since language is the vehicle in which meaning is most fully articulated, the spoken and written word are of special importance in the development and the clarification of religion.

By its word, religion enters the world mediated by meaning and regulated by value. It endows that world with its deepest meaning and its highest value. It sets itself in a context with other meanings and other values. Within that context it comes to understand itself, to relate itself to the object of ultimate concern, and to draw on the power of that relationship to pursue the objectives of proximate concern all the more fairly and all the more efficaciously.

Before it enters the world mediated by meaning, religion is the prior soundless word God speaks to us inasmuch as he floods our hearts with his love. That prior word pertains, not to the world mediated by meaning but to

---

13 [Rudolf Otto, *The Idea of the Holy* (see above, p. 39, note 20).]
14 [See D. MacKenzie Brown, *Ultimate Concern: Tillich in Dialogue* (New York: Harper & Row, 1965).]
15 [Karl Rahner, *The Dynamic Element in the Church*, *Quaestiones disputatae* 12 (Montreal: Palm Publishers, 1964) 131–36. The 'Notes' indicate that the previous seven paragraphs are taken from 'Religious Commitment' 57–58, and the remainder of the paper except the last paragraph from ibid. 62–64.]

the world of immediacy, to the unmediated experience of the mystery of love and awe. The outwardly spoken word is historically conditioned: its meaning depends on the human context in which it is uttered, and such contexts vary from place to place and from one generation to another. But the prior word in its immediacy, though it differs in intensity, though it resonates differently in different temperaments and in different stages of religious development, has an orientation of its own. It withdraws man from the diversity of history by moving out of the world mediated by meaning and towards a world of immediacy in which image and symbol, thought and word, can lose their relevance and even disappear.

Still, one must not conclude that the outward word is something incidental. It has a constitutive role. When a man and a woman love each other yet do not avow their love, they are not yet properly in love. Their very silence means that their love has not yet reached the point of self-surrender and self-donation. It is the love that each freely and fully reveals to the other that brings about the radically new situation of being in love and that begins the unfolding of its lifelong implications.

What holds for the love of a man and a woman also holds in its own way for the love of God and man. Ordinarily, the experience of the mystery of love and awe is not objectified. It remains within subjectivity as a vector, a fateful call to a dreaded holiness. Perhaps after years of sustained prayerfulness and self-denial, immersion in the world mediated by meaning will become less total, and experience of the mystery will become clear and distinct enough to awaken attention, wonder, inquiry. Even then in the individual case there are not certain answers. All one can do is let be what is, let happen what in any case keeps recurring. But then as much as ever one needs the word – the word of tradition that has accumulated religious wisdom, the word of fellowship that unites those that share the gift of God's love, the word of the gospel that announces that God has loved us first and has revealed his love in Christ crucified, dead, and risen.

The word, then, is personal. *Cor ad cor loquitur.* Love speaks to love, and its speech is powerful. The religious leader announces in signs and symbols what is congruent with the gift of love that God works within us. The word, too, is social. It brings into a single fold the scattered sheep that belong together because at the depth of their hearts they respond to the same mystery of love and awe. The word, finally, is historical. It is meaning outwardly expressed. It has to find its place in the context of other, nonreligious meanings. It has to borrow and adapt a language that more easily speaks of this world than of what transcends it; and all such languages and contexts vary with time and place to give words changing meanings and to give statements changing implications.

It follows that religious expression will move through the various stages of meaning and speak in its different realms. But any attempt to outline the successive stages of meaning and its different realms lies beyond the scope of the present paper. Such an attempt would have to account for the prior background of the Old Testament, the diverse layers within it, intertestamental thought and speech, the diverse layers in the New Testament, the Apostolic Fathers, ante-Nicene Christian writers, the style of post-Nicene writing, the developments in the West during the medieval period, during the Renaissance and Reformation periods, in subsequent dogmatic theology, and in contemporary ecumenism.[16] The only point I wish to make here is that religious thinking is the product not only of religious experience but also of the culture of religious thinkers and writers. What accounts for the differences between religious thinkers is far less differences in their religious experience and far more differences in the culture in which their thinking and writing is embedded.

To go into these differences pertains to religious studies. To study them in the light of the commitment to a single faith is the task of a theologian. Into such matters I cannot now go, but if any of you feel called to take them, let me assure you that the fuller your preparation in languages and literatures, in the natural and the human sciences, in philosophy and above all a good life, the greater may be your hope for the successful completion of your appointed task.

Question:[17] I talk a lot about knowledge, and development of knowledge, and so forth. Does that make any contribution towards relating different religious traditions, particularly insofar as they are mystical traditions such as yoga, Zen, and so on?

Response: It makes a contribution of what you're not to attend most to. In other words, you know what you can set aside. Because the mystical tradition insofar as it is properly mystical is something with a content, but not a content derived from the world of experience. As they say, those that know do not speak and those that speak do not know. It's when they start to speak that you

---

16 [The paper from which Lonergan read has 'in contemporary theology,' but his spoken words were 'in contemporary ecumenism.']
17 [Two questions were recorded. In each case, Lonergan repeated the question, and the wording here is his.]

can begin to discover where the difference is, what the contribution of the culture is, and something else besides. William Johnston, an Irish Jesuit who has been in Japan for over twenty-five years teaching at the University of Sophia, speaks about a retreat that Christians and Zen Buddhists made in a Zen monastery, and how they all understood one another as far as religion went but their way of talking about it was quite different. Raymond Panikkar, who has a Spanish mother and and an Indian father, both a European and an Indian culture, speaks of a fundamental theology, and he sees it in a dialogue between people of profound religious experience who are seeking to understand one another without hoping to arrive at a common formulation. The formulation will depend upon the cultural background. Further questions can be asked on that, but we won't go on to them immediately, unless someone wants to.

Question: These successive stages, the level of experience, of understanding, of judgment, of action, of being in love, are they chronologically successive? Are they comparisons from the viewpoint of value, hierarchy? Do the later depend on the earlier, or vice versa? And so on.

Response: Fundamentally they are comparative. You need them all to have any in a sense, to be an adult in any. But the relation between them properly is what I mean by sublation. And it's giving another twist to Hegel's *Aufhebung*, which has four different meanings all at once. We won't go into Hegel's four. But take a simple example. Relate understanding to sensibility. And imagine a bug walking across the table. I say it's a bug, and people who know as little about insects as I do would say it's a bug. But an entomologist would tell you a hundred things about that particular type of bug. And you wouldn't know what his words meant. He's developed a whole vocabulary to deal with all the various features. His use of intelligence sharpens his senses. It doesn't blur his sensations. It refines them. It leads to differentiations that otherwise would not occur. That's the meaning of sublation. You go beyond, you set up a new principle, namely, understanding, what the scientist was aiming at. You become master of a far greater range of data that are just a blur to you otherwise. You move from the level of understanding to the level of judgment. There are all the different theories you can get historically, and then the Babel at any present time, but insofar as you make judgments and say this is right and those are wrong, there is a vast simplification. You are moving to a higher level. You have a better control. Then there is the level of action. You are not merely knowing, you are also doing. What's the good of it? You're finally reaching the answer to the question that's put to people that are specializing in any field. It doesn't seem to butter anyone's bread, does it? And on the level of action there are all sorts of competitions as to what one is to do, and if you're religious you find that religion provides criteria regarding values. It's love and hatred that makes values and disvalues really effective. And that again is the point of sublation: the heart has reasons that reason does not know.

Now chronologically, moral self-transcendence is more likely to occur if religious self-transcendence has occurred. Intellectual self-transcendence is more likely to occur if both religious and moral self-transcendence have occurred. It's through the lower that you advance to the higher, yes, but God's grace isn't conditioned by going through the lower. He gives his grace to whom he pleases. In other words, what is true is interdependence.

18

The Human Good[1]

My title is 'The Human Good,' and what I have to say comes from a book on *Method in Theology*.[2] It is an attempt to give theologians something more concrete to think about than usually has been the case in the past. What do I propose to offer? Not a definition. A definition always gives you something abstract, and the good is never an abstraction; it is concrete. And a definition presupposes an appropriate system of technical terms. Plato's early dialogues tried to define the virtues, and they always concluded that no one there could define them, not even Socrates himself. But in the *Nicomachean Ethics* two generations later, Aristotle defined all the virtues and all the vices. How could he define them when neither Plato nor Socrates could? By setting up a system of technical terms. You move into a different world when you can define. You are using technical terms.

---

1 This lecture was given at a conference, 'Beyond Relativism,' sponsored by the Institute of Human Values, St Mary's University, Halifax, Nova Scotia, 8-10 September 1976; it was delivered on 10 September. Selections from the lecture (and others of the conference) were broadcast on the CBC program 'Theatre for Ideas,' on 11 March 1977. The CBC tape has been converted to compact disc at the Lonergan Research Institute. Transcriptions of the full taped lecture have been made by Nicholas W. Graham. Another transcription of the taped conference lecture was published in *Humanitas* 15 (February 1979) 113–26. Unfortunately, there are many errors in this published version. We rely here on the tape of the lecture and on Graham's transcription. All notes are editorial.
2 Bernard J.F. Lonergan, *Method in Theology* (see above, p. 12, note 2).

So what do I offer? It is not a description of reality. Is there any reality that is good? Where do you find examples of it, realities? Reality is always doubtfully good or disputably good. And it is not a hypothesis to be verified in reality. What, then, is it? Well, I will give you an example from Henri-Irénée Marrou, an expert in Hellenistic education. He wrote a book at the end of his career, *De la connaissance historique*. It was unfortunately translated with the title *The Meaning of History*,[3] but it is about historical knowledge, and in it he speaks of ideal types, and his example of an ideal type is Fustel de Coulanges, *La cité antique*.[4] He says it is not a description of any Greek city, it is not a description of the most common type of Greek city, but it is the most *explanatory* account. And what is the use of this? It sets forth a narrative of origins, structures, processes, and though they are not the most common features, they are the most connected and explanatory set of features. They provide illumination, insight into such features when they are found, when you can get the documentary evidence for them; but they are also extremely helpful in the contrary case. The Greek city most removed from Fustel de Coulanges's *Cité antique* was Sparta, and taking the *Cité antique* as an ideal type for studying Sparta you get all sorts of clues as to the things to be investigated about Sparta that the book does not account for at all. These clues stimulate the investigation, they provide a lead for the investigation, they provide questions. If you are familiar with Collingwood, you know that history is a matter of questions more than answers.[5]

That is an example out of history. You can take another example if you are familiar with physics: the marvelous way they use differential equations and boundary conditions and tell you what is going to happen, although they don't know the law.

It is something like that that I am going to attempt: a set of variables, namely, skills, feelings, values, beliefs. They are all variable: different skills you will find all over; feelings are a great variety; values – various meanings and various valuations; and beliefs. I will also present a structure.

3 Henri-Irénée Marrou, *De la connaissance historique*, 2nd ed. (Paris: Editions du Seuil, 1955); trans. Robert J. Olsen, *The Meaning of History* (Baltimore and Dublin: Helicon, 1966).

4 Numa Denis Fustel de Coulanges, *La cité antique* (Paris: Librairie Hachette, 1864, 1912); a translation by Willard Small in 1873, *The Ancient City*, has been published in Doubleday Anchor Books (Garden City, NY: Doubleday, 1956).

5 R.G. Collingwood, *The Idea of History* (Oxford: Clarendon, 1946, and New York: Oxford University Press, 1956) 269–74, 278–82.

	1 *Individual* *Potentiality*	2 *Actuation*	3 *Social*	4 *Ends*
A	capacity, need	operation	cooperation	particular good
B	plasticity, perfectibility	development, skill	institution, role, task	good of order
C	liberty	orientation, conversion	personal relations	terminal value

This structure is on the page that has been reproduced,[6] in which we have eighteen terms, defined implicitly. The terms fix the relations between them, and the relations fix the terms; it is an attempt at implicit definition. After speaking about this structure, I will speak of motion: progress, decline, and recovery.[7] Finally, there is the historical: it is process in which we are involved, by which we are challenged.

1   Skills

First of all, skills. I get my notion on skills from Jean Piaget who, with collaborators, has put out about thirty books on the development from zero months up to about fifteen years.[8] In British and American circles, for some time

6 The structure is from a one-page outline and explanation (Archives, Lonergan Research Institute, Toronto) provided for the lecture. It is similar to the structure given in *Method in Theology*, p. 48 (see above, p. 147), but adds column numbers and row letters, to which Lonergan will refer in his explanation of the structure later in the lecture.

7 In an abstract drawn up by Lonergan himself for the lecture, he uses the word 'time' instead of 'motion': 'The paper concludes by adding the fourth dimension, time, and considering the mechanisms of progress, decline and recovery' (Archives, Lonergan Research Institute, Toronto). The term 'motion' suggests the movement of history, while 'time' is intrinsic to history. Undoubtedly, the significance of the variant wording bears further exploration; see the comment by Frederick Crowe, *Lonergan Studies Newsletter* 13 (June 1992) 18.

8 Several previous papers in this volume have mentioned Piaget. For Piaget's works in English translation, see the bibliography of John R. Phillips, *The Origins of Intellect: Piaget's Theory* (San Francisco: W.H. Freeman & Co., 1969) 139–40. Lonergan gives his own bibliography in *Topics in Education*, vol. 10 in Collected Works of Bernard Lonergan, ed. Robert M. Doran and Frederick E. Crowe (Toronto: University of Toronto Press, 1993) 193–95.

pedagogues were content to repeat his experiments and say, 'He's right, he's right!' Later on, they started getting into his theory: how did he get these notions? Well, I will just give you a few clues how his notions originated.

First, what we call 'trial and error' he expressed more concretely in terms of assimilation and adjustment. Assimilation: the child uses an operation he has already performed, a performance which is spontaneous or which he or she has already learned. And if it doesn't work, then one adjusts it and by trial and error arrives at a differentiated operation.

Then there is the combination of differentiated operations, and a higher notion, the grouping of spontaneous, differentiated, and combinations of differentiated, operations. Grouping is a mathematical term. You have a group when from any one in the set you can move to any other and back again. When the toddler first is called from mother to daddy, and then mother calls him back again, he doesn't know he is coming back; he comes back, he has a referent to which he goes. Combining, ordering space, is the matter of being able to go anywhere and come back again and knowing what you are doing. That is grouping. And by different levels of groups Piaget defines stages of development. He was able to say that at the age of eight or about the age of eight children are able to do such and such and not before. Or boys of twelve can operate on propositions, hardly before, easily afterwards, and so on. By this grouping, he succeeds in setting stages of development from zero months to fifteen years.

He has a further distinction that admits a terrific expansion, a distinction between immediate operations and mediated operations. Immediate operations: you operate on what you can touch, what you see, what you feel, and so on. Mediated operations: you operate immediately with respect to a sign, a symbol, an image, and by the mediation of the sign, the symbol, the image, you operate with respect to the referent. That distinction leads to a distinction in the development of culture. The infant lives in a world of immediacy. As the child learns to speak, goes to school, goes to work, marries, he moves more and more into a world mediated by meaning and motivated by values, and it is an entirely different world, enormously larger, a world not merely of fact but also of fiction, involving truth but also falsehood.

This world mediated by meaning is mediated by a meaning in which the meanings aren't very well controlled; and in that first stage when meanings aren't very well controlled, you have the multiplication of myths and magic, of rituals. Myths and magic deal with the penumbra or the dark part, whatever is beyond the horizon. As with classicism, the meanings are controlled by universal principles; you have the perennial philosophies, the immortal works of art, the laws and customs that are the product, the distillation, of the prudence and of the wisdom of mankind; and nothing changes. In the modern world, the controls of meaning are ongoing, they are developing. You move into human historicity.

The distinction between the world mediated by meaning and the world of immediacy sets the fundamental problems in philosophy, because you have there two meanings of the word 'real,' two meanings of the word 'objectivity,' and two sets of criteria about what it is to be real and what it is to really know. You can get fundamental philosophic conflicts out of those two worlds.

So much for skills.

2   Feelings

What I have to say about feelings comes largely from Max Scheler, mediated by Dietrich von Hildebrand's book on *Christian Ethics*[9] and Manfred Frings, a phenomenologist teaching at Duquesne University in Pittsburgh.[10] There is a fundamental distinction between nonintentional feelings – we have an example of that in hunger where even before the biological level there is an attraction to obtain things that a thing needs – and intentional responses. There are nonintentional states and trends: states like fatigue, irritability, bad humor, anxiety; trends like hunger, thirst, sexual discomfort. States have causes, trends have goals, but both are nonintentional; they are not evoked by objects, they do not evoke objects. You feel hungry, but you have to discover that the trouble is that you need something to eat. These are two distinct things: feeling hungry and knowing what the trouble is.

In contrast, there are intentional responses that are evoked by objects and that evoke objects. They respond to what is perceived, imagined, represented. They relate us not just to a cause or goal, but to an apprehended object or an imagined object; and they give intentional consciousness, they give this world mediated by meaning, its mass, momentum, drive, power. Without feelings, this world mediated by meaning would be paper thin, just the sort of stuff that is in books. Feelings make it alive, and make it terrifically alive.

Intentional responses are of two basic kinds: self-regarding and self-transcending. The self-regarding regard what is agreeable, disagreeable, satisfying, unsatisfying. The self-transcending are vital values: values of health, and so on; social values: the vital values of the group; cultural values: not on bread

9 Dietrich von Hildebrand, *Christian Ethics* (see above, p. 13, note 3).
10 Manfred Frings, *Max Scheler* (see above, p. 140, note 3).

alone does man live; personal values: the realization in oneself of vital, social, and cultural values; religious values: relations to the cosmos, to the totality of things – not finding the universe absurd.

Again, values are ontic or qualitative: the ontic value of the person, the qualitative value of understanding, truth, beauty, virtuous acts, noble deeds. And values stand not in isolation but in a scale of preference. Apprehensions of values are not only transient feelings; they can be permanent or quasi permanent states like being in love, hatred, and so on.

Feelings are fundamentally spontaneous; they are not like moving one's hand. One moves one's hand whenever one pleases; one cannot evoke feelings in that fashion. But still, there is an education or aberration of feelings; they can be reinforced by approval, curtailed by disapproval, given a subterranean existence by repression.

So we have skills, command of language in a world mediated by meaning, feelings that bring the world mediated by meaning alive.

3   Values

I have two sections on this topic: the notion of value and judgments of value.

3.1   The Notion of Value

I use the word 'notion' not uniformly, but, at times, in a special sense. A notion: there are different types of questions in which we intend an object without knowing it. We ask the question, Why? What? What for? How? not because we know what or why, but because we want to know. We are intending an intelligibility that we want to know but do not know, and that is a notion. These notions are not abstract; they are comprehensive. These questions keep recurring as long as there is something I have not yet understood. And because, of themselves, they are comprehensive, they are not abstracting from any intelligibility, they are intending intelligibility and they keep on intending it.

Similarly, when we have understood, we ask, 'Is it so?' I once spoke to a group of psychiatrists on *Insight*, and at the end one of the doctors said: 'Our patients have all sorts of insights; the trouble is they are wrong!' Insights are a dime a dozen; you need a very large number of them to get things right. So besides understanding, there is the question, Is that so? The man from Missouri comes on the stage and says, 'Show me!' You want the evidence, and that is a different type of question. A notion of truth is involved and, beyond that, a notion of reality, the reality that is mediated by meaning.

Finally, there is the question about the good. If it is good, is it worth while? It can be good in the sense of the self-regarding good. But is it worth while? The question we have been discussing, well, we are very interested in all this, but is it really worth while? Couldn't we find something better to do with our time, so many of us? The question that stops us is the question of the good.

Now, these notions, as I've said, are relevant to all we understand, all we agree with or disagree with, all we approve or disapprove of (and we are continually approving and disapproving, we are always praising or blaming this or that; that is the staple of human conversation). They are also normative. They not only ask; they also know when you have the answer. You ask why, and someone gives you an explanation and you say, 'Yes, but what about this?' They are recurrent, and they keep on recurring. Any defect in understanding, and there are further questions for understanding. Any defect in evidence, and there are further questions about the truth: 'Is it really so?' Any defect in goodness, and you can criticize; you needn't do it; that is the standard argument for freedom. Courses of action are not demonstrable. How do you decide to do something? You intervene, you put in your own vote.

So the wonder of the investigator, the restlessness of the doubter, the disquiet of the uneasy conscience keep moving us. Wonder moves us from the level of experience to understanding and formulation; doubt to the level of truth and knowledge of reality as mediated by meaning; and the uneasy conscience to making good resolutions, which don't change the future; you can't decide now what you are going to do tomorrow; whether you actually do it will depend on tomorrow.

So much for the notion of value. It is what may be called a transcendental notion. It seems to be another abstract concept, but it isn't; it is dynamic, recurrent, comprehensive.

3.2 Judgments of Value

Next, judgments of value. These are of two kinds: simple and comparative. Simple: *A* is good; comparative: *A* is better than *B.* You can compare judgments of value with judgments of fact. The question of value judgments is a question that came to the fore with the development of empirical science. This development, which concentrated on questions of fact (Is that so?), brought to light that there is another type of judgment. Fundamental judgments were all supposed to be self-evident. Well, judgments of value are even more evident than those of fact, and they were lumped together – there was that tendency anyway, at least in the traditions.

If we compare the two, we find that they differ in content but are similar in structure. They differ in content: one may not affirm something that doesn't exist. 'Is there an elephant in the room?' Wittgenstein's question. Well, you can't affirm that there is, if there isn't one. But you can approve something that doesn't exist. You can say that Utopia is a wonderful thing, even though it doesn't exist. So they differ in content.

They are similar in structure. Both involve some claim to objectivity, objectivity in the world mediated by meaning and motivated by values. And in what does that objectivity consist? It derives its claim from self-transcendence: the sense in which objectivity is authentic subjectivity, the subjectivity of a person who is attentive, intelligent, reasonable, responsible – authentic human subjectivity. You get into a box very quickly if you try to explain objectivity in terms of seeing what is out there. Anybody who knows anything about perception will do it for you.

True judgments of value take one beyond the realm of the purely cognitive in the sense of empirical science. They introduce one into a moral realm; you have the beginnings of moral responsibility. But they fall short of moral achievement. As Ovid put it, 'Video meliora proboque, deteriora autem sequor.'[11] You can make fine judgments of value, but leave it up to Jones to do it.

There are three components in the judgments of value. That ties in with a question that came up yesterday afternoon, namely, Can we learn ethics from the study of animals? There is the apprehension of values and their scale. In feelings, there is that apprehension of values. A beautiful illustration of it is in a slim book by Roger Poole, *Towards Deep Subjectivity*.[12] In the front of it there is a picture of three soldiers seated on a park bench. At right angles a young man and a girl are seated on another bench. The soldiers are looking straight ahead; they were of the occupying army. And the young man and young lady are glaring at them. It was a picture, according to the author, of ethical space. You could see that the soldiers felt they had no right to be there; they were looking straight ahead. And the occupied people glaring at them were telling them by their glare, 'You have no right to be here!' This is communicating an ethical judgment in a picture. It is not strictly an ethical judgment; it is an ethical feeling; but it ties in very closely with judgments of value. It is the apprehension of values in feeling, in intentional feelings of the self-transcending type. So you have the apprehension of values in intentional responses, the notion of value in the

11 [Ovid, *Metamorphoses* 7, 21: 'Video meliora proboque, Deteriora sequor.']
12 Roger Poole, *Towards Deep Subjectivity* (see above, p. 322, note 8).

query, Is it truly good? Is it really worthwhile? and the evaluation in the judgment of value itself. When you make the judgment of value about your own concrete situation, you are moving yourself into the moral realm. Whether you will stay there or not depends upon how you actually behave.

Such judgments of value have their presuppositions. Knowledge of reality, and especially of human reality in its actuality, its possibilities, its probabilities is presupposed. Without that knowledge of reality and of human reality, you get into moral idealism, beautiful ideas with terrific appeal, but unfortunately, if they were put in practice, the results would be disastrous. You have to have knowledge of reality. And a tendency from which the modern world suffers is the gimmick, the pressure group, and the slogan, which becomes the law. Such is largely moral idealism.

Human development is of two types. There is development from below upwards: experience, understanding, judgments of fact, judgments of value. That is the way we appropriate, make things our own. On the other hand, there is development from above downwards, the benefits of acculturation, socialization, education, the transmission of the tradition. Without that transmission of the tradition we would all still be at the earliest stage of the preliterate tribe, and we would have no possibility of getting beyond it because there would be no transmitting what anyone did achieve; we would always start at square one. So there is the presupposition of the transmission of past achievement, and that is from above downwards. It is insofar as one belongs to the group, is attached to the group, attached to its ways, that you have the transmission. On the other hand, if there is simply tradition without that personal appropriation of drawing upon one's own personal experience, having one's insights validated by one's own experience, then one is not on one's own.

Finally, there are stages in the development and deliberate stages in the development. There is horizontal development within the horizon one has already attained, and there is vertical development when one has moved beyond one's present horizon, when someone pulls the rug from underneath your world and you have to move into another world.

4   Beliefs

Fourthly, there are beliefs. The modern term is the sociology of knowledge. You can read Berger and Luckmann, *The Social Construction of Reality*.[13] The

13 Peter L. Berger and Thomas Luckmann, *The Social Construction of Reality* (Garden City, NY: Doubleday, 1966).

social construction of reality: we do not construct our world, we get it, we learn about it. Again, Thomas Kuhn, *The Structure of Scientific Revolutions*: this book provoked a considerable controversy, and in a postscript[14] he discussed various opinions and criticisms, and said that if he were rewriting the book, he would make its basis the scientific community; the revolution is in the scientific community. People thought he was being irrational in his view of scientific revolution, because he held that really it was a vote in the scientific community that decided whether a new theory was going to be accepted or not. But that is where the science resides. A deductive science as conceived by Euclid or Aristotle can be tucked as a habit in the mind of a single man, but a modern science is not that sort of thing. It is in the group and in the tools and libraries of the group, and it is an ongoing reality.

If you want a justification of that ongoing dimension, you start talking about belief. There is immanently generated knowledge in virtue of one's own inner and outer experience, one's own insights, one's own judgments of fact and value which one has made oneself on the evidence that one knows. But immanently generated knowledge is just a small fraction of what any civilized man knows or thinks he knows. Immediate experience is filled out by reports of what others have experienced at other places and times. One's own insights are complemented by the insights of others, and one doesn't really recapitulate them in oneself. One's own judgments are formed within the context of the judgments of others, from what one has been believing from childhood, in school or in college or in university or in the press or in the journals of opinion, and so on. And this immanently generated knowledge and the beliefs are not in two separate compartments. You can't separate them out; there is a symbiosis. We have no possibility of sorting out how much of each of our judgments rests on what *we* know and how much is influenced by the context given us by our language, our milieu over the years, what has been accumulated over the centuries, the millennia.

An engineer whips out his slide rule – I suppose he would use a computer or calculator now; in the old days he would pull out a slide rule – and performs a very intricate calculation. He knows exactly what he is doing, and he knows why it works. It is based on logarithmic and trigonometric tables, and he has never calculated out those tables for himself. He leaves it to the mathematicians, to the tradition that has handed down these tables from the time of Napier (or whoever it was). He has never calibrated his slide rule against the tables. That is

14 Thomas Kuhn, *The Structure of Scientific Revolutions* (see above, p. 134, note 11); the postscript is on pp. 174–210 of both the second and third editions.

not immanently generated knowledge, and no one blames the engineer for not repeating all these calculations and calibrating his slide rule.

We know about the relative positions of the cities in Canada and the United States. We've seen maps and the tiny little circles with the names of the cities opposite them, and we know where they all are. But did we check all this ourselves? No. We know the people who have traveled around. A cloud of witnesses will tell us the maps are right; and all exchanges of property depend upon the maps. But did the mapmaker know? Well, the mapmaker probably depended upon a series, a large number of small maps made by surveyors. The surveyors believed one another, and the mapmaker put the maps together. Human knowledge is not an individual enterprise; it is a common fund on which everyone draws according to his capacity, and everyone checks and disputes when he finds it wrong.

Can believing be defended? In general you can defend it because the alternative is to go back to the earliest stage of the most preliterate tribes and remain there. Otherwise, you don't have accumulation over the generations. In any particular case you have to take all the precautions you ever were taught about the credibility of witnesses and check them. In the purgation of mistaken beliefs you don't have to throw out all your beliefs; you would have nothing left. You don't know where beliefs begin and end. What you do when you find you have been mistaken in a belief is to start a bit of an investigation. Are there other beliefs you have from the same source? Are they connected? Are they equally reliable or unreliable? You can start working from a mistaken belief, and after you have finished with the mistaken belief you can perhaps do some work on the mistaken believer. He may have some responsibility too.

I have considered the variables: skills, feelings, values, beliefs. We want to put the foregoing into a structure. How does it fit together? That's the page I gave you.[15] In it you will find at the top numbers 1, 2, 3, and 4: individual, social, and ends. The individual breaks down into two parts, potential and actual. And there are three rows: A, B, and C. On the top, row A, numbers 1, 2, and 4: capacity, need, operation, the particular good; and those tie together in implicit definition. Individuals use capacities to operate and thereby meet needs with instances of the particular good. By a need is not meant a necessity; it is anything anyone wants. The instance of the particular good is anything that people do want that is a particular instance. And the operation is what gets it.

15 This is the one-page outline of the structure (see above, p. 334). Lonergan refers to it in the explanation that follows.

A, B, in the third column: cooperation, institution, role, task. With individuals living in groups, operations become cooperations inasmuch as members assume roles and perform tasks within institutional frameworks, that is, already understood and commonly accepted manners of cooperating. When you speak of an institution you begin thinking of all the written legal documents. Well, long before any of those documents you had institutions, namely, already understood – you don't have to explain it – and commonly accepted manners of cooperating. That is what goes on in the home without any institutions, and in general that is the way things run smoothly anywhere.

The second row [B], columns 1, 2, and 3: the potential of the individual is plastic and perfectible. The human infant can hardly do anything at first. But think of Nadia Comaneci[16] bouncing around on the beam, the acrobat, the concert pianist, the skills that people require. The calf, as soon as it is born, can walk around; the infant takes months before it is able to walk. But it is plastic, it is perfectible, it can acquire endless varieties of skills: that is the plasticity and perfectibility of the human being. One develops skills, and the skills fit in with the roles and tasks of the already understood and commonly accepted manners of cooperating.

B, 4: the good of order. We heard about it yesterday in terms of the ecosystem, or the super ecosystem. The good of order is not the institution; the good of order is the institution that works, that is working well. The same institution of marriage can be a source of misery or bliss. In one case you have the good of order, and in the other it is missing, something is missing. The same economy can mean prosperity or slump, depression. The good of order at one time is functioning. The good of order is the proper functioning, and it is something concrete, what actually is occurring in this society, in this group.

And finally the third row [C]: liberty, orientation, conversion, personal relations, terminal value. Conversion is from a self-regarding to a self-transcending orientation. It is an exercise of vertical liberty – that conversion – and transforms the personal relations rising upon institutional roles and tasks. Institutional roles and tasks set up personal relations of all sorts, with all the people you meet from morning to night.[17]

16 The reference is the Romanian gymnast who, with perfect scores, was the darling of the Summer Olympic Games in Montreal in 1976. Having later defected to the West, she now lives in Montreal.
17 At this point, the cassette tape is switched to side 2, and a sentence or two may have been omitted, especially regarding terminal value. Here the one-page handout is helpful: 'C, 1–4: Conversion is from a self-regarding to a self-transcending orientation. It is an exercise of vertical liberty and transforms

This has been an attempt, a first approach, at indicating not a description of reality so much as a source from which you can develop hypotheses about a reality.

5   Motion: Progress, Decline, Recovery

Finally we have to introduce the element of motion: progress, decline, recovery.

There is a cyclic and cumulative process that results when situations give rise to insights revealing new possibilities. New possibilities lead to new courses of action, new courses of action produce new situations, and new situations give rise to further insights revealing still further possibilities, and so on: a cyclic and cumulative process. Now this process is in the sciences as well, only it doesn't work out, in the concrete, the way this one does.

Of itself, this process admits an indefinite unfolding, but its actual course will depend upon a people's freely chosen orientation, and specifically on the self-transcending or self-regarding character of that orientation. Insofar as the orientation is self-transcending, intelligence will take the lead and good will will follow. In Toynbee's creative minority, the rank and file are glad to fall in, and everybody's happy. At each turn of the cycle, the mistakes of the past are eliminated to some extent, and intelligence is effectively guiding another part or aspect of the social process. At each turn of the cycle, you see that insight is revealing the mistakes of the past, bringing them to light, revealing possibilities for correction, and indeed bringing to light new courses of action. Challenge-and-response is an ongoing process.[18]

On the other hand, insofar as the orientation of people is self-regarding, intelligence again will lead, but the private interest of individuals will balk, and the special interest of groups will encourage, promote, even impose its own special type of intelligence: mainly the intelligence that discovers and implements what is to a particular group's advantage, even though not conducive to the well-being of all. In this fashion the social process is biased; development occurs, but it restricts its favor to some and neglects the rest. The longer the bias is maintained, the smaller the group it favors and the larger

the personal relations rising upon institutional roles and tasks. Again, it is the originating value whence flows the terminal value of a truly worthwhile good of order.' For a fuller treatment of this part of the structure, see *Method in Theology* 50–52.

18 Arnold J. Toynbee, *A Study of History*, vol. 3: *The Growths of Civilizations* (London: Oxford University Press, 1962) 217–48.

the group it neglects, then the greater will be what Toynbee calls the 'schism in the body social' (one of the big sections in the first six volumes),[19] the more distorted will be the economic and political situation, the less will that situation provide an intelligible base on which still further development can be built. What intelligence will discover in this situation is its lack of intelligibility, not new sources, new possibilities of creativity.

To material, economic, and political distortion there probably will be added cultural distortion as well. For social institutions and processes are man-made, they are constituted in the world mediated by meaning and motivated by values. They stand in need of cultural legitimation, and never is that need of legitimation greater than when social institutions and processes suffer from aberrations. That is when you really need legitimation; the defects are a little too glaring to do without it.

Now what do we do in that kind of situation? Well, the first type of solution is Paul Ricoeur's hermeneutic of suspicion and hermeneutic of recovery.[20] Hermeneutic of suspicion: in the manner of Marx, Nietzsche, Freud, you find the seeds of the aberration, the bias, where things went wrong. And the hermeneutic of recovery: there is something good about it or it wouldn't have happened. This is in hermeneutics, in interpretation; it's more complex in concrete situations. Together, however, in interpretation and at least in understanding the situation, the two constitute a means of discernment that sets the ideological goats on the left and the nonideological remainder on the right. But this is just a first step, for any given operator of discernment may well suffer from a bias of his own; a certain amount of ideology will function in his discernment, and consequently a certain amount of objective ideology will pass for real, fine gold. At this point the problem takes the form of the function of the complex variable, the function of $x + iy$. Only in this case you don't exactly know what the i means. There is no clear notion of which is the source of the complexity in the variables because the judges, the discerners, also can be subject to the error.

Can one say more about it? Well, of course, one could go on – especially a theologian could go on! What we are talking about is not simply process but historical process. It is not something of the past; it is something we are part of, it is human history, it is something in which we are involved now and for the rest of our lives. And in this the one great delusion, to my mind, is the belief

19 Ibid. vol. 5: *The Disintegrations of Civilizations* (1962) 35–376.
20 Paul Ricoeur, *De l'interprétation, Essai sur Freud* (see above, p. 263, note 6) 32–36.

that there is an island of safety called 'method.' If you follow the method, you will be all right: in the sense that there is some algorithm, some set of rules, some objective solution, independent of each man's personal authenticity, honesty, genuineness. And that does not exist. The only solution lies in 'the good man.' With that, I think we can leave this enormous topic to your reflection.

Comments by Fr William A. Stewart, s.j. [21]

Perhaps I could begin my own comments by furthering something of what Dr Bourke himself has said when he mentioned Thomism and its revival. If I can use the distinction between Scholasticism and Thomism, without trying to explain it here, I think much of Scholastic philosophy traditionally was taught in a very deductive way: you began with self-evident principles, you plucked values, you might say, out of some noetic heaven, and then imposed these and, starting with your self-evident principles, then you could deduce the whole system. I think the great characteristic of Fr Lonergan's approach, as distinct from this, is that it is an experimental one; it's rather inductive: he proceeds from experience through intelligent grasp and reasonable affirmation to deliberation, decision, and choice. So the discovery of values is not something written on the wall out there for all to see, but something that is discovered rather by the collaboration of many people in an ongoing process. Man is what he makes of himself, as he says at one point in *Insight*, through his own free decisions;[22] and I think that what Fr Lonergan has been telling us this morning is illustrative of this business of the discovery of values and arriving at principles which are not self-evident at the start by any means, as so often occurs in traditional Scholasticism, but are the result, the generalizations, you

21 At the time of the lecture, Fr Stewart was Professor of Philosophy and Acting Dean of Arts, St Mary's University, Halifax, Nova Scotia. He was the second of two respondents to Lonergan's lecture. The first was Dr Vernon Bourke, then Professor of Philosophy at St Louis University. Dr Bourke's comments did not evoke any response from Lonergan, and so they are omitted here.
22 Lonergan, *Insight* 633–42. The general references cited indicate where the substance of Fr Stewart's quotation may be found; Lonergan is more specific in later writings, for example, 'The Subject' (1968), in *A Second Collection: Papers by Bernard J.F. Lonergan, S.J.*, ed. William F.J. Ryan and Bernard J. Tyrrell (London: Darton, Longman & Todd, 1974) 79: 'By his own acts the human subject makes himself what he is to be, and he does so freely and responsibly; indeed, he does so precisely because his acts are the free and responsible expressions of himself.'

might say, of human living and human experience. So we build up our scale of values accordingly.

I might repeat a favorite story of mine because I think it does illustrate a point – though perhaps it is a sad story. There were these two good Scots in swimming together one day, and each bet the other a penny that he could swim under water the further. Both of them drowned! I think we laugh because the scale of values is a bit at odds with our own scale of values, or perhaps with your preferential scale of values: we don't equate a penny with a human life. But it's a long process we take, I think, to arrive at that scale of values; and our feelings as responses to values give us a scale of preferences, and the preferences, in turn, give us a scale of values. And this, as I say, to me is a very ongoing and collaborative process.

One point I might make before turning over to Fr Lonergan is to address the topic of this conference, 'Beyond Relativity';[23] and nowhere have we heard, at least in today's talk, the discussion of relativity and the absolute, and so on. I just mention this without trying to answer it myself because I've heard the criticism that, if one relies merely on the conscience of the virtuous man, of the good judge, then one is making values entirely a matter of relativity. Without going into *Insight*, of course, and its answer to relativism in chapter 11, I think it is a point that we could reflect upon and perhaps Fr Lonergan himself might like to say a word about it.

Lonergan's Response to Fr Stewart

I think you have to accept the vicious circle. Aristotle could speak empirically of ethics by presupposing the existence of virtuous men; and if you don't know what a virtuous man is, well, you can hardly usefully talk about ethics. Another point he made, of course, was that ethics is a subject for older people; it requires experience of life, and it's something one develops towards, it's a stage of human development. I drew a distinction between the self-regarding and self-transcending feelings, and it's a stage in one's development. Kohlberg distinguishes stages in moral development, and to move to a life dominated by values is his sixth level in moral development.[24] For these things to be not

23 As indicated in n.1 above, the title of the conference was 'Beyond Relativism.' Fr Stewart is using the word 'relativity' in that sense. He speaks of 'relativism' a couple of sentences later; and Lonergan, in any event, clarifies the difference between the terms in his remarks which follow.
24 Among various articles, see 'Moral Development,' in *International Encyclopedia of the Social Sciences* (New York: Crowell, Collier & MacMillan, 1968) 483–94.

simply, as Newman would call them, notional apprehensions but real apprehensions, things you've appropriated, made your own, is a matter of development, and not simply of definition.

With regard to relativity and relativism, a distinction is to be drawn: anything anyone understands is related to something else, it's involved in a relativity, and history reveals a terrific relativity. But the mere fact that you are writing history, that you can have a historical science, means that your historical differences are put in an understood continuum, or you are trying to get them into an understood continuum or discontinuities, as the case may be. You are setting up relations, and by setting up the relations you move to understanding, and you find that while it differs in this and this respect, still it's the same in this and this respect, and so on.

Relativity is not relativism; relativism means that nothing is true. The doctrine of internal relations was taught by certain British idealists towards the end of the nineteenth century, namely, that everything is related to everything else; you can't make a true statement about anything without making all the true statements about everything, because everything is related to everything else, and that relation is intrinsic to its reality. That is a theoretical statement of relativism, that you can never know anything. It presupposes that in this world nothing is contingent, nothing is merely statistical. 'The cup is on the table' does not depend upon the nebula of Andromeda; it can be on the table or off the table, and the nebula of Andromeda remains exactly the same, as far as the statement, 'The cup is on the table,' goes. In other words, there are contingent events, and concrete judgments of fact are in that category. That's the question of relativism, and relativity is an entirely different thing.

Question: I'd like to question Fr Lonergan on the whole notion that he brought up about the nature of progress and the nature of decline. I really don't understand it. It seems we have a situation which then gives rise to insights, which then eventually give rise to a new situation. But according to Fr Lonergan the correct insights are derived if we accept certain principles, and these include 'Be reasonable,' 'Be responsible,' 'Be attentive,' 'Be intelligent.' But these four commands are part of the original situation. Now, why should our insights not be of a nature that they question these four original principles by which we come to the correct insights? And that would turn the whole cycle of progress into a cycle of decline. And I think in fact that that is exactly what we are experiencing in the present; the values which over the last few hundred years have given rise to the progress that we have experienced are now being eroded by the very progress which we have made; and that's the dilemma which we're in at the moment. How would you explain that or resolve that?

Response: Insights aren't total. In other words, decline is also involved in insights, but they are the insights of the biased mind. What a man understands, what seems really tops, is, 'Six percent is better than five, seven better than six,' and so on: intelligent self-interest – that's the kind of intelligence that's been recommended. Of course, it worked much better two centuries ago than now, but you have the cultural distortion coming in, in economic theories, and so on. In other words, insight is not one thing; 'Be intelligent' means a steady, ongoing flow of insights. Your creative minority can become a dominant minority; it's just remaining in the saddle although it has no more ideas, it's no longer meeting the issues. Try Toynbee's *Study of History*, which is principally a lot of ideal types; people object it isn't empirical history; well, okay, but it's ideal types at least. He was a terrific humanist. Am I meeting your question at all, am I understanding it?

Question: I think you touched on it when you said the biased mind fouls up progress.

Response: That's part of the problem, eh?

Question: In that case, I would have to suggest that the danger of progress ruining itself is still present.

Response: Oh sure, I have no doubt about it whatever!

Question: Every mind must be biased in the sense that it cannot see the full consequences of its actions.

Response: Oh well, yes, but that isn't the same as bias. Bias is concerned with the self-transcending and the self-regarding – that distinction. Self-transcendence: to know, to be objective in your judgments of fact, you have to be authentic; objectivity in the world mediated by meaning is the fruit of authentic subjectivity. Authentic subjectivity is being attentive, intelligent, reasonable, responsible. And it's *being* that, and letting that function, which is a tussle: you don't start off that way; knowledge makes a bloody entrance.

Question: I still don't think that is enough to prevent someone from having the same effect on your system that a biased person would.

Response: I'm not offering a system. The answer to this problem of bias, the only answer, is that there's no system, there's no method, there's no island, on which you can climb. What you need is the honest man, all honest men; if they are all honorable men, then they can go on, you see: get on or get honest, people in the third stage.

Question: I understood you to say that judgments of fact and judgments of value are similar in structure but differ in content. Precisely how are they similar in structure?

Response: They are similar in structure insofar as both proceed from self-transcending subjectivity, from attention, intelligence, reasonableness, and responsibility; insofar as both claim to be objective; insofar as the judgment of value is an *as*sent rather than a *con*sent, and the judgment of fact also is an assent: 'That is so.'

Question: When you speak of objectivity – 'both claim to be objective' – what do you mean?

Response: That's what's so.

Question: What do you mean by 'objective?' Let's be very concrete. I say, 'John is a white man,' and a second proposition, 'John is a good man.' Now I can see a similarity in structure there, namely, a grammatical similarity: '*X* is *Y*.' But does the similarity go beyond this, and if so, where?

Response: It isn't a similarity in content. In other words, the white man has to exist for your statement to be true. But you can talk about the good man even though you don't believe that such a person exists.

Question: Wait a minute now. The statements are both existential. 'John *is* a good man.' 'John *is* a white man.' Both are using 'is.'

Response: Oh yes, but 'is' is not univocal.

Question: Well in that case, we're not univocal with 'white' or 'good' either. So that doesn't help. Let's not add problems. Let's get down to the important thing. The similarity in structure, where they both claim to be objective: in other words, you want to say something like this, as G.E. Moore did. When I say, 'John is a white man,' 'John is a good man,' what makes John 'good' is that there's some property out there in John which makes John good, just as there's some property out there in John which makes John white. And if he didn't have that property of 'good,' he wouldn't be good, just as if he didn't have the property of 'white,' he wouldn't be white. Is that what you mean by being similar in structure and being objective?

Response: I distinguish two worlds: the world of immediacy and the world mediated by meaning, and consequently two sets of criteria of objectivity. There is the objectivity of what you can put your paw on, the sure and firm-set earth on which I tread, in which Macbeth took refuge when he saw the dagger. And there is objectivity in the sense of what satisfies the exigences of the subject as attentive, intelligent, reasonable, responsible. That's another sense of objectivity, and it's in that sense of objectivity that your judgments of fact and your judgments of value are similar in structure.

Question: Well, you lost me on that last one. Could you be a little more concrete?

Response: That's as concrete as you can get. Your attention is something that's concrete even though you can't put your paw on it. Your intelligence, your asking questions, is something concrete, and it's something that's recurrent. It will keep on until you get satisfying answers. And you want to get the truth of the matter. There's another meaning to 'objective,' and to get those two distinct is essential to philosophy.

19

Questionnaire on Philosophy: Response[1]

1 Please describe briefly the present state of philosophy and of philosophical studies in your country or region: tendencies, schools, impact, importance given to philosophical studies, etc.

I am not particularly competent to speak of English-speaking Canada since eleven years of my studies and over twenty of my teaching were done elsewhere. But taking the University of Toronto as a paradigm, the traditional core is the presentation of ancient and modern philosophies. This tradition has been infiltrated and, in part, overcome by the linguistic analysts. The impact of philosophy seems small and its importance little appreciated. The best students do mathematics and natural science.

---

1 [The questionnaire to which Lonergan responded was distributed to Jesuit professors of philosophy around the world, in preparation for a symposium on philosophy that was eventually held at Villa Cavalletti near Rome, 8–18 September 1977. Lonergan did not attend the symposium. Twenty-three questionnaires were distributed, and nineteen responses, often very detailed, were received by the Faculty of Philosophy at the Gregorian University. The responses were to be made by 30 September 1976, so we can presume that Lonergan's response was composed sometime prior to that date.

'Questionnaire on Philosophy: Responses by Bernard J.F. Lonergan, s.j.,' edited by Frederick E. Crowe, was first published in *METHOD: Journal of Lonergan Studies* 2:2 (October 1984) 1–35.

The autograph can be found in the Lonergan Archives, A2801. Bracketed footnotes in this edition are editorial. The other footnotes are Lonergan's, written into the autograph not precisely as footnotes but as references or as notes set off at the appropriate places in the text.]

2.1 Against this background describe the present state of Jesuit philosophical studies in your region, as to extent, content, and methods.

In 1930 the Jesuits of Upper Canada opened a house of philosophy in Toronto. The professors were good men, faithful to the assigned textbooks, apparently unaware of the exigences of *Deus scientiarum Dominus*, but very generous in spending their weekends in Toronto and neighboring parishes. After about twenty-five years it was decided to discontinue studies of philosophy in Toronto and to send our scholastics to the Oregon Province for their philosophy.

2.2 In comparison with the situation before the Thirty-first General Congregation of the Society of Jesus (1965) do you notice a decline, a simple change, or even an improvement of philosophical studies? What do you think are the reasons for this phenomenon?

As studies of philosophy in English-speaking Canada were discontinued well before 1965, there has since been no change whatever. However, attitudes towards philosophy have suffered incidental losses and enjoyed incidental gains. The incidental loss is the widespread conviction that philosophy is a waste of time. The incidental gain is the breakdown of the old regimentation.

In both cases the underlying and longstanding causes are: (1) the radical shift in the notion of science in the seventeenth century; and (2) the radical shift in the notion of history in the nineteenth century.

On the scientific revolution Herbert Butterfield has said:

> Since that revolution overturned the authority in science not only of the middle ages but of the ancient world – since it ended not only in the eclipse of scholastic philosophy but in the destruction of Aristotelian physics – it outshines everything since the rise of Christianity and reduces the Renaissance and Reformation to the rank of mere episodes, mere internal displacements, within the system of medieval Christendom. Since it changed the character of men's habitual mental operations even in the conduct of the non-material sciences, while transforming the whole diagram of the physical universe and the very texture of human life itself, it looms so large as the real origin both of the modern world and the modern mentality that our customary periodisation of European history has become an anachronism and an encumbrance.[2]

2 Herbert Butterfield, *The Origins of Modern Science: 1300–1800*, rev. ed. (New York: The Free Press, 1966) 7–8.

Of the 'historical revolution' Alan Richardson has written:

> We should never forget that it was one and the same movement of
> critical enquiry which first culminated in the seventeenth-century
> scientific achievement and later in the emergence of the fully devel-
> oped historical critical method of the nineteenth century. The critical
> faculty, once awakened, could not rest satisfied with the successful
> exploration of the realm of nature; it was bound to go on from there to
> the critical investigation of the more intractable realm of human
> nature, and, when the idea of development was fully understood, to
> seek to understand scientifically how, in fact, man and his institutions
> have come to be what they are. Since the nineteenth century it has
> been an axiom of Western thinking that men and their institutions
> cannot be understood apart from their history ... The historical revolu-
> tion in human thinking, which was accomplished in the nineteenth
> century, is just as important as the scientific revolution of two centu-
> ries earlier. But they are not two separate revolutions; they are aspects
> of the one great transitional movement from the mediaeval to the
> modern way of looking at things.[3]

So much for the underlying and longstanding causes.

The proximate cause is to be sought, in my opinion, not in a total unaware-
ness of the scientific and the historical revolutions, but in a failure to grasp
their radical character and to acknowledge that far more than piecemeal
concessions are needed to meet the issue. We have acknowledged the transformation of our knowledge of nature and of our knowledge of man, not as a
single momentous event demanding an equally momentous development in
philosophy, but as a series of regrettable aberrations that unfortunately were
widely accepted.

*3.1 In the light of what you think to be the nature of philosophy (and of theology) can you
state clear reasons why philosophical studies should be a necessary part of preparation for
the priesthood and/or the training of a Jesuit?*
I shall attempt to answer this question in two main stages with suitable
subdivisions: *3.11* my opinion on the nature of philosophy; *3.111* the view
commonly derived from Aristotle; *3.112* its inadequacy; *3.12* an alternative

---

3 Alan Richardson, *History, Sacred and Profane* (London: SCM Press, 1964) 32–33.

view; *3.121* its relevance to theology; *3.122* its relevance to the formation of priests and of Jesuits.

3.11 In general, I should say that philosophy is the basic and total science, the *Grund- und Gesamtwissenschaft*, and for this reason it fulfils an essential mediating role between theology, other sciences, human cultures and societies.

3.111 On a traditional view, commonly derived from Aristotle's *Posterior Analytics*, science is certain knowledge of things through their causes, *certa rerum per causas cognitio.*

The dependence of this view on Aristotle's writings is manifest enough. For if the *Posterior Analytics* begin by asserting (1) an element of necessity, truth, certainty and (2) an element of causality, understanding, explanation, still these two are given immediately their technical objectification in the demonstrative syllogism, where the premises are true and certain, while the middle term assigns the necessary ground of the predicate pertaining to the subject.

Once this view of science is accepted, it is not difficult to conclude that the basic and total science must be metaphysics. Metaphysics is the science that sets forth necessary principles and conclusions about being as being. These principles and conclusions must hold for every being. And so metaphysics must be the total and basic science.

3.112 However, this view of science is challenged both by the scientific revolution of the seventeenth century and by the historical revolution of the nineteenth century.

For the view that metaphysics is the basic and total science supposes that other sciences derive their basic concepts and principles by some further specification of the basic concepts and principles of metaphysics. But the development of modern natural science revealed that empirically established correlations yielded sets of basic terms and basic relations, and these terms and relations were far more fruitful than anything that could be derived from Aristotelian metaphysics.

Further, while the *Posterior Analytics* began from the view that we think we understand when we know the cause, know that it is the cause, and know that the effect cannot be other than it is, still this initial interest in reality promptly gave way to its expression in demonstrative syllogisms and in an unfolding of the numerous interesting properties of demonstrative syllogisms. Moreover, neither the fourteenth-century Scholastics nor their subsequent followers showed much concern to submit their syllogistic conclusions to empirical tests. So there arose loud complaints against Aristotelian verbalism, and, at the same time, the new scientists subscribed to a rule to entertain no questions that could not be settled by an appeal to observation and/or experiment.

This rule of empirical verification had ulterior implications. For if Newton, Laplace, Maxwell, not to mention the pamphleteers, expressed no serious doubts about the necessity of natural laws, it remains that Euclid, once assumed to be unique and indubitable, has given way to Riemann's manifold of geometries, Newton has yielded to Einstein, Laplace to Darwinian probabilities of emergence and survival, Maxwell to Heisenberg's principles of uncertainty or indeterminacy. Nor is this simply the rediscovery of the Scholastic distinction between metaphysical and physical necessity. What the empirical scientist discovers is not the intelligibility of what must be but the intelligibility of what may or may not be. For that reason, verification is of the essence of empirical science.

As Aristotelian science was knowledge of the necessary, so also it was knowledge of the universal. But modern science, while it uses universals, conceives them not as scientific objectives but merely as tools that, through successive and ever more determinate approximations, bring us ever closer to knowledge and control of the concrete.

Finally, this concern with the concrete brings to light a further difference between the modern and the Aristotelian notion of science. Because Aristotelian science was to be an ordered set of demonstrative syllogisms, it could be a habit tucked into the mind of an individual. But no individual knows the whole of any modern science. Knowledge of the whole of modern mathematics, or modern physics, or modern chemistry, or any other modern field, resides not in the minds of individuals but in the aggregate resources of the respective scientific communities. So Thomas Kuhn in the postscript to the second edition of his *The Structure of Scientific Revolutions* began by remarking that, if he were rewriting the book, he would begin from the notion of the scientific community.[4]

While the seventeenth-century scientific revolution was anti-Aristotelian, the nineteenth-century historical revolution was opposed to Aristotle only inasmuch as Aristotle could not conceive history as a science. Historians do not derive their basic terms and relations either from a metaphysic or from empirically validated laws; they are content to extend the ordinary language of their own place and time to include the ways of thought and feeling of the period they are investigating. They do not demonstrate their conclusions but

4 [Thomas Kuhn, *The Structure of Scientific Revolutions*, 2nd ed. (see above, p. 134, note 11) 174–81.]

find them confirmed by the available documentary and other evidence. They do not discover the intelligibility of what must be but uncover the intelligibility of what was, though it might not have been. They use universals but only as tools towards reaching the concrete with which they are concerned. Their knowledge, finally, has its locus not in the mind of each historian but only in aggregate resources of the ongoing community of historians.

3.12 I have been setting forth the divergence between the idea of science formulated in Aristotle's *Posterior Analytics* and the achievement of scientific and historical investigation in recent centuries. I have now to ask, in the light of the new idea of science, what the basic and total science is to be. Essentially my answer is simple: the basic and total science is not just metaphysics but the compound of (1) cognitional theory, (2) epistemology, (3) the metaphysics of proportionate being, and (4) existential ethics. Let us say a few words on each of these.

Cognitional theory tells just what one is doing when one is coming to know. It includes the whole genesis of common sense, of the sciences, of exegetical and historical studies, of the philosophies. It will be radical enough to leave room for future scientific, scholarly, and philosophic developments. It insures our basic and total science against objections from the sciences of the past and leaves it open to the discoveries of the future.

Epistemology tells why performing the operations set forth in cognitional theory is knowing. It takes the reader or student beyond the mistaken views on knowledge and reality which men of common sense, scientists, scholars, and philosophers so easily and frequently maintain.

From knowing what we do when we know and knowing why doing that is really knowing there follows a corollary, namely, a metaphysics that sets forth what in general we know when we perform cognitional operations. Such a metaphysics will be no more than a metaphysics of proportionate being, of the world of our experience. But it is from that world we must start if we are to understand the modern question of God, since modern science has given us knowledge confined to this world, and to go beyond that knowledge we have to be fully and explicitly aware of what we are doing.

Of existential ethics, finally, something will be said in our next section, for it regards man in this world, and that falls within the traditional domain of theology.[5]

5 The foregoing view I have developed in two works, *Insight: A Study of Human Understanding* [see above, p. 3, note 2] and *Method in Theology* [see above, p. 12, note 2].

3.121 A Christian theology thematizes the Christian religion on the level of the times in which the theology is composed.

So theologies are distinguished by their time, and people speak of biblical theology, patristic theology, medieval theology, and modern theology, of their respective characteristics and differences, of their relations to one another and to their times.

In the Christian religion as lived but not yet thematized there may be distinguished three moments. First, there is the ontic present of God's love flooding our hearts through the Holy Spirit he has given us. Second, there is the objective past in which God's revelation of his love to us through Christ Jesus has been mediated down the ages by the ongoing Christian community. Thirdly, there is the eschatological consummation and, on the way, the command and the duty to preach the gospel to every class in every culture.

The Christian religion as lived enters human living both on the side of the object and on the side of the subject. On the side of the object it enters human history and penetrates human cultures as the word of God in and about and through Jesus Christ, his life and his work. On the side of the subject it is a transformation of existential ethics. By existential ethics I mean the ethical living that has not yet emerged inasmuch as one just drifts through life – that is, just does and says and thinks what everyone else is doing and saying and thinking, and everyone else is drifting too. Positively, I mean the ethical living that begins indeed when one finds out for oneself that one has to decide for oneself what one is to do with one's life, but that becomes established when one lives in love with those nearest one and in loyalty with one's fellow men about one. Now such existential ethics undergoes a transformation when God's love floods our hearts through the Holy Spirit he has given us: for such love is unrestricted; it is with all one's heart and all one's mind and all one's strength; further, it is comprehensive, loving God above all, and one's neighbor as oneself, and the world in which we live, with all it contains, as God's own world. It is the love described by St Paul in the thirteenth chapter of his first letter to the Corinthians; it is the love to which Ignatius of Loyola directs those that follow his *Spiritual Exercises.*

If I may use the terms 'sublate' and 'sublation' in the sense indicated in *Method in Theology*[6] one may say that the Christian religion sublates the whole of human living. For what sublates goes beyond what is sublated; it adds an entirely new principle, sets a new goal, a new task, a new criterion, liberates what is sublated from its limitations and directs it to higher ends, yet in no way

6 Lonergan, *Method in Theology* 237–44, 314–18, 340–44.

stunts it, interferes with it, robs it of its integrity. So sensitivity sublates vegetal living; intelligence sublates animal living; rational judgment concentrates the creativity of intelligence on truth and reality; deliberation, evaluation, decision, praxis integrate knowing and feeling in the pursuit of the good, of the truly worthwhile. The Christian religion as lived adds a further stage in this process of sublation: within the individual it is God's love flooding his heart and thereby transforming his existential subjectivity; within the ongoing human community it is the objective revelation of God's love in Christ Jesus, the mediation of that revelation through the Christian community, and the mission to preach the gospel to all nations until the consummation of all in all.

I have been speaking of the Christian religion as lived in order that I might speak of it as thematized, as the concern of theology. We have seen that the Christian religion as lived is the sublation of the whole of human living. It follows at once that to thematize the sublation of the whole of human living is a task beyond the competence of theology as a particular science or particular discipline, that theology can perform that task only by broadening its horizon by uniting itself with philosophy as the basic and total science.

To put the point in other words, one may note that particular sciences are specializations, that interdisciplinary studies build bridges between specializations to give us physical chemistry, biophysics, biochemistry, psychologies of the unconscious, and social psychologies, that the ultimate ground of all interdisciplinary work is the basic and total science that results from understanding both in their similarities and in their differences the several methods of the particular sciences and, as well, the procedures of common sense. Only in virtue of such understanding is the theologian capable of thematizing adequately the Christian religion both in itself as a principle of sublation and in its effects upon the whole of human living.

As the reader will have noted, I am restating in the contemporary context the traditional view that philosophy is the handmaid of theology. In the medieval context logic was the norm and measure of science and by that standard metaphysics was the basic and total science. But in the contemporary context method is the norm and measure of science, and so it is from an understanding of methods in their similarities and their differences that one attains the basic and total science.

There remains a final point, for in the new context the relations between theology and philosophy are particularly simple and clear. Theology is the sublation of philosophy. For philosophy is the basic and total science of human living. The Christian religion as lived is the sublation of the whole of human living. Hence the Christian religion as thematized is the sublation of the basic and total science of human living.

3.122 We have come to the end of this long answer and have now to conclude with an opinion on the relevance of philosophical study in the preparation of candidates for the priesthood and in the training of Jesuits.

First of all, then, I do not see any relevance in any antiquated philosophy, and I consider antiquated any philosophy with a cognitional theory inadequate to account clearly and accurately for the procedures of common sense, of mathematics, of the natural sciences, of the human sciences, and of human studies.

Secondly, competence in a contemporary discipline pertains not to individuals but to groups, and, in like manner, competence in a set of disciplines pertains to a group of groups. This feature of our world results from specialization, and specialization results from the fact that modern disciplines aim at knowledge, not of abstract universals, but of ever closer approximations to the concrete. Moreover, as knowledge advances, specializations multiply, and as they multiply they tend to get narrower and narrower. Eventually narrowness succumbs to decreasing returns and the need for 'generalists' as well as specialists is felt. So in West Germany at Bielefeld there has been instituted a university for interdisciplinary studies, while in America Ludwig von Bertalanffy has launched a movement with his General Systems Theory.[7] Within this context, theology as the sublation of philosophy is of supreme importance. For if one believes that the Christian religion is the sublation of the whole of human living, the theological thematization of this religion must be granted first place in significant studies.

Thirdly, as it is only in the university that all aspects of human living are under study, it is in the Christian university that theology can attain its full development and exercise its full influence. In the past indeed it claimed to be the queen of the sciences, but then its deductivist notion of science misled it into making dictatorial claims. In the present proposal its influence will be exercised, not by laying down premises and demonstrating conclusions, but by promoting interdisciplinary understanding through its philosophy and through its sublation of philosophy.

Fourthly, as I argued in my paper on 'The Response of the Jesuit as Priest and Apostle in the Modern World,'[8] the New Testament emphasis on the

---

7 See Ervin Laszlo, ed., *The Relevance of General Systems Theory* (New York: George Braziller, 1972).

8 In *A Second Collection* [see above, p. 22, note 12] 165–87, especially 179–80.

function of priests is that they are to be leaders, teachers, preachers. In the measure that a diocese or a religious order wishes to provide the church with leaders, teachers, preachers, it will do all it can to make the leaders far-seeing, the teachers profound, the preachers wise. The formula for that is simple: they will themselves live the Christian life that is the sublation of the whole of human living, and they will know a theology that thematizes the sublation of the whole of human living. In this fashion they will preach what already they practice.

Fifthly, resources both human and material are limited. Doing all one can at times may be little. But even then the ideal can be maintained. What one individual lacks can be made up by another, for in modern studies what counts is not the learning in the individual mind but in the group. Further, genuine Christian humility excludes the *ressentiment* that belittles the learning one does not oneself possess; and it is such *ressentiment* that erodes ideals.

3.2 Do you think that philosophical studies for Christians and/or especially for candidates for the priesthood should be different from philosophical studies 'tout court,' and if so, why?

Perhaps I should mention that I have written on this issue in my *Philosophy of God, and Theology*[9] and in a paper on 'Philosophy and Theology.'[10]

Briefly, I may say that the basic principle seems to me to be that human development occurs in two distinct modes. If I may use a spatial metaphor, it moves (1) from below upwards and (2) from above downwards.

It moves from below upwards inasmuch as it begins from one's personal experience, advances through ever fuller understanding and more balanced judgment, and so attains the responsible exercise of personal freedom.

It moves from above downwards inasmuch as one belongs to a hierarchy of groups and so owes allegiance to one's home, to one's country, to one's religion. Through the traditions of the group one is socialized, acculturated, educated to become in time either (1) a member of the tribe or clan or (2) an inheritor of the classicism of ancient Greece and Rome or (3) a participant in the modernity that is familiar with the variety of human cultures and literatures, the achievements of modern mathematics and science, the expertise of the contemporary exegete and historian, the reflections of philosophers and theologians.

9 See above, pp. 157–218.
10 Bernard Lonergan, 'Philosophy and Theology,' *Proceedings of the American Catholic Philosophical Association* 46 (1970) 19–30; reprinted in *A Second Collection* 193–208.

These two modes of development are interdependent. Both begin from infancy. But only through the second does the first take one beyond the earliest prehistoric stages of human development. Only through the first is there any real assimilation and appropriation of the second.

Such interdependence, as it supposes distinction, so too it opposes separation. In philosophy (and particularly in its basic phase of cognitional theory, epistemology, metaphysics, and existential ethics) the overwhelming emphasis is upon personal appropriation of one's own intelligent, rational, and responsible being. In theology (and particularly with regard to the mysteries of faith that Aquinas did not see his way to treating in the first three books and so relegated to a fourth in his *Contra Gentiles*) the major emphasis is on the Christian tradition. But differences in emphasis are one thing. Systematic separation is another, and, as it seems to me, it is less a product of Christian wisdom or prudence than of Cartesian universal doubt and of the eighteenth-century Enlightenment's identification of tradition with prejudice and abuse.

Summarily, then, the theoretical shift is from philosophy as it would be worked out by men *in statu naturae purae* to philosophy that along with modern science is concerned not with abstract universals but with concrete realities.

Practically it would seem that the development of those not due to study theology would be enriched perhaps by some philosophical theology but more probably by an 'extension' or popular course in theology. On the other hand, those due to study theology have little to gain from an artificial abstraction from the Christian world in which they were born and brought up.

4.1 In view of the answer to question 3.1, what does the study of philosophy involve in relation to content?

4.11 Is there a necessary (minimum) content for the philosophical studies to be done by one who will be a priest and a Jesuit?

I should say that, while one may assign a minimum core requirement, still the further additions to that core have to be based on the needs and dangers of particular places and times, and are best determined on the advice of people on the spot.

The minimum core I would describe as religious, moral, and intellectual conversion. By religious conversion, which is the foundation of the other two, I mean the habitual acceptance of God's gift of his love flooding our hearts through the Holy Spirit he has given us (Romans 5.5). By moral conversion I mean the existential decision to guide one's decisions and one's actions not by satisfactions but by values, by what truly is worth while. By intellectual conversion I mean an adequate understanding of the difference between the world of immediacy (in which the infant lives) and the world mediated by meaning and motivated by values (into which the child, the adolescent, the adult gradually enter). Along with an understanding of this difference there would be required practical knowledge of all the symptoms of the infantile regression which confuses the real with the immediately given and pronounces the meaningful to be unreal, or abstract, or controversial, and so on.

Such conversions involve radical shifts of horizon, and horizons underpin all that is thought, said, done. Moreover, in the history of Christianity may be discerned quite different styles in which the same basic horizon finds expression, and a brief survey of these differences will serve to indicate different ways in which the core requirement may be expressed and communicated.

The universal style is the symbolic. Its language is instinct with feeling. At its liveliest it is poetry. At its profoundest it is rhetoric. It lacks neither attention to detail nor keen insight nor balanced judgment nor responsible decision. But it has all these, not stripped of feeling but permeated with feeling. The calm, the detachment, the clarity, the coherence, the rigor, of the logician, the mathematician, the scientist – these are just beyond its horizon. Such by and large is the language of the New Testament, which employs parable and aphorism and apocalyptic to shift thought and meaning from man's everyday world to the world of religious meaning. Such also in the main was the language of the church Fathers, and down the ages it has remained the straightforward simple language of mainstream Christianity.

A second style is the analytic. It is a variant on the foregoing introduced to meet emergencies in which a clarification of the basic Christian message became imperative. I call it analytic because it anticipates the discovery of the linguistic analysts that ordinary language fixes the meaning of words, not by definitions, but by showing how the word may be used appropriately. Now it would seem to be precisely this device that was employed in resolving the trinitarian controversies of the fourth century and the christological controversies of the fifth. Athanasius was revealing how the term *homoousios* was used appropriately when he stated: 'omnia de Filio quae de Patre dicuntur excepto Patris nomine.'[11] Similarly, the same procedure takes a more concrete form in the Preface to the Mass of the Trinity: 'Quod enim de tua gloria, revelante te, credimus, hoc de Filio tuo, hoc de Spiritu sancto sine differentia discretionis sentimus.'[12] Finally, the classical *communicatio*

11 [everything that is said of the Father is said of the Son, except the name 'Father']
12 [What we believe because of your revelation about your glory, the same we

idiomatum[13] in Christology is speech about appropriate usage, and it appears as early as the *Formula unionis* in the spring of 433, some eighteen years before Chalcedon: 'Evangelicas autem et apostolicas de Domino voces scimus deiloquos viros aliquotiens consociantes tamquam de una persona dictas, aliquotiens autem dividentes tamquam de duabus naturis et has quidem Deo condecentes secundum deitatem Christi, humiles autem secundum humanitatem tradentes.'[14]

A third style prolongs the second by attempting definitions. So Augustine explained heuristically that the word 'person' names what there are three of in the Trinity. Boethius drew upon Aristotle's *Categories* to define a person as 'individua substantia rationalis naturae.'[15] Richard of St Victor refined on this with his 'divinae naturae existentia incommunicabilis.'[16] Aquinas proposed 'subsistens distinctum in natura intellectuali.'[17]

But with the mention of Richard and of Aquinas we move into a new world. The speculative genius of Anselm lacked the factual material on which it might fruitfully work. The hardheadedness of Abelard's *Sic et non* revealed contrasts and contradictions in the Christian tradition but did not attempt to bring about their reconciliation. It was the theologians of the twelfth and thirteenth centuries that brought data and intelligence together by developing the technique of the *quaestio* and by applying it to the materials assembled in collections, commentaries, books of sentences. When they discovered that the solutions to their many questions would themselves be coherent only if underpinned by a coherent conceptuality (*Begrifflichkeit*), theology became a science. By adopting and adapting the Aristotelian corpus it underwent a transformation that can be paralleled only by Galileo's demand that nature be mathematicized, by Newton's development of the calculus, by Darwin's intro-

---

   accept of your Son and of the Holy Spirit, without any discrimination, any
   difference. This translation is based on one Lonergan once gave; see *Philo-*
   sophical and Theological Papers 1958–1964, vol. 6 in Collected Works of
   Bernard Lonergan ed. Robert C. Croken, Frederick E. Crowe, and Robert
   M. Doran (Toronto: University of Toronto Press, 1996) 260.]
13 [interchange of properties]
14 [DS 273: As for the words of the gospels and the apostles about the Lord, we
   know that theologians sometimes predicate all of them without distinction to
   the one person (of Christ), but at other times apply them separately to his
   two natures, referring those that are appropriate to God to the divinity of
   Christ but the lowly attributes to his humanity.]
15 [individual substance of a rational nature]
16 [incommunicable existence in divine nature]
17 [distinct subsistent in an intellectual nature]

duction of evolution into biology. Unfortunately this matching of systematic intelligence with a wealth of positive information was short-lived. It was derailed by the Augustinian-Aristotelian conflict of the late thirteenth century. When the controversies subsided, a cult of the minimum took over. The rest of Aristotle was dismissed. Theologians were content with his logic.[18] The decadence of Scholasticism had begun: it left theology quite unprepared to deal both profoundly and opportunely with the already mentioned scientific and historical revolutions.

Today Scholasticism is barely mentioned and neo-Scholasticism a lost cause. It remains that something must be devised to be put in their place. For what they achieved in their day was to give the mysteries of faith that limited and analogous understanding (DS 3016) that helped people find them meaningful. Today that help is not forthcoming. The bold pronounce the traditional formulations meaningless. The subtle discern in them an admixture of Christian doctrine with a Heideggerian forgetfulness of being.[19] Nor is there any general consensus to expound and vindicate them, for the theological and philosophic basis for a consensus no longer seems to exist.

I have been indicating different ways in which the horizon of religious, moral, intellectual conversion found expression in the past. I have done so because the question, as I understood it, desired a statement on a necessary minimum for ordination to the priesthood, and, as I believe in cultural pluralism, as I have written a booklet on *Doctrinal Pluralism*,[20] so I would not close the door to the priesthood on unphilosophic minds.

At the same time I must insist that thinking in terms of the minimum leads to minimal results. The minimum is dull and uninspiring. It offers no challenge. It brings no real benefit. It is regarded as drudgery, and it is endured only because it is authoritatively stated to be a *conditio sine qua non* of ordination. Once the condition is fulfilled, it is forgotten, and the only regret people have is that they had to put up with it.

Consider, on the other hand, the advantages of planning a maximum, of providing brilliant teachers, of encouraging all to make the most of their

18 The minimal results have been described by Konstanty Michalski, *La philosophie au xiv⁴ siècle: Six études*, long difficult to obtain but re-edited in 1969 by Kurt Flasch (Frankfurt: Minerva).
19 See Bernhard Welte, 'Die Lehrformel von Nikaia und die abendländische Metaphysik,' in *Zur Frühgeschichte der Christologie, Quaestiones disputatae* 51 (Freiburg: Herder, 1970) 100–117. [Lonergan has treated Welte's paper in some detail in 'Theology and Praxis,' in *A Third Collection* (see above, p. 214, note 22) 185–88, 192–94.]
20 See above, pp. 70–104.

opportunity, of keeping students at the books only as long as they are making progress (or perhaps long enough for them to discover their limitations).

4.12   Is a thorough presentation permitting an understanding of Marxism an essential element in the preparation of priests today?

The modern world has been dominated by then one and now by another theory of history. From the eighteenth century came the liberal doctrine of progress. From the nineteenth came the Marxian doctrine of dialectical materialism.

It has long been my conviction that if Catholics and, in particular, if Jesuits are to live and operate on the level of the times, they must not only know about theories of history but also must work out their own. The precepts of the moral law, while rich and detailed in prohibitions (*malum ex quocumque defectu*),[21] are of extreme generality in their positive content (*bonum ex integra causa*).[22] But what moves men is the good; the good is concrete; but what the concrete good of Christian living is, we shall come to know only by thematizing the dynamic of Christian living in this world, in itself and in its relations to liberal progress and Marxian dialectic. To put it bluntly, until we move onto the level of historical dynamics, we shall face our secularist and atheist opponents, as the Red Indians, armed with bows and arrows, faced European muskets.

Elsewhere, and at some length, I have indicated the main lines of this dynamic. It is dialectical in the sense that it has to do with the concrete, with action, with contradiction. It may be unfolded scientifically in terms of successive approximations, or philosophically in terms of position, its negation, and the negation of the negation. The first approximation, or the position, determines what happens when people ever are attentive, intelligent, reasonable, and responsible. The second approximation, or the negation, adds what happens insofar as people are inattentive, unintelligent, unreasonable, irresponsible. The third approximation, which negates the negation, raises the question of the conditions of recovery or redemption.

The first approximation, the position, is progress. By progress I mean a cyclic and cumulative process in which concrete situations give rise to insights, insights to new courses of action, new courses of action to changed situations, and changed situations to still further insights.

The second approximation, the negation of the position, is decline, the opposite of progress. Progress results only if people are attentive to the results

21   [Failure in any part renders the whole defective.]
22   [The good of the whole results from the order of all the parts.]

of previous action, only if they are intelligent in devising remedies for previous mistakes, only if they are reasonable and responsible in their decisions to act and to cooperate. But such attentiveness, intelligence, reasonableness, and responsibility are distorted or even blocked by the egoism of individuals and groups and by the bias of practical men of common sense, who are ever prone to fancy themselves omnicompetent. Now in the measure that men are inattentive, unintelligent, unreasonable, irresponsible, in the same measure their actions and the consequent situations will be marked by the unintelligibility of their oversights, their mistakes, their irrationality. Further, the more that objective situations are distorted by unintelligent and irrational actions, the less are they capable of giving rise to fresh insights, since all that intelligence can discern in the unintelligible is its lack of intelligibility. So with creativity blocked, the body social becomes the victim of warring egoisms and blundering shortsightedness. Then amoralism raises its ugly head. It sets aside the moralists and appeals to the efficient causes of modern science, for it proposes to be really practical, to be effective, to get things done. But the cult of efficiency in politics and economics easily becomes oppression, revolution, warfare. So we learnt about the liquidation of the opponents of Machiavelli's *Principe*, the liquidation of the feudal remnants blocking the expansion of bourgeois liberalism, the liquidation of the bourgeoisie in the Peoples' Republics.

There remains the third approximation, the negation of the negation. The liquidation of individuals, classes, nations does not go to the root of the matter, for the problem of warring egoisms keeps recurring as long as inattentiveness, obtuseness, unreasonableness, irresponsibility keep producing and augmenting the objective social surd of the unintelligible and irrational situation. What alone goes to the root of the problem is the new man, the man converted at once intellectually, morally, religiously. Above all, religiously. For the new man will have to be a man of faith, for only faith can triumph when reason has been discredited, and reason was discredited by the ongoing process of rationalization put forward in defence of amoralism. The new man will have to be a man of hope, for only hope can release people from the hopelessness of warring egoisms and blundering shortsightedness. The new man will have to love God above all and his fellows as himself, for evenhanded justice becomes merely destructive once injustice has penetrated the very fabric of a society.[23]

The foregoing analysis proceeds in terms of ultimates. Attentiveness, intel-

---

23 For a fuller account of the foregoing, see *Insight* 242–69, 650–53, 710–25, 740–70. For the historical background, see *Grace and Freedom* [see above, p. 238, note 21].

ligence, reasonableness, responsibility are the conditions of possibility of human authenticity. These conditions are excluded by inattention, obtuseness, unreasonableness, irresponsibility, and such exclusion is the root and substance of human unauthenticity, of man's alienation from his true being. Finally, man's salvation even in this life is the otherworldliness of the theological virtues of faith, hope, and charity.

Now both the liberal doctrine of progress and the communist doctrine of dialectical materialism stand in explicit disregard of otherworldliness. The liberal is a secularist who does not suspect that religion is a key vector in social dynamics. The Marxist is an avowed and militant atheist. This exclusion of religious otherworldliness is part of their this-worldly efficiency, but it has the implication that, while their doctrines may be simply progressive, they may also be some mixture of progress and decline. In the latter case, their abandonment of religion leaves them without the remedy for overcoming decline.

In fact, in the capitalism of the liberals one may discern both the principle of progress and the seeds of decline. There is the principle of progress in Adam Smith's metaphor of 'the invisible hand' that produces a harmonious synthesis out of the manifold and independent initiatives of capitalist enterprise. For what the metaphor refers to I have analyzed in *Insight* (chapters 4 and 8) as a conditioned series of more or less probably emerging and surviving schemes of recurrence. This process I refer to as emergent probability, and I find it relevant to the genesis of atoms, molecules, crystals, solids, larger bodies; relevant again to the evolution of plant and animal species and to their ecologies; relevant finally to human history, in which human ingenuity puts together natural and human resources to bring about institutional and, in particular, economic schemes of recurrence. Among such schemes are capitalist enterprises; their harmonious fitting despite their independent origins appears the work of 'an invisible hand' but really results because human insight into concrete situations continues a process that runs through the whole of nature.

But if I believe that the liberal was right in speaking of human progress, I cannot but find him over-sanguine in handing over the motivation of capitalist process to enlightened self-interest. For enlightenment is given many meanings. There is the enlightenment of the mystic, of the seven sages, of the philosophers. But what the self-interest of the capitalist must have is profit, for the alternative to profit is loss, and sustained loss means bankruptcy. In such a context enlightened self-interest easily comes to mean really profitable self-interest. And when the mathematical economists draw up their design for utopia, the best of all possible worlds is seen to result from maximizing profits.

In this fashion an ambiguous term betrays capitalist enterprise into complicity with the forces of decline. Profit as a criterion encourages the egoism of individuals and of groups; individual and especially group egoism is a bias that generates inattention, obtuseness, unreasonableness, and social irresponsibility; what initially appeared to be a 'scientifically' efficient and efficacious motivation has turned out to be an engine of decline.

A similar compound of progress and decline may be discerned in Marxian thought. Basically Marx was reacting against his predecessors in philosophic, political, and economic thought. But if his reacting was sound, his implementation appears faulty. First, from Hegelian idealism he moved to world-historical praxis. This was a real advance, but its benefit was compromised by Marx's arguing against idealism and concluding to materialism; today one might well prefer a realism realistic enough to have learnt much from the scientific and the historical revolutions. Secondly, it remains that these revolutions were not intrinsic to Hegelian thought. Hegel propounded a philosophy of nature that claimed to be a product of speculative reason, something far profounder than the lowly scientific understanding. But it has been scientific understanding that has survived, and, in like manner, Hegel's apriorist approach to history was the position successfully negated by the German Historical School. Thirdly, Marx was right in feeling that the Hegelian dialectic needed to be adjusted, but he was content to turn it upside down. What it needed, I should say, was to be turned inside out. Instead of endeavoring to insert movement within logic, the relatively static operations of logic had to be inserted within the larger ever-ongoing context of methodical operations. Fourthly, Marx has much to say about alienation. It is a topic with an undertow as deep and strong as the problem of evil. But I find it difficult to find the Marxian analysis in terms of capitalism and the Marxian remedy in 'true communism' to be more than a trivialization of the issue. Sin is the irrational component in the human condition, and God's remedy is in the grace of Christ Jesus our Lord. Such is the dialectic in which all men are involved; it cannot be acknowledged by a militant atheist; and so I find it contradictory to speak of a Christian Marxism. Fifthly, Marx had a sound and, it would seem, original intuition into the nature of capitalist profit; it is this intuition that gives Marxian thought its fascination and its power. It remains that Marx expressed his intuition confusedly and emotionally in terms of surplus value and of exploitation. But its accurate expression is in macroeconomic terms,[24] and it is on the basis of such

24 See Michal Kalecki, *Selected Essays on the Dynamics of the Capitalist Economy: 1933–1970* (Cambridge: Cambridge University Press, 1971); Joan Robinson

accurate expression and in the context of Christian praxis that a solution is to be sought.

Such Christian praxis is the dynamic of human creativity and freedom in which individually men make themselves and collectively they make the world in which they live. In that dynamic must be recognized (1) developing intelligence as the principle of progress, (2) the evils of individual and group egoism and the arrogance of omnicompetent common sense as the principles of alienation and decline, and (3) faith, hope, and charity as the principles of recovery from alienation and decline. Finally, there is needed up-to-date technical knowledge of economic and political theory and their respective histories; perhaps the great weakness of Catholic social thought is its apparent lack of awareness of the need for technical knowledge.[25]

In brief, what priests need today is, not an understanding of Marx, but an understanding of the dynamics of history and of the vital role that Christians are called upon to play.

4.13   What is the place (if any) of the human sciences, and their relationship to the study of philosophy?
For me, philosophy is the basic and total science because it is the adequate cognitional theory. Specialists in the particular sciences perform cognitional operations but attend to objects. The philosopher's job is to thematize the operations that the specialists perform and, no less, to thematize the operations performed by men of common sense.

It is well to distinguish between human sciences, engaged in discerning universal laws, and human studies, such as interpretation and history, engaged in understanding particular texts and particular processes.

Both human sciences and human studies are cognitional activities that the philosopher has to thematize, but there must be two separate thematizations. The human sciences are analogous to the natural sciences, but human studies are analogous to the development of common sense.

It is of considerable importance that the analogy between natural and human science be clarified. There is identity insofar as man is an animal. There is difference insofar as man sublates his animality and lives in a world mediated by meaning and motivated by values. Insofar as man is an animal, the human sciences will follow the same methods as physicists, chemists, biolo-

---

and John Eatwell, *An Introduction to Modern Economics* (Maidenhead, Berkshire: McGraw-Hill Book Co., 1973).
25 See Christian Duquoc, *Ambiguité des théologies de la sécularisation* (Gembloux: Duculot, 1972) 103–28.

gists, animal psychologists. But insofar as man sublates his animality and lives in a world mediated by meaning and motivated by values, then the relevant methods are those of human studies; and it is only by postulating continuity in accepted meanings and values that the human scientist can extrapolate from the past to the future. Hence, Gibson Winter in his *Elements for a Social Ethic* was led to distinguish four styles in sociology – the physical, the functional, the voluntarist, and the intentional – and to assign each its area of competence.[26] The physical style assumes that the methods of natural science are the only scientific methods: it is positivist, behaviorist, reductionist. The functional style understands social structures and processes by grasping the functions of parts in the whole: it is intellectualist. The voluntarist style stresses power, conflict, and ideology. The intentional style, finally, is phenomenological: its subjective dimensions are the constituting intentionalities of embodied consciousness; the objective dimensions are the forms in which this world appears for this consciousness.

An alternative procedure is to conceive the human sciences as instrumental: they set forth the limitations under which human freedom operates and the options among which freedom may choose. Once free choices have been made, the human scientist becomes the technician determining the steps to be followed to obtain the desired result. Something along these lines has been worked out for economics by Adolph Lowe, *On Economic Knowledge: Toward a Science of Political Economics.*[27]

Finally, both the human sciences and human studies suffer from a flight from philosophic, moral, and religious issues. They are aware that scientific procedures cannot handle these issues. They know of no consensus on these issues. They opt for a scientific approach and endeavor to justify it by isolating areas from which the philosophic, moral, or religious issues are excluded or held in abeyance.

An exposition of Max Weber's view on value-free science and arguments against it from a traditional viewpoint may be found in Leo Strauss's *Natural Right and History.*[28] My own position would be to follow the lines laid down in my *Method of Theology*: there exist scientific techniques to be followed in works of interpretation and in the writing of history; but these techniques do not

---

26 Gibson Winter, *Elements for a Social Ethic* (see above, p. 138, note 13).

27 Adolph Lowe, *On Economic Knowledge: Toward a Science of Political Economics* (New York and Evanston: Harper Torchbooks, 1965; reprint of volume xxxv of Ruth Nanda Anshen's series, *World Perspectives*).

28 Leo Strauss, *Natural Right and History* (Chicago: University of Chicago Press, 1953) 35–80.

preclude differences arising from the philosophic, ethical, and religious views of those that employ them; hence interpretation and history have to be regarded as functional specialties to be completed by such further specialties as dialectic and foundations in which radical differences can be dealt with, not indeed automatically but at least openly and clearheadedly.

4.14 In case you would prefer different philosophical studies for those who do not have philosophical talent, or whose studies are directed to other fields than professional philosophy and theology, please indicate what should be the minimum content of such studies.

For those said not to have philosophical talent, I do not desire or prefer different philosophical studies. I would urge better teachers and simplified studies (see below § 4.21). Everyone can attain a certain measure of self-appropriation, of knowing just what happens when he is coming to know and coming to choose. Not everyone can specify the ramifications and complications of such coming to know and to decide, through the various fields of knowledge, of moral growth, of religious development. The big block will not be a total absence of philosophical capacity but the novelty of training teachers that (1) can thematize their own conscious activities and (2) help their pupils to do likewise.

For those destined to specialize in other fields, I would have no objection to their dropping the so-called 'professional' aspects of philosophy or theology, but I would profoundly deplore any tendency to let them be satisfied with anything less than all the understanding of philosophy and of theology of which they are capable. Without that development only too easily will they tend to be not only specialists in other fields but also secularists, unable to bring their special knowledge within a Christian context and so give the Christian community (in its effort to sublate the whole of human living) the advantage of the technical knowledge they possess and the community wished them to attain. Unless Christian specialists are something of generalists, they are like the seed that does not fall into the ground to die but itself remaineth alone.

4.2 In the light of the answer to § 3.1, what does the study of philosophy involve in relation to method?

4.21 What method (of thinking rather than of teaching) should be used in the philosophical formation of our men?

The basic step is learning to give basic terms and relations the meaning they possess as names of conscious events and conscious processes.

Everyone has insights. They are occurring all the time. But few people are aware of the fact. The problem is to make them aware and fully aware both of the occurrence of insights and of the series of other consciously occurring events.

The general lines of the solution have been set forth by Abraham Maslow in his *Religions, Values, and Peak-Experiences*.[29] What he says of 'peaking' and 'peak experiences' also holds for the whole of intentionality analysis. I quote a few sentences.

> All this implies another *kind* of education, i.e., experiential education ... it also implies another kind of communication ... What we are implying is that in the kind of experiential teaching which is being discussed here, what is necessary to do first is to change the person and to change his awareness of himself. That is, we must make him aware of the fact that peak-experiences go on inside himself. Until he has become aware of such experience and has this experience as a basis for comparison, he is a non-peaker; and it is useless to try to communicate to him the feel and the nature of peak-experience. But if we can change him, in the sense of making him aware of what is going on inside himself, then he becomes a different kind of communicatee. He now knows what you are talking about when you speak of peak-experiences; and it is possible to teach him by refer-ence to his own weak peak-experiences how to improve them, how to enrich them, how to enlarge them, and also how to draw the proper conclusions from these experiences ...
>
> Part of the process here is an experiential-educational one in which we help the patient become aware of what he has been experiencing without having been aware of it ... Until that point is reached at which he has a detached, objective, conscious awareness of the relationship between a particular name or label or word and a particular set of ineffable, subjective experiences, no communication and no teaching are possible ... In all of these we may use the paradigm that the process of education (and of therapy) is helping the person to become aware of internal, subjective, subverbal experiences so that these experi-ences can be brought into the world of abstraction, of conversation, of communication, of naming, etc., with the consequence that it immediately becomes possible for a certain amount of control to

29 Abraham Maslow, *Religions, Values, and Peak-Experiences* (New York: Viking Press, 1970).

be exerted over these hitherto unconscious and uncontrollable processes.[30]

In the foregoing, while it is reasonably clear what the author is attempting to convey, it has to be admitted that he has not yet worked out a consistent vocabulary, particularly with regard to what is conscious but not thematized and, on the other hand, what is conscious but has become explicitly thematized. But there can be little doubt that this contrast and transition is what he wishes to communicate, and, I believe, it will be found that the thematization of this distinction becomes meaningful only after one has had, and repeatedly had, the experience of the transition itself. Experience comes first. Only afterwards does meaningful thematization arise. Indeed, in my book *Insight* it is only in chapter 11 that there is attempted an explicit account of the transition from merely being conscious to actually knowing.

Of course, I have done no more than indicate the basic rudiments of methodical philosophic thought. But further aspects of the matter will conveniently be treated in the next three questions, §§ 4.22, 4.23, 4.3.

4.22 Is there a minimum knowledge of philosophic methods necessary for a priest and a Jesuit?

Knowledge of method becomes a necessity when false notions of method are current and more or less disastrous.

For example, there have been theologians that held, perhaps innocuously enough, that the dogmas of the church were revealed not explicitly but implicitly. Many thought this to mean that the dogmas could be deduced from revealed propositions to be read in the sacred scriptures. Such an interpretation did no harm either among those not very good logicians or among those not much interested in scripture. However, with the revival of logical and scriptural studies we have been hearing that, after all, the dogmas were not revealed at all. Or again, that the dogmas have been revealed, not in a revelation contained in scripture but in an ongoing and still continuing process of revelation in the church. Or again, that the dogmas express, not simply what has been revealed but what has been revealed as apprehended and expressed within a particular culture so that, if that particular culture proves alien to us or outmoded, then the dogmas are to be revised.

Common to all of these views is the unavowed assumption that logic is ultimate and, indeed, absolutely ultimate. Now it is ultimate with regard to the clarity of terms, the coherence of propositions, the rigor of inferences. But it is

30 Ibid. 89–90.

not absolutely ultimate even in human discourse, for there are many actual and many more possible 'universes of discourse'; and it always is possible to introduce still one more universe of discourse in which fresh distinctions are introduced, terms become clearer, different propositions are found coherent, and different conclusions are inferred.

We reach the notion of method when we ask how does one effect the transition from one universe of discourse to another or, more profoundly, how is there effected the transition from one level or stage in human culture to another later level or stage or, vice versa, from a later to an earlier level or stage. Obviously, the operations involved in such transitions are not ruled by the logic of clear terms, coherent propositions, rigorous inferences. Quite different, though quite common, types of operation have to be considered, and considered just as explicitly as the logical operations that from Aristotle to Hegel were thought to control legitimate mental process.

These further operations are attending to the data of outer and inner experience, precise descriptions of what is given, stumbling upon oddities, the formulation of problems, the search for solutions, the discovery of new viewpoints, the formulation of hypotheses, the deduction of their suppositions and of their implications, the planning of processes of control by observations and/or experiments, the confirmation of the hypothesis or the need for revising it and, in that case, the recurrence of the methodical process.

Still, such further operations occur and combine differently in different disciplines. In each discipline one learns to perform the operations readily, easily, with satisfaction, in the lecture rooms, the laboratories, the seminars of a university. In the main, such learning is much more learning what is done than why it is done. It remains that the proficient, the future leaders and successful teachers and great pioneers, will owe their superiority to the fact that they have taken the time to pause and reflect and discern just why things are done and even how they might better be done.

There is still one more step. If there is to be in the twentieth century a basic and total science, it will have to be a basic and total method. When the particular sciences were supposed to be certain knowledge of things through their causes, then the basic and total science could be certain knowledge of being through its causes. But now that the particular sciences offer no more than the best available opinion, now that they are ruled in the last resort not by their basic principles and laws but by the methods by which their current principles and laws may be revised, it becomes necessary for the basic and total science to be the basic and total method.

As any other method, the basic and total method is a normative pattern of related and recurrent operations with cumulative and progressive results. But it is a method that is reached only through performing the operations of such particular disciplines as mathematics, natural science, common sense, human studies, adverting to the operations so performed and thematizing them, adverting further to the dynamism linking related operations and thematizing that dynamism, thereby arriving at a normative pattern for each of the particular methods and, through them, to the common core of all methods, namely, the dynamic structure of human coming to know and coming to decide.

In this fashion a philosophic theory of knowledge is attained, and from it one moves with relative ease to an epistemology, a metaphysics of proportionate being, and an existential ethics.

The attainment may be maximal or minimal or in between these extremes. It moves towards a maximum, materially, as one advances in competence in particular disciplines and, formally, as one's increasing competence both broadens and refines one's grasp of all cognitional styles. It moves towards a minimum, materially, as one's competence in other disciplines decreases and, formally, as one's grasp of the common core narrows and coarsens.

4.23   In what sense, if any, should the philosophy taught our scholastics be systematic?

Thought is systematic if all its terms are defined.

Terms are basic or derived. Derived terms are defined by employing basic terms. Basic terms are defined implicitly by their relations to one another. Such relations may form a closed circle, an interlocking set, an ongoing progression, or an open analogy such as Aristotle's proportion between potency and act.

Propositions constructed out of basic terms and their defining relations are 'true' by definition and in that sense are named analytic propositions.

Analytic principles must be distinguished from analytic propositions. They are true not only by definition but also by verification. For the basic terms and relations in their defined sense have been verified.[31]

The distinction between analytic propositions and analytic principles is of the essence of empirical science. However, verification falls short of proof: for in verification the argument runs, not from affirming the hypothesis to affirming its implications but from affirming the verified implications to affirming the hypothesis. Such an argument is cogent if and only if the hypothesis in question is the only possible hypothesis; and proof of such unique possibility commonly is not available.

31 See *Insight* 329–34.

Hence, in general, empirical science is systematic, not in the sense that it offers a system valid for all time but in the sense that it offers a succession of provisional systems, where each later system satisfies the known data better than its predecessors.

Besides the methods of the particular empirical sciences, there is the generalized empirical method born of the reflective interplay between acting out the operations of the particular disciplines and thematizing the operations one is acting out. In this interplay the basic terms and relations of intentionality analysis both are given their meaning and are verified. They are given their meaning, for what the terms mean is the operations one is consciously performing, and what the relations mean is the conscious dynamism of sensitive spontaneity, intelligent creativity, rational reflection, and responsible freedom, that promotes us consciously from one operation to the next. They also are given their verification, for there are actually occurring the conscious operations and there is actually unfolding the conscious dynamism to which the terms and relations refer.

Such verification has singular properties. In the ordinary case, the hypothesis is the antecedent, its implications are the consequent, and the confirming data correspond directly only to the consequent. But in generalized method both antecedent and consequent are given in experience: the antecedent in the thematized operations and processes; the consequent in the publicly performed methods of particular disciplines. Again, in the ordinary case, revision involves change in a theory but not a change in the object to which the theory refers. But the revision of the central core of generalized method involves a change not only in a theory about human knowledge but also in the occurrence, or in the consciousness, or in the thematization, of conscious and thematized operations and processes.

It follows that the basic and total science is empirical yet in some sense it is not strictly hypothetical, and in some sense its central core of experiencing, understanding, and judging is not open to revision.

Now the structure of knowing is isomorphic with the structure of the known: as our knowing combines elements of experience, elements of intelligence, and elements of rationality, so the objects of the particular sciences will be compounded of a potential element, corresponding to experience, of a formal element, corresponding to intelligence, and of an actual element, corresponding to rational judgment.[32]

---

32 See Lonergan, *Insight* 456–60; and 'Isomorphism of Thomist and Scientific Thought,' in *Collection* [see above, p. 76, note 7] 133–41.

Similarly, the structure of our knowing and doing expresses the conditions of being an authentic person; but this structure is a matter of being attentive, being intelligent, being reasonable, being responsible; accordingly, there are four basic precepts that are independent of cultural differences. Moreover, since the actuation of the structure arises under social conditions and within cultural traditions, to the four there may be added a fifth, Acknowledge your historicity.

It would seem, then, that empirical science and empirically established cognitional theory are equal to the task of accounting for the invariants in human knowledge, in human conduct, and in the structure of reality proportionate to man's native powers. It remains that down the ages there have been rationalists claiming a priori knowledge independent of empirical tests and absolute idealists endeavoring in their peculiar way to vindicate the claims of speculative reason. But in the past such efforts have not succeeded in anticipating the pronouncements of empirical science, and, as empirical science, from the nature of its verification, is ever open to change, at the very least we must await radical change in the methods of science before we may anticipate a successful resurgence of apriorist philosophy.

So much then for systematic knowledge. But we must not overlook the fact that not all human knowledge and not even, often enough, the majority of man's concrete certitudes are systematic. For systematic thinking defines explicitly – or implicitly in a very technical sense of 'implicitly.' But common sense does not define, as Socrates discovered in Athens millennia ago, and the linguistic analysts at Oxford have rediscovered more recently. Moreover, the spontaneous development of understanding, which is the hallmark of common sense, recurs in the operations of exegetes and historians.[33]

4.3 How do we maintain intellectual coherence for philosophical studies without denying freedom to philosophical inquiry and to teachers of philosophy? What pluralism in systems and methods in any one faculty is compatible with this coherence?
The problem of freedom may be narrowed down to manageable limits by beginning from a list of the varieties of pluralism and then considering the problems that arise within each variety.

First, there is the knowledge that arises from the spontaneous development of human intelligence. In English it is apt to be called 'common sense,' in French 'le bon sens,' in German 'gesunder Menschenverstand.' What is common to all instances of it is not content but procedure: it always is the

33 See *Insight,* chapters 6 and 11; and *Method in Theology,* chapters 7, 8, and 9.

result of spontaneous intellectual development; but the results vary from village to village, region to region, country to country, culture to culture, and there are corresponding differences in the endless ordinary languages in which these results are expressed. Fortunately, ordinary language does not express systematic thought, and so if philosophy is agreed to be systematic, the problems arising from this type of pluralism need not concern us.

Secondly, the knowledge of exegetes and of historians would seem to be an enormously learned extension of spontaneously developed intelligence, in brief, the common sense of one time and place catching on to the common sense of another. Here there arises the problem of perspectivism, for exegetical and historical techniques do not suffice to master the minutiae of variations in common sense. But from the nature of the case such differences are minor, and in any case they are more or less irremediable.

There are graver difficulties that arise from philosophic, moral, and religious differences among exegetes and among historians. But such pluralism can be mitigated by the device of conceiving exegetical and historical techniques to be functional specialties and by the addition of further functional specialties, such as dialectics and foundations, to objectify these graver differences and in some fashion to deal with them equitably and not without some hope of progress.

Thirdly, there are systematic types of thought, and, roughly, it will suffice to consider two types. There are the systems that are apriorist, that claim validity universally or absolutely, that take their stand on the clarity of their ideas, the coherence of their assertions, the rigor of their inferences, and the cogency of the evidence they present.

Now as long as there is only one such system, the problem of pluralism does not immediately arise. But as soon as there are two or more of such systems, not only does a problem of pluralism exist but also it bids fair to be insoluble. Obviously an appeal to experience will offer no solution, for these systems are apriorist; they are true by the truth of their definitions, and they do not acknowledge any higher truth that rests on appeals to mere experience. Further, an appeal to logic will not solve the problem; the various types of Riemannian geometry are all perfectly coherent; and so it does seem likely that different apriorist philosophies might be equally coherent in their respective contents yet radically opposed when one is compared with another. Finally, an appeal to method has the disadvantage either of being an apriorist method, and so coherent with one philosophy but automatically rejected by another, or else of being an empirical method, and so rejected automatically by all apriorist philosophies.

It remains, however, that apriorist philosophies are contentious. They dispute without end but also without fruit. Eventually, the age dominated by logic comes to a close, if not from the exhaustion of the opposing parties, at least from the ever decreasing size and interest of their audience. Finally, there comes the 'coup de grâce' when logical operations are seen to be but a minor part within the larger whole of methodical operations. With that change there arises a totally new situation and the insoluble problem of apriorist but divergent philosophies may happily be forgotten.

There remain, finally, the philosophies that are not only systematic but also methodical, not methodical in some apriorist sense but empirical, with their method a generalization of the methods employed in the particular sciences and, at the same time, fixing the meaning and verifying it by thematizing the operations and processes of cognitional and moral consciousness.

Now in the sciences in which an empirical method is accepted there are available and accepted empirical controls. Everyone is free to advance understanding of the field, to formulate discoveries in hypotheses, to plan and execute programs of research and/or experimentation, to publish his findings and thereby submit them to the judgment of his peers.

It remains that empirical methods in the particular sciences are not capable of resolving ultimate issues in cognitional theory, in ethics, in religion. So it is that philosophies of science are often mistaken while moral and religious issues are systematically evaded. Accordingly an empirical method in philosophy has to go to the root of this problem if it is not to be bankrupt from its inception.

Here, to my mind, the key notions are horizon and conversion. By horizon is meant the totality, the *Umgreifendes*, within which understanding is sought, judgments of fact are made, and evaluations accepted. Such a totality dominates our knowing and deciding from the very fact that our questions have their origin in the a priori desire to understand, to reach the truth, to know the real, to do what is worth while; that this desire of itself is both comprehensive and concrete, but its specification is attained only through specific questions and through the accumulation of specific answers. It follows that our specification of the horizon easily enough falls short of the objective at which the comprehensiveness and concreteness of our a priori desire aims. It further follows that we have to be converted from assumptions about the real and the good that suffice for the infant, and have to complete the development begun as the child, the adolescent, the adult moves into a world mediated by meanings and motivated by values. Finally, it follows that teachers of cognitional theory, epistemology, the metaphysics of proportionate being, and existential ethics (1) should themselves be converted, and (2) should be able to organize their courses so as to communicate their own conversion to their charges.

This may appear a tall order. But intellectual conversion is a topic that admits full objectification in terms of positions and counterpositions,[34] while moral and religious conversions have their root in God's gift of his love, a gift that alone is a sufficient grace for salvation, and so a grace granted to all by God's universal salvific will.

Perhaps we may now address ourselves to the questions raised in § 4.3, and we begin by noting that inasmuch as both coherence and pluralism are desired, some sort of analogy has to be invoked.

The prime analogate, I suggest, conceives philosophy as the basic and total science, defines sciences materially by their fields and formally by their methods, and finds the method of the basic and total science to be the generalized empirical method reached inasmuch as particular methods are explained and understood by thematizing the conscious operations and processes of the scientist.

On this conception of philosophy, inquirers and teachers are free as long as they are following the method; and as soon as they really depart from the method, then they no longer are philosophers in the defined sense.

Following the method, of course, is not a matter of deduction but of creativity. Such creativity may enrich the thematization of experiencing, understanding, judgment, deliberation that already has been achieved; it may also add quite new dimensions to it, as has Robert M. Doran, s.j., in his doctoral dissertation *Subject and Psyche: A Study in the Foundations of Theology.*[35]

Further, it is to be noted that accepting this or any other method rests on a judgment of value. The value in question is the value of intelligence and of collaborative and sustained advance towards truth. Such a primacy of the judgment of value (1) contradicts any rationalist primacy of reason or intellect, (2) breaks away from the ambiguities of Aristotle's *Nicomachean Ethics* (VI, 2, 1139b 4), (3) rests on intentionality analysis in which it becomes clear that the level of deliberation is the sublation of previous levels, (4) finds itself in congenial continuity with religious faith and theology, in which the basic horizon is one of love and of value, and (5) opens the way for theology, other human disciplines, and the common sense (purged of its common nonsense) of every culture, region, and village, to inspire and direct the already described (§ 4.12 above) Christian dynamic of history.

34 See *Insight*, Index, Positions, vs. counterpositions.
35 See below, p. 390, note 13.

So much for the prime analogate. Variants may be constructed by working backwards to its less complex predecessors, in which, nonetheless, there were expressed religious, moral, and intellectual conversion.[36]

5 How should future professors of philosophy be prepared?

First of all they must be equipped with the essential tools: languages and mathematics. The more generous the time and effort spent on these preliminary tasks, the richer will be the future professor's cultural initiation, the profounder will be his cultural perspective across the present and into the past, and the greater will be his facility in understanding the natural sciences.

Secondly, they must gradually come to understand how arduous is their task. They are to be generalists: (1) not only knowing the objects but thematizing the operations so precisely defined in mathematics, so dynamically unfolding in physics, so dialectically involved with common nonsense in common sense, so eruditely extended to the common sense and nonsense of other places and times in interpretation and history, etc., etc.; (2) through such thematizing, attaining the appropriation of their own cognitional, affective, and deliberative operations to the point where, as Aristotle put it, they no longer need a teacher but operate on their own; (3) advancing from intentionality analysis to epistemology, the metaphysics of proportionate being, and existential ethics; (4) entering into a symbiosis with theology inasmuch as theology sublates philosophy to define its special categories while it derives from philosophy its general categories;[37] and (5) fulfilling its mediating functions by enabling theology to enter into interdisciplinary work with the sciences and with human studies, as well as utilize them in its great task of communications.[38]

Thirdly, as already has been noted (§ 3.112 above), the carrier of a modern science is not the individual but the ongoing scientific community, and similarly the carrier of interdisciplinary studies is the relevant set of scientific communities. Now what holds for specialists, *mutatis mutandis* also holds for generalists.

Their proper domain is thematizing, intentionality analysis, epistemology, metaphysics of proportionate being, and existential ethics. In that proper domain individually they have to be masters according to the level of their

36 See § 4.11 above on a minimum core; or *Method in Theology*, chapter 12, §§ 5 and 7, on the 'Ongoing Discovery of Mind'; or Eric Voegelin, 'Equivalences of Experience and Symbolization in History,' in *Eternità e Storia* (Florence: Vallecchi, 1970) 215–34.

37 *Method in Theology*, chapter 11, §§ 6 and 7.

38 *Method in Theology*, chapter 14.

times. Again, individually, each must have sufficient knowledge of other fields to derive from them what is essential to his own proper domain. On the other hand, it will be not the individual generalist but the group that through different members attains expertise in the various departments of interdisciplinary work; in other words, the group of generalists includes some expert in theology, others in mathematics, others in natural science, others in human science, others in human studies, others in communications.

Fourthly, it cannot be stressed too strongly that the mediation of the generalists is intelligent rather than logical. By logical mediation I understand the process from universal concepts to particular instances as just instances; by intelligent mediation I understand the process from understanding the universal to understanding the particular. The difference between the two is a difference in understanding: in logical mediation, one understands no more in the instance than one did in the universal; in intelligent mediation, one adds to the understanding of the universal a fuller and more determinate understanding of the particular case. The generalist that is just a logical mediator turns out to be an obtuse intruder; the generalist that is an intelligent mediator speaks not only his own mind but also the language of his interlocutor.

Fifthly, there is an ambiguity to the terms 'theme,' 'thematic,' 'thematize.' They can be given a naïve-realist interpretation, and then to thematize is to observe carefully and to describe accurately. But they also can be given a critical realist interpretation: then from the experience of operations one advances to the bestowal of names; from the experience of process (sensitive spontaneity, intelligent inquiry and formulation, rational reflection, responsible deliberation and freedom, where each later mode sublates those that go before) to the understanding of the structure within which the operations occur; from such experience and understanding to judgment on the difference between such self-appropriation and the formation and verification of hypotheses about subatomic particles.

When thematizing follows the naïve-realist model, it is an unending task. When it is a matter of experiencing, naming, understanding, judging, it quickly reaches the building blocks that can be recombined in a great variety of manners to reveal the diverse structures of diverse procedures and methods.

Sixthly, any attempt to introduce a new program of studies will find itself involved in the dialectic of progress, decline, and redemption. For if the new program is worth while, it will attempt progress. If it runs into undue opposition, there will be some failure to attend, to understand, to be reasonable, or to be responsible. And so there will be need of charity, of hope, and of faith.

20

Reality, Myth, Symbol[1]

I believe that each of the three terms – reality, myth, symbol – gives rise to questions. I have no doubt that the questions that are raised are quite different. But I venture to treat all three because in my opinion the style or method of reaching solutions in each case is fundamentally the same.

1   Reality

Now let me state this a bit more fully. There arise problems about reality not

---

1 A paper given on 29 March 1978, at Boston University as part of a symposium, 'Myth, Symbol, Reality,' held at the Institute for Philosophy and Religion of the University, 27–29 March. Other speakers in the symposium included Elie Wiesel and Alasdair MacIntyre.

   The autograph text of the paper is extant in the archives of the Lonergan Research Institute, Toronto, Batch xiii, file 766, item A2926. At the top of the first page Lonergan typed, 'Read at 1.00 pm on Wednesday, March 29, 1978.' Lonergan's paper, together with other papers of the symposium, was published in *Myth, Symbol, and Reality*, ed. Alan M. Olson (Notre Dame: University of Notre Dame Press, 1980) 31–37. Both the published version of the paper and the autograph have been used here, but with reliance especially on the autograph. The autograph text contains no division into titled subsections, but regards what here are the first three sections as the first section. A set of asterisks distinguishes that 'first' section from what follows, which here begins with section 4. A division into titled sections was also provided in the Olson edition, but both the division and the titles have been changed in the present text. The autograph also contains no footnotes, although there are some references in the text. Thus all footnotes here are editorial.

merely because people make mistakes and even live their lives in error, but more radically because they have lived in two worlds without adverting to the fact and grasping its implications. There is the world of immediacy of the infant. There also is the world of the adult, mediated by meaning and motivated by values. The transition from one to the other is a long process involving a succession of stages. We are familiar with the stages, say, learning to talk, learning to read, learning to write, learning to be good, and so on. But that very familiarity is apt to dissemble the fact that the criteria employed in coming to know the world mediated by meaning and in coming to behave in the world motivated by values are quite novel when contrasted with the more spontaneous criteria that suffice for orienting oneself in the world of immediacy. Samuel Johnson's refutation of Berkeley's acosmic idealism by kicking a stone appealed to a criterion of the world of immediacy but has been thought inefficacious against an elaborate world mediated by meaning. At the same time Berkeley's principle, *esse est percipi*, being is being perceived, was an attempt to make the world of immediacy a world mediated by meaning. Hume's radical empiricism was a radical use of the criteria of the world of immediacy to empty out the world mediated by meaning and motivated by values and so revert to the simpler world of immediacy. Kant and the absolute idealists rightly saw that the criteria of the world of immediacy were insufficient to ground a world mediated by meaning and motivated by values. Again, they were right in seeking the further criteria in the spontaneity of the subject. But the worlds they mediated by meaning are not the worlds of common sense, of science, or of history. So it is that I wish to suggest to your consideration that it is in the immanent criteria of the knowing subject that we may perhaps manage to discover why there are many opinions about reality and even which is probably the correct opinion.

Indeed, since I am not writing a detective story, let me say briefly what I fancy these immanent criteria to be. A principle may be defined as a first in an ordered set. So there are logical principles, that is, propositions that are first in a deductive process. Again, there are principles that are realities: for example, Aristotle defined a nature as an immanent principle of movement and rest. Now our ability to raise questions is an immanent principle of movement and rest: it is a principle of movement as long as the inquiry continues, and it becomes a principle of rest when a satisfactory answer has been reached. Further, there are three distinct types of question. There are questions for intelligence asking what, why, how, what for. There are questions for reflection asking whether our answers to the previous type of question are true or false, certain or only probable. Finally, there are questions for deliberation, and deliberations are of two kinds: there are the deliberations of the egoist asking what's in it for me or for us; there are also the deliberations of moral people, who inquire whether the proposed end is a value, whether it is really and truly worth while.

2   Myth

Let us now turn to myth. For the rationalist, myth was simply the product of ignorance, if not of waywardness. But a more benign view has been gaining ground in this century. Indeed Plato composed myths, insisting that they were not the truth but gave an inkling into the truth. Aristotle in a later letter confessed that as he grew older he became less a philosopher, a friend of wisdom, and more a friend of myths.

What is the justification of such views? I would suggest that since man's being is being-in-the-world, he cannot rise to his full stature until he knows the world. But there is much that is obscure about the world. People easily enough raise questions for intelligence, for reflection, for deliberation. But we can have hunches that we cannot formulate clearly and exactly, so we tell a story. Stories, as is being currently affirmed, are existential: there are true stories that reveal the life that we are really leading, and there are cover stories that make out our lives to be somewhat better than in reality they are. So stories today and the myths of yesterday suffer from a basic ambiguity. They can bring to light what truly is human, but they can also propagate an apparently more pleasant view of human aspiration and human destiny.

3   Symbol

So we are led from myth to symbols, for there, it would seem, lie the roots of the hunches that myths delineate. But I am not a professional depth psychologist, and so I do no more than direct your attention to the writings of Ira Progoff, specifically to his *Death and Rebirth of Psychology*,[2] which reviews the positions of Freud, Adler, Jung, and Otto Rank, and assigns the laurels to Otto Rank. Rank was for long years a disciple and collaborator of Freud's but ended with a posthumous work, *Beyond Psychology*,[3] which contended that human destiny is

2 Ira Progoff, *The Death and Rebirth of Psychology* (New York: Julian Press, 1956; McGraw-Hill, 1973).

3 Otto Rank, *Beyond Psychology*. Published privately by friends and students of the author, Camden, NJ: Haddon Craftsmen, 1941; later, New York: Dover Publications, 1958.

much more than is dreamt of in the worlds of the depth psychologists. There followed Progoff's *Depth Psychology and Modern Man.*[4] It stressed what Bergson would have named the *élan vital*, the formative power that underpins the evolution of atomic elements and compounds, of the genera and species of plant and animal life, of the spontaneous attractions and repulsions of human consciousness that, when followed, produce the charismatic leaders of social groups, the artists that catch and form the spirit of a progressive age, the scientists that chance upon the key paradigms that open new vistas upon world process, the scholars that recapture past human achievement and reconstitute for our contemplation the ongoing march of human history, the saints and mystics that, like the statue of Buddha, place before our eyes the spirit of prayer and adoration, and, I would add, the Christ, the Son of God, whose story is to be read in the Gospels and the significance of that story in the Old Testament and the New.

Let me recapitulate. There arise questions about reality, about myth, about symbol. In each case the questions differ. Nonetheless, I would suggest that in each case the style or method of solution is fundamentally the same. It appeals to what has come to be called intentionality analysis. It reduces conflicting views of reality to the very different types of intentionality employed by the infant, the *in-fans* that does not talk, and the adult that lives in a world mediated by meaning and motivated by values. It accounts for the oddity of the myth by arguing that being human is a being-in-the world (an *in-der-Welt-sein*), that one can rise to full stature only through full knowledge of the world, that one does not possess that full knowledge and thus makes use of the *élan vital* that, as it guides biological growth and evolution, so too it takes the lead in human development and expresses its intimations through the stories it inspires. Symbols, finally, are a more elementary type of story: they are inner or outer events, or a combination of both, that intimate to us at once the kind of being that we are to be and the kind of world in which we become our true selves.

4   Personal Background

So far I have been merely outlining my own views on reality, myth, and symbol. But an outline is not a proof, and I may be asked for proof. Unfortunately, what proof there is is not deductive but inductive, and the induction is long and

---

4 Ira Progoff, *Depth Psychology and Modern Man* (New York: Julian Press, 1959; McGraw-Hill, 1973).

difficult. The best I can hope to do is to attempt a Platonic *deuteros plous*, a second best, and tell something of the story by which I arrived at my views.

My fundamental mentor[5] and guide has been John Henry Newman's *Grammar of Assent*.[6] I read that in my third year of philosophy (at least the analytic parts) about five times and found solutions for my problems. I was not at all satisfied with the philosophy that was being taught, and found Newman's presentation to be something that fitted in with the way I knew things. It was from that kernel that I went on to different authors.

A first step had already occurred when I was a second-year student of philosophy. I became convinced that universal concepts were grossly over-rated, that what really counted was intelligence. At the time I thought myself a nominalist, but a few years later I got beyond that verdict on reading J.A. Stewart's *Plato's Doctrine of Ideas*,[7] which contended that for Plato an idea was something like the Cartesian formula for a circle. Obviously that formula, $(x^2 + y^2) = r^2$, is the product of an act of understanding. And I was to elaborate that point later at considerable length in my *Verbum* articles in *Theological Studies*, later published in book form.[8]

A second and related source was Peter Hoenen, a Dutch professor of philosophy in Rome, who during the thirties was writing articles and eventually brought out a book on the nature of geometrical knowledge.[9] I was already familiar with the recurrent lapses from logic in Euclid's *Elements*. But Hoenen was a former pupil of Lorentz of the Lorentz-Einstein transformation and had a far wider range. The example that sticks with me is the Moebius strip. He explained how the strip was constructed, how it was to be cut, how unexpected was the result of the cutting, only to ask whether the result would always be the same when the same procedure was repeated. His answer was a development of the theory of abstraction: just as intellect abstracts universal terms from images, so too it abstracts the universal connection between the universal terms. It was an answer that fitted into the context of Aristotelian logic. But I had shifted somewhat from that context. I believed, not in the abstraction of universals, but in the understanding of particulars and, provided the particu-

---

5 This paragraph does not appear in the autograph text. Obviously, Lonergan added it at a later date.
6 John Henry Newman, *An Essay in Aid of a Grammar of Assent*, first published London, 1870; currently available in an edition with an introduction by Nicholas Lash (Notre Dame, IN: University of Notre Dame Press, 1979).
7 John A. Stewart, *Plato's Doctrine of Ideas* (Oxford: Clarendon Press, 1909).
8 See above, p. 65, note 26.
9 Peter Hoenen, *De noetica geometriae origine theoriae cognitionis*, volume LXIII, Analecta Gregoriana (Rome: Gregorian University Press, 1954).

lars did not differ significantly, in the generalized formulation of that understanding.

I followed this up in the forties with two historical studies, the first concerned with Aquinas's views on willing, the second with his views on knowing. These labors put my thought in a medieval context. The further labor of transposing it to a contemporary context began when I was invited to give a course on 'Thought and Reality' at the Thomas More Institute for Adult Education in Montreal. The Institute was founded at the end of the Second World War in 1945. I lectured one evening a week for two hours. In November forty-five were attending the course. At Easter time forty-one were still coming. Their interest and perseverance assured me that I had a book. Eventually in 1957, it appeared under the title *Insight: A Study of Human Understanding*.[10]

While *Insight* had something to say on evolution and historical process, it did not tackle the problem of critical history. But with this issue I was confronted in its multinational form when I was assigned to a post at the Gregorian University in Rome. When I had been a student there in the thirties, the big name in Christology was de Grandmaison, and on the Trinity Jules Lebreton. Unfortunately, when it became my job to present these doctrines in the fifties, de Grandmaison and Lebreton were regarded as apologists rather than historians. So I found myself with a twofold problem on my hands. I had to extend my theory of knowledge to include an account of critical history, and I then had to adjust my ideas on theology so that critical historians could find themselves at home in contributing to theology. Finally I managed to publish a book on *Method in Theology* in 1972.[11]

5   A Threefold Conversion

More significantly, the book on method has already provided a basis for a distinct advance. In writing on *Insight* and on *Method* I had to develop a doctrine of objectivity that was relevant to a world mediated by meaning and motivated by values. My position was that objectivity was the fruit of authentic subjectivity, and authentic subjectivity was the result of raising and answering all relevant questions for intelligence, for reflection, and for deliberation. Further, while man is capable of authenticity, he also is capable of unauthenticity. Insofar as one is unauthentic, there is needed an about-turn, a conversion and, indeed, a threefold conversion: an intellectual conversion

---

10   See above, p. 3, note 2.
11   See above, p. 12, note 2.

by which without reserves one enters the world mediated by meaning; a moral conversion by which one comes to live in a world motivated by values; and a religious conversion when one accepts God's gift of his love bestowed through the Holy Spirit.

6   A Fourth Conversion

The advance to which I wish to allude comes from Robert M. Doran of Marquette University. He affirms a fourth conversion. It occurs when we uncover within ourselves the working of our own psyches, the *élan vital*, which according to Ira Progoff has two manifestations. There are the dynatypes and the cognitypes. The cognitypes are symbols. The dynatypes are the root of the life-styles to which we are attracted, in which we excel, with which we find ourselves most easily content.[12] By the dynatypes our vital energies are programmed; by the cognitypes they are released. The spontaneity that has been observed in the hummingbird for the first time building a nest also has its counterpart in us. But in us that counterpart is complemented, transposed, extended by the symbols and stories that mediate between our vital energies and our intelligent, reasonable, responsible lives.

Now it is in the realm of symbols and stories, of what he terms the *imaginal*, that Professor Doran finds a deficiency in my work. With me he would ask, 'Why?' 'Is that so?' 'Is it worthwhile?' But to these three he would add a fourth. It is Heidegger's *Befindlichkeit* taken as the existential question, 'How do I feel?' It is not just the question but also each one's intelligent answer, reasonable judgment, responsible acceptance. And on that response I can do no better than refer the reader to Professor Doran's current writing.[13]

12 Progoff, *Depth Psychology and Modern Man* 182–88.
13 Robert M. Doran, 'Aesthetics and the Opposites,' *Thought* 52 (1977) 117–33; 'Psychic Conversion,' *The Thomist* 41 (April 1977) 200–36; *Subject and Psyche: Ricoeur, Jung, and the Search for Foundations* (Washington, DC: University Press of America, 1977); 'Subject, Psyche, and Theology's Foundations,' *The Journal of Religion* 57 (1977) 267–87; 'Jungian Psychology and Lonergan's Foundations: A Methodological Proposal,' *Journal of the American Academy of Religion* 47:1, Supplement (1979) 23–45. [The first, second, fourth, and fifth of these items have been reprinted in Robert M. Doran, *Theological Foundations*, vol. 1: *Intentionality and Psyche* (Milwaukee: Marquette University Press, 1995), and the third has been reissued in a second edition entitled simply *Subject and Psyche* (Milwaukee: Marquette University Press, 1994).]

21

Philosophy and the Religious Phenomenon[1]

The question suggested for this symposium reads: 'How, from the viewpoint of the lecturer, does philosophy view the religious phenomenon in terms of the viability or validity of that phenomenon?'

1 [A paper prepared by Lonergan for a symposium sometime in late 1977 or early 1978. It was discovered posthumously in file 725 of Lonergan's papers. The file contains several items, but this one is also the title of the file itself. It was edited by Frederick E. Crowe and published with an Editor's Preface in METHOD: *Journal of Lonergan Studies* 12 (1994) 121–46. As Crowe says in his preface, 'The curiosity is that PRP itself seems, in a sense, to have been discarded. Its content shows it was written as a contribution to a symposium and in response to a request, but there is no symposium, so far as we know, where it was delivered, nor have we found any correspondence inviting a response to the question as quoted. The paper seems to have been written and set aside, to be discovered only fifteen years later.' Crowe finds a clue to the date of the paper in the fact that at one point Lonergan says that 'twenty years ago' Duméry's philosophy of religion was put on the Catholic Index of Forbidden Books, but then types in the interlinear space 'not quite.' 'Not quite twenty years' might date the writing of the essay in early 1978 or late 1977 (see the next note), which would mean that the symposium in question would be dated most likely some time in 1978. Crowe conjectures that the conference in question may well be one on 'Contemporary Religious Consciousness' held at Carleton University, Ottawa, in October 1978. By February of 1978 Lonergan had settled on presenting an earlier paper, 'Prolegomena to the Study of the Emerging Religious Consciousness of Our Time.' Crowe concludes: 'In any case the essay stands on its own, without need of any context except that of its date. The latter, however, is important, not only because it puts the essay toward the end of Lonergan's career, and records advances in several points of his thinking, but also because it is part

A first topic is philosophy and, indeed, not any philosophy but philosophy from the viewpoint of the lecturer. To this topic a certain clarification may perhaps be contributed if I contrast the Scholastic or neo-Scholastic views on which I was brought up with my present position.

On a Scholastic view, then, philosophy was concerned with ultimate, naturally known truths about the universe. It was concerned with the universe: in other words, its material object was unrestricted. It was concerned with truths: it did not aim at setting up a theory in the perpetual hope of later arriving at a still better theory, as do the natural and human sciences; it aimed at determining for all time just what was so. It was concerned with naturally known truths: for it acknowledged the existence of supernaturally known truths, but left that domain to theology. Finally, it was concerned with ultimate, naturally known truths, and thereby it distinguished itself from the sciences concerned with proximate truths about the various parts and levels of the universe.

Clearly on Scholastic soil a philosophy of religion could not flourish. Either it confined itself to naturally known truths, and then it overlooked the one true religion, which is supernatural. Or else it vainly attempted to include the supernatural within its purview, and then its inevitably inadequate viewpoint led to a misrepresentation and distortion of the one true religion. So it was that not quite twenty years ago Henry Duméry's scholastically trained judges placed his account of a critical philosophy of religion on the *Index librorum prohibitorum*.[2]

However, since the Second Vatican Council the *Index* has been dropped and the prestige of Scholasticism has practically vanished. At this point accordingly there become operative the terms of reference, 'philosophy, from the viewpoint of the lecturer.' On these terms, if I understand them correctly, I am to be my little self.

---

of a series of essays and lectures in the area of religious studies that occupied him in his final years.'
   A number of Crowe's editorial notes are preserved in the footnotes here. All bracketed notes are editorial. The asterisks that punctuate the text at several spots are Lonergan's.]

2 [Three of Duméry's books were put on the *Index* on 4 June 1958. It should be remembered that Lonergan, in his Gregorian University courses, had referred to Duméry's work with great respect, while noting a deficiency; see his *De Verbo incarnato*, 3rd ed. (Rome: Gregorian University Press, 1964) 16: 'illud notate quod huic philosophiae, tam acute quam erudite elaboratae, unum deest, scilicet, illud verum absolute positum quo innotescit ens'; also his *De Deo trino*, vol. 1, 2nd ed. (Rome: Gregorian University Press, 1964) 60, 274.]

From my viewpoint, then, a contemporary philosophy is under the constraint of an empirical principle. This principle means that there always is required some empirical element in any judgment of fact or of possibility or of probability. In the natural sciences the empirical element is the relevant data of sense. In the human sciences the empirical element is the relevant data of sense and of consciousness. In a foundational logic, a foundational mathematics, a foundational methodology, the relevant data are the immanent and operative norms of human cognitional process, a process that is both conscious and intentional, and as conscious provides the data of its own proper and improper proceeding.

For a fuller account of the nature and implications of this empirical principle, I must refer to my little book *Insight*.[3] My present concern is a philosophic approach that is open to the inclusion of a philosophy of religion.

To this end I note that a foundational methodology involves three successive sections. First, there is a cognitional theory, answering the question, What are you doing when you are knowing? Secondly, there is an epistemology, answering the question, On what grounds is doing that really knowing? Thirdly, there is a metaphysics, answering the question, What do you know when you do it?

A series of observations is now in order.

First, foundational methodology on this showing covers all that is basic in philosophy. One may or may not choose to include other issues within philosophy, but one cannot treat them in any sound and thorough fashion without settling – or presupposing as settled – the issues of cognitional theory, epistemology, and metaphysics.

Secondly, from the viewpoint of foundational methodology metaphysics is not the first science. It is not the *Grund- und Gesamtwissenschaft*. Though I have the honor of having my name associated with that of Fr Emerich Coreth and of being included with him when transcendental Thomists are mentioned,[4] still on the matter of the priority of metaphysics we have disagreed, we have

---

3   [See above, p. 3, note 2.]
4   [Coreth, Lonergan, and Rahner are a recurring trio in discussions of transcendental Thomism, but with varying emphases; see Vernon Bourke, '*Esse*, Transcendence, and Law: Three Phases of Recent Thomism,' *The Modern Schoolman* 52 (1974–75) 49–64, where it is Rahner and Coreth who are discussed, with Lonergan added; or William J. Hill, 'Thomism, Transcendental,' *New Catholic Encyclopedia*, vol. 16 (Supplement 1967–74) 449–54, where Rahner and Lonergan are discussed, with Coreth added. But regularly it is Joseph Maréchal who is the focus.]

disagreed publicly,[5] and we still do disagree. I am quite willing to grant that in a philosophy primarily concerned with objects metaphysics must be the first science, for it is the objects of metaphysics that are both most basic and most universal. But in a philosophy that primarily is concerned not with objects but with operations, metaphysics cannot be the first science. What now is both most basic and most universal are the operations, and these are studied in cognitional theory. Secondly, comes the validity of the operations, and such is the concern of epistemology. Only in the third place does there arise the question of objects, which is the concern of a metaphysics.

Thirdly, this shift from the priority of a metaphysics of objects to the priority of a theory of cognitional operations has an interesting implication for a philosophy of religion. For the distinction between naturally known objects and supernaturally known objects can now both retain all of its validity and, at the same time, lose the rather absolute priority it enjoyed in Scholastic thought. For its priority in Scholastic thought presupposed the priority of metaphysics, and on our present showing the priority of metaphysics no longer exists. Metaphysics finds its proper place not on the primary, not even on the secondary, but only on a tertiary level.

Fourthly, the shift we have been discussing is a shift from logic to method. Logic regards particular systems in their clarity, their coherence, and their rigor. Method regards movement, movement from nonsystem into systematic thinking, and from the systematic thinking of a given place and time to the better systematic thinking of a later time, whether at the same or at another place.

Here a comparison with Hegel may not be out of place. Hegel rightly felt that logic was too static to deal with a universe in movement. But the solution to that problem, we feel, does not consist in the invention of a logic of movement. Rather we would leave logic to its traditional tasks, which are essential to working out the coherence of any system and thereby bringing to light its shortcomings. But we would confine the relevance of logic to single stages in the process of developing thought, and we would assign to method the guidance of thought from each less satisfactory stage to each successive

5   [Lonergan may be thinking of Philip McShane, ed., *Language Truth and Meaning: Papers from The International Lonergan Congress 1970* (Dublin and London: Gill and Macmillan, 1972); see in that volume 33–48: E. Coreth, 'Immediacy and the mediation of being; an attempt to answer Bernard Lonergan,' and 306–12, at 311: 'Bernard Lonergan responds.' The original element in the exchange was Lonergan's review article on Coreth, 'Metaphysics as Horizon,' *Collection* (see above, p. 76, note 7) 188–204.]

more satisfactory stage. In brief, the relevance of logic is at the instant, when things are still. The guide of philosophy and science over time is method.

We may cut short the argument here to offer the conclusions to this first section of our paper. Such conclusions are three.

First, since philosophy has been identified with foundational methodology, there no longer holds the peremptory Scholastic argument against a sound philosophy of religion.

Secondly, as philosophy is foundational methodology, so philosophy of religion is the foundational methodology of religious studies.

Thirdly, a foundational methodology of religious studies will be able to pronounce on the viability or validity of this or that method of religious studies. But such a foundational methodology would go beyond its competence if it ventured to pronounce on the nonmethodological aspects of religious studies.

Therewith we arrive at a first conclusion on the topic before us. A philosophy of religion has much to say on the method of religious studies. The religious studies themselves, however, are not mere deductions from the method but applications of the method; and the attentiveness, intelligence, and reasonableness with which the applications are carried out are the responsibility, not of the methodologist but of the student of religion. Accordingly, philosophy as foundational methodology can pronounce, not immediately and specifically but only remotely and generically on the validity or viability of the results of religious studies.

***

Let us now attempt to carry the argument a step further.

The priority of metaphysics in the Aristotelian tradition led to a faculty psychology. For other sciences were subordinate to the first science; from it they derived their basic terms and theorems; and so Aristotelian psychology had to be a metaphysical psychology in terms of potencies, forms, and acts.

But once the priority of metaphysics is rejected, there also is rejected its implication of a faculty psychology. When philosophy is conceived as a foundational methodology, and when cognitional theory is its basic step, the empirical principle demands that cognitional theory take its stand on the data of cognitional consciousness. But cognitional consciousness is of operations and of the normative tendencies linking operations together. Cognitional theory, accordingly, will consist of terms and relations, where the terms name operations and the relations name normative tendencies. In this fashion faculty psychology gives way to an intentionality analysis.

This shift is of considerable importance. As long as psychology is basically a discussion of faculties or potencies, there arise questions regarding the relative priority or importance of the sensitive, the conative, the intellectual, and the volitional components of human living and acting. Moreover, since clear-cut solutions to these questions do not exist, there result unending complaints about the one-sidedness of the other fellow's stand.

In contrast, intentionality analysis transposes these issues into a new form that automatically settles questions of precedence and importance. For now there are compared, not potencies, but levels of operation. The levels are sharply distinguished by operators that promote the conscious and intentional subject from a lower to a higher level. The operators are manifested by questions. So from a first level to a second the promotion is effected by questions for intelligence; such questions are: what? why? how? what for? how often? They arise with respect to data, and they lead to insights and thence to the expression of insights in concepts, definitions, hypotheses, theories, systems. From a second to a third level the promotion is effected by questions for reflection; such questions ask: is that so? are you certain? From a third level to a fourth the promotion is effected by questions for deliberation; they ask whether a proposed course of action is truly or only apparently good, whether it is really worth while or not; and such fourth-level questions lead to the operations of evaluating, deciding, acting.

Now the relation between successive levels may be named sublation, not in the proper Hegelian sense of *Aufhebung* but in a related sense I have found in Karl Rahner's *Hearers of the Word*.[6] One reaches this related sense by distinguishing between sublated and sublating operations, and by defining the sublating operations as going beyond the sublated, introducing a radically new principle, respecting the integrity of the sublated, and bestowing upon them a higher significance and a wider relevance.

So questions for intelligence go beyond the data of sense and/or the data of consciousness. They head for insights that contrast radically with the mere givenness of data. They not merely respect the integrity of data but make

6 [In 'Faith and Beliefs' (see above, p. 36, note 12) Lonergan gives a more precise reference: '*Hörer des Wortes* (Munich: Kösel, 1963) 40'; there was a personal copy of this book in his room when he died, with sidelining on page 40. But it is not at all clear to what extent he owed his concept of sublation to Rahner and to what extent he conveniently found support in Rahner; the page referred to in *Hörer des Wortes* does not suffice as source for Lonergan's own view. In any case in *Insight*, completed in 1953, Lonergan had already distanced himself from Hegel: 'Hegel's sublation is through a reconciling third concept, but our development is both the accumulation of insights ... and the reversal of ... aberrations' (*Insight* 447).]

possible ever more comprehensive and more exact apprehensions of data. Finally, they promote data from the status of conscious occurrences in a subject to the beginnings of an apprehension of a universe.

Similarly, questions for reflection go beyond the concepts, definitions, hypotheses, theories, systems thought out by intelligence. They direct conscious intentionality beyond mere understanding towards truth and reality. They lead to operations that effect the transition from objects of thought to real objects, and thereby they bestow an essentially new significance and importance on experience and understanding.

In like manner questions for deliberation sublate the previous three levels. They are concerned with the good. They end the one-sidedness of purely cognitional endeavor to restore the integration of sense and conation, thought and feeling. They not merely ask about a distinction between satisfaction and value but also assume the existential viewpoint that asks me whether I am ready, whether I am determined, to sacrifice satisfactions for the sake of values. Having put the question of moral authenticity, they reward acceptance with a good conscience, and they sanction rejection with an uneasy conscience. Finally, they push the requirement of authenticity to the sticking point: good decisions must be complemented by good conduct and good actions; and failure in this respect is just the inner essence of hypocrisy.

Now from the viewpoint of intentionality analysis and sublation, the old questions of sensism, intellectualism, sentimentalism, voluntarism merely vanish. Experience, understanding, judgment, and decision all are essential to human living. But while all are essential, while none can be dropped or even slighted, still the successive levels are related inasmuch as the later presuppose the earlier and complement them, and inasmuch as the earlier are ordained to the later and need them to attain their human significance.

Such an introduction of hierarchy naturally calls for a series of notes and corollaries.

First, while we have spoken of successive levels, of earlier and later, of lower and higher, such terms are merely initial signposts. The real meaning is neither spatial nor chronological. The real meaning is in terms of sublating and sublated operations, and the meaning of sublation is the meaning already defined and illustrated.

Secondly, the hierarchy that intentionality analysis brings to light justifies traditional complaints about the one-sidedness of intellectualism, of an exclusive emphasis on the cognitional elements in man's makeup. While it is true that observation, understanding, and factual judgment are immediately under the guidance of the subject's attentiveness, his intelligence, his reasonableness, while it is true that this guidance excludes interferences from feelings and wishes, still this guidance is not the activity of some putative faculty named speculative intellect or pure reason. It is the guidance of the norms immanent and operative on the first three levels of conscious and intentional operations, and it is a guidance that attains its proper stature when formulated in a method and implemented by a decision to dedicate some part of one's life to scientific, scholarly, or philosophic pursuits.

However, while acknowledging the one-sidedness of an exclusive intellectualism and the incompleteness of an intellectualism that is not subordinated to a deliberately chosen method, one must not accept the common complaint that intellectualist products are abstractions. They are not. The so-called 'abstract' is usually the incompletely determined apprehension of the concrete, and all human apprehension is incompletely determined. Indeed, intellectualist apprehension is more complete than the apprehensions of undifferentiated consciousness, and it is just the ignorance of undifferentiated consciousness that complains about the abstractness of the intellectual.

Thirdly, the hierarchy of sublated and sublating operations reveals the significance of the existential. For the level of deliberation, decision, action has two aspects. Insofar as it affects other persons and objects, it is practical. But insofar as it is the locus where the subject decides for or against his own authenticity, it is existential.

Note that the two aspects, the practical and the existential, are not separable. However practical any decision is, it reveals and confirms and intensifies the authenticity or unauthenticity of the practical subject. Inversely, however existential any decision is, it attains substance and moment in the measure that it transforms one's conduct and pursuits.

Note again that the man of common sense, without any aspiration to science or scholarship or philosophy, is spontaneously existential and practical for the simple reason that he has no notion and much less any attainment of the scientific, the scholarly, or the philosophic differentiations of human consciousness. But at the same time note that while undifferentiated consciousness does not need to be told to prefer orthopraxis to orthodoxy, it is prone to underestimate orthodoxy, while a just balance is to be had only by a consciousness that is multiply differentiated, that has a proper appreciation of orthodoxy, and that learns to rank orthopraxis higher still.

Fourthly, a foundational methodology can function as a philosophy of religion only by moving beyond the levels of experience, understanding, and judgment and including the higher significance and relevance of deliberation, evaluation, decision, and action. For every religion is involved in value judgments, and value judgments pertain to the fourth level of intentional consciousness. Specifically, Catholic theologians consider the act of religious belief to proceed from judgments of credibility and credentity; in plainer English, the object of belief not only can but also should be believed; and to judge that it should be believed is a value judgment.

To be noted here is that this extension of foundational methodology to include the subject as existential and practical, while it runs counter to older philosophies that thought in terms of speculative intellect or pure reason, merely follows out the implications of what already has been noted. For the austere detachment of purely cognitive or intellectual operations is itself the product of a free choice and implemented by the acceptance of a method. And the higher integration of an orthopraxis that justly appreciates an orthodoxy is a complement to which experience, understanding, and factual judgment are ordained and which they need.

In this connection it is only proper to note that the view we are propounding draws support from Talcott Parsons's account of the development of the sociology of religion away from an initial hostility and towards a recognition of the high role of religion within an action system.[7] For the early hostility was against a view of religion as essentially cognitive, and the later friendliness views religion as predominantly noncognitive.

A final note to this section will be a simple contrast with the Hegelian program, which was to sublate religion by philosophy. It was a sublation strongly resisted especially by Catholic theologians on the obvious ground that it rejected the subordination of the natural to the supernatural, and so the subordination of philosophy to religion and theology. If, however, we fully agree with our Catholic predecessors in rejecting the Hegelian program, we cannot do so precisely on the grounds that they offer. For the distinction between natural and supernatural resides within a metaphysical context, and for us a metaphysical context is not primary or even secondary but only tertiary. But this does not imply that our opposition to the Hegelian sublation of religion is only tertiary. For our opposition rests on our own primary context of intentionality analysis, in which one finds such cognitive or putatively cogni-

---

7   Talcott Parsons, 'The Theoretical Development of the Sociology of Religion,' in *Essays in Sociological Theory Pure and Applied* 197–210. See also his 'The Dimensions of Cultural Variation,' in Parsons et al., *Theories of Society: Foundations of Modern Sociological Theory*. Also the initial and final essays in Robert N. Bellah, *Beyond Belief: Essays on Religion in a Post-Traditional World*. [For all the book references in this note, see above, p. 311, notes 18 and 19.]

tive operations as a Hegelian dialectic subordinated to the operations of the existential and practical subject. In a word, Kierkegaard had a point.

***

Our intentionality analysis distinguished the four levels of experience, understanding, factual judgment, and existential decision. We must now advert to the fact that this structure may prove open at both ends. The intellectual operator that promotes our operations from the level of experience to the level of understanding may well be preceded by a symbolic operator[8] that coordinates neural potentialities and needs with higher goals through its control over the emergence of images and affects. Again, beyond the moral operator that promotes us from judgments of fact to judgments of value with their retinue of decisions and actions, there is a further realm of interpersonal relations and total commitment in which human beings tend to find the immanent goal of their being and, with it, their fullest joy and deepest peace.

So from an intentionality analysis distinguishing four levels one moves to an analysis that distinguishes six levels. Moreover, the two added levels are particularly relevant to religious studies. The symbolic operator that shapes the development of sensibility and, in its ultimate achievement, guides the Jungian process of individuation, would seem highly relevant to an investigation of religious symbols. And the soul of religion has been seen to lie in a total commitment that embraces the universe and frequently does so in adoration of a personal God.[9]

From a specifically Christian viewpoint, I have characterized the total commitment of religious living as 'being in love in an unrestricted manner'; I have associated it with St Paul's statement that 'God's love has flooded our inmost heart through the Holy Spirit he has given us' (Romans 5.5); and I have noted that the Christian case of the subject being in love with God is complemented

---

8 For the notion of symbolic operator I am indebted to conversations with Robert M. Doran, s.j. See his 'Paul Ricoeur: Toward the Restoration of Meaning,' *Anglican Theological Review* 55 (October 1973) 443–58 (reprinted in Doran, *Theological Foundations 1: Intentionality and Psyche* [see above, p. 390, note 13] 1–24). On the individuation process, Gerhard Adler, *The Living Symbol: A Case Study in the Process of Individuation* (New York: Pantheon, 1961. Bollingen Series, 63).

9 On the nature of religion, see Joseph P. Whelan, *The Spirituality of Friedrich von Hügel* (New York: Newman, 1971) 131–33. [Lonergan's reference: 'pp. 131 ff.' He was relying, perhaps, on excerpts he had taken from pp. 131–33; for a wider basis, see Whelan's extensive index under 'religion,' 'religious experience,' 'religious sense.'] Bernard Lonergan, *Method in Theology* (see above, p. 12, note 2) chapter 4.

by God's manifestation of his love for us in the death and resurrection of Christ Jesus.

But attention to Christian religion does not exclude attention to other religions. Indeed the transition to the others may be effected in two manners. The first has specifically Christian premises. It appeals to the rule: 'By their fruits you shall know them' (Matthew 7.16). It notes the scriptural text that favors the affirmation of God's will to save all men (1 Timothy 2.4). It notes that those God wills to save will be given the charity described in the thirteenth chapter of the First Letter to the Corinthians, even though as yet they have no explicit knowledge of Christ the mediator.

The second manner of proceeding towards a universalist view of religion may begin with Raymond Panikkar's conception of a fundamental theology that takes its stand on the lived religion or mystical faith that is prior to any formulation and perhaps beyond formulation.[10] Again, it may take its rise from empirical studies of religious phenomena that come to discern a convergence of religions.[11] Finally, it may seek to bring these two standpoints together into a single integrated view.

In concluding this section I would recall that we have been conceiving the philosophy of religion as foundational methodology, that in a first section we attempted to surmount the incapacity of a Scholastic philosophy to be the philosophy of what it considered the true religion; in a second section we extended the range of foundational methodology to include value judgments; and in this third section we have introduced two further extensions. First, we mentioned the possibility of a symbolic operator that, through image and affect, headed psychic process to its own and to higher ends; and an exploration of this area we felt highly relevant to an account of religious symbolism. Secondly, we adverted to a topmost level of interpersonal relations and total commitments, a level that can be specifically religious, a level that in one of its actuations is easily verified in New Testament doctrine, that conforms to the view of all Scholastic schools that without charity even the infused virtues are unformed, that provides a basis for explicitating the universalism

---

10 Raymond Panikkar, 'Metatheology or Diacritical Theology as Fundamental Theology,' *Concilium* 46 (1969; J.B. Metz, ed., *The Development of Fundamental Theology*) 43–55, at 54.
11 William Cenkner, 'The Convergence of Religions,' *Cross Currents* 22 (Winter 1972 through Winter 1973) 429–37. Robley Edward Whitson, *The Coming Convergence of World Religions* (New York: Newman Press, 1971). [There is extensive sidelining in Lonergan's personal copy of Whitson's book in the Archives, Lonergan Research Institute, Toronto.]

of Christianity and relating it positively to other religions. As a final note to this section one may add that what in a philosophic context I have named being in love in an unrestricted manner, in a theological context could be paralleled with Karl Rahner's supernatural existential.

***

Up to now we have been working our way out of a traditional Scholastic context – in which a sound philosophy of religion is a contradiction in terms – and into a contemporary context in which philosophy, by becoming foundational methodology, regains both its universal significance and its universal function.

As already remarked, basic foundational methodology consists of three parts: cognitional theory, epistemology, and metaphysics. Moreover, as argued in *Insight*, from this viewpoint metaphysics is, not knowledge of all being but the integral heuristic structure within which one operates methodically towards knowledge of all being.

Such an integral heuristic structure has both a ground and a consequent. Its ground is the self-appropriation of the experiencing, intelligent, reasonable, free, responsible, and loving subject. Its consequent is the application of this ground to the guidance of methodical inquiry in a fashion analogous to the application of mathematics in the inquiry of modern physics.

My present purpose is limited. I cannot offer a full exploration of the heuristic structure of religious studies. I can only indicate two items in such a heuristic structure. One of them I shall be content to mention, for I have treated it sufficiently elsewhere. The other I shall sketch to some extent; I have treated it elsewhere as well, but here I shall attempt a different and perhaps more accessible approach.

The first element, then, in a heuristic structure for religious studies arises from the distinction between authentic and unauthentic. The distinction is relevant both to the object of religious studies and to the subject. It is relevant to the object, for the followers of a given religion may represent it authentically or unauthentically to provide contradictory evidence on the nature of the religion under investigation. It is relevant to the subjects carrying out religious studies, for they may be humanly or religiously authentic or unauthentic and so offer contradictory interpretations of the same data.

This problem is not new. But it has been evaded either by abstracting from the values exhibited by the religion, or by attending to these values but refraining from any judgment that either approves or disapproves of them.

While these devices satisfy the requirements of empirical science, it is not impossible to doubt that they meet the exigences of a science of religions.

Simply to ignore the values exhibited by a religion seems to ignore a principal element in the religion. It seems as unacceptable as a Scholastic philosophy of religion that considers any religion except insofar as it resembles what the Scholastics held to be the one true religion.[12] On the other hand, to exhibit the values presented by a religion while abstaining from any value judgment of one's own is a hazardous procedure; it is like undertaking a value-free theory of values, and that resembles a theory of knowledge that prescinds from the knower. Such procedures are precritical.

However, if empirical science bogs down in the empirical facts that follow-ers of a religion follow differently and that interpreters of religion interpret differently, it remains that a philosophy of religion can resolve the issue. Paul Ricoeur has advocated the combination of a hermeneutic of suspicion with a hermeneutic of recovery, so that unauthentic religion can be repudiated and authentic religion maintained. I myself in *Insight* and again in *Method in Theology* have proposed a dialectic in which investigators are urged both to expand what they consider authentic in the followers of a religion they are studying and, as well, to reverse what they consider unauthentic. The result will be a projective test in which interpreters reveal their own notions of authenticity and unauthenticity both to others and to themselves. In the short run both the more authentic will discover what they have in common, and so too will the less authentic. In the long run the authentic should be able to reveal the strength of their position by the penetration of their investigations, by the growing number in the scientific community attracted to their assump-tions and procedures, and eventually by the reduction of the opposition to the hard-line dogmatists that defend an inadequate method no matter what its deficiencies.

In brief, for the long run I am relying on the course that Thomas Kuhn has found to prevail in physics, namely, that mistaken ideas that once were

12 [This sentence has puzzled readers. Some have wondered whether there should be a word (such as 'unacceptable') between 'religion' and 'except,' and in a similar vein others have suggested that 'except' should be changed to 'only.' Such tampering would change Lonergan's meaning. He means just what he says. A Scholastic philosophy of religion, Lonergan said earlier, is incapable of being 'the philosophy of what it considered the true religion,' because philosophy for the Scholastics 'was concerned with naturally known truths ... it acknowledged the existence of supernaturally known truths, but left that domain to theology.' Just as religious studies modeled on empirical science abstracts or prescinds from the values exhibited by the religion, so Scholastic philosophy of religion abstracts or prescinds from what the Scholastics held to be the one true religion and what resembles the one true religion.]

dominant are not so much refuted as abandoned. They vanish when they prove incapable of gaining competent disciples.

***

There is a second contribution that, I believe, a philosophy of religion can make to religious studies. For the most part I have referred to it as differentiations of consciousness, but I now find that an equivalent point can be made and parallel results obtained in a less abstruse approach.

The issue in hand is the need of some account and ordering of the various contexts in which, first, religious living occurs and, secondly, investigations of religious living are undertaken. Such an ordered account is again a dialectic, not indeed in the meaning of dialectic in the previous section, which turns on the opposition of authenticity and unauthenticity, but rather a dialectic in the style of Collingwood as interpreted by Louis Mink.[13]

In such a dialectic there are the terms whose meaning shifts in the course of time, and further, there are the terms that denote the factors bringing about such shifts in meaning.

The terms whose meaning shifts are social contexts and cultural contexts. Social contexts are the already understood and accepted modes of human cooperation grouped under such headings as family and mores, community and education, state and law, economics and technology. Cultural contexts are the areas of interest in which social frameworks find explanation, justification, a goal: such areas are art, religion, science, philosophy, history.

Now the further one turns to the past, the shorter become the lists of social headings and cultural areas, while the realities to which they refer become simpler in structure and more comprehensive in scope. So, for example, the more ancient the religion, the less sharply will its role be distinguished from other roles, and the more notable will be the position it occupies in the sociocultural matrix.

It remains that earlier forms may be found in later periods, so that mere chronology does not provide even a preliminary ordering. On the other hand, differentiation is not independent of language, and, in fact, not a little relevance is found when one distinguishes four stages: the linguistic, the literate, the logical, and the methodical.[14]

13 [Louis Mink, *Mind, History, and Dialectic: The Philosophy of R.G. Collingwood* (Bloomington, London: Indiana University Press, 1969).]
14 [While elsewhere there are three 'plateaus' ('Natural Right and Historical Mindedness,' *A Third Collection* 169–83, at 177–80), namely, 'meanings such as prove operative in men of action; further meanings that involve a familiarity with logical techniques; and a still further plateau of meanings that attain

Each of these stages includes those that precede but adds a new factor of its own. In the linguistic stage people speak and listen. In the literate they read and write. In the logical they operate on propositions; they promote clarity, coherence, and rigor of statement; they move towards systems that are thought to be permanently valid. In the methodical stage the construction of systems remains, but the permanently valid system has become an abandoned ideal; any system is presumed to be the precursor of another and better system; and the role of method is the discernment of invariants and variables in the ongoing sequences of systems.

Now in the later periods the scope of earlier stages may be enhanced: so the radio extends speech and hearing; the cinema extends the drama; television extends both. Again, the invention of printing extends reading and writing. Further, a symbolic logic provides an intermediate step between traditional logic and the digital computer.

At the same time this distinction of stages in no way suggests that the later stages are universal. The invention of writing does not stamp out illiteracy. The discovery of logic leads to technical languages without displacing 'ordinary' language in ordinary living. The illusion of permanently valid systems is not automatically dispelled with the emergence of scientific or philosophic method.

Now the distinction of stages involves different apprehensions of social arrangements and cultural achievements. Moreover, it involves differences in the social arrangements that are projected and realized as well as in the cultural achievements that are ambitioned and brought to birth.

Further, the fact that the stages are not universalized, that there may live together people who can and people who cannot read and write, people who can and people who cannot operate on propositions and construct systems of thought, people who can and people who cannot grasp that systematic constructs last their little day eventually to pass away in favor of better constructs – this complex fact has the twofold consequent of stratification and alienation.

It leads to stratification, for those in the more advanced stages are far more capable of initiating new and perhaps better social arrangements and of

-----

their proper significance and status within a methodical approach that has acknowledged its underpinnings in an intentionality analysis' (180) or the 'three stages' of *Method in Theology* 85–99, 108), namely, common sense, theory, and interiority, still the distinction between linguistic and literate is not new; it was used for differentiations of consciousness in *Philosophy of God, and Theology* (see above, p. 209), but becomes in the present paper the basis for still more fundamental divisions in human living.]

providing appropriate cultural justifications for their new social arrangements.

It leads to alienation. For inasmuch as the more advanced devise the social arrangements and invent their cultural justification, the less advanced find themselves living in social arrangements beyond their comprehension and motivated by appeals to values they do not appreciate. Inversely, inasmuch as the less advanced assume the initiative, the more advanced are alienated by *simpliste* social thought and crude cultural creations.

I have been sketching in bold outline – an outline that admits almost endless differentiations and refinements – (1) eight headings of social arrangements, (2) five areas of cultural interest, (3) four stages diversifying the scope of social and cultural initiatives, and (4) the increasing tendency of these stages to bring about stratification and alienation.

It is within these varying social and cultural contexts that religion discovers itself, works out its identity, differentiates itself from other areas, and interacts with them. But in its linguistic stage religion will manifest itself as myth and ritual. In its literate stage it becomes religion of the book, of the Torah, the gospel, the Koran. In the logical stage it may reduplicate itself with the reflection on itself that would end dissension by dogmatic pronouncements and would seek overall reconciliation by systematic theologies. In the methodical stage it confronts its own history, distinguishes the stages in its own development, evaluates the authenticity or unauthenticity of its initiatives, and preaches its message in the many forms and styles appropriate to the many social and cultural strata of the communities in which it operates.

Over the years each earlier stage brings to light an exigence for the next. To meet that exigence there forms an elite and, when its work is not merely abstruse and difficult but in some measure unsuccessful, the steadfast representatives of earlier stages express their alienation by voicing their grievances.

So Christianity began and spread through the words and deeds of Christ and his apostles. But by the end of the second century there had emerged an elite that studied the scriptures and read Irenaeus in Gaul, Hippolytus in Rome, Tertullian in North Africa, Clement and Origen in Egypt.

The spoken word objectifies transiently. The written word objectifies permanently. It can regard a larger area and underpin a sustained scrutiny. So Irenaeus, Hippolytus, Tertullian, Clement, and Origen propounded Christianity in its opposition to a Gnosticism that belittled and even ridiculed the creator God of the Old Testament who also was God the Father of Jesus Christ, the Savior of mankind.

Now even the linguistic stage of a religion will be concerned not only with 'doing the truth' but also with the particular form of 'doing' that is 'saying the truth.' So scholars have discerned brief formulas of faith embedded in the New Testament, and the First Epistle of John is thought to be opposing a form of Gnostic docetism. But apologetics and controversy lead into the logical stage of religion. The anthropomorphisms of the Old Testament had to be explained not as literal but as symbolic statements; and to express literally the Christian apprehension of God the Father, Christian resourcefulness turned to the achievements of the Greeks. For Origen, God the Father was strictly spiritual and strictly eternal; and the same was true of his Son and Word.

Now an entry into the logical stage admits no logical retreat from it. Worse, arguments for one position can be matched by other arguments against it. There followed the councils. The Arians were rejected at Nicea, the Macedonians at Constantinople, the Nestorians at Ephesus, the Monophysites at Chalcedon. The doctrines of the Trinity and the Incarnation were formulated in all their austerity, and dangers of alienation were warded off inasmuch as literate minds were permitted to regard the dogmas as laws, while the masses in the linguistic stage enshrined them in confessions of faith and liturgical prayers.

As there is a transition from 'doing the truth' to 'saying the truth,' so there is a further transition from 'saying the truth' to reaching some understanding of it. Even though the truth expresses mystery, at least it should not involve contradiction. This concern, of course, brings forth a further and still smaller elite. It had made a momentary appearance in Origen's comparison of the generation of the Son to the origin of willing from knowing. It had attained a brief but still compelling realization in Gregory of Nyssa's *Ad Ablabium* that explained the difference between the generation of the Son and the procession of the Spirit. It found a respected vehicle in Augustine's lengthy and largely rhetorical and logical *De trinitate*. But it became the occupation of a large and ongoing intellectual community in medieval Scholasticism. The inspiration of Scholasticism was Anselm's faith seeking, though hardly attaining, understanding. Its schoolmaster was Abelard's *Sic et non*. Its achievement was the collected works of Aquinas. Its tragedy was that a spontaneous method, stemming from the practice of *lectio et quaestio*, was led astray by the ineptitude of Aristotle's *Posterior Analytics*.

Scholasticism declined. Its decline was greeted by the alienation of the *devotio moderna*, which would rather feel compunction than define it, by the ridicule of the humanists in a new revival of learning, and by the invention of printing, which gave new life and vigor to religion of the book. On this wave rode the Reformation. Breasting it stood the Council of Trent. But if the

Reformation rejected *en bloc* the ambiguities of Scholasticism, if it stressed the scriptures, still it remained faithful to the Greek councils and so was committed to a logical stance, and in time to a Scholasticism of its own.

It remains that Protestant insistence on scripture kept open a door. Through that door in due course there entered into scriptural studies the application of new, nineteenth-century methods to historical investigation and textual interpretation. So there came to light the differences between the mind of the scriptures and the mind of the councils, and there followed doubts that conciliar dogmas could be attributed to divine revelation. The problem surfaces in nineteenth-century liberal Protestantism, in early twentieth-century modernism, and for a third time in the wake of the Second Vatican Council, when even Catholic theologians find the definition of Chalcedon questionable and wish to change both our traditional understanding of Christ and our profession of faith in Christ.

The problem, indeed I should say the crisis, is one of understanding. However radical its content, its roots are ancient, for problems of understanding are problems of method. Scholasticism went astray when its questions arose, not from its sources in scripture and tradition but from the conflicts between theological systems. The sixteenth century went astray when its incomprehension of doctrinal development divided Christendom into the archaists, that pronounced developments corruptions, and the anachronists, that read later developments into earlier documents. Catholics went astray both by their long-sustained opposition to advanced methods in historical investigation and textual interpretation, and by an uncritical transposition of Scholasticism into the milieu of modern thought.

***

My discussion falls into two parts. In the first I sought to set up a philosophy of religion by conceiving philosophy as foundational methodology, and philosophy of religion as foundational methodology of religious studies. This first part fell into three sections: in the first section there was effected a transition from the priority of metaphysics to the priority of cognitional theory; in the second, we moved from faculty psychology to intentionality analysis; in the third, we added the parts of intentionality analysis specifically relevant to religious studies.

The second part of the paper was concerned with heuristic structures in religious studies: a first concern was with the methodical handling of value problems; the second was with the ordering of the differences due to developments.

22

Horizons and Transpositions[1]

Professor Gerald McCool of Fordham University has recently given us a quite thorough study of the reasons that led Pope Leo XIII to write the encyclical *Aeterni Patris*, and thereby to impose the doctrine of Aquinas upon Catholic

1 [A lecture given at the Lonergan Workshop, Boston College, on Thursday evening, 21 June 1979. The theme of the workshop, 18–22 June, was 'Crisis of Liberal Education.'

A tape recording was made of the lecture and brief question period, and a transcription of the recording by Nicholas Graham is in the library of the Lonergan Research Institute, Toronto. The recording has been converted to compact disc by Greg Lauzon. The Institute library has a photocopy of an autograph typescript marked 'preliminary draught' (file 963); file 773 of Batch XIII in the Archives contains the original of the same document without the 'preliminary draught' indication. The editing relies on all of these materials. Bracketed footnotes here are editorial. The autograph gives references, not in notes but in the text.

The taped lecture began with the following introductory remark. 'The topic is "Horizons and Transpositions." The idea came to me when Professor Lawrence was responding to Fr McCool at a meeting of the Catholic Theological, and McCool could see no logical connection between my position and that of St Thomas. Professor Lawrence explained that I did not talk about a conclusion but a transposition. The idea was worth elaborating.' Lonergan's reference is to the Annual Convention of The Catholic Theological Society of America, held in Toronto, 15–18 June 1977. More specifically, the reference is to McCool's address, 'Theology and Philosophy,' in the *Proceedings of the Thirty-second Annual Convention of the Catholic Theological Society of America* (1977) 72–89; and to Fred Lawrence, 'A Response (1) to Gerald McCool,' ibid. 90–96.]

teaching of philosophy and theology.[2] Moreover, to his book he has added an article on twentieth-century Scholasticism, on its initial vigor and on its decline since the pastoral council, Vatican II.[3]

Both the book and the article are relevant to our topic, for the word 'horizon' denotes the range or field of a person's interests and knowledge, and Fr McCool's studies have set before us not only many different persons but also not a few different horizons, and even a few changes of horizon.

Now a change of horizon takes us out of the field of deductive logic. As long as one is simply logical, one remains within the same horizon. As soon as one changes one's horizon, one begins to operate in virtue of a minor or major change in one's basic assumptions. Such a change may be just a jump but also it may be a genuine transposition, a restatement of an earlier position in a new and broader context. Einstein's special relativity[4] was a transposition of Newton; it included Newton's general gravitation as a particular case. The differences were minimal when the velocity between two frames of reference was not comparable to the velocity of light, and no new measurements had to be made. All the old measurements held; you might have to add a few decimal points, but you weren't able to measure them really. This is an example of a restatement of an earlier position in a new and broader context.

Our present concern is to illustrate the notion of genuine transposition. So first we ask whether there was anything genuine about the process that transplanted the gospel from the religious soil of Palestine to the arid context of Greek speculation. Next we shall ask what constituted the golden age of Scholasticism, and what led to the breakdown of theology in the fourteenth and fifteenth centuries. Finally we shall ask whether there were oversights in the nineteenth-century resurgence of Thomism that account for the debacle that followed the pastoral council, Vatican II.

Finally, be it observed that a change of horizon cannot be demonstrated from a previous horizon. So the genuineness of transpositions cannot be a simple logical conclusion. What is basic is authenticity. It is a summit towards which one may strive, and only through such striving may one come to some imperfect participation of what Augustine and Aquinas named Uncreated Light.

2 Gerald A. McCool, *Catholic Theology in the Nineteenth Century: The Quest for a Unitary Method* (New York: Seabury, 1977).
3 Gerald A. McCool, 'Twentieth-Century Scholasticism,' *The Journal of Religion* 58 (Supplement, 1978) s198–s221.
4 [In the lecture, Lonergan adds the rest of this paragraph to the autograph text as an example of a genuine transposition.]

1   The Transition from a Palestinian to a Hellenistic Horizon

It has long been[5] a commonplace for the followers of the History of Religions School that the high Christology of the church emerged under the dominance of a Hellenistic milieu. In the recent decade, however, the commonplace has been attacked both on its Palestinian and on its Hellenistic front.

1.1 Hengel and Voegelin

Martin Hengel, a specialist in comparative studies of Judaism and Christianity, in his inaugural lecture at the University of Tübingen in 1973 (a lecture revised and published in German in 1975 and in English in 1976),[6] has argued vigorously that the letters of Paul to Galatians, to 1 and 2 Corinthians, and to Romans (a) are the earliest, certainly authentic Christian documents we possess, (b) teach a high Christology, and (c) are expressed in language of Palestinian origin.

So extensive is the erudition displayed in this lecture (it's a book, mostly footnotes) that some time will elapse before scholars will have assimilated its viewpoint and evaluated its contribution. But its immediate implication is that it calls in question the supposition of Harnack and the School of the History of Religions that the high Christology of the church emerged under the dominance of a Hellenistic milieu. If it did emerge in that manner, then, according to Hengel, its emergence was prior to the authentic Pauline letters, and more happened in the first two decades of Christian history than in the subsequent seven centuries.[7]

Nor is Professor Hengel's lecture the only twist that has been given to our present topic. The History of Religions School, like the German Historical School, was anti-Hegelian. Its ideal was not a history deduced from a philosophic dialectic but a history laboriously pieced together from empirical research. It was radically suspicious, not only of myths and legends but also of

---

5 [This paragraph is in the autograph text, but was not part of the lecture.]

6 Martin Hengel, *The Son of God: The Origin of Christology and the History of Jewish-Hellenistic Religion* (Philadelphia: Fortress Press, 1976).

7 Ibid. 2. [This paragraph and the next were not in the autograph. Rather, after listing Hengel's three contentions, Lonergan wrote, 'While his scholarship cannot be summarized, I must be content to repeat his contention that, if high Christology emerged under the dominance of a Hellenistic milieu, then more happened in the first two decades of Christian history than in the subsequent seven centuries.']

metaphysics. Hegel and the Scholastics, the early and the later Scholastics, the Scholastics and the Greeks, were apt to be taken as so many instances of metaphysical philosophy, or if you prefer, ideology.

Eric Voegelin, a historian and not a metaphysician, has written a highly illuminating article entitled 'Reason: The Classic Experience.' I quote:

> I shall not deal with the 'idea' or a nominalist 'definition' of Reason but with the process in reality in which concrete human beings, the 'lovers of wisdom,' the philosophers as they styled themselves, were engaged in an act of resistance against the personal and social disorder of their age. From this act there emerged the Nous as the cognitively luminous force that inspired the philosophers to resist and, at the same time, enabled them to recognize the phenomena of disorder in the light of a humanity ordered by the Nous. Thus, Reason in the noetic sense was discovered as both the force and the criterion of order.[8]

I have been reproducing the second paragraph of Voegelin's article. It states clearly and succinctly his viewpoint. For him, the *Sitz im Leben* of Platonic and Aristotelian philosophy was personal morality and social order. Yet to reach that interpretation of the high point of Greek philosophy one has to be acquainted, *from personal experience*, both with what Michael Polanyi refers to as 'tacit knowledge'[9] and with the signs and symbols of the transition from what is tacit to what becomes explicitly expressed. Or again, one has to be aware both of Robert Doran's primary process and of the intermediate zone that lies between it and his secondary process.[10] Or to speak with Wittgenstein, one has to place Polanyi's tacit knowledge as the starting point for one's trying to show what as yet one cannot say. Or again with Doran and Vernon Gregson,

---

8 Eric Voegelin, 'Reason: The Classic Experience,' *The Southern Review* 10 (Spring 1974) 237–64, at 237. [The article was included later in Eric Voegelin, *Anamnesis*, trans. and ed. Gerhart Niemeyer (Columbia and London: University of Missouri Press, 1978) 89–115; the quotation is found on p. 89.]

9 [Michael Polanyi, *The Tacit Dimension* (Garden City, NY: Doubleday Anchor, 1967).]

10 [See Robert M. Doran, 'Primary Process and the "Spiritual Unconscious,"' in Fred Lawrence, ed., *Lonergan Workshop* 5 (1985) 23–47; reprinted in Doran, *Theological Foundations*, vol. 1: *Intentionality and Psyche* (Milwaukee: Marquette University Press, 1995) 447–79. Doran's paper had been available for the 1979 Lonergan Workshop at which this lecture was delivered.]

one has to grasp how exactly they are speaking when they refer to my book *Insight* as a set of exercises in intellectual therapy.[11]

1.2 A Contemporary Context

Let me briefly recall how my own intellectual therapy has advanced since writing *Insight*, before I proceed to a brief outline of key elements in Voegelin's earlier and longer paper on 'The Gospel and Culture.'

Traditionally 'nature' has been described as an immanent principle of movement and of rest. But for present purposes we are led from such generality to what is more specific and multiple. To think of human nature, we distinguish a series of horizontal processes traversed by a vertical process. Each horizontal process has its own principle, yielding moments, first of movement and then of rest, on the successive levels of sensitivity, intelligence, reasonableness, and responsibility. The vertical process springs from an undifferentiated eros, commonly referred to as the unconscious, influences in turn each of the horizontal movements, and finds its proper goal beyond them in a self-transcending being-in-love that begins in the home, reaches out to the tribe, the city-state, the nation, mankind, and finds its anchor and its strength in the agape of the New Testament.

The basic horizontal process is the spontaneity of our sensitivity. Undifferentiated eros, pregnant with dreams or fantasies, memories or anticipations, is oriented by our perceptions of persons or things, and is powered by our feelings of desire and fear. But spontaneous vitality can shift to give place to the wonder and detachment of intelligence. Such a pause is in itself tacit, but it may come to be expressed in such questions as why? what? how? how often? what for? Whether tacit or expressed, the wonder tends to insight, which may be manifested merely in a quiet smile or in an Archimedean shout of triumph.[12]

11 [See Vernon Gregson, *Lonergan, Spirituality, and the Meeting of Religions* (Lanham, MD: University Press of America, 1985) 10–15. Lonergan had read all or most of this work, Gregson's dissertation, by the time of preparing this lecture.]

12 [In the spoken lecture, Lonergan read several lines somewhat different from what appears in this paragraph, but that material is crossed out in the autograph. It reads as follows. 'This process begins from outer stimulus and continuously returns to it. But our responses proceed from the spontaneity of our sensitivity: our perceptions of persons and things, our feelings of desire and fear, our memories, our anticipations, our fantasies. But if such spontaneity is the most conspicuous component in our consciousness, it is

The occurrence of one insight normally leads to the occurrence of further, complementary insights, and it may do so tacitly or explicitly: tacitly in the genesis of common sense, methodically and elaborately in the genesis of science. There is a tacit process of learning by watching others, endeavoring to imitate them on our own, failing perhaps and watching some more until we have acquired some skill or mastered a technique or made successful performance into a routine. There is an explicit process when we formulate just what the insight adds to the data and select from the data as much as is needed for the recurrence of that insight, when we go on to work out the presuppositions of the insight and to deduce its implications, when we undertake elaborate processes of testing that may eliminate unnecessary suppositions or add others that are needed, that determine whether the consequences all follow whenever the data needed for the insight are present, and whether they may equally follow when some of the conditions are dropped – the process of experimentation that leads to a verification.

On the accumulation of insights a new principle supervenes. There is the pause of reflection, which ceases to be tacit and becomes explicit when we ask, Is that possible, probable, certain? In philosophy, such questions demand elaborate answers. In the sciences, there is a continuity in which reorganizations and even revolutions preserve what is sound in previous work, so that, if the new explains more than the old, it has a claim to greater probability. In common sense, abstract principles give way to reassuring proverbs (usually contradictory: 'Look before you leap,' 'He who hesitates is lost'), universal affirmations and negations are not very seriously entertained, amusement at mistakes discourages their repetition, and familiarity with one's daily tasks, with relatives, friends, acquaintances, with the spontaneous process of teaching and learning that silently goes forward in any group and field, give birth to the security to which Macbeth appealed when, in the dagger scene, he addressed 'Thou sure and firm-set earth on which I tread.'[13]

The addition of reflection and judgment to accumulated insights places us in a world of greater or less truth and reality, and then there supervenes the question for responsibility. It takes successive forms. The self-regarding form

---

far from the whole of it. The data of sense give rise to the wonder of intelligence, a wonder that in itself is tacit but may come to be expressed in questions such as what, why, how, what for, how often. Whether tacit or expressed the wonder tends to insight which may be manifested merely in a quiet smile or in a shout of triumph.']

13 *Macbeth*, Act 1, sc. 7, l. 56.

asks, What is in it for me? The legalistic form asks, What does the law say, what does it imply, what does it enforce? The strictly moral form raises the question of value: Are my goals worth while? Are my decisions making me a person that is worth while?[14]

Such are the successive horizontal processes of discrete principles towards movement and then to rest. But running through them all is the vertical drive from undifferentiated eros to agape. It transmutes our sensitivity from a biological function into the carrier of artistic inspiration, into an instrument of practical and theoretical intelligence, into an embodiment of wisdom's concern for the true and the good.

1.3   Voegelin: 'The Gospel and Culture'

I have been attempting an explicit summary of a contemporary context for Voegelin's account in 1974 of the classic Platonic and Aristotelian experience of reason. But that paper followed on another and longer paper entitled 'The Gospel and Culture.'[15] There he asks why Christianity could come to dominate the decaying ecumenic empire of Rome and the subsequent history of Europe, yet today experiences an inability to gain a hearing in the modern world. His answer comes out of the introduction to Justin's *Dialogue with Trypho*. Justin had tried to live by many philosophies but set them aside when he discovered in Christianity, not something opposed to philosophy but philosophy in its state of perfection. But what Justin could discern, our age cannot, for if the answer is still available, still the question has been lost. We ask about the meaning which must be given to the fact of existence, but existence is not a fact. Rather, it '... is the non-fact of a disturbing movement in the In-Between of ignorance and knowledge, of time and timelessness, of imperfection and perfection, of hope and fulfilment, and ultimately of life and death.'[16]

On the ultimate, life and death, Voegelin stresses the ambiguity disturb-

---

14   See Walter Conn, 'The Ontogenetic Ground of Value,' *Theological Studies* 39:2 (1978) 313–35, and Elizabeth A. Morelli, 'The Sixth Stage of Moral Development,' *The Journal of Moral Education* 6:2 (1978) 97–108.

15   Eric Voegelin, 'The Gospel and Culture,' in Donald G. Miller and Dikran Y. Hadidian, eds., *Jesus and Man's Hope* (Pittsburgh: Pittsburgh Theological Seminary, 1971) 59–101. [In the lecture Lonergan added parenthetically, 'It was the 175th Anniversary of the foundation of the Pittsburgh Theological Seminary, and a number of scholars from all over took part.']

16   Ibid. 63.

ingly stressed by Euripides: 'Who knows if to live is to be dead, and to be dead to live?'; by Jesus: 'Whoever would save his life will lose it, and whoever loses his life for my sake will find it'; by Paul: 'If you live according to the flesh, you are bound to die; but if by the spirit you put to death the deeds of the body, you will live.'[17] In brief, 'There is a direction in existence; and as we follow it or not, life can be death, and death be life eternal ... The question expressed by the double meaning of life and death is the question of every man's, not only the philosopher's, existence.' It is a question buttressed by 'the authority of the representative death suffered by Socrates for its truth. Plato's *Apology* concludes with the ironic parting word to the judges: "But now the time has come to go. I go to die, and you to live. But who goes to the better lot is unknown to anyone but the God."'[18]

In the Gospel of John, when a group of Greeks approach the apostles with the Greek names, Philip and Andrew, in the hope of speaking with Jesus, the symbolic meaning of life and death is applied to the divine sacrifice: 'Most solemnly I tell you, unless a grain of wheat falls into the earth and dies, it remains only a single grain, but if it dies it bears much fruit. Who loves his life loses it, but who hates his life in this world, keeps it for life eternal. If anyone serves me, he must follow me, and wherever I am, my servant will be too.' And some verses later, 'And I, when I am lifted up from this earth, will draw all men to myself.'[19]

Voegelin considered this double meaning of life and death as the symbolism engendered by man's experience of being pulled in various directions and his need to choose between them. For Plato,

> When opinion leads through reason (*logos*) towards the best (*ariston*) and is more powerful, its power is called self-restraint (*sophrosynê*), but when desire (*epithumia*) drags us (*helkein*) towards pleasures and rules within us, its rule is called excess (*hybris*)' (Phdr 238A). The pulls are in conflict, dragging us up or down. A young man may be 'drawn (*helkein*) towards philosophy' (Rep 494E), but social pressure may divert him towards a life of pleasure or success in politics. If he follows the second pull, however, the question of meaning is not settled for him, for the first pull continues to be experienced as part of his existence. By following the second pull he does not transform his existence into a question-free fact, but into a recognizably questionable course of life. He will sense the

17 Ibid. 66–67.
18 Ibid. 67.
19 See ibid. 68–69.

life he leads as 'not his own and true life' (495C) – he will live in a state of alienation. The play of the pulls, thus, is luminous with truth. By following the wrong course one does not make it the right one, but slides into existence in untruth. This luminosity of existence with the truth of reason precedes all opinions and decisions about the pull to be followed. Moreover, it remains alive as the judgment of truth in existence whatever opinions about it we may actually form.[20]

For Voegelin, 'the terms seeking (*zêtein*) and drawing (*helkein*) do not denote two different movements but symbolize the dynamics in the tension of existence between its human and divine poles. In the one movement there is experienced a seeking from the human, a being drawn from the divine pole.'[21] Such experience is prior to the emergence of what we call classic philosophy. 'Only from the travail of this movement there emerges man as the questioner, Aristotle's *aporon* and *thaumazon* (Met 982b 18), and God as the mover who attracts or draws man to himself, as in Plato's *Laws* x or Aristotle's *Metaphysics*.'[22]

Now this experience of being at a loss and wondering is not something peculiar to a few fourth-century Greeks. It does not fit into the rationalistic segregation and separation of the natural and the supernatural, so that we can speak of Plato and Aristotle as merely pagans, and banish their thinking from the Christian religion pure and undefiled. For the ascetical and mystical tradition that belongs to the upper reaches of Christian thought and practice has a millennial familiarity with the pulls and counter-pulls that constitute the tension of Christian existence, of their ambiguities, of the need for a discernment of spirits if one is to follow the call of God's grace, even of different rules to be applied under different circumstances.[23]

There seems to be some evidence, then, for the claim of Justin Martyr that Christianity is philosophy in its state of perfection, though, of course, this is true only of philosophy in its original sense, namely, the love of wisdom. But it

20 Ibid. 71.
21 Ibid.
22 Ibid.
23 On this topic, for a brief account, *Sacramentum mundi: An Encyclopedia of Theology*, vol. 2, ed. Karl Rahner et al. (Montreal: Palm Publishers, 1968) 89–91. For a fuller treatment, *Dictionnaire de spiritualité ascétique et mystique*, articles on 'Consolation spirituelle' (2: 1617–34), 'Démon' (3: 141–238), 'Direction spirituelle' (3: 1002–1211), 'Discernement des esprits' (3: 1222–91).
    On the key to discernment in the Ignatian *Spiritual Exercises*, consolation without a previous cause, a notable study recommended with a preface by Karl Rahner is Harvey D. Egan, *The Spiritual Exercises and the Ignatian Mystical Horizon* (St Louis: The Institute of Jesuit Sources, 1976).

still may be questioned whether we have to go beyond existential truth and wisdom, and include the commitment to some sort of metaphysics implicit in the Greek councils and the better Scholastic writers. But while we shall be directly concerned with this issue only in the third part of our paper, there remains that something be said at once on the issue that gives rise to metaphysical thought.

1.4 Evidence of Monotheism

In a collection of *Ancient Near Eastern Texts* relating to the Old Testament and edited by James B. Pritchard in 1950,[24] there is included the translation of excerpts from a hymn to *Amon as the Sole God.* It is taken monotheistically by Voegelin in his paper on 'The Gospel and Culture,' where Amon is the God above the cosmic and national gods, the source of their dignity and power, but unknown not only to men but even to those known gods.[25] It is this unknown God that is for Christians the Father of Jesus Christ and by them identified with the Creator God of the Old Testament, but by Gnostics, at least in their anti-Semitic writings, set in opposition to Yahweh and above him.

Now it also happens that John A. Wilson, who translated the excerpts from Egyptian texts, also contributed to a symposium held at the University of Chicago and published by the University Press in 1946.[26] In the chapter in which he discusses the Amon hymn, he begins with the question whether the ancient Egyptians acknowledged any difference of substance among men, gods, and other elements in the universe. His personal answer was that a man seems 'to be one thing and the sky and a tree another. But to the ancient Egyptians such concepts had a protean and a complementary nature. The sky might be thought of as a material vault above the earth, or as a cow, or as a female. A tree might be a tree or the female who is the tree-goddess.'[27] After several further examples, he notes that his line of argument will be 'that to the ancient Egyptians the elements of the universe were consubstantial ... The first claim for the argument that the elements of the universe were of one substance is the principle of free substitution, interchange, or representa-

24 James B. Pritchard, ed., *Ancient Near Eastern Texts* (Princeton: Princeton University Press, 1950).
25 Voegelin, 'The Gospel and Culture' 84–85.
26 H. and H.A. Frankfort, John A. Wilson, Thorkild Jacobsen, William A. Irwin, *The Intellectual Adventure of Ancient Man, An Essay on Speculative Thought in the Ancient Near East* (Chicago: University of Chicago Press, 1946).
27 Ibid. 62.

tion. It was very easy for one element to take the place of another. The person who had died wanted bread, ... he might be supplied with real loaves ... but if stealing occurred, then a wooden loaf of bread might do, or a picture of bread, or even the written or spoken word, "bread."'[28] Eventually, he turns to the Amon hymn, and he admits that it has been considered a prime document for the thesis of essential monotheism. But he would preface such an interpretation by insisting that it is not a matter of a single god but of a single nature of observed phenomena in the universe, with the clear possibility of exchange and substitution. With relation to gods and men the Egyptians were monophysites: many men and many gods, but all ultimately of one nature.[29]

Obviously between these scholars, Voegelin and Wilson, there is some difference of opinion. But I should say that it is underpinned, not by Polanyi's tacit knowledge but by the pre-metaphysical and the post-metaphysical expressions of tacit knowledge. The pre-metaphysical expression is mythical. The post-metaphysical is controversial. It exhibits the need for Paul Ricoeur's twofold dialectic, a dialectic of suspicion in search of the unauthentic, and a dialectic of recovery that uncovers the authentic.

But there is no easy solution. To recognise and acknowledge the authentic, one already must be authentic. If already one is unauthentic, such recognition and acknowledgement is beyond one's effective reach. Such is the moral impotence of man, the concrete fact of original sin, not the remote origins of original sin (*peccatum originale originans*), but the present fact (*peccatum originale originatum*). To confront that issue as the basic issue is to come to grips with St Paul's Letter to the Romans, chapters 5, 6, 7, and 8.

So much, then, for that first point: Is there any connection between the Gospels and certain aspects of Greek culture?

2   The Medieval Rise and Fall of Scholasticism

I would attribute the medieval rise of Scholasticism in the twelfth and thirteenth centuries to the emergence of a theological method, and I would attribute the medieval fall of Scholasticism in the fourteenth century to the decline of method and the dominance of deductive logic. Such is, so to speak, my thesis. I hope to develop it under five headings, namely, (1) the initiators, (2) the emergence of method, (3) the problem of coherence, (4) the turn to Aristotle, and (5) the ambiguity of the *Posterior Analytics*.

28 Ibid. 63.
29 Ibid. 66.

2.1 The Initiators

The initiative, I believe, may be attributed to three men: St Anselm of Canterbury, Peter Abelard, and Gilbert de la Porrée.

Anselm was the thinker. His interest centered on all the profoundest problems in Christian theology: the Trinity, the end of the Incarnation, the fall of the angels, original sin, divine foreknowledge and predestination, grace and liberty. But his solutions were brilliant constructions without a solid underpinning in revealed sources or in theoretical exploration.[30]

Abelard was the investigator. His *Sic et non* was a series of one hundred and fifty-eight propositions, and each of them he undertook both to prove and to disprove by appealing to the scriptures, the Fathers, and reason. His emphasis in this work underscored what was lacking in Anselm: a critical review of tradition.

Gilbert de la Porrée established a cardinal point in what was to be Scholastic method. He set forth the conditions for the existence of a question: a question exists when solid grounds from scripture, tradition, or reason can be advanced to establish *both* an affirmative *and* a negative answer.

2.2 The Emergence of Method

Taken together, the three initiators offer the speculative originality of Anselm, the positively grounded problems of Abelard, and the technical rule of Gilbert. When these three are added to the practice of the monastic schools of reading followed by reflection (*lectio* and *quaestio*), we are at the origins of Scholastic method. The *lectio* was clarified by glosses, extended by commentaries, organized by collections of passages taken from different sources but bearing on distinct and ordered topics. Such collections were known as *Books of Sentences* (*Libri sententiarum*). A number of them came into existence, but the most celebrated was Peter Lombard's, and on it commentaries were written up to the time of Estius at the beginning of the seventeenth century.

The commentaries were not modern in their style. They did not aim at the historical reconstruction of the original meaning of the texts. They simply applied to the collected materials the technique of the *quaestio*. With regard

---

30 See Bernard Lonergan, *Grace and Freedom: Operative Grace in the Thought of St Thomas Aquinas*, Collected Works of Bernard Lonergan, vol. 1, ed. Frederick E. Crowe and Robert M. Doran (Toronto: University of Toronto Press, 2000) 7–10.

to any particular topic several questions might be distinguished. They were enunciated. In turn, their existence was established by listing authorities or reasons, first for a negative answer (*Videtur quod non*), and then for a positive answer (*Sed contra est*). There followed a statement of principles for a solution (*Respondeo dicendum*) and finally an application of these principles to each of the authorities or reasons that showed the question to exist.

There resulted a method, for it attracted a group of specialists following a common procedure in a determinate field of investigation.[31] Its results were ongoing and cumulative: previous solutions often were only partial, to give rise to further questions that were to be tackled by later writers; and the later writers would complement their predecessors yet, by that very fact, give rise to new questions. The process has been exhibited in detail by the writings of Arthur M. Landgraf on early Scholastic opinions on grace, and by Otto Lottin on early Scholastic accounts of liberty.[32] So we find that the questions Aquinas raised in his *Scriptum super Libros Sententiarum* stand at a notable distance from those suggested by the text of the Lombard under consideration. Between the text and the commentary there had occurred a century-long process of refinement, development, transposition.

2.3 The Problem of Coherence

It remains that the method needed to be complemented by some overarching vision. It yielded solutions that reconciled endless apparent oppositions. But of itself it was powerless to make the many solutions coalesce into some coherent whole of precisely related meanings expressed by appropriately univocal or even analogous terms. To offset the multiplicity of basic issues, there was needed at least some preliminary but comprehensive view which might interact with the many solutions and, by modifying them, also modify itself into the wanted synthesis.

The solution to this superordinate issue seems to have come simply from the cultural ecology of medieval Europe. Besides Christian thinkers there were Arabic scientists and philosophers, and behind them both was the heritage from ancient Greece. Moreover, it was first through translations from

31 Bernard Lonergan, 'Aquinas Today: Tradition and Innovation,' *The Journal of Religion* 55 (1975) 166–69; reprinted in *A Third Collection* (see above, p. 214, note 22), where the relevant pages are 36–40.
32 For bibliographic references to Landgraf and Lottin, consult their names in the index to Lonergan, *Grace and Freedom.*

the Arabic that Christian theologians came into contact with such thinkers as Aristotle and Plotinus. And as Greek thought moved into an Arabic horizon by translation into Arabic, so also there was a Latin and Christian horizon that had a twofold need to cultivate Greek achievement. The first and more obvious need was apologetic. The second and more fundamental was to provide Scholastic method with its overarching vision.

2.4 The Turn to Aristotle

The first of Aristotle's works to be accepted by the theologians was his logical *Organon*. But through the thirteenth century there was an ever deeper penetration of Aristotelian categories into Christian theology. Three examples will suffice.

A traditional view had been that, since justifying faith supposed free consent, baptised infants were freed from guilt yet did not receive justifying faith. But early in the century a papal document, after recalling the traditional view, added the opinion of some that baptized infants not only were free from guilt but also received the habit, though not the use, of justifying faith (DS 780). A century later the second opinion had become the more probable view in an official document (DS 904).

Again, throughout the twelfth century theologians had been at a loss to say what was meant by grace: everything was a free gift of the Creator. As that was a somewhat preposterous account of what scripture meant by grace, several less general views were proposed but none that coincided with the later view of the supernatural habit or act. At the same time, there was a great problem of reconciling human liberty with the necessity of divine grace: if man was free, grace could not be absolutely necessary; and if it were absolutely necessary, man could not be free. There was[33] the philosopher's definition of liberty as freedom from necessity, and the theologian's: liberty was that which enabled man to do what was right when God gave him the grace and didn't enable him when God didn't give the grace. A series of ever better proposals early in the thirteenth century culminated in the solution of Philip the Chancellor of the University of Paris, who posited an entitative disproportion that set grace above nature, faith above reason, charity above friendliness, and merit before God above the opinion of men. Nature, reason, friendliness, and the good opinion of men resulted simply from being human. But grace, faith, charity,

33 In the lecture, this sentence was added to the autograph text.

and merit before God were the free gift of God's love for those he had made his own adopted children. Faithful love of one person for another is a gift of oneself to another. Even in men and women, however much supported by natural spontaneity, principally it is the fruit of a free and personal decision. What principally is true of human love, entirely is true of divine. Such is the meaning of God's grace as supernatural, even though current English usage is apt to equate the supernatural with the spooky.[34]

Finally, the high point of medieval Scholastic method was reached in the writings of Aquinas. For over twenty years he wrote and rewrote. On some topics his opinion at the end was much the same as it had been at the beginning, but on others there can be discerned a series of stages. First on one aspect and then on another, the thought of his predecessors was clarified, adjusted, partially transformed. Eventually a whole set of interlocking issues would be so modified as to constitute a new position. In the end a coherent set of new positions was reached to constitute a new paradigm for inquiring minds.[35]

2.5 The Ambiguity of the Posterior Analytics

As Max Planck has testified and Thomas Kuhn has exemplified, new paradigms provoke resistance. What is true of the twentieth century also was true of the late thirteenth, where the work of Aquinas led to the explosive controversy between Augustinians and Aristotelians. The plaint of the Augustinians at its boldest was that Aquinas used Aristotle as though he were a Father of the Church. It is not quite in those words, but it is a complaint of Archbishop John Peckham of Canterbury in a letter to the pope.[36] But if the issue is judged by its results, it would seem to lie in the fact that, while Aquinas appealed ultimately to wisdom, his opponents appealed to the notion of science (*epistêmê*) set forth in the *Posterior Analytics*.

In the latter work (1, 2) it is said that we think we understand when we know the cause, know that it is the cause, and know that the effect cannot be other than it is. This descriptive account of understanding is immediately transposed into the technical language of Aristotle's scientific syllogism (*syllogismos*

---

34 Lonergan, *Grace and Freedom* 14–20.
35 Again, Lonergan, *Grace and Freedom*, and *Verbum: Word and Idea in Aquinas* (see above, p. 65, note 26).
36 Bernard J.F. Lonergan, *De Deo trino, Pars systematica* (Rome: Gregorian University Press, 1964) 49.

epistêmonikos, syllogismus faciens scire). Such a syllogism reveals a predicate to pertain necessarily to a subject when its premises are 'true, primary, immediate, better known than and prior to the conclusion, which is further related to them as effect to cause.'[37]

But how do we acquire knowledge of such premises? Aristotle met this issue only in the second book of the *Posterior Analytics* in the nineteenth chapter. His conclusion was that knowledge of the primary and immediate premises is 'neither innate in a determinate form, nor developed from other higher states of knowledge, but from sense-perception. It is like a rout in battle stopped by first one man making a stand and then another, until the original formation has been restored. The soul is so constituted as to be capable of this process'[38] and such constitution will be by way of intuition.[39]

However, the contemporary reader, familiar with the reformulation of Euclidean geometry (Hilbert) and with the invention of n-dimensional geometries of any curvatures (Riemann), will feel that in mathematics, as in the sciences, intuitions are just insights. They are not intrinsically certain, they may be revised, and they admit alternative views. Even Gödel's argument that a formalized deductive system either admits further developments or else is inconsistent or incomplete has been thought to rest its final generalization on an insight.

One should not, I think, leap to the conclusion that Aristotle's position precludes such a view. He distinguished conclusions as science, premises as principles grasped by intellect, intelligence (*nous*), but the truth of principles he reached by wisdom. Such is the position in the *Nicomachean Ethics*.[40] But it is presented in an even more fundamental fashion in the *Metaphysics*, where the importance of wisdom becomes the ground of the importance of philosophy, the love of wisdom. The topic is recurrent in the first four books but a single sample has to suffice for the present occasion.

> It is right also that philosophy should be called knowledge of the truth. For the end of theoretical knowledge is truth, while that of practical knowledge is action ... Now we do not know a truth without its cause; and a thing has a quality in a higher degree than other things if

37 Richard McKeon, ed., *The Basic Works of Aristotle* (New York: Random House, 1941) 112.
38 Ibid. 185.
39 Ibid. 186.
40 Ibid. 1027–28; Aristotle, *Nicomachean Ethics*, VI, 6, 1140b 31 – 1141a 7; VI, 7, 1141a 17–19.

in virtue of it the similar quality belongs to the other things as well ...;
so that that which causes derivative truths to be true is most true.
Hence the principles of eternal things must be always most true (for
they are not merely sometimes true, nor is there any cause of their
being, but they themselves are the cause of the being of other things),
so that as each thing is in respect of being, so it is in respect of truth.[41]

This passage is a source of such once familiar Latin tags as 'propter quod
unumquodque tale, et illud magis,'[42] and 'sicut est ordo rerum in esse, ita et
in veritate.'[43] From them follows the Thomist contention that to know what is
meant by being and not being, by whole and part, and the other consequents
of the meaning of being (from which are constituted first principles), pertains to wisdom.[44]

Now this basic concern with wisdom and with the love of wisdom is not to be
expected as the principal motive of the Augustinian-Aristotelian controversy
that exploded at the end of the thirteenth century in the *Correctoria fratris
Thomae* and the *Correctoria corruptoriorum fratris Thomae*. Again, one misses such
concern in the distinction between the *potentia Dei absoluta* and the *potentia Dei
ordinata*, which enquires about divine omnipotence as though it could lack
the ordering derived from divine wisdom. It contributes to an understanding
of the fourteenth-century breakdown of Scholastic method, which degener-
ated first towards skepticism and eventually into decadence, as Yves Congar
teaches in his *History of Theology*.[45]

2.6   Horizon and Wisdom

Let us conclude this section on the rise and fall of medieval Scholasticism
with a note on the similarity and the differences of the notions 'horizon' and
'wisdom.' Horizon is the field of one's interests and knowledge. Wisdom and,
more modestly, philosophy has the function of ordering all things and passing judgment on them. 'Horizon' is the more general term: its range may be

---

41 McKeon, *The Basic Works of Aristotle* 712–13; Aristotle, *Metaphysics*, II, 1, 993b
19–31.
42 [That which is the cause that a certain quality is found in everything else has
itself that quality and in a higher degree.]
43 [As the order of things is in their being, so is it also in their truth.]
44 See Lonergan, *Verbum* 57, 70.
45 Yves Congar, *A History of Theology*, trans. Hunter Guthrie (Garden City, NY:
Doubleday, 1968) 137–43.

extended or contracted; its interests may be ruled by self-interest or, to a greater or lesser extent, by values, by what really is worth while. Wisdom regards all that exists to exclude human aberrations, and its judgments are not swayed by 'what's in it for me' but endeavor to conform to what truly is of value. The rise and fall of medieval Scholasticism was a succession of horizons. The rise culminated, in the judgment of many, in the wisdom of Aquinas. The fall would seem to have been brought about by an initial contentiousness, followed by an overmastering concern for science strictly so-called, *scientia stricte dicta*, a notion of science set forth in the greater part of Aristotle's *Posterior Analytics*.

It may not be amiss to note that such a concern was not dominant in Aquinas's own thinking. His most personal work, I feel, was his *Contra Gentiles*. It begins with a sequence of chapters on wisdom that justify the plan of the work. He distinguishes between objects of human knowledge and objects of faith. Some arguments are demonstrations and others are only probable. He proposes to demonstrate what can be demonstrated. He will combine arguments from authority and probable arguments where this is possible in theology, notably in the third book, in which he treats the end of man, the vision of God, divine providence, divine law, and the grace of God. Finally, where faith rests only on authority, he attempts to understand how what is revealed might be so, that thereby revelation be shown not necessarily to involve a contradiction. This is the procedure in the fourth book, which treats of the Trinity, the Incarnation, original sin, the sacraments, the resurrection of the body, the final state of men and women.[46]

3   Some Elements in a Transposition to the Post–Vatican II Horizon

The Second Vatican Council was explicitly a pastoral council. At its inception Cardinal Siri, Archbishop of Genoa, voiced the opinion that all councils had been pastoral, that the function of councils was to set forth truths revealed by God, and the function of pastors was to transmit conciliar decisions from their pulpits. It was a view that did not prevail, and perhaps the most eloquent exponent of the contrary view was Marie-Dominique Chenu, o.p., who objected that the eminent cardinal was putting the cart before the horse. What comes first is the word of God. The task of the Church is announcing the good

---

46 Here Lonergan adds parenthetically in the taped lecture, '... where there are what are called arguments of convenience, known by students as proofs that don't prove.'

news, preaching the gospel. That preaching is pastoral. It is the concrete reality. From it one may abstract doctrines, and theologians may work the doctrines into conceptual systems, but the doctrines and systems, however valuable and true, are but the skeleton of the original message. A word is the word of a person, but doctrine objectifies and depersonalizes. The word of God comes to Christians through Jesus Christ, the Son of God. The church has to mediate to the world not just a doctrine but the living Christ.[47]

Now I feel that Chenu's position is unanswerable, and in fact I include the pastoral function as the crowning specialty in my *Method in Theology*. But I would suggest that an outstanding characteristic of the post–Vatican II horizon is a certain disregard of doctrinal issues. No doubt my own *déformation professionelle* gives me an excessive sensitivity to such disregard but, at the same time, I am inclined to fancy that not a few among you will feel that the pastoral office will suffer if we simply jettisoned our doctrinal past.

3.1 Secularism

A first issue is secularism. Aquinas sharply distinguished philosophy and theology, but he did not separate them. In fact, the finer points of his philosophic thought have to be dug out of his theological investigations. But the separation of philosophy and theology was brought about very effectively by Descartes with his doctrine of methodic doubt. The one necessary step towards sound philosophy was to doubt everything, in the sense of supposing nothing that could be questioned. Descartes found the indubitable in the fact that he thought, and from that fact he felt he could conclude to his own existence.

Kant took the matter a step further. His *Religion within the Bounds of Pure Reason* (1793) is secularist. It not only separates philosophy from theology; it denies that there is any need for a being superior to man if man is to recognize his duty and, as well, it denies that there is any need for any motives other than the moral law itself for man to fulfill his duty.[48]

Now from a variety of causes secularism had been gaining ground from the end of the Middle Ages, mostly in ecclesiastical and state politics, and one can detect a trace of it in one of the provisional schemata of the First Vatican

---

47   Marie-Dominique Chenu, *La parole de Dieu*, vol. 2, *L'Evangile dans le temps* (Paris: Editions du Cerf, 1964) 655–72.
48   See Frederick Copleston, *A History of Philosophy*, Image Books, vol. 6, pt. 2 (Garden City, NY: Doubleday, 1964) 135.

Council. There one can read an anathema against anyone who denied that through created things God's existence could be known with certainty by fallen man.[49] In the final draft the words 'by fallen man' were omitted, and common doctrine has it that the council was considering not a question of fact but a question of right, a question that regarded the capacity of human reason as such, and not a question that settled the conditions under which this capacity could be actuated.

The significance of the point comes to light when one shifts one's thinking from human nature to the existential human subject, from the conditions of possibility assured by human nature to the conditions of actuality permitted by the aberrations of human history. The former was the viewpoint of Vatican I. The latter is the question that becomes uppermost when one turns from abstract human nature to the concrete task of preaching the gospel to all nations. Human nature is capable of wisdom, but mankind in its historical existence is open to the conviction that talk about wisdom is a flight into fantasy. Nor is this true only of our own day. The ancient Stoics were inclined to expound their doctrines in terms of what the wise man would say or do. Their opponents would ask, Where does this wise man live? Will you introduce him to us? And, as I have already contended in the question period on Tuesday, we have to be prepared to use Paul Ricoeur's double dialectic, the dialectic of suspicion to eliminate what appears excellent but is fraudulent; and a dialectic of recovery that uncovers what really is excellent underpinning a position that has become deformed.

3.2 Where Does Philosophy Begin?

A second point comes out of Voegelin's paper, 'Reason: The Classic Experience.' Aristotle asks somewhere whether an inquiry should begin from what is first in itself or first for us. He answers that we have to begin from what is first for us, not from the sphericity of the moon which can be deduced from its phases, but from the phases from which the sphericity of the moon is deducible. But the Scholastic tradition, by and large, has been wont to consider 'being' first, though 'being' is not first for us but first in itself. I think a clarification can be had from Voegelin's contention that classic philosophy began from the pulls and counter-pulls of existential experience. From that base can be developed the love of wisdom that is philosophy. But that base is

49 See Bernard Lonergan, 'Natural Knowledge of God,' in *A Second Collection* (see above, p. 22, note 12) 118.

not explicit but rather tacit knowledge. It becomes explicit only in the practical rules for the discernment of spirits and, theoretically, only in contemporary intentionality analysis. But, now that it is in the open, it supports the view of (1) beginning from a phenomenology of coming to know as a series of acts and (2) using that as a basis for an epistemology that explains why such acts constitute knowledge and (3) concluding with a metaphysics of proportionate being that is critical in the sense that its terms and relations have their empirical counterpart in the experienced terms and experienced relations of cognitional theory.

3.3   The New Notion of Science

The first point was secularism; the second, where does philosophy begin? Does it begin with being or does it begin with the existential subject, with what is first for us? A third point is the recognition of the breakdown of the ideal of science expounded in the *Posterior Analytics* and echoed by Aquinas in such statements as 'science is concerned with the universal and the necessary.' In fact, modern science is concerned mainly, not with the intelligibility of the necessary but with the intelligibility of the possible. Science proceeds through hypotheses to more or less probable theories. Again, while natural science aims at theories that are universally valid, it is no less concerned with the further determinations that bring about an ever closer approximation to the concrete, and it reserves a notable role for statistical laws, which speak simply of concrete events that are likely to occur.

3.4   History as Wissenschaft

A fourth point is the recognition of history as a *Wissenschaft*. I use the German term because it embraces not only physical science but also hermeneutics and history. In English it happens that the word 'science' has come to be preempted by physicists, chemists, biologists, geologists, and the like. Since possession is said to be nine points of the law, let us distinguish human studies and human science. Human studies have their basis in hermeneutics and history. Human sciences follow the positivist precept that one reaches a scientific understanding of man only if the same understanding may be applied to a robot or at least to a rat.

Now history, as a department of human studies, made a slow entry into Catholic thought. The first to be received were the church historians. Next came patristic and medieval studies. The last to be welcomed into the fold were biblical scholars, who in 1943 in the encyclical *Divino afflante Spiritu* received a long-denied official recognition.

The reason for these delays and piecemeal recognitions lay in the new notion of critical or scientific history. On the old view, history was a matter of distinguishing between credible and incredible testimonies, piecing the credible testimonies into a continuous narrative, and consigning the incredible to the waste basket or the flames. On the new view, history was not a matter of beliefs at all. Its model might be said to be the detective who finds all testimonies to be false and all clues to be planted, seeks the cause of these multiple deceptions, and finds their author to be the criminal. However, the point to this model is simply to underscore the point that the historian, as historian, is not a believer but a highly intelligent investigator. The first part of his investigation is devoted to a detailed study of his sources, of their strengths and weaknesses, of relying on them where he finds they are reliable in their approach and understanding, and also relying on their weaknesses as indirect evidence for the opposite of their views. Only when such critical work is completed does he attempt to write his narrative; and even then the writing will often provide an occasion for revising his critical conclusions.

3.5 Method

A fifth and final point is method. The word has two quite different meanings. On the common meaning, a method is like the recipes in a cookbook, and its characteristic is that, if one follows the method, then ideally one obtains always the same results. A recipe for lemon pie yields lemon pie, and no one expects it to result in a chocolate cake. But the function of a method in an academic discipline or science is to yield a cumulative series of different and better results. Copernicus's speculation on the celestial orbits led to Tycho Brahe's measurements of the successive positions of the planet Mars. Gallileo's experiments led to the formulation of the law of falling bodies. Newton's generalization yielded a planetary system that accorded with Copernicus's view of the celestial orbits.

Further, just as Aristotle's *Posterior Analytics* set the mold for all deductivist systems, so method sets the mold for all modern sciences and academic disciplines. They all have their principles, but the principles change, and the change is brought about by the method that earlier had led to the principles.

Again, just as the Aristotelians acknowledged the existence of different subjects and conceived their development as an effort towards a deductivist presentation, so too they subsumed all subjects under the principal subject, metaphysics, which was the science of being as being. In like manner, empirical method as developed in the natural sciences can be expanded into a generalized empirical method that yields an 'Ongoing Genesis of Methods'[50] to meet the exigences of different fields of inquiry and, at the same time, calls for interdisciplinary studies that move the many fields towards a unified view.

Such, I believe, is the contemporary situation, and it was to help fit theology within that situation that I spent a number of years trying to work out a method in theology. But to elucidate that effort calls for a different occasion. However, I think it a fitting conclusion to this and previous points to quote Irenaeus of Lyons, bishop and martyr, who remarked that facility at discourse does not show greater faith, and little ability to speak does not prove that one's faith is less.[51]

Question: Were you suggesting that in the dispute between the Augustinians and Thomas the Augustinians were championing Aristotelian science and Thomas was championing wisdom?

Response: No. The Augustinians were defending their own position, the position they had prior to additions from other works of Aristotle besides the *Organon*. They didn't want a new paradigm. Einstein's relativity in 1905 was greeted with all sorts of incomprehension even in encyclopedias. It takes time for a new idea to get across. The same was true of quantum theory in 1926. Carl Becker, a historian, read a paper on 'What Are Historical Facts?' at Princeton and at Cornell in 1926. He never published it; it was published posthumously. But it has been remarked on, that if it had been published in 1926 it would have left the historians in the same disarray as quantum theory left the physicists. New ideas take time, just as knowledge makes a bloody entrance. And to complicate matters, they had the question of faith: 'This is what we believe, and this is why we believed it, and this man's quoting Aristotle just as if he were quoting the saints!' He wasn't; what he was doing was getting materials, ideas, for a synthesis, from a man who had a partial synthesis. And that's a hard idea to get ahold of, and it doesn't develop by a controversy. As a matter of fact, when the Thomists, the Dominicans, first made Aquinas the obligatory source of all their teaching of theology, the question was, What work of Aquinas? You can't have the whole thing. And they picked the *Sentences*,

---

50 See Bernard Lonergan, 'The Ongoing Genesis of Methods,' in *A Third Collection* 146–65.
51 Irenaeus, *Adversus haereses*, I, 10, 3; Harvey I, 94–96. See above, p. 183, note 10.

which was the first work. It is Pelagian on grace, and it has other defects, but they didn't do historical study of Aquinas at that time.

Question: I was just thinking about your comments about the post-Vatican II period, and the suspicion of doctrines not being completed by recovery of doctrine. Perhaps you might want to say a couple of words on that.

Response: It would take a lot of words! The quest for the humanity of Jesus: there is a lot of quite inadequate thinking about the formal constituent of the Incarnation, and so on. In fact, the only theory I agree with is my own! But if you make the issue of the quest for the humanity of Jesus the basis for throwing out the Council of Chalcedon, without being aware that Chalcedon just flows right out of Ephesus, and then throwing out Ephesus which is based simply on Nicea, it doesn't help you to agree with it. And you carry on the discussion on the basis of schemata. The word used by Schoonenberg – the German translation – is *Modell*, different models. And that idea is used very well by Grillmeier, contrasting the *Logos-Sarx* Christology with the *Deus-Homo* Christology – the difference between the Alexandrians and the people in Asia Minor. And it's the way they spoke that he's talking about. He finds a different model. In the New Testament there are all sorts of christologies. There are christologies that start from the man Jesus; there are christologies that go on to add the crucifixion, resurrection, and 'seated at the right hand of the Father.' There are other christologies that go further back and that speak of Jesus coming down to this earth. They are all in the New Testament with different layers. So the question can be endlessly complex, and if one starts speculating on the basis of a Dutch philosophy, one gets into bad problems. The greatest Dutch philosopher, I always tell Dutchmen, was Spinoza.

Question: You said that Ricoeur's hermeneutics of suspicion and of recovery require the prior authenticity of the subject for them to work. Would you have more to say about that in terms of how Ricoeur uses these themes?

Response: There is a considerable amount of writing on Ricoeur, and I think that's the place to go.

Question: Well, I have read some of that and I wondered whether you had anything more to say.

Response: No.

Lexicon of Latin and Greek Words and Phrases

Latin Words and Phrases

an sit? quid sit? an honestum sit?: is it? what is it? is it right?

fides fiducialis: a faith of confidence, trustful faith

ignorantia elenchi: ignorance of (the point) of the argument

lectio et quaestio: reading and reflecting

mysterium fascinans et tremendum: fascinating and terrifying mystery

nihil amatum nisi praecognitum: nothing is loved unless it is first known

obiter dicta: said in passing

omni et soli: (applicable) to all instances and to them alone

potentia Dei absoluta: absolute power of God

potentia Dei ordinata: power of God as ordered (by divine wisdom)

principia per se nota: principles known of themselves, self-evident principles

priora quoad nos: the things that are first in regard to us

priora quoad se: the things that are first in themselves

quidquid recipitur ad modum recipientis recipitur: whatever is received is received in the way proper to the receiver

respondeo dicendum quod: in reply I maintain

sed contra est: but against that

ultra vires: beyond the scope of or in excess of legal power and authority

unum necessarium: the one thing necessary

verbis et rebus: in word and reality

videtur quod non: it seems not

Greek Words

aporon: puzzled
homoousion, homoousios: consubstantial
thaumazon: wondering

Index